Knowledge Politics

Knowledge Politics

Nico Stehr

Paradigm Publishers

Boulder • London

Published in the United States by Paradigm Publishers, 3360 Mitchell Lane Suite C, Boulder, CO 80301 USA.

Paradigm Publishers is the trade name of Birkenkamp & Company, LLC, Dean Birkenkamp, President and Publisher.

ISBN 1–59451–086–5 (hardcover)

Library of Congress Cataloging-in-Publication Data has been applied for.

Printed and bound in the United States of America on acid-free paper that meets the standards of the American National Standard for Permanence of Paper for Printed Library Materials.

Designed and typeset by Straight Creek Bookmakers.

09 08 07 06 05 5 4 3 2 1

Contents

Preface

Anxieties and concerns about the harmful social consequences of new scientific knowledge and novel technologies are not of recent origin. Nor are elusive promises of the blessings of science for humankind and the mitigation of human suffering that scientific advances will bring. Indeed, few individuals are ready to reject the most common rationale for spending public monies on scientific projects huge and small. The widely shared rationale was and is that scientific projects have the potential to transform our lives into healthier, longer, wealthier, safer, and generally more pleasant lives. In a word, the advancement of knowledge functions to improve the human condition.

But a persuasive case can be made that we have reached a new stage in our understanding of the social role of new knowledge. The first controlled genetic experiment did not occur until 1972. The first human being conceived outside a woman's body was born in 1978. We are now in the midst of controversial discussions about recombinant DNA and embryonic stem cells; genetically modified foods and "precision agriculture"; the prospects of lethal and "nonlethal" biotechnology weapons; neuroscience, neurogenetics, and genetic engineering of the human germline; reproductive cloning and the reconstruction of the human ancestral genome; and, last but not least, visions of a fusion of nanotechnology, biotechnology, information technology, transgenic human engineering, and cognitive science whose products may, as its boosters claim, someday cure disease, slow the aging process, eliminate pollution, and generally enhance human performance. Although for now we have to live with much smaller and mundane gains such as stain- and wrinkle-resistant slacks, the more general prospects and promises exemplify the novel issues we are confronting in vigorously contested scientific and public debates.

While many are persuaded that utopias have been relegated to the dustbin of history—perhaps as recently as a couple of decades ago with the collapse of the empire that attempted to put them into practice—utopian and dystopian visions are resurfacing that bet on biology and its ability to transform forms of life.

Concerns about the societal consequences of an unfettered expansion of (natural) scientific knowledge are being raised more urgently and are moving to the center of disputes in society—and thus to the top of the political agenda. In the preamble to the charter of fundamental rights in the draft of the treaty establishing a *Constitution for Europe,* which was adopted by consensus by the European Convention in the summer of 2003, we find the following statement. It can be interpreted both as an affirmation of the need by the European Union to engage in knowledge politics and also as an expression of anxiety about the impact of science and technologies on individuals and society: "It is necessary to strengthen the protection of fundamental rights in the light of changes in society, social progress, and scientific and technological developments, by making those rights more visible in a Charter."

Governments will have to engage in new political activity and will be held accountable to new standards. But the state clearly will not be the only relevant actor in the context of knowledge politics. And public conflicts, frictions, and disputes over the implementation of knowledge, which are seen by at least some as attacks on science and the deliberate creation of excessive fear among the public, will no longer take place mainly *a posteriori.*

For it is no longer uncommon that the discussion of the role of new scientific knowledge in modern societies leads to demands that such knowledge and its impact be in some way managed, regulated, or even suppressed. The question that has now become pertinent—and that is no longer prompted only by the possible consequences of nuclear science and technology—is: How can we avoid being devoured by a marvelously powerful science? It would be too easy to dismiss calls for intervention as an irrational or antimodern response. The questions being raised and the resistance being mobilized refer back, of course, to the image that we have of ourselves, according to which we arrange our lives—an image that appears to be under threat.

In listing only some of the perplexing issues that will characterize and constrain knowledge politics, it is evident that we are just at the beginning of unprecedented and challenging disputes and decisions: Which knowledge needs to be regulated, and whose responsibility is it? Are the regulatory regimes now in place to control the risks of chemicals, for example, sufficient in the case of emerging forms of knowledge in biotechnology? And what knowledge do we require in the context of regulative knowledge politics? Do we need to regulate new scientific knowledge as closely as, or even more strictly than, one regulates traffic, for instance? If not, on what grounds? If so, for what reasons, and to protect what interests? How do we resolve conflicts about competing goals that knowledge should serve? If strict restrictions apply, could absolute prohibitions, for example, of human germline gene therapy, be enforced? Is knowledge about to become a private good (again)? What will be the identity of some of the major actors involved, and how will knowledge politics be organized?

Critics will be prompt to argue that knowledge politics is neither new nor dissimilar from other fields of contemporary or past regulatory political activity. Social scientists not only have to confront this argument, but also must acknowledge the sense in which the critics are correct. If the world of phenomena that social scientists confront deserves to be differentiated from phenomena constructed by and attended to by other disciplines in the scientific community, the differentiation, in my view, stems from the extent to which the social sciences are always challenged and embarrassed by the *noncontemporaneity of the contemporaneous*. It is impossible to escape the dilemma of the simultaneity of conflicting manifestations of social phenomena. What is argued here is that knowledge politics is a societal process that gradually supersedes (in the sense of *aufheben*) existing ways of dealing with new capacities of action or knowledge.

I am interested in the bases of the clashing approaches and perspectives in debates about the policing of knowledge, as well as the methods and chances of regulating new knowledge in modern and increasingly fragile societies. Decisive for the possibilities and limits of knowledge politics are dynamic social, cultural, political, and economic settings, often at the macro rather than micro level, such as laboratories, theories, and experiments. The context-specific matrix changes rapidly, for example, as a result of the loss of power of large, modern societal institutions, such as the state, the church, corporations, or science. Yet large social institutions continue to present themselves, despite their growing weaknesses, as systems of effective societal control. Robust scenarios for knowledge politics are difficult to generate and are not at all obvious. The burden of this study is nevertheless to show on the one hand, how and why knowledge politics is set to emerge as an arena of significant political activity and choices, and on the other, that much can be anticipated. Knowledge politics will have a major impact on what future societies will look like.

A substantial part of this study was finished during fellowships at the Hanse Wissenschaftskolleg, Delmenhorst, Germany, and the Kulturwissenschaftliche Institut, Essen, Germany, from 2000 to 2004. The productive atmosphere in these two centers for advanced study contributed greatly to this work. I am also grateful to a large number of friends and colleagues who have read and commented on parts of or the bulk of the manuscript, to patient audiences who listened and responded to public presentation of some of the issues discussed in this volume, and also to readers of brief newspaper and magazine articles that addressed one or another issue dealing with modern knowledge politics. I would like to thank Gernot Böhme, Aant Elzinga, Andrew Feenberg, Steve Fuller, Reiner Grundmann, Kevin Jones, Maurice Richter, Gene Rosa, Barry Schwartz, and Justin Stagl for their critical and constructive comments. The remaining deficiencies are my responsibility.

Overview

This book is organized as follows: In the Introduction which follows this brief summary of the argument of the book, an effort is made to show that a new field of political activity is emerging that responds to public concerns about and objections to the use of mainly new scientific and technical knowledge in modern societies. Knowledge politics as conceptualized here evolves in reaction to fundamental questions raised about the social, political, and moral utility of new discoveries and inventions.

The first, longer section of my study deals with the central concepts of my analysis and offers observations about "Knowledge of Knowledge." The concept of knowledge is one of the most widely used concepts in everyday life and in scientific discourse. The idea that we are living in a knowledge society is gaining acceptance, as is the notion that the modern economy is knowledge-based and that the world of work is both transformed by and based on knowledge and information. But what knowledge is exactly and how it perhaps differs from information, human capital, and other cognitive skills and competencies is quite contentious.

Thus, it is self-evident that one needs to spend time and care examining the central notion of knowledge in knowledge politics. This requires, as I will try to argue, a sociological conception of knowledge concerned, in this context, not so much with the traditional question of the sociology of knowledge—namely its social bases—but rather with the kind of "work" knowledge performs in the context of social action. What is at issue therefore is not to emphasize yet again that knowledge is a negotiated product of human inquiry, but to apprehend the social impact such knowledge has and to respond to its likely social, economic, and cultural effects. This includes a discussion of when it is that knowledge acquires an active function in social action and how knowledge may assimilate to power.

By the same token, in this section on knowledge about knowledge, I will discuss the difference between knowledge and information, recognizing the regularity with which the two concepts are conflated in everyday and scientific discourse.

1

Of particular relevance to the issue of knowledge politics is the question of whether knowledge has some built-in protective attributes or whether it seems to operate according to a kind of self-realizing process. In both cases, the impact, if not the very possibility, of knowledge politics is at stake. Finally, I will refer to the famous metaphor that knowledge is power, and especially to its often repeated variant—that cutting-edge knowledge is only of immediate use to elites. In this context, I will discuss theoretical perspectives that, in my opinion, systematically overestimate the extent to which knowledge gravitates toward the powerful in society and can easily be deployed by them to cement their privileges and control. In other words, a differentiated understanding of some of the salient attributes of knowledge assists in significant ways the exercise of passing judgment on the question of whether knowledge politics in democratic societies is even possible or, for that matter, sensible.

In order to disentangle the frequent, uncritical linkage of power and knowledge, I would like to offer, first, some observations about the attributes of knowledge that could account for its power in practical circumstances. And what better theoretical treatise to examine for answers to this question than John Maynard Keynes' extraordinarily influential *General Theory of Employment, Interest, and Money,* first published in 1936.

In the second part of my discussion of the power of ideas, I will refer to various recent theoretical perspectives that see the power of knowledge closely linked to certain attributes of knowledge that are embedded in all forms of knowledge emerging from the scientific community. I will analyze another set of answers to the question of the reasons for the power of knowledge, which assign responsibility instead to specific social forces. It follows that adherents of both perspectives must be highly skeptical that knowledge politics is possible in democratic societies or, for that matter, likely to even emerge given the strength with which power and knowledge are associated.

In the following, equally extensive chapters, "The Governance of Knowledge" and "Rules, Regulations, and Restrictions," I plan to discuss a broad set of issues, including motives, methods, and institutional possibilities for arriving at collective decisions in democratic societies on sets of knowledge issues that represent new challenges, and yet refer back to intentions and practices that are by no means novel.

Knowledge politics and knowledge policies—the control and regulation of the social, cultural, and economic use of (not only newly added) knowledge, and therefore of the kind of impact knowledge and technical artifacts have on the social fabric that deploys rules and sanctions—have always been a part of modern regulatory apparatuses of societies, put into place by different social institutions and organizations, and widely accepted as part of "doing business." However, since the 1970s there has been an explosion in the volume of regulation and the range of activities that are subject to regulatory regimes in modern societies. Environmental policy is one such growing field of government regulation in recent decades. The approaches taken to regulation, the scope and coverage of regulation, as well as the regulatory standards and regulatory apparatus, vary considerably from country to country—for example, in the forms of regulatory jurisdiction, implementation, enforcement, sanctions, and supervision.

It therefore is not contradictory to stress that numerous social activities have been subject to state-imposed control and command for decades and even centuries, and yet argue that the field of knowledge politics is for the most part a newly emerging political and societal agenda. New technological developments have always induced the need to regulate their use. But the rules and norms that were formulated *followed* the implementation of new technologies and the discovery of problems related to the introduction of new technologies. Even the more recent field of environmental policy and regulation—including the growing number of international environmental agreements—aims for the most part at fixing existing and not anticipated externalities. In contrast, knowledge politics is an emergent form of responding to and dealing with *novel* forms of knowledge that have yet to be put into practice. Societies will have to experiment with new ways and methods of resolving these disputes and demands for the implementation of new techniques and new forms of knowledge.

The discussion of motives and methods of governing knowledge in modern societies in the second and third chapters merges with the following section on the "Moralization of the Markets." My examination of what I call the moralization of the markets has multiple purposes in the context of an analysis of knowledge politics. The moralization of the markets—that is, the gradual but growing transformation of the motives that govern market decisions by investors, consumers, and producers—has the purpose of underlining the observation that knowledge politics cannot be left to a state-centered analysis of the social control of knowledge. Market forces play a significant role. It is not only the state and legal apparatuses that have a central role in modern knowledge politics. Knowledge politics also results from what might be conceptualized as the unintended outcome of intentional (economic) action. Decisions by consumers, investors, and producers in the marketplace amount to a form of knowledge politics that is highly significant and that, at least initially, does not rely on a state-based regulatory system. State regulation may follow the marketplace. Under the heading of the moralization of the markets, I will discuss the nature of economic exchange in market capitalism and its transformation into a knowledge-based economy. I will discuss the "material" basis for a change of the motive structure of marketplace decisions and refer to the unique historical experience of advanced societies: Nothing in the history of the industrialized countries of Western Europe and North America resembles their experience between 1950 and 1985. By the end of that period, the perpetual possibility of serious economic hardship, which had earlier always hovered over the lives of three-quarters of the population, now menaced only about one-fifth of it. Although absolute poverty still existed in even the richest countries, the material standard of living for most people had improved almost without interruption and often very rapidly for thirty-five years. Above all else, these are the marks of the uniqueness of the experience. The immense change in the existential conditions of millions of people provides one foundation, perhaps the most important, for the moralization of the markets in advanced societies.

At the center of the section on the moralization of the markets, then, are observations mainly about the market of consumer goods and the formation of the *use value* of goods and services. The symbolic determination of the value of goods and services is increasingly influenced by new values that are attached to a product or service and which then impact their use value in the marketplace. The new values displace more "rational" or economic motives of decision-making in the marketplace. These transformations of the moral basis of economic conduct amount, as it were, to a form of market-driven modern knowledge politics.

In our day and age, inasmuch as social, economic, political, scientific, and cultural processes operate not merely within national boundaries but are subject to the now much-discussed globalization process, knowledge politics cannot be treated in isolation from globalization. Thus, in the last section of the study, the coupling of globalization and knowledge politics is at issue. If a society wants to protect itself against the consequences of the implementation of new knowledge, it will be necessary not only to assure that all efforts to implement a particular procedure are stopped within a given society, but also to reach agreements that extend such prohibitions well beyond the boundaries of a single country. All of this produces immense challenges and perhaps insurmountable obstacles. Whether or not globalization processes under way will enhance such barriers to knowledge politics is one of the themes raised in the last section of the book.

Introduction: A Millsian World of Knowledge

In this introduction, I will try to make the case that a new field of political activity is emerging, the field of knowledge politics. It is a response to growing public concerns about and objections to the use of new scientific and technical knowledge in modern societies. Knowledge politics as conceptualized here has evolved in reaction to fundamental questions raised about the social, political, and moral utility of new discoveries and inventions. I will indicate in greater detail what developments are responsible for the emergence of knowledge politics. Of course, knowledge politics is not practiced in a historical vacuum; it has distinctive links to past motives and methods. But it also represents a break with the past.

However, my examination of knowledge politics has no immediate connection to observations that natural scientific and technical knowledge is "under siege" in a very different sense in modern society, fostered perhaps not only by science studies but also by such notions as the "risk society." Countless empirical studies of the fabrication of scientific and technical knowledge have shown that it does not in fact live up to its image of an authoritative and uncontested source of advice and insight into the workings of nature. Actors who rely on science and technology are increasingly cognizant that scientific knowledge is uncertain, often essentially contested and not always helpful for providing closure to public controversies. In this manner, science studies have provided a major extension of the classical sociology of knowledge and have closely examined the social basis of natural scientific knowledge (Stehr, 2002b).

While students of scientific activity entered the laboratories in which science is done and showed how allegedly extraneous factors and processes impact the construction of scientific knowledge, a much smaller group of researchers asked what implications the new understanding of scientific knowledge has for public debates on the uses of science. This group of scholars advocated that the new understanding of science, if it had not already penetrated public consciousness, ought to enter into the public understanding of science and the ways in which social institutions in modern societies approach science. One was able to infer from these observations about the nature of science that doubts expressed toward science are legitimate, that science should not be seen as a single, authoritative voice, and that other forms of knowledge may well claim to speak to contentious public issues as well.

This study of knowledge politics does not aim to make essentially the same points yet again, nor to express concern about degrading the traditional image of the social efficacy of knowledge. It does not immediately matter what public image science may have acquired in today's advanced societies, nor whether traditional epistemological views are under siege. It is more likely that the public image of science will be affected by debates and disputes that center on demands to control the social role of knowledge. What matters more, initially, is that knowledge is a capacity to act, and that knowledge, not alone of course, can alter reality.

Moreover, what is at issue here is the shift from regulating and policing normality or identity (Foucault) to the growing concern in knowledge societies with efforts to police novelty and differences.[1] Technological and scientific innovation often is seen as driven by the need of corporate and state agencies, operating in tandem, to manage and regulate their immensely enlarged domains of control and profitability. In the end they diminish the individual's role in democratic participation; they intensify isolation, threaten individual privacy, heighten the sense of individual helplessness, and erode the differentiation between private and public spheres of life. But knowledge politics as discussed here is not about the alleged complicity of knowledge and power and the gains from new knowledge that inevitably flow to the powerful.[2] The interest here is in how novel knowledge is regulated and controlled by a whole range of actors in modern society and why such control includes conduct that has the unintended consequence of regulating knowledge.

The main questions therefore are: Will what can be done always be done? What is knowledge for? I plan to discuss what I take may well become one of the most significant and contentious issues for intellectual, legal, public, scientific, and political discourse during the century that has just begun:[3] the growing pressure to regulate or police *novel* knowledge—or, in other words, the emergence of a new field of political activity, namely knowledge politics and policies.[4] What is at stake is more than merely the vague feeling that we need a slowdown or consolidation in the fabrication of new knowledge.

Knowledge politics, or the governance of knowledge, is about attempts to channel the social role of knowledge, to generate rules and enforce sanctions pertaining to relevant actors and organizations, to affix certain attributes (such as property restrictions) to knowledge, and—likely the most controversial strategy—to restrict the application of new knowledge and technical artifacts.[5] These efforts, of course, will be mainly located *outside* the immediate boundaries of the scientific community.[6] The essence of knowledge politics consists of strategic efforts to move new scientific and technical knowledge, and thereby the future, into the center of the cultural, economic, and political matrix of society.[7] Despite what the term may appear to suggest on the surface, knowledge politics is not inherently prohibitive.

The regulation of knowledge—in the general sense of attempts to control knowledge, and not merely through statutory enactments and administrative regulations and decisions—also extends to efforts designed to enhance and enlarge the options and opportunities for the use of new knowledge in society. Many segments of civil society want governments to enact measures aimed at satisfying their ideas or demands for the future use of knowledge, be it in the field of health care, education, the environment, or social policies in varied fields within and across nations. As a matter of fact, as long as at least some societies continue to place a strong emphasis on the virtue of individual initiative and decisions based on self-interest, the institutions, if only passively, encourage the use of novel scientific knowledge and technical devices (Green, 1976: 171).[8]

However, in the context of this study I will focus on the control of knowledge (which suggests that knowledge generated by molecular genetics, for example, may involve "adverse" individual or collective consequences which justify its regulation on these grounds), rather than on the extension of methods of deploying knowledge in modern society. Although one should not underestimate the persistence of governance regimes once institutionalized, an analysis of the governance of knowledge in modern society has to be cognizant of the general practical incompleteness, fragility, obsolescence, and often failure of projects aimed at governance in modern societies, as well as, more narrowly, the possibility that rapid deregulation will follow on the heels of regulatory efforts (as was the case in the field of genetic engineering in the early 1980s).[9] The tempo at which knowledge evolves may be a further reason why specific attempts to regulate knowledge become obsolete. Regulative politics is surpassed by the dynamics of knowledge.[10] Hence this study, in response to these questions, can be only an interim report.[11]

Why is a knowledge politics emerging? Why are there growing efforts to exert power over knowledge? Why are we, perhaps in growing numbers, not prepared simply to accept the apparently "natural" progression and to take for granted the relentless exponential development of scientific knowledge, and of technical artifacts and their application, as a key to unlocking the mysteries of the world, as a release from pain and freedom from suffering, as the basis for a better and just society, and as a means for greater prosperity? Or to believe that more knowledge simply represents an emancipation from all kinds of troubling ills and harsh constraints? The straightforward, or at least traditional, assumption that specialized knowledge ought to command respect in general, and that any increase in knowledge automatically brings with it an increase in benefits to humankind in particular, is becoming porous and vulnerable.[12] However, the idea that the uselessness of science is a virtue and that the uses that humans "have drawn from science have contributed to their misery" (Chargaff, 1975: 21), or that the fruits of gene technology will simply not amount to improvements in the human condition (Callahan, 2003), or that science threatens our existence (Rees, 2003), are still marginal voices, rarely heard.

Still, the optimistic faith, nurtured in a period of unprecedented economic growth in the 1950s and early 1960s, that a constant expansion of knowledge might even prompt a displacement of politics and ideology (Bell, 1960, 1973; Brooks, 1965; Lane, 1966) has been thoroughly demystified (King and Melanson, 1972). After a couple of centuries of widespread certainty that progress in science and technology equaled progress in society, the development of the "techno-sciences," as Lyotard (1989: 9) suggests, is increasingly seen as "a means of increasing disease, not of fighting it."

If one no longer regards the fabrication and use of additional scientific knowledge as a humanitarian project, "as an unquestioned ultimate good, one is willing to consider its disciplined direction" (Sinsheimer, 1978: 23). Fears that we know too much, or that we are about to assume the role of God, or are going to commence a "self-transformation of the species" (Habermas, 2001: 42)[13] or "self-engineering" (Jonas, 1982), are increasingly replacing the concern that we do not know enough, and that we are to a large degree poorly informed or have difficulties coping with scientific knowledge which is uncertain. Apprehension and alarm replace the rhetoric of hope and aspiration that until recently dominated societal discourse about new developments in science and technology in modern societies (Mulkay, 1993: 735–739).[14] The nature of the empowerment, for example, in the field of biotechnology, that accompanies the enlargement of knowledge is now looked upon with growing misgivings: "If we are to understand what biotechnology is for, we shall need to keep our eye more on the new abilities it provides than on the technical instruments and products that make these abilities available to us" (President's Council on Bioethics, 2003: 2).

The concern that we know too much is no longer—as was the case in the seventies of the last century, for example—that we are amassing a large store of trivial and practically irrelevant knowledge at a high price that promises no useful gains (Lübbe, 1977: 14). The worry that our conduct persistently lags behind the development of knowledge has been replaced by concerns about the accumulation of novel knowledge that appears to have questionable social and cultural consequences. In that sense, at least, current concerns about science represent a return to conflicts that science has experienced in the past. But in contrast to past disputes, when discussions about the societal consequences of science were driven by complaints about its deficient social and economic utility in tackling major social problems of the day, today's concern is directed at a surplus of effects—especially with respect to traditional world views, established life-worlds, and the limits to what can be manipulated in nature and society. I will try to offer some realistic answers to these and associated questions about the regulation of knowledge in modern societies, such as the possibilities, foundations, prospects, and effectiveness of (modern) knowledge politics in an age of increasing globalization.

One can ask, for example: Would knowledge permitting an extension of average human life expectancy be applied almost instantly after its discovery as a capacity for action? Once medical intervention is possible prior to the onset of a disorder, why wait until someone falls ill? But should we not fear, on the other hand, a much-improved predictability of individual life expectancy or a therapy that precedes an illness? Might such predictability of the lifespan of the individual eliminate much of the spontaneity of action, or even lead to horrible mistakes individuals feel prompted to undertake that are irreversible? Do we want to live in a world in which control of all conquerable genetic defects is possible? In what ways will the state or other corporate actors intervene between prospective parents and their ability to decide the genetic makeup of their children? Should the prerogative of individual autonomy prevail in these cases, or should collective prerogatives govern decision-making about the potential utilization of new knowledge? Even more generally, will new genetic technologies intensify existing social inequalities and inequities? The legend of Faust resonates with the ambivalence that accompanies the fascination of science's persistent quest for missing answers and the fear of what such a pursuit of the unknown may engender.

All of these issues become even more interesting and perplexing in light of the observation that we are in fact living in an age of deregulation and that those who advocate the withdrawal of the state by pushing a neoliberal policy agenda have won the day. At least within the developed world, there appears to be no exception to the strong support for neoliberal policies that promote deregulation efforts, be it by freeing labor markets, by lowering taxes, or by withdrawing from strong welfare-state policies (Cerny, 1991).

The politics of regulating new knowledge and novel technical devices is bound to upset the established line of political conflicts and in many instances may well create "strange political bedfellows" in the form of novel and quickly changing political coalitions. Central emotionally and politically charged debates in modern society about the authority of science, medicine, or experts—and also about politics and control of the body, the desirable relations between nature and society, the meaning of technology and human agency, and the linkages between ethics and knowledge—will not only be symbolically recast and heavily strained, but also reinvented.

It is necessary from the outset to define a distinction that I will try to sustain as far as possible, though this may be difficult in some instances—namely, the difference between science policy and knowledge policy. My interest focuses on knowledge, not science policies. For instance, the contested issue of human embryonic cell research, much in the public eye in recent months, is a question that goes to the heart of science policy.[15] Science policies regulate and control *research*. Science policy as conducted by governments, firms, and foundations refers directly to the creation of scientific knowledge—the individuals who produce such knowledge; the social context within which knowledge is fabricated; incentives such as tax policies, tariffs, and subsidized research and development; and the alleged benefits of science for society, which legitimate various efforts to "manage" science. Science and technology policies are drawn up and implemented using a variety of instruments, some of which I have just listed, in social systems outside the scientific community. The goal, of course, is to gain leverage in the fabrication of scientific knowledge and the development of technologies. Most recently, control and constraints on research were recommended by a panel of biological scientists of the U.S. National Academy of Sciences and justified for national security reasons; specifically, the panel recommended "prior review of experiments [by a local and a federal committee in seven areas of biology] that could help terrorists or hostile nations make biological weapons."[16]

In contrast, the capacities to act on the knowledge generated by research on (embryonic) stem cells extracted from human embryos—which have the potential to grow into any cell or tissue in the human body and therefore might be instrumental, as proponents suggest, in curing degenerative diseases such as Parkinson's, Alzheimer's, heart disease, kidney failure, and diabetes—pertains to the emerging field of knowledge politics. As the report of the U.S. National Bioethics Advisory Commission (1999: 20) emphasizes, many diseases, such as Parkinson's disease and juvenile-onset diabetes mellitus, are triggered by the death or dysfunction of just one cell type, or of only a few cell types. A substitution of cells grown in the laboratory could offer effective treatment and even cures for such illnesses. Widespread applications in this case and other medical ones may indeed remain a long way off, but discussions and disputes about the effects, benefits, and risks will take place in tandem with ongoing research.[17] Summing up, knowledge policies refer to what knowledge can do and to what it is; science policies refer to how knowledge can be produced, in the first instance.

But the promise that research efforts utilizing embryonic stem cells are likely to yield considerable therapeutic benefits makes it probable that a liberal mix of science and knowledge policy disputes will occur.[18] One set of disputes refers to science policy matters, such as resource allocation, while others already anticipate new knowledge claims and instrumental abilities that will become central to knowledge policy discussions. A bill passed by the U.S. House of Representatives in late July 2001 that prohibits the cloning of embryonic stem cells ("therapeutic cloning")[19] and human cloning ("reproductive cloning")—a ban now supported by more than sixty of the world's leading science academies[20]—directly affects research in this field.[21] Nonetheless, it is entirely possible that knowledge policies will become indistinguishable from research policies, as intentions and agendas of the former extend into and intervene directly or indirectly in the production of knowledge in the scientific community. Moreover, as knowledge politics becomes more widely instituted, the "nature" of research likely will change, moving toward what might be called a much more reflexive mode of scientific research, in which critical societal responses and consequences are taken into consideration.

A less entangled example of knowledge policy, in contrast to science policy, was the curtailment in 1975 by the government of a Harvard-based genetic screening program for XYY chromosome patterns. The genetic work, using known techniques, was controversial because it pursued the idea that there was a significant correlation between deviant behavior and the presence of the XYY chromosome. Pressure from the Children's Defense Fund and similar groups brought about a ban enacted by the Reagan administration.

In addition, the formulation of agendas and the nature of specific science and knowledge policies likely depend on common sociopolitical convictions or trends, such as the resolve either to pursue strongly interventionist science and knowledge policies or to support and strengthen the autonomy of the scientific community and market forces. The discursive, heuristic distinction between science and knowledge policy does not imply that new knowledge is, in the context of societal change, the outcome of an exogenous process. Novel knowledge results from endogenous social processes. It does not fall from the sky nor appear by accident on the scene.

A second, immediately relevant distinction helpful in delineating the issues at hand refers to the regulation of existing forms of knowledge and the regulation of additional knowledge that still has to be realized. Culture, in a most general sense, constitutes control. Culture dictates and regulates, and it has done so from the beginning. What is new is the tempo at which new knowledge is generated—additional knowledge that needs to be assessed and controlled in some fashion.

Among the growing number of recent news items that illustrate the issue of knowledge policy, I refer at this point to just a few relevant announcements: In September of 2001, the acting head of the ethics committee of the American Society for Reproductive Medicine announced that in his view, it would sometimes be acceptable for couples to choose the sex of their children by selecting either female or male embryos, and discarding the rest. One group of fertility clinics was quick to respond; the chairman of the board of the Center for Human Reproduction indicated that the center would offer the procedure immediately.[22] In another example, the U.S. Food and Drug Administration indicated in early June of 2001 that it did not want meat or milk from cloned livestock sold to consumers. First, it would have to be established that the food was "safe" and that the technology did not "harm" the environment or the animals. A study carried out by the National Academy of Sciences was supposed to provide answers to these questions.[23] Also in June, the German ministry of consumer affairs and agriculture announced that a particular brand of genetically engineered corn seed (Artius) would not be permitted for commercial uses on German farms. The seed in question was resistant to a particular herbicide. If that herbicide was used, it destroyed other plants and left the corn unaffected. Further studies by a state research institute are required. The genetically engineered brand of corn seed would have been the first such seed permitted to be sold and freely used.[24]

An unambiguous observation about the societal regulation of power (in the Weberian sense of the term) by John Kenneth Galbraith (1983: 83) offers the following proposition: "The precision and effectiveness of the regulation of the use of condign power are, perhaps, the clearest index of the level of civilization in a community, and they are extensively so regarded in practice." If this is the case and if, as I will assert, new or additional knowledge is among the growing sources of power in modern society, then by analogy the regulation of the use of such knowledge becomes an indicator of the civility of social relations in modern society. Knowledge politics will be a strongly contested form of regulative politics, but that there will be knowledge politics is a certainty. We should not have any excessive hopes, however, that our ability to anticipate (in any robust sense) the social impact of the use of novel capacities to act (knowledge) will be very impressive. Similarly, knowledge politics will be enacted even though the ability to forecast the consequences of intervention in systems *other* than the political system is likely quite limited (Luhmann, [1991] 1993: 155).

Thus, for a variety of reasons, it is important to reflect more directly and intensively about the kind of knowledge we need, as well as about the use we make of the knowledge we have. I will concentrate on the importance of the use of incremental, new knowledge in society. Such a focus extends, of course, to what is now sometimes called "biopolitics," inasmuch as the term suggests that it is the function of the political system to regulate nothing less than the way we deal with the nature of life, especially in response to new capacities that would affect the ways this system could act on our life and that of others.

The emergence of knowledge politics occurs with some delay in response to the exceptional growth and speed with which knowledge and technical capacities are added in modern societies. Appropriating Adolph Lowe's (1971: 563) astute insights, the change is from social realities in which "things" simply "happen" (at least from the point of view of most people) to a social world in which more and more things are "made" to happen. Advanced society may be described as a knowledge society because of the penetration of all its spheres by scientific and technical knowledge.[25] In knowledge societies, the potential capability of what an individual can do and be is considerably enhanced. The societal changes I have in mind can also be described in the following way: In the case of large and influential social institutions, but also in the case of individuals and small social groups, the weight in the relation of autonomy and conditionality is shifting. The sum total of conditionality and autonomy is not constant. Both autonomy and conditionality of social action are capable of growing. They may also decline. In knowledge societies, the degree of apprehended autonomy of individuals and small social groups increases, while the extent of conditionality shrinks. In the case of large collectivities such as the state, large corporations, science, the church, etc., the extent to which their conduct is conditioned may decline as well, but their autonomy or ability to impose their will does not increase in proportion. While the limits of what can be done are rewritten, the responsibility for the changes that are under way must be shared by a larger segment of society.[26]

The boundaries of what once appeared to be solidly beyond the ability of all of us to change, to alter, or to manage are rapidly being moved and penetrated. This applies, for example, to the possibility that in the not too distant future, we may come to review the validity of the Lamarckian idea that deliberately induced genetic transformations in one individual may be passed to one's offspring. The result, of course, is that new knowledge and new technical abilities as capacities to act are also perceived as a peril posed to every woman, man, and child, as a burden and as a threat, not merely to privacy, the status quo, the understanding of what life is, and the course of life, but also as a danger to the very nature of creation. As the biologist Robert Sinsheimer (1976b: 599) put it, shortly after the discovery of the possibility of genetic engineering by recombinant DNA techniques:

> With the advent of synthetic biology we leave the security of that web of natural evolution that, blindly and strangely, bore us and all of our fellow creatures. With each step we will be increasingly on our own. The invention and introduction of new self-reproducing, living forms may well be irreversible. How do we prevent grievous missteps, inherently unretractable? Can we in truth foresee the consequences, near- and long-term, of our interventions? By our wits mankind has become the master of the extant living world. Will shortsighted ingenuity now spawn new competitors to bedevil us?

The growth of knowledge and technical capacities is not prompted merely by sheer curiosity interested in penetrating the secrets of nature and society but is also driven by economic and military interests. In deploying novel knowledge and technical artifacts for economic growth and military purposes, the social costs and environmental burdens produced are treated as exogenous and ex post developments. As the term "exogenous costs" signals, perceived burdens and costs are mitigated as far as possible only after the realization of new knowledge. A growing gap between perceived benefits and burdens, of course, will enhance calls for the proactive regulation of new knowledge and technical capacities. Vanderburg, for example, refers to the existence of a "labyrinth of technology" in modern societies, meaning the extent to which these civilizations are trapped within the dilemma of first creating burdens of various kinds as the result of making use of science and technology and then mitigating these costs. The labyrinth of technology necessitates the "creation of an approach for the engineering, management, and regulation of modern technology that proactively prevents social and environmental burdens" (Vanderburg, 2000: xi).

However, in order to gain a better understanding of the social role of knowledge in modern society, it is necessary to spend some time critically examining our knowledge about knowledge.

Notes

1. Nor is the political field that I identify as "knowledge politics" immediately connected with the often felt and ambivalent sense of crisis in modern societies, based on what is apprehended as the overproduction and/or mass production of knowledge. The tension between the volume of knowledge production in advanced societies and the limited capability of the individual person to assimilate the huge amount of knowledge available, was vividly described by Georg Simmel ([1907] 1989) in the final chapter of his *Philosophy of Money*. For Simmel, the tragedy of culture manifests itself in the cleavage between objective culture made independent and the obstinacy of subjective culture. The problem of the policing of knowledge is not related to the overproduction of knowledge—however that may be defined—but rather to incremental knowledge, which is a scarce resource and apprehended as capable of changing reality in dramatic ways.

2. In a later section on the "power of ideas," I will briefly address the question of why Michel Foucault's perspective on the marriage of knowledge and power is not immediately relevant to my study.

3. Dorothy Nelkin (1995: 447–456) has published an informative typology of public controversies in the United States in recent years in which segments of the scientific community were involved.

4. A report issued by the Rand Corporation (Fukuyama and Wagner, 2000:1; also Fukuyama, 2002) anticipates in an analogous sense that in the early part "of the twenty-first century, the technologies emerging from the information and biotechnology revolutions will present unprecedented governance challenges to national and international political systems." The report deals with the governance of both research and knowledge policies. Harriet Zuckerman (1986: 342), as well, has written about the need to examine critically how we use the knowledge we have.

5. Anxieties and concerns about the social consequences of new scientific knowledge and novel technologies are not of recent origin (Rüstow, 1951). Dystopian novels such as Aldous Huxley's *Brave New World* or George Orwell's *1984* represent but one genre among multiple cultural critiques of the societal consequences of modern science and technology. And, as Steve Fuller (2000a: 121) has pointed out, deliberate attempts to at least discourage or to impose restrictions on the implementation of new discoveries and inventions for the workplace were part of the industrial policy of the New Deal in the United States during the Depression years. As the Depression reached it peak, a key function of the New Deal industrial policy in the United States was to curb chronic unemployment. In order to ensure that unemployment would not grow even more, industrial policies of the day discouraged engineers from developing even more efficient forms of automation that would displace workers, and regulations were introduced that restricted the deployment of such innovations into the workplace.

6. I emphasize that knowledge politics is instigated mainly outside the scientific community; however, there are significant exceptions and responses from within the scientific community to knowledge politics. For example, to take a recent case, the *New York Times* reports that "more than 20 leading scientific journals [including *Science* and *Nature*] have made a pact to censor articles that they believe could compromise national security, regardless of their scientific merit" ("Journals to consider U.S. security," February 16, 2003). The policies adopted by the journal editors were in response to the debates about open access to publications in the wake of the anthrax attacks in the United States in 2001. Critics were quick to call these policies a step in the wrong direction, since journal editors have no conclusive and realizable way of assessing the potential practical outcomes of new knowledge.

7. A discussion of the economics of biotechnology and why that can no longer be uncoupled from ethical, environmental, legal, and political considerations may be found in Gaisford, Hobbs, Kerr, Perdilis, and Plunkett, 2001.

8. Taking the opposite position, Niklas Luhmann ([1991] 1993: 173) observes, perhaps reflecting an "old European" political perspective and experience, that the pressure to act characterizes the political system: "Politics presents itself as a system of societal control. This alone may dispose it to action rather than inaction. We seldom find mere inaction entered on the credit side of governmental balance sheets."

9. The conservative Thatcher government in Great Britain issued a White Paper in which deregulation efforts were seen as the best way to support the biotechnology industry of the country. It argued that the support of the biotechnology industry required the removal of "regulatory constraints inhibiting biotechnology development, such as burdensome health and safety regulations" (Gottweis, 1995:202).

10. A case in point could be the discovery of a highly versatile group of adult stem cells isolated from the bone marrow, which may make obsolete much of the discussion of the use of techniques that rely on embryonic stem cells (see "Scientists herald a versatile adult cell," *New York Times,* January 25, 2002). Moreover, it is possible, as recent findings suggest, that embryonic stem cells may be acquired not with the aid of embryos but with the help of unfertilized cells (see "Forscher entdecken neue Quellen für embryonale und adulte Stammzellen, *Die Welt,* April 24, 2003).

11. The interim nature of this study is at least partly an outcome of the unprecedented rapidity with which new technical artifacts are developed and move to market, and with which new forms of knowledge are fabricated. As a consequence, many of the discussions and disputes regarding the social impact of novel knowledge can now be found in the media, especially in daily or weekly publications that are able to respond in a more timely

fashion to rapid developments. For this reason, I will make more frequent reference than is customary in studies of this kind to news items, comments, and contributions in the "fast" press, rather than in conventional academic journals or books. One also has to be cognizant of the possibility that there may be a deep rift between the knowledge-based future scenarios discussed in the fast media and developments that can, in fact, be realized in practice. Finally, it is, of course, impossible to anticipate what knowledge and what artifacts will form the substantive reference for disputes, conflicts, and debates surrounding their anticipated impact on the individual and society.

12. Now that the idea that progress in science must invariably equal progress in human affairs is no longer widely taken for granted, it is worth briefly mentioning that the equation that has fallen into disrepute did not find strong support until the age of Francis Bacon, who himself did much to expedite its acceptance and promotion. Bacon was very cognizant that the identification of advances in science and society could not be taken for granted, but rather had to be established, especially among the ruling classes. In much of antiquity the idea of progress was completely absent, and in the Middle Ages human progress was not expected either to arrive with or to derive from the secular sciences (cf. Böhme, 1992).

13. Jürgen Habermas ([1998] 2001:164) opposes human cloning and raises the analogy to slavery, on the grounds that no "person may so dispose over another person, may so control his possibilities for acting, in such a way that the dependent person is deprived of an essential part of his freedom. This condition is violated if one person decides the genetic makeup of another." The difference between cloning and "standard" human reproduction is, however, difficult to detect in respect to the moral prohibition Habermas wants us to observe. As one might formulate it, birth is always "determined" not by the individual that is born but by others.

14. For example, an essay collection that challenges the societal merits of biotechnologies warns, "Today's biotechnologies are products of a very particular social context: a market-dominated, hypercompetitive capitalist society in which virtually all the social decisions that affect most people's lives are driven by powerful, unaccountable political and economic institutions ... [The] biotechnology industry seeks to commodify all of life, to absorb all that is alive into the sphere of products to be bought, sold, and traded in the commercial marketplace. The institutions that are developing genetic engineering and other biotechnologies appear to be seeking nothing less than the private ownership of all life on earth" (Tokar, 2001:217–218).

15. Since 1995, the U.S. Congress has every year attached a ban to its appropriations legislation disallowing support of stem cell research with public monies. Research funds raised from private sources may be used for stem cell research in the United States. As a result, James A. Thompson (e.g., 1998) of the University of Wisconsin—the discoverer of the method to isolate embryonic stem cells (from frozen embryos that were no longer wanted by couples who created them to have children)—carries out his research on stem cells in a separate laboratory supported by private research funds (see "Scientist's stem cell work creates uproar," *New York Times,* July 10, 2001). The type of political considerations (see Brave, 2001: 7) that play a role in decisions for or against public support for research on embryonic stem cells can be gleaned from a report in the *New York Times* ("Bush aides seek compromise on embryonic cell research," July 4, 2001). The decision for or against stem cell research with the aid of federal funds will also be carefully judged—by presidential advisors and observers—against the background of declining support for President Bush as reflected in surveys during his first months in office in the summer of 2001, mainly because the President was seen as too conservative. The presidential advisors argued against making research funds available. But due also to the low approval ratings of the president

prior to September 1, 2001, the political decision has been postponed and newly debated. Whatever the decision will be, some portion of the American voting public will be disappointed.

16. "Science panel urges review of research terrorists could use," *New York Times*, October 9, 2003.

17. How far away such treatments are—whether in the distant future or close at hand—is difficult to judge. See for example "Gene therapy used to treat patients with Parkinson's," *New York Times*, August 19, 2003, reporting about the first experimental cases of patients who received gene therapy for Parkinson's.

18. A report issued by the National Institutes of Health (NIH) in June of 2001 praises stem cell research and promises a "dazzling array" of treatments for various diseases that at present defy therapy (see "U.S. study hails stem cells' promise," *New York Times*, June 27, 2001). The report not only praises the almost limitless benefits of stem cell research, but also advocates its more or less unrestricted practice supported by federal funds, without analyzing ethical, legal, or social issues (see also NIH, "Institute and centers answer the question: 'What would you hope to achieve from human pluripotent stem cell research,'" www.nih.gov/news/stemcell/achieve.htm).

19. Lanza et al. (2000: 3175), who attempt to make an ethical case for therapeutic cloning, suggest that the term "therapeutic cloning," although widely used, is misleading because it "brings to mind images of the replication of a single genome for reproductive purposes. In therapeutic cloning, however, no such replication is involved." The description Lanza and his colleagues advance refers to therapeutic cloning as a new biomedical technology that "involves the transfer of the nucleus from one of the patient's cells into an enucleated donor oocyte for the purpose of making medically useful and immunilogically compatible cells and tissues." Both human reproductive cloning (duplicating an entire human organism) and therapeutic cloning currently begin by creating a human embryo.

20. "Scientists call for international ban on human cloning," *Guardian*, September 23, 2003.

21. Therapeutic cloning (or cell replacement by means of nuclear transfer) implies that embryos are created in order to experiment with them or use them to treat disease. In Great Britain, therapeutic cloning is legal, but not in the United States (see "House backs ban on human cloning for any objective," *New York Times*, August 1, 2001). President Bush has urged the U.S. Senate to follow the lead of the House of Representatives and ban cloning. The restrictions on "cloning research" has prompted some scientists to warn that *limiting science* is "cutting off hope," namely the hope of patients to obtain relief from advances in research in this field. The controversial issue of cloning human embryos has been reignited as the result of the announcement on November 25, 2001, by scientists at Advanced Cell Technology (ACT), a privately held company in Worcester, Massachusetts, that they had used cloning techniques to make several early human embryos, each from a cell taken from an adult (see "Mass. firm's disclosure renews cloning debate," *Washington Post*, November 27, 2001, p. A03). The company made it clear that the cloned embryos were solely produced for research purposes and not to produce adults. Within fourteen days, the embryos, activated oocytes, would be destroyed in the process. During a December 4, 2001, U.S. Senate hearing, the CEO and the chief ethicist of ACT (a professor of religion at Dartmouth) told a subcommittee that life does not begin until two weeks after conception or, in the case of the cloning process, the timing of the nuclear transfer. Why did the representatives of ACT choose the two-week period? At that juncture, known as the gastrulation or the formation of the primitive streak, the embryo "clarifies" whether it will become a single or two persons. Gastrulation takes place about two weeks after conception. At that point, the em-

bryonic mass organizes or aligns itself into layers. The layers form the first outline of an organism or, in the case of twins, two organisms. The CEO of ACT, Michael West, explained, "If the proposition was that we would clone a developing human being, I would [agree] with Sen. Brownback we shouldn't cross that line. We have a line here. It's the primitive streak ... Primitive streak, I think is an effective line to draw and say that that is the beginning of a human being, and prior to primitive streak we should use some other terminology ... because this is not an individualized human being" (as cited in William Saletan, "Everyone's a twinner," *Slate,* December 27, 2001; see also Lanza et al., 2000). In his article, Saletan points to the logical flaws in the position of the proponents of therapeutic cloning and the specific cut-off point they have identified that accounts for the beginning of human life. The flaw involves the accomplished cloning itself, for it represents evidence that the possibility of more than a single person emerging from a particular embryo is not finally determined at the two-week stage of the growth of the embryo. The (later) clone would be another person. The debate and the public relations struggle over cloning are by no means closed. It will become one of the central issues for knowledge politics. The dispute is bound to intensify in the future (see "Dispute over cloning experiments intensifies," *New York Times,* March 6, 2002). But *The Economist* already comments despairingly, "Many ethicists ... are paid consultants to the growing biomedical industry, and not a few scientists in this area are religious believers with a doctrinal agenda" (March 14, 2002, "Should we lock the door on cell science?").

22. The ruling refers to selection procedures using preimplantation genetic diagnostics, and not other techniques (compare "Fertility ethics authority approves sex selection," *New York Times,* September 29, 2001). The September 2001 decision of the ethics committee of the American Society for Reproductive Medicine was revised six months later. In a more restrictive opinion, the society suggested that couples should be discouraged from creating embryos using preimplantation genetic diagnostics, then selecting some while discarding others, solely because they had a child of one sex and wanted one of another. The society demanded that fertility clinics abide by the decision, and most indicated that they would ("Fertility society choosing embryos just for sex selection," *New York Times,* February 16, 2002). However, other techniques of sex selection, for example, "sperm sorting," were not affected by the society's ruling.

23. "Cloned livestock subject of review," *International Herald Tribune,* June 6, 2001, p. 3. In 2003, eight types of animal were successfully cloned using the so-called "Dolly method" first used in 1996, the most recent a cloned mule (see "Another clone milestone as a mule is born in Idaho," *New York Times,* May 30, 2003).

24. "Zulassung von Genmais vorerst gestoppt," *Frankfurter Allgemeine Zeitung,* June 6, 2001, p. 4.

25. It is in this general sense that the perspective advocated here and elsewhere in my analysis of modern society as a knowledge society (Stehr, 2001; 2002) is part of a broader theoretical orientation that has been called the *cultural turn* in the social sciences. The cultural turn in the social sciences emphasizes the socially constitutive role of cultural practices and signification, including of course the socially constitutive role of knowledge, and therefore fresh ways of looking at familiar social forces. For an analysis and exemplification of the cultural turn in the social sciences, see Steinmetz, 1999.

26. I have examined these changes in modern societies and their consequences in greater detail in *The Fragility of Modern Societies* (Stehr, 2001a).

Chapter 1

Knowledge about Knowledge

> One can easily be reproached for making a trivial observation if one suggests that the modern era is the age of science. Among the innumerable observations at which we have ceased to be amazed are the facts of the existence and the extraordinary impact of science, which affects our consciousness and conditions our life—in fact, makes it possible in the first place.
>
> *Hans Blumenberg,* The Legitimacy of the Modern Age[1]

The first section of my study deals with the central concept of my analysis—knowledge—and offers observations about our knowledge of knowledge. The concept of knowledge is one of the most widely used concepts in everyday life and in scientific discourse. The idea that we are living in a knowledge society is gaining acceptance, as is the notion that the modern economy is knowledge-based and that the world of work is both transformed by and based on knowledge and information. Thus, Hans Blumenberg's observation that our identity and our existential conditions are profoundly affected by knowledge is apt, as is his observation that our consciousness and our life represent realities created by our knowledge.

But what knowledge exactly is and how it perhaps differs from information, human capital, and other cognitive skills and competencies is a contentious matter. Thus, it is almost self-evident that one needs to spend time and care examining the central notion of the term "knowledge" in knowledge politics. This requires, as I will try to argue, a sociological conception of knowledge, concerned not so much with its social bases but with the kind of "work" knowledge performs in the context of social action. This includes a discussion of when it is that knowledge acquires a function in social action and how knowledge may assimilate to power.

19

By the same token, I will discuss the difference between knowledge and information, recognizing the regularity with which the two concepts are conflated in everyday and scientific discourse. Of particular relevance to the issue of knowledge politics is the question whether knowledge has built-in protective attributes or whether knowledge can be seen to operate according to a kind of self-realizing process. In both cases, the impact of the very possibility of knowledge politics is at stake. Finally, I will refer to the famous metaphor that knowledge is power and discuss perspectives that overestimate either the extent to which knowledge gravitates toward the powerful in society or to which it can easily be deployed by the powerful to cement their privileges.

In order to demonstrate fully the significance of knowledge for societies and social action, particularly for advanced societies—and therefore the assertion that knowledge is not merely the key to unraveling the secrets of nature and society but rather the becoming of a world—it is necessary first to formulate a *sociological* concept of knowledge that differentiates between what is known, the content of knowledge, and knowing itself. What is it, then, that we know, and what does it mean that we know? Some examples, taken from the *Oxford Dictionary of Current English,* are: "Every child knows that two and two make four. He knows a lot of English. Do you know how to play chess? I don't know whether he is here or not." These examples show that knowing is a relation not only to things and facts, but also to laws and rules. In any case, knowing is some sort of participation: knowing things, facts, and rules means to "appropriate" them in some manner, to include them in our field of orientation and competence. Rather than suggesting that knowledge is something that people have in their possession or are able to obtain with relative ease—a notion that is more appropriate for the term "information"—knowing is better seen as an activity, as something that individuals do (cf. Blackler, 1995: 1023). Knowledge can, of course, be objectified; that is, the intellectual appropriation of things, facts, and rules can be established symbolically, so that to know, it is not necessary to get into contact with the things themselves, but only with their symbolic representations. This is the social significance of language, writing, printing, and data storage. Modern societies have made dramatic advances in the intellectual appropriation of nature and society. There is an immense stock of objectified knowledge that mediates our relation to nature and to ourselves. In a general sense, this advancement used to be called, in earlier contexts, modernization or rationalization, leading to a "unity of civilization."[2] This secondary nature is overgrowing the primary nature of humans. The real and the fictional merge and become indistinguishable; theories become facts, but not vice versa. Facts, for example, cannot police theories. A sociological concept of knowledge has to accept the intrinsic "impurity" of knowledge, its rootedness in all social institutions (including science) and in cultural processes, its entanglement with power and interests, and its enormous variability.

It is only after a sense of the societal significance of such opposites and oppositions has been acquired that the full sociological significance of knowledge begins to emerge. Such a perspective leads to the realization that knowledge is increasingly the foundation of authority, and that access to knowledge becomes a major societal resource and the occasion for political and social struggles.

Although knowledge has always had a social function, it is only recently that scholars have begun to examine the structure of society and its development from the point of view of the production, distribution, and reproduction of knowledge.[3] Applied to present-day society, the question is whether knowledge can provide the principle for social hierarchies and stratification, for the formation of class structures, for the distribution of chances of social and political influence, and for the nature of personal life; and, finally, whether knowledge may also prove to be a normative principle of social cohesion and integration, even though the variations and alterations in the reproduction of knowledge appear to be enormous. Paradoxically, efforts to entrench necessity in history, or to eliminate chance from history, have produced its opposite, at least at the collective level. The role of chance, ambiguity and, as I will stress, "fragility" at the collective level, continues to be an increasingly important part of the way society comes to be organized.

One of the first comprehensive sociological analyses of societies in which the knowledge-producing sector attains decisive importance for the dynamics of social relations is Daniel Bell's *The Coming of Post-Industrial Society* (1973). Radovan Richta's theory of the scientific-technical revolution, formulated at roughly the same time, constitutes the "socialist" counter-image to Bell's theory of modern society as a postindustrial society. Bell (1973: 212) argues that postindustrial society is a *knowledge society* for two major reasons: (1) "The sources of innovation are increasingly derivative from research and development (and more directly, there is a new relation between science and technology because of the centrality of theoretical knowledge)," and, (2) "The weight of the society—measured by a larger proportion of Gross National Product and a larger share of employment—is increasingly in the knowledge field." The pace and scale of the translation of knowledge into technology provide the basis for the possibility of modernity. Thus, if there is a "radical gap between the present and the past, it lies in the nature of technology and the ways it has transformed social relations and our ways of looking at the world" (Bell, 1968: 174).

Science has been the site where most currently circulating concepts of knowledge have originated during the past centuries. But in the attempt to elaborate and come to a shared understanding of knowledge, scientific discourse has developed a taken-for-granted attitude toward its own knowledge. The number of well-explicated categories of knowledge has therefore been limited. We have not moved far beyond the different forms of knowledge proposed by Max Scheler ([1925] 1960) in his essays on the sociology of knowledge in the 1920s: namely, the distinction between (1) knowledge of salvation (*Erlösungswissen*); (2) cultural knowledge, or knowledge of pure essences (*Bildungswissen*); and (3) knowledge that produces effects (*Herrschaftswissen*).

Even those scholars who have elevated knowledge to some kind of new axial principle of modern society, like Daniel Bell with his notion of a postindustrial society, treat knowledge in effect as a black box, and especially as a disembodied phenomenon. Bell and many sociological theorists before him saw every reason, typically in polemically charged circumstances, to defend positive knowledge as nonproblematic—inherently practical, uncontested, efficient, powerful, and even ethical.[4]

A more appropriate explication of the concept of knowledge requires one, as I have argued, to distinguish between what is known, the content of knowledge, and knowing itself. Knowing is a historical relation to things and facts, but also to rules, laws, and programs. Some sort of participation is therefore constitutive for knowing: knowing things, rules, programs, and facts is "appropriating" them in some sense, including them in our field of orientation and competence (also Lave, 1993: 3–32). The intellectual appropriation of things can be made independent or objective. That is, symbolic representation of the content of knowledge eliminates the necessity to get into direct contact with the things themselves (cf. also Collins, 1993). The social significance of language, writing, printing, data storage, etc., is that they represent knowledge symbolically or provide the possibility of objectified knowledge. Most of what we today call knowledge and learning (by doing) is not direct knowledge of facts, rules, and things, but rather objectified knowledge. Objectified knowledge is the highly differentiated stock of intellectually appropriated elements of nature and society that constitute the cultural resource of a society. Knowing is, then, *grosso modo* participation in the cultural resources of society.[5] However, such participation is subject to stratification; life chances, lifestyle, and the social influence of individuals depend on their access to the stock of knowledge at hand.

Knowledge is a most peculiar entity, with properties generally unlike those of commodities or secrets, for example. A secret that is known to everyone is a secret no longer. When revealed, knowledge does not lose its influence. Knowledge known to all still performs its function. If sold, knowledge enters other domains and yet remains within the domain of its producer. Knowledge exists in objectified and embodied forms. Knowledge does not have zero-sum qualities. On the contrary, knowledge represents a positive-sum game. Knowledge grows. Everyone is able to win. However, there is no guarantee that everyone will win to an equal extent; nor is there any assurance that the *practical* gains some actors may be able to realize will not mean the contraction of resources or utilities other actors command. Moreover, commanding a volume of knowledge similar to or better than that of an opponent or competitor, for example, is not the sole prerequisite for influence and competent conduct.

Knowledge is a public, as well as private, good. At times, knowledge may be a "positional" good. The value of positional goods, as Fred Hirsch (1977) argues, is conditional on others failing to gain access to them. The value of knowledge is tied to its scarcity. As I will discuss as part of this section, the proposition that scarcity of knowledge determines its exchange value already signals that at least some forms of knowledge (not subject to scarcity and depletion) must have properties that move such knowledge (at least in terms of economic reasoning) close to the attributes that public goods typically share.[6]

While it has been understood for some time that the "creation" of knowledge is fraught with uncertainties, the conviction that its application is without risk and that its acquisition reduces uncertainty has only recently been debunked. Unlike money, property rights, and symbolic attributes such as titles, knowledge cannot be transmitted more or less instantaneously. Its acquisition does not take place in a vacuum; it takes time and is typically based on intermediary cognitive capacities and skills. But acquisition can be unintended and can occur almost unconsciously. Both the acquisition and the transmission of knowledge are typically not easily visualized. Once knowledge has been "mastered," it is difficult to arrest and return it. The development, mobility, and reproduction of knowledge are difficult to regulate. It is "troublesome" to censor and control knowledge. It is reasonable to speak of limits to growth in many spheres and resources of life, but the same does not appear to hold for knowledge. Knowledge has virtually no limits to its growth, but it takes time to accumulate.

The assertion that growth of knowledge is without discernable limits (compare Weber, [1919] 1922: 534–535) is by no means without its dissenting voices, at least when it comes to the growth of basic (natural) scientific knowledge. In 1872, Emil de Bois-Reymond, in a lecture entitled "On the limits of nature science," offered widely discussed ideas about the limits of science. It is with respect to the limits of the growth of basic scientific knowledge that a few contemporary scientists—to the dismay of many other scientists—have voiced the opinion that science will not grow significantly any more, or has only limited room for additional growth. The narrative that speaks of a lack of limits to the growth of scientific knowledge fails to see, as the proponents of the existence of a law of diminishing returns in science argue, that we have uncovered the major secrets of nature; science has solved its main problems. Science *works*; it mirrors reality well (Stent, 1969; Glass, 1971, 1979). Moreover, "given how far science has already come, and given the physical, social, and cognitive limits constraining further research, science is unlikely to make any significant additions to the knowledge it has already generated. There will be no great revelations in the future comparable to those bestowed upon us by Darwin or Einstein or Crick" (Horgan, 1996: 16).[7] In addition, there may be limits to the growth of scientific knowledge generated by socioeconomic constraints, due to the increasing expense of future research endeavors (Rescher, 1978: 193–207).[8] The contentious issue evidently involves, first and foremost, the question of the growth of *basic* knowledge. Even if one limits the discussion to the difference between basic and applied knowledge, proponents of the thesis that the growth of scientific knowledge is not immune from the law of diminishing returns concede that applied science will continue to grow for a long time.[9] Therefore, the contentious and risky claim that the growth of scientific knowledge is limited does not constitute a central challenge to this study, which is mainly concerned with what is traditionally seen as applied knowledge.

Knowledge is typically seen as a collective or communal commodity par excellence; for example, the ethos of science demands that it be made available to all in the scientific community as a public good, at least in principle. But is the "same" knowledge available to all? Is scientific knowledge, when transformed into technology, still subject to the same normative conventions? The answer provided by one economist is that technology must be considered a "private capital good." In the case of technology, disclosure is uncommon, and rents for its use can be privately appropriated (cf. Dasgupta, 1987: 10). But the potentially unrestricted availability of knowledge to all makes it, in peculiar and unusual ways, resistant to private ownership (Simmel, [1907] 1978: 438).

Modern communication technologies ensure that access to knowledge and information will become easier, and may even subvert remaining proprietary restrictions. The ease with which knowledge and information become available engenders fears, such as the fear of bioterrorism (see Lane and Fauci, 2001). However, concentration, rather than dissemination, of knowledge is also distinctly possible and is certainly a worrisome development to many observers, including Marshall McLuhan (also Ginsberg, 1986: 127). It is equally possible to surmise, however, that in the end, the increased social importance of knowledge will undermine efforts at exclusiveness. Yet the opposite appears to be the case, therefore raising anew the question of the persisting basis of the power of knowledge. Despite its reputation, knowledge is virtually never uncontested.[10] Unlike the conviction displayed by the classical functionalist theory of social differentiation, science is in many instances incapable of offering cognitive certainty. This is to say that scientific discourse has been depragmatized; it cannot offer definitive, or even true, statements (in the sense of proven causal chains) for practical purposes, but only more or less plausible and often contested assumptions, scenarios, and probabilities (see Stehr, 1992a). Instead of being the source of reliable trustworthy knowledge, science becomes a source of uncertainty (Grundmann and Stehr, 2000).[11] The uncertainty linked to scientific findings is not an expression of ignorance, or of a temporary deficit of knowledge. Uncertainty is a constitutive feature of knowledge, as it is of the contexts in which knowledge must operate.[12] And contrary to what rational scientific theories suggest, this problem cannot be comprehended or remedied by differentiating between "good" and "bad" science (or between pseudoscience and correct, i.e., proper, science).

In the context of some philosophies of science, the contestability of scientific claims is seen as one of its foremost virtues. In practical circumstances, the contested character of knowledge is often repressed by or conflicts with the exigencies of social action.

Knowledge as a Capacity to Act

I would like to characterize knowledge as a generalized *capacity to act* and as a model *for* reality.[13] Knowledge creates and changes existential conditions.[14] My definition of the term "knowledge" is indebted to Francis Bacon's famous observation that knowledge is power (a somewhat misleading translation of Bacon's Latin phrase *scientia est potentia*).[15]

Bacon suggests that knowledge derives its utility from its capacity to set something in motion. Knowledge as a symbolic "system" structures reality. Knowledge is a model for reality. Knowledge is discovery. The added value of knowledge should be seen as a capacity to illuminate and to transform reality.[16] Knowledge as an effective or productive model for reality, of course, requires knowledge of reality.

The term *potentia,* meaning *capacity,* is employed by Francis Bacon to describe the power of knowing. Knowledge is becoming.[17] More specifically, Bacon asserts at the outset of his *Novum Organum* (I, Aph. 3) that "human knowledge and human power meet in one; for where the cause is not known the effect cannot be produced. Nature to be commanded must be obeyed; and that which in contemplation is the cause is in operation the rule." The success of human action can be gauged from changes that have taken place in social reality (Krohn, 1981; 1987: 87–89),[18] and knowledge acquires *distinction,* last but not least because of its apparent ability to transform reality. As a result, (most of) the reality we confront, and increasingly so, arises from and embodies knowledge.[19]

Science is not merely, as was once widely thought, the solution to the mysteries and miseries of the world; it is, rather, the becoming of a world. The idea that knowledge is a capacity for action that transforms, or even creates, reality is perhaps almost self-evident in the case of social science knowledge, but less persuasive in the case of the natural sciences. In the case of contemporary biology, however, one is more prepared to acknowledge that biological knowledge extends to the fabrication of new living systems. Biology does not simply study nature. Biology transforms and produces novel natural realities. Biology and biotechnology are closely linked.

Knowledge, as a generalized capacity for action, acquires an "active" role in the course of social action only under circumstances where such action does not follow purely stereotypical patterns (Max Weber), or is strictly regulated in some other fashion.[20] Knowledge assumes significance under conditions where social action is, for whatever reasons, based on a certain degree of freedom in the courses of action that can be chosen.[21] The circumstance of action I have in mind may also be described as the capacity of actors to alter, transform, or change a specific reality (*Gestaltungsspielraum*). The capacity to alter and affect reality is not symmetrical with the capacity to act (knowledge). Knowledge may be present but for a lack of the capacity to transform, knowledge cannot be employed. Actors may have the necessary authority, power, or material resources to change reality, and yet lack the capacity to act.

In much the same sense, Karl Mannheim ([1929] 1936) defines the range of social conduct generally, and therefore contexts in which knowledge plays a role, as restricted to spheres of social life that have not been routinized and regulated completely.[22] For, as he observes, "conduct, in the sense in which I use it, does not begin until we reach the area where rationalization has not yet penetrated, and where we are forced to make decisions in situations which have as yet not been subjected to regulation" (Mannheim, [1929] 1936: 102).[23] Concretely,

> The action of a petty official who disposes of a file of documents in the prescribed manner or of a judge who finds that a case falls under the provisions of a certain paragraph in the law and disposes of it accordingly, or finally of a factory worker who produces a screw by following the prescribed technique, would not fall under our definition of "conduct." Nor for that matter would the action of a technician who, in achieving a given end, combined certain general laws of nature. All these modes of behavior would be considered as merely "reproductive" because they are executed in a rational framework, according to a definite prescription entailing no personal decision whatsoever (Mannheim, [1929] 1936: 102).

For Mannheim, the question of the relation of theory to practice is then restricted precisely to situations which offer a measure of discretion in social conduct, and which have not been reduced to a corset of strictly ordered and predictable patterns of social action. It cannot be ruled out, however, that even under circumstances where situations are repeated with routine regularity, elements of "irrationality" (that is, openness) remain.[24] The ability to deploy new knowledge is just as crucial as is the process of finding knowledge.

Without becoming entangled in long terminological debates, I would like to deal with the concept of "knowledgeability," which Giddens (1984: 21–22), for example, uses. In the first place, he means practical knowledge (practical consciousness), and thus knowledge as a "normal" or everyday point of reference of social action, shared by many and tacit, or not immediately apparent (Giddens, 1984: xxiii). Knowledge, so defined, is a condition for social action. Giddens appeals principally to this universalistic aspect, and not to the questions taken up in this study—how and why knowledge increases; how knowledge is distributed in modern societies; how the knowledge-based professions mediate knowledge; how knowledge gives rise to authority, solidarity, or economic growth; or what influence knowledge has on the social power structures. Giddens' interest centers on the community of knowledge among actors against the backdrop of the unintended consequences of their actions (Giddens, 1981: 28); my interest focuses on the knowledge that is not at hand, even if only temporarily, and must again and again be obtained by the actor. Giddens presents an ontological thesis. I am basically concerned with the fact that an actor does not content himself with knowing, but rather wants to know more than his fellow-actor, and thus with the problem that knowledge in social contexts is a stratifying phenomenon of social action.

The definition of knowledge as a capacity for action has a number of advantages. For example, it implies that knowledge for action always has multi-faceted implications and consequences. The term *capacity* for action signals, as I have already hinted, that knowledge may be left unused, may be employed for irrational ends, or may not be mobilized to change reality. The thesis that knowledge is invariably pushed to its limit in the absence of friction, that it is realized and implemented almost without regard for its consequences (as argued, for instance, by C.P. Snow [cf. Sibley, 1973]), represents a view that is not uncommon among observers of the nature of technological development, for example. However, the notion that science and technology inherently and inevitably force their own realization in practice fails to give proper recognition to the context of implementation by assuming such automaticity in the realization of technical and scientific knowledge. Any conception of the immediate practical efficacy of scientific and technological knowledge (for example, in the sense that "there is nothing as practical as a good theory") overestimates the "built-in" or inherent practicality of knowledge claims fabricated by science. Suffice it to say at this point that the implementation of knowledge as a capacity for action relies upon existing frameworks of social action.

It would be equally misleading to conclude that the conception of knowledge as a capacity for action and not as "something," using the most traditional contrasting image that we know to be true, thereby supports a reversal of the metaphor "knowledge is power" into "power equals knowledge." Indeed, the implementation of knowledge requires more than knowing how to put something into motion. The capacities for action and for power, or better, control over some of the circumstances of action, are allies. The relation is not symmetric. Knowledge does not always lead to power. Power does not lead to knowledge, and power does not always rely on knowledge.

If one refers to "society as a laboratory," as Krohn and Weyer (1989: 349) do, in order to capture the idea that research processes and the risks associated with them are moved outside the established boundaries of science into society—for example, in the case of nuclear technology, the planting of genetically modified seeds, or the use of chemicals with certain undesirable side effects—this viewpoint also alerts us to the necessity that the replication of laboratory effects outside the laboratory requires as a basic precondition the ability to control the conditions under which the effect was produced or observable in the first instance. It is only then that the initial observation of an effect can be duplicated. This also means that every "realization" of knowledge, not only of major experiments, requires the ability to control the circumstances of action. Put differently, the "application" of scientific knowledge in society demands an adjustment to the existing conditions of action, or else the social conditions have to be transformed according to the standards set by science (Krohn and Weyer, 1989: 354).

In the sense of my definition of knowledge, *scientific and technical* knowledge clearly represent "capacities for action." But this does not mean that scientific knowledge should be seen as a resource that is incontestable, is not subject to interpretation, travels without serious impediments (for example, in the sense that knowledge travels even more effortlessly than money and spreads instantly),[25] can be reproduced at will, and is accessible to all. Nor does it infer that scientific and technical knowledge primarily convey unique and generally effective capacities for action.

What counts in modern societies—especially in the sense of gaining advantages in societies that operate according to the logic of economic growth and are dependent on the growing wealth of significant segments of the population—is access to and command of the *marginal additions to knowledge* rather than the generally available stock of knowledge (cf. Kerr, 1963: vii).[26] Knowledge need not be perishable. In principle, a consumer or purchaser of knowledge may use it repeatedly at diminishing or even zero cost.

Additional Knowledge

The differentiation between common sense or everyday knowledge and expert or scientific knowledge is the most frequent difference among forms of knowledge that one typically encounters both in everyday life and in the scientific community. The difference is most often asymmetrical. Objective knowledge enhances and embellishes itself by pointing to the deficiencies of common-sense knowledge.

The deficits of nonscientific knowledge are legion. Everyday knowledge is superficial, if not unreflective and false. In many analyses, as a result, the elevated *social role* of scientific and technological knowledge is almost invariably tied to its superior attributes. The deficiencies of common-sense knowledge in turn account for its inferior, or even declining, status and function in modern societies. But one certainly must wonder how it is that everyday knowledge, given such inherent deficiencies, has managed to survive in modern societies. In response, I do not want to collapse the difference between everyday and scientific knowledge (see Shapin, 2001). But in contrast to the common-sense distinction between lay and expert knowledge, I want to make the case that the many characteristics that justify the rise of scientific knowledge above the multiple insufficiencies of common-sense knowledge are helpful in accounting for what is undoubtedly the greater social, intellectual, and economic importance of scientific knowledge in modern societies.

The science system in modern societies is by definition part of an innovative set of societal institutions. The prestige, the exceptional social, economic, and intellectual importance of scientific knowledge, is firmly associated with the capacity of the social system within which it is embedded to fabricate *additional knowledge* claims. In modern societies, scientific and technical knowledge is uniquely important because it produces *incremental* capacities for social and economic action, or an *increase* in the ability of "how-to-do-it" that may be "privately appropriated," at least temporarily.[27] In social institutions other than science, routinized, habitual conduct and the interpretation and defense of established intellectual perspectives are constitutive. For science, innovation is the prime function.

In the case of the economic importance of knowledge in general and additional knowledge in particular, contrary to neoclassical assumptions, the unit price for knowledge-intensive commodities and services decreases with increased production, reflecting "progress down the learning curve" (cf. Schwartz, 1992; also, the economic implications of learning by doing, Arrow, 1962b). Incremental knowledge is just as inhomogeneous as is widely accessible knowledge. Thus it is entirely conceivable that some particular pieces of incremental knowledge at any given time may be "key findings" that prove to be especially valuable in many respects, as for example in economic, military, or political contexts. Which knowledge will become key knowledge can only be determined empirically (see Stehr, 2000a).

Knowledge constitutes a basis for power. Knowledge excludes. As John Kenneth Galbraith (1967: 67) stresses with justification, power "goes to the factor which is hardest to obtain or hardest to replace . . . it adheres to the one that has greatest inelasticity of supply at the margin." But knowledge as such is not a scarce commodity, though one feature of some knowledge claims may well transform knowledge from a plentiful into a scarce resource: What is scarce and difficult to obtain is not access to knowledge *per se,* but access to *incremental knowledge,* to a "marginal unit" of knowledge. The greater the *tempo* at which incremental knowledge ages or decays, the greater the potential influence of the social system within which additional knowledge is produced and the greater the social importance and prestige of those who manufacture or augment knowledge—and correspondingly, of those who transmit such increments to other social systems.

If sold, knowledge enters the domain of others; yet it remains within the domain of the producer, and can be spun off once again. This signals that the transfer and the absorption of knowledge do not necessarily include the transfer of the cognitive ability to generate such knowledge—for example, the theoretical apparatus, the technological regime, or the required infrastructure that yields such knowledge claims in the first place, and on the basis of which they are calibrated and validated. Cognitive *skills* of this kind, therefore, are scarce. It is often taken for granted by economists that the fabrication of knowledge is expensive, while the dissemination is virtually without costs. This view is further supported by the common conviction that technological knowledge is nothing but a blueprint that is readily usable at nominal cost to all.

However, the acquisition of the kinds of cognitive skills needed to comprehend knowledge and technology can be quite expensive. For example, in many cases, only the rough outlines of technical knowledge are objectified or codified by nonpersonal means of communication (cf. Berrill, 1964). As a result, some economists suggest that the dissipation and absorption of knowledge, at least of some forms of knowledge, is more costly than its production (see Stigler, 1980: 660–641). Such a conclusion, as well as evidence supporting the observation (Teece, 1977), raises the question of whether the fabrication and the dissemination of knowledge, in the sense of its reproduction, can be really separated at all.

The progressive elimination of time and space as relevant elements in the production of knowledge has paradoxically injected the importance of time and location into the interpretation and use of (objectified) knowledge. Since mere understanding and the validation process of knowledge cannot refer back, except in rare circumstances, to the original author(s) of the claim, the separation between social roles makes the interpretive tasks carried out by "experts" more crucial. Knowledge must be made available, interpreted, and linked to local, contingent circumstances. The complexity of the linkages and the volume of resources required to enact capacities for action delineate the limits of the power of scientific and technical knowledge. Such limits are an inevitable part of the fabrication of scientific knowledge, and explain why the knowledge work performed by the stratum of experts in knowledge-based occupations, generally speaking, attains greater and greater centrality in advanced society. The social prestige and influence of experts is heightened, moreover, if their claim to expertise is uniquely coupled to access to additional knowledge.

The centrality of knowledge-based occupations or, to use a narrower term, "experts," in knowledge societies does not mean that we are on the way, as social theorists have feared in the past, to a technocratic society. A technocratic model of society and its major social institutions, which "sees technicians dominating officials and management, and which sees the modern technologically developed bureaucracies as governed by an exclusive reliance on a standard of efficiency" (Gouldner, 1976: 257), be it a nightmare or a utopia, is a counterintuitive scenario. It is doubtful that the crucial choices modern societies will be forced to make are more about the technical means and less about the competing ends of social action. Quite a number of arguments can be deployed to demystify the threat of technocracy and a new ruling class made up of faceless experts. The most persuasive argument is social reality itself, which has failed to support the transformation of society in this direction. The long-predicted emergence of technocratic regimes has not materialized. The diagnosis of an imminent and menacing technocratic society was greatly overdrawn.[28]

Michael Crozier offers a less obvious argument in his study of the bureaucratic phenomenon. Crozier ([1963] 1964: 165) argues that the power of an expert is self-curtailing and self-defeating: "The rationalization process gives him power, but the end results of rationalization curtail his power. As soon as a field is well covered, as soon as the first intuitions and innovations can be translated into rules and programs, the expert's power disappears. As a matter of fact, experts have power only on the front line of progress—which means that they have a constantly shifting and fragile power." The objectification and routinization of incremental knowledge curtails the power of knowledge. Yet knowledge assimilated to power is most likely incremental knowledge. Crozier's vision of the "natural" limits of the power of experts, however, is still animated, if only implicitly, by the idea that experts—temporarily and exclusively—command uncontested knowledge, that their clients fully trust expert knowledge, and that experts therefore do not get enmeshed in controversies.

But the growing importance of knowledge-based occupations in modern society does not mean that the trust of the public in experts, advisers, and consultants (cf. Miller, 1983: 90–93) is growing at the same pace or is not contingent on relationships (Wynne, 1992). On the contrary, we believe less and less in experts, although we employ them more and more.[29] Yet without some element of trust exhibited by ordinary members towards experts, expertise would vanish. Nonetheless, experts today are constantly involved in a remarkable number of controversies. The growing policy field of setting limits to the presence of certain ingredients in foodstuffs, of safety regulations, risk management, and the control of hazards, has had the side effect of ruining the reputation of experts. As long as an issue remains a contested matter, especially a publicly contentious matter, the power and influence of experts and counter-experts is limited (see Mazur, 1973, 1987; Nelkin, 1975, 1987). However, once a decision has been made and a question settled, the authority of experts becomes almost uncontested as well. The work required to transform a contested matter into an uncontested issue is linked to the ability of experts to mobilize social and cultural resources in *relevant* contexts (see Limoges, 1993).

How knowledge and its role are defined in a particular context is determined by individual actors as well as by the legal, economic, political, or religious constructs that have gained authority. Moreover, the nature of the interaction, whether private or public (see van den Daele, 1996), the issue or practices at hand, and the audiences concerned are crucial in deciding what knowledge is mobilized and how it is enacted. Increasingly it is the job of experts, counselors, and advisors to define the role of knowledge. The group of occupations designated here as counselors, advisers, and experts is required to mediate between the complex distribution of the changing knowledge and the seekers for knowledge. Ideas tend to travel as the baggage of people, as it were, whereas skills, in the sense of know-how and rules of thumb, are embodied or inscribed in them.[30] A chain of interpretations must come to an "end" in order for knowledge to become relevant in practice and effective as a capacity for action. This function of ending reflection, or healing the lack of immediate practicability of scientific and technical knowledge as it emerges from the scientific community for the purpose of action, is largely performed by various groups of experts in modern society.

Knowledge and Information

In the context of an examination of some of the important properties of knowledge, it is necessary to take up the contentious question of the relation between knowledge and information (see Machlup, 1983). Before attempting to differentiate between knowledge and information, the initial puzzle that has to be addressed is whether, at this juncture, it is even possible and sensible to distinguish between them. The conceptual distinction between information and knowledge, at best a relative one,[31] appears to be most difficult, if not impossible, to sustain in light of the fact that these notions are often employed as virtual equivalents (for example, Stewart, 1977; Faulkner, 1994: 426).

Many dictionaries simply define information as a certain kind of knowledge. A similar equation of information and knowledge is evident if one defines information as "knowledge reduced and converted into messages that can be easily communicated among decision agents" (Dasgupta and David, 1994: 493). In other definitions of information and knowledge, information is simply conceptualized as a subspecies, as an element or the raw material of a number of knowledge forms. For example, information is seen as codified knowledge as well as indirect knowledge (see Borgmann, 1999: 49), or knowledge is defined as the cumulative stock of information (Burton-Jones, 1999: 5). Similarly, knowledge in general is seen to extend to "tacit knowledge" (cf. Polanyi, 1967: 204–206) and other categories of knowledge (Dosi, 1996: 84). But is there such a phenomenon as "tacit" information? The outcome of many efforts to define knowledge and information appears always to remain the same—knowledge and information become indistinguishable (see Wikström and Normann, 1994: 100–11). The extent to which such widespread indiscriminate usage of the terms information and knowledge has made them indistinguishable raises, last but not least, the problem of the futility of any alternative effort that aims not at conflating, but at distinguishing their meanings and referents.

Nonetheless, from time to time efforts are launched to differentiate between information and knowledge. Starbuck (1992: 716), for example, suggests that knowledge refers to a stock of expertise and not a flow of information. Thus, knowledge relates to information in the way that capital or assets connect to income. Kenneth Boulding (1955: 103–104) warns that we should not regard knowledge as a mere

accumulation of information. Knowledge has, in contrast to information, a structure—sometimes it is a loose network, sometimes a quite complex set of interrelations. Fritz Machlup (1983: 644) refers to the possibility that one may acquire new
knowledge without receiving new information. Summing up the distinction between knowledge and information, Machlup (1983: 644) prefers to claim that "information in the sense of telling and being told is always different from knowledge
in the sense of knowing. The former is a process, the latter a state. Information in
the sense of that which is being told *may* be the same as knowledge in the sense of
that which is known, but *need* not be the same. " The act of delivering (information) is one side of the coin, the "object" that is being delivered (knowledge) the
other (also Machlup, 1979: 63–65). Only rarely does one find, in definitions designed to differentiate between information and knowledge, any reference to practical usefulness or correctness as salient characteristics of knowledge and information.

If there is another side to the ledger, it is the unease with the practice of liberally
conflating information and knowledge both in everyday life and in scholarly reflections, and reducing or extending them to an all-inclusive "mental material," as
viewed by many. It is, of course, the case that one rarely finds in public places such
as airports, shopping centers, or train stations a counter or booth marked "knowledge," rather than "information." It is likely, however, that prevailing practices of
conflating knowledge and information, for example in legal discourse (cf.
Easterbrook, 1982), will prove to be more persuasive than efforts designed to distinguish between them. After all, who is able to clearly distinguish between the
information and the knowledge society?

An equally formidable barrier to any new or renewed attempt sociologically to
separate knowledge and information (and/or point to their commonalities) is the
almost insurmountable mountain of competing conceptions of knowledge and/or
information embedded in and indebted to multiple epistemological perspectives or
pragmatic purposes. Knowledge and information may be distinguished based on
economic considerations or other social points of reference: the different ways in
which they are produced, stored, diffused, consulted, and applied; their typical
carriers; or the distinct social consequences they may be seen to have in society. I
will refer to some relevant conceptions of knowledge *and* information, thereby
recognizing the tremendous difficulties faced in efforts to sustain and codify differences between knowledge and information.

One of the more traditional and, in many languages, entrenched distinctions
among knowledge forms is the opposition between *knowledge of acquaintance*
and *knowledge-about* (in theory). Though these terms appear to be somewhat clumsy
in English, they signify an asymmetrical dichotomy available in many languages,
for example, as the terms *connaître* and *savoir, kennen* and *wissen,* or *noscere* and
scire indicate. And as William F. James (1890: 221) observes with respect to this
opposition of forms of knowing, "I am acquainted with many people and things,
which I know very little about, except their presence in the places where I have met
them. I know the color blue when I see it, and the flavor of a pear when I taste it; I
know an inch when I move my finger through it; a second in time, when I feel it

pass; an effort of attention when I make it; a difference between two things when I notice it; but *about* the inner nature of these facts or what makes them what they are, I can say nothing at all."

The differences between knowledge of acquaintance and knowledge-about also suggest a possible distinction between information and knowledge whereby information becomes less penetrating and consequential—a more superficial and fleeting cognizance of the attributes of a process or object. Knowledge of acquaintance or knowledge of attributes (World Bank, 1999: 1)—for example, the quality of a product, the diligence of a worker, or the profitability of a company—refer to the presence or absence of information among market participants about relevant economic "data." In this sense, economic discourse has always made reference to the importance of information, but also to incomplete information and its function in pricing mechanisms or market transparency, for instance.

But the distinction between knowledge and information, even in its most elementary sense, is not only an asymmetrical dichotomy but also a difference that is supposed to have its dynamic, even progressive, elements.[32] For what might be called knowledge-about becomes acquaintance-with as knowledge develops, matures, or becomes more explicit and articulate. James (1890: 221) indicates as much when he observes that the two kinds of knowledge are "as the human mind practically exerts them, relative terms." As a result, the distinction moves, as later interpretations of James show as well (for example, Park, 1940), closer to the dichotomy of scientific knowledge in the sense of formal, analytic, rational, and systematic knowledge, and "information."

Given the attention paid to Daniel Bell's (1979) theory of postindustrial society and the extent to which knowledge is constitutive of such a society, it is worth paying some attention to the definitions of information and knowledge advanced by Bell. First, Bell refers to what is an anthropological constant, namely that knowledge has been necessary for the existence of any human society. What is therefore new and distinctive about postindustrial society "is the change in the character of knowledge itself. What has now become decisive for the organization of decisions and the control of change is the centrality of *theoretical* knowledge—the primacy of the theory over empiricism, and the codification of knowledge into abstract systems of symbols that can be utilized to illuminate many different and varied circumstances. Every modern society now lives by innovation and growth, and by seeking to anticipate the future and plan ahead" (Bell, 1968: 155–156). However, the distinction between forms of knowledge that have run their course because they "informed" industrial society and theoretical knowledge constitutive of postindustrial society does not necessarily affect Bell's general differentiation between information and knowledge, to which I now turn.

By information, Bell (1969: 168) suggests, "I mean data processing in the broadest sense; the storage, retrieval, and processing of data becomes the essential resource for all economic and social exchanges (in postindustrial society)." Bell's conception of information is indistinguishable from the technical conception of communication in which the meaning, exchange, and transfer of a piece of information are independent of the carriers (source and receiver) of information. By knowledge, in contrast, he means "an organized set of statements of fact or ideas, presenting a reasoned judgment or an experimental result, which is transmitted to others through some communication medium in some systematic form" (Bell, 1979: 168).[33] It would appear that the technical conception of communication applies to knowledge as well, although Bell makes implicit reference to the distinct epistemological status (or value) of knowledge and information, which results in a hierarchical and asymmetrical gradient between knowledge and information. As a result, information is easily dubbed "mere" information, while knowledge is methodically generated, sorted, and judged. Nonetheless, the dichotomy has strong disembodied strains. That is, there is no reference to the contingent character of information and knowledge, or to the need to interactively render knowledge and information intelligible and negotiate whether it is valuable or appropriate. At least implicitly, the concepts depict innovation and the fabrication of incremental knowledge as a fairly smooth, well-behaved process. Given Bell's scientific and technological conception of the communication and acquisition of knowledge and information, the strong assumption is that both knowledge and information travel virtually unimpeded. In addition, the linkages, if any, that may exist between information and knowledge remain ambivalent. At best, it would seem that Bell's conception of knowledge and information contains the claim that information is the handmaiden of knowledge. Moreover, this notion tends to be overly confident about the (uncontested?) authority, trustworthiness, and power of information and knowledge. According to Bell, knowledge is primarily abstract, disembodied, formal, individual—and aspires to be universal. It seems to me that Bell's interpretation raises more questions than it answers.[34]

A different perspective, offered by an economist, conflates the notion of information with what Bell considers to be the very characteristics that distinguish information from knowledge. Information, Dosi suggests, "entails well-stated and codified propositions about 'states of the world' (for example, 'it is raining'), properties of nature (for example, 'A causes B'), or explicit algorithms on how to do things." On the other hand, knowledge includes cognitive categories, codes of interpretation of information, tacit skills and problem-solving, and search heuristics that can be reduced to explicit algorithms (Dosi, 1996: 84). On the basis of this dichotomy, information comes close to or is identical with what many conceptualize as codified knowledge; while knowledge, in this case, is close to the notion of tacit knowledge.[35]

Nonetheless, a discussion of the interrelation between knowledge and information provides an opportunity to summarily rehearse some of the comments I have made about the role of knowledge in social affairs. Knowledge, as I have defined it, constitutes a capacity for action. Knowledge is a model for reality. Knowledge enables an actor, in conjunction with control over the contingent circumstances of action, to set something in motion and to structure reality. Knowledge allows an actor to generate a product or some other outcome. Knowledge is ambivalent, open, and hardly blind to the specific meaning knowledge claims contain. But knowledge is only a necessary, and not a sufficient, capacity for action. As indicated, in order to set something into motion or generate a product, the circumstances within which such action is contemplated must be subject to the control of the actor. Knowledge that pertains to moving a heavy object from one place to the next is insufficient to accomplish the movement. In order to accomplish the transfer, one needs control over some medium of transportation useful for moving heavy objects, for example. The value that resides in knowledge, however, is linked to its capacity to set something into motion. Yet knowledge always requires some kind of attendant interpretive skills and a command of the situational circumstances. In other words, knowledge—its acquisition (see Carley, 1986), dissemination, and realization—requires an active actor. Knowledge involves appropriation rather than mere consumption. It demands that something be done within a context that is relevant beyond being in the situation within which the activity happens to take place. Knowledge is conduct. *Knowing,* in other words, is (cognitive) doing.[36]

The function of information is, as I would see it, both more restricted and more general. Information is something actors have and get. It can be reduced to "taking something in." Information can be condensed into quantifiable forms. It therefore is possible and sensible to conclude that someone has more information than another individual. It is much more difficult and contentious to conclude that someone commands more knowledge than another person.

In its compacted form, information can migrate more easily. Information does require sophisticated cognitive skills, but places fewer intellectual demands on potential users. Information is immediately productive but not necessarily politically neutral (Burke, 2000: 116–148). This applies, for example, to a map, a timetable, legal records, charts, bibliographies, a census, questionnaires, directories, etc. In many instances, there is no need to be the master over the conditions of its implementation, as is the case for knowledge as capacity for action. Information is more general. Information is not as scarce as knowledge. It is much more self-sufficient. Information travels and is transmitted with fewer context-sensitive restrictions. Information is detachable. Information can be detached from meaning. It tends to be more discrete than knowledge. In addition, the access to and the benefits of information are not only (or not as immediately) restricted to the actor or actors who come into possession of information. Information is not as situated as knowledge.[37]

Information, in comparison to knowledge, can have a very high depreciation pace over time. The information that the share X is a good buy rapidly loses its value. The information about the value of purchasing the share quickly depreciates, and it does so as a result of its wide communication and the possibility that many will follow the advice. If one wants to assure that information quickly depreciates, one should act and encourage others to act according to the information.

The use of knowledge can be quite restricted and limited in its use-value, however, because knowledge alone does not allow an actor to set something into motion, though information may be a step in the acquisition of knowledge. The acquisition of knowledge is more problematic. In general, a simple and quite straightforward model of communication is appropriate for the purposes of tracing the "diffusion" or transfer of information. Whether it is even possible to speak of a transfer of knowledge is doubtful. The "transfer" of knowledge is part of a learning and discovery process that is not necessarily confined to individual learning.[38] Knowledge is not a reliable "commodity." It tends to be fragile and demanding, and has built-in insecurities and uncertainties.

Good examples of information are price advertising and other market information, such as the availability of products (i.e., its *signaling* function).[39] Such information is easy to get and easy to have and can certainly be useful. In the context of the modern economy, it is very general and widely available, but the consequences of having such information are minimal. From the point of view of a consumer, price information combined with knowledge about the workings of the marketplace may constitute a capacity to effect some savings. But information about prices does not enable one to generate insights into the advantages or disadvantages of different economic regimes within which such prices are generated. A comparative analysis of distinct economic systems and the benefits they may have for different groups of actors requires special economic knowledge.

Not unlike language, information has attributes, especially on the supply side, which assure that it constitutes, certainly to a greater extent than is the case for knowledge, a public good. It is not enabling, in the sense of allowing an actor to generate a product. Information merely reflects the products from which it is abstracted.

The Contingency of Knowledge

It is undoubtedly the case that the knowledge communicated by the scientific community to the public is rarely acknowledged to be problematic, partial, contingent, uncertain, and conflicting. If knowledge is *not* contingent, then attempts to police knowledge, as I would like to emphasize, are bound to be futile. In the following three sections, I will therefore focus on various conceptions of knowledge, information, and technology that appear to deny *a priori* that knowledge and technological artifacts can be, or for that matter, need to be controlled. Any discussion of the emergence of knowledge politics in modern societies is based on one fundamental premise. The possibility of control of knowledge relies, aside from allowing for the difference between knowledge and action, on the notion that evolving knowledge cannot automatically realize itself, is not self-protecting, and can only be exploited by the powerful in society, especially those actors who control large rationalized organizations. The anxieties that find expression in the formula that the economic (and other) fruits of science and technology almost automatically benefit only rich and powerful individuals and corporate actors in society also hint at another concern: that we are witnessing a growing concentration of the ownership of the right to knowledge, and therefore a switch in the nature of knowledge from a "public good" to a private resource.

Knowledge politics requires the ability to limit or enlarge the opportunities for the use of knowledge as a capacity for action. However, if one is persuaded that the realization of knowledge is guaranteed in principle, perhaps is even inevitable because such a "fate" is part and parcel of emergent knowledge, then the notion of knowledge politics makes no sense whatsoever. The only meaningful response to knowledge as capacity for action that knows no limits is adaptation to the social, economic, and political consequences that knowledge invariably produces. A second perspective, which rules out the need to control incremental knowledge, would be directly related to the assertion that knowledge and information is largely *self-protecting*. The third view, which denies the possibility of knowledge politics, relies on the underlying assumption that the use of knowledge invariably benefits the powerful and sustains the status quo in society.

The Self-Realization of Knowledge

As far as I can see, there are two basic pathways, one immediate and the other indirect, that lead to the expectation that knowledge—quite independent of the context—cannot really be stopped from realizing itself. The immediate trajectory that invariably assures the realization of knowledge, and therefore defeats any efforts to control it, is seen as being built right into the very structure of knowledge itself. In other words, there is an essential, necessary coupling of theory and practice that already occurs, or is added, in the production process of knowledge itself. The fabrication of knowledge implies its realization. The less immediate route to the self-realization of knowledge points to the possibility, as Brave (2001: 3) suggests with respect to new genetic knowledge, that "no matter what roadblocks might be placed in the way, the human genome is now and forever in our midst, and its manipulation will be difficult to simply prohibit. Neither the relatively small-scale technology required nor the individual or societal belief in biological benefits will be easily reined in by a regulatory body." As Richard Dawkins[40] argues in this context, the discovery of the code of the human genome ought to be considered a triumph of the human spirit, and as the benefits of the genome project will become increasingly evident during our lifetimes (which will be extended), the practicalities of the genome persuasively speak for themselves. Any calls for a social regulation of the genome will likely be viewed with suspicion.

In the case of technical artifacts, a species of determinist logic prevails in the imagery of technological developments that assure from the beginning that the technological objects have a built-in-destiny (i.e., technical necessity) that disallows ambiguous, or even alternative, paths of elaboration and therefore the "interpretative flexibility" (Pinch and Bijker, 1984: 419–424) of technical objects.[41]

First, the fact that science is pursued in this self-realizing fashion is evident, for example, from the once widely discussed notion of different knowledge-guiding *interests* that prevail in science (Habermas, 1964). The different, quasi-transcendental, knowledge-constitutive interests are anchored in the human species as a whole. From the beginning, we are engaged in the dual project of interacting with our fellow human beings (interaction) and in providing for the physical necessities of life (work). The category of a technical knowledge-guiding interest—aside from the practical and emancipatory (and literally innate) cognitive interests as the forms of knowledge pursued by scientists—suggests that it constitutes a form of knowledge that literally has a built-in urge to be realized in a certain fashion, namely as knowledge that is useful or instrumental in practice. At least my interpretation of Habermas' ([1965] 1971: 309) own characterization of the nature of the technical knowledge-guiding interest leaves no other conclusion: "Theories of empirical science disclose reality subject to the constitutive interest in the securing and expansion, through information, of feedback-monitored action. This is the cognitive interest in technical control over objectified processes." Any other kind of (natural) science and technology is not possible.[42] The boundaries between theory and practice diminish; in the practice of science, a coupling of theory and practice emerges or has to take place.

The decisions that occur in the course of the development of technical devices are hidden in the conception Habermas advances; and as long as they remain invisible, the image of a technologically constrained and determined social order—for example, in the sphere of production—is projected and justified. Orientation toward one of these cognitive interests, representing almost natural constraints, allows for the possibility of knowing; these interests establish the perspectives from which one is able to apprehend reality in the first instance. Knowledge generated under the auspices of a particular interest remains, of course, hostage to that interest and to the ways in which only it can be realized. A kind of self-reinforcing spiral is set into motion: The rationalization of social contexts with the help of knowledge claims constituted on the basis of a technical interest lead, according to this perspective, to an increasing neutralization of social action—and thereby an increase in the demand for knowledge produced as the result of instrumental knowledge-guiding interests. In the end, society soon resembles a laboratory.

The idea that knowledge is invariably pushed toward practical implementation is certainly a time-honored conception, and not merely an invention of the postwar era. The conception that knowledge carries within itself a kind of built-in pressure toward utilization is encountered in efforts to legitimate the very enterprise of science. Karl Dunkmann (1929: 7), for example, refers to the legitimation of *applied* sociology in the following terms: "It is impossible to point to theoretical research that is *solely* carried out on its own terms and that does not at the same time imply its own practical realization. As a matter of fact, one can go one step further and suggest that all theory originates with the motive of achieving some practical end" (also Lynd, 1939: ix).

A conception that has a historical dimension to it—in that it refers to changes in the nature of the production of scientific knowledge itself—also suggests that the once firm difference between theory and practice (in premodern times) is not merely blurred, but has become indistinguishable; and that the two dimensions are "now fused in the very heart of science itself, so that the ancient alibi of pure theory and with it the moral immunity it provided no longer hold" (Jonas, [1976] 1979: 35). Hans Jonas justifies the case for the fusion of theoretical and practical knowledge on the following grounds: (1) Much of scientific knowledge now "lives" on the intellectual feedback it receives from its technological application. (2) The impetus for research stems from practical problems that need to be solved. (3) Science uses advanced technology to generate new knowledge. The interlocking of technology and science is symmetrical. (4) The costs of the science infrastructure must be underwritten by external sources that expect a return on their investments. In sum, "it has come to be that the tasks of science are increasingly defined by extraneous interests rather than its own internal logic or the free curiosity of the investigator" (Jonas, [1976] 1979: 36). All of these arguments over the fusion of theoretical and practical knowledge seem to imply that any control and regulation of knowledge becomes impossible once scientific discoveries have been made. It does not matter much whether new scientific knowledge proves to be irresistible to the marketplace or some other interests; the built-in utility of knowledge assures that what can be shown, will be done.

Second, a less immediate trajectory implying that attempts to police knowledge are bound to be futile refers to social, economic, or cultural processes that assure the realization of knowledge despite resistance. For example, as one observer relates, "This is an age of consumption—if it can be bought, it will be" (Appleyard, 1998: 10). In the second chapter, I will refer to a couple of prominent social theorists who focus on intervening societal processes—though their concerns about the power of knowledge and technology also resonate with and stem from conceptions that assign enormous practical efficacy to modern science and technology.

But I will address first a number of assertions that focus attention on what are seen as necessary, even inevitable, trajectories leading from the production of knowledge to its implementation. Assertions of a kind of automaticity with which knowledge realizes itself are by no means indistinct reflections on the future role of knowledge in society. Reference here is therefore to the peculiar powers of knowledge itself, and its fruits in practice, that exempt it from regulation. As is argued, not only is the enlargement of knowledge without limits, but so too is the application of the "knowledge explosion" without any apparent limits.[43]

Edward O. Wilson was one of the first contemporary scholars who expected, well before the fall of the Soviet empire, an end to history. In his view, dramatic knowledge advances, designed to rescue humankind, are paradoxically bound to destroy that which has been demystified. That is, Wilson (1975: 574–575) closes his lengthy and controversial treatise on sociobiology with a few guardedly ambivalent thoughts about the future (cf. Caplan, 1978). More precisely, he speculates about the completion of social evolution, probably by the end of the twenty-first century.[44] By that time, humankind will have achieved an ecological steady state, and the "internalization of social evolution" will be accomplished. What does he mean? First of all, reference is made to rapid intellectual advances, a kind of knowledge explosion in biology and sociology. However, the state of affairs Wilson (1975: 575) has in mind is by no means restricted to a perfection of the sciences. He envisions the evolution of a "planned society, the creation of which seems inevitable in the coming century."

In the planned society, as far as I can see, the contribution of evolutionary biology will be to offer the foundations not only for monitoring the genetic basis of social behavior, but also for the deliberate intervention in the gene pool of humankind to *steer* the world's population past "those stresses and conflicts that once gave the destructive phenotypes [aggression, dominance, violence] their Darwinian edge," in which case "the other phenotypes [cooperativeness, creativity] might dwindle with them." And in this "ultimate genetic sense, social control would rob man of his humanity" (Wilson, 1975: 575). The "evolution" of knowledge achieves a kind of solipsistic completion, according to Wilson, since the new neurobiology that yields enduring first principles for sociology offers us, at the same time, efficient ways of intervening into our "cognitive machinery."

More specifically, social evolution is complete; it is finished, and as Wilson maintains, has to be consummated by the application of the advances of our knowledge to ourselves. The principle of natural selection becomes social selection. There is little ambiguity in his scenario. As Wilson (1975: 575) stresses, the results might be difficult to accept, but "to maintain the species indefinitely we are compelled to drive toward total knowledge, right down to the levels of the neuron and gene" (cf. Keller, 1992). At the very end of his massive treatise, Wilson does hesitate a moment or two. He cites Albert Camus, in order to point to the absurdity of his claims, or perhaps of life itself. Human agency is empowered to eliminate humanity. And under such circumstances, it hardly makes sense to discuss the notion of knowledge politics.

Another perspective that might also be counted among the string of views that argue for a kind of automaticity in the realization of knowledge—but one that I will not discuss extensively in this context—concerns speculations about the disappearance of any significant time-lag between processes of fabricating knowledge and its practical implementation. More specifically, the interpretation and transformation of reality literally merge, denying that the famous Marxian metaphor about the need to change rather than merely interpret the world is still meaningful and applicable in the modern world. Francis Fukuyama's observations about the end of history resonate with similar notions. More specifically, if history does not repeat itself, and if there is, as a result, a singular directionality to social evolution, then there must be a universal mechanism that accomplishes this goal. For Fukuyama (1992: 72), the only mechanism among the range of human endeavors that could assure such directionality is modern, cumulative natural science: "Scientific knowledge has been accumulating for a very long period, and has had a consistent if frequently unperceived effect in shaping the fundamental character of human societies." In such a setting, the unfolding and realization of modern natural science is driven by an automatic, irrepressible process.

The Self-Protection of Knowledge

Economists have been concerned with the issue of the difficulties of appropriating as private profits any of the direct and indirect (social) benefits that the inventor and disseminator of knowledge generates, because knowledge is not consumed by its use and may be transmitted almost without cost. Kenneth Arrow (1962a: 614–615) alludes to the now conventional economic perspective on the fragile nature of the value of knowledge and information by emphasizing that "the cost of transmitting a given body of information is frequently very low ... In the absence of special legal protection, the owner cannot, however, simply sell information on the open market. Any one purchaser can destroy the monopoly, since he can reproduce the information at little or no cost."[45] In this context, I will set aside the question of whether it is sensible to differentiate between information and knowledge. Instead, I would like to refer to another, often implicit, premise of neoclassical economic discourse concerned with knowledge as a commodity:

As both the notion of the exclusive and rival (or divisible) use of knowledge and the idea of knowledge as self-protecting indicate, the implicit legal framework of property (in order to generate an incentive for the production of knowledge, that is, value) and contract (in order to facilitate the exchange of value) often employed by economists has to be extended to *social contexts,* such as markets or firms in which knowledge is embodied,[46] both as a "more promising implicit framework for analysis of the ways in which competition produces and transmits valuable information" (Kitch, 1980: 723) and as a perspective that allows for a more promising analysis of how knowledge policies in fact operate.[47]

The probability of fabricating incremental knowledge and enjoying the economic advantages that flow from such knowledge is, of course, a stratified and contingent process. Within technological regimes, techno-economic networks (cf. Freeman, 1991; Callon, 1992),[48] or theoretical "paradigms," the advantage goes to those who already have made, and therefore command, significant elements of incremental knowledge. Technological regimes or paradigms may be embedded within a company, a network of firms, research institutes, etc. In analogy to Robert Merton's observations about the operation of the Matthew principle in the process of accumulating reputation and prestige in science, it is possible to stipulate a similar principle for the stratification of incremental knowledge.

Incremental knowledge is most easily obtained by those who are able to benefit disproportionately from what they already know. The notions of knowledge as a productive force ("input") and of tacit knowledge further testify to the idea that knowledge or information is by no means all that easy to transmit and reproduce. The competitive advantages that may accrue to individuals or firms that generate and manage to control incremental knowledge are, without question, limited in terms of time. Thus, such companies must continuously strive to stay ahead in the fabrication of knowledge: "Once they are imitated and their outputs standardized, then there are downward wage and employment pressures" (Storper, 1996: 257), as well as a decline in profitability.[49]

In contrast to incremental knowledge, and employing the attributes of rivalry and excludability of economic goods for the purposes of this discussion (cf. Cornes and Sandler, 1986; Romer, 1993), the general mundane and routinized stock of knowledge consists mostly of knowledge that is nonrival as well as nonexcludable; that is, these forms of knowledge may very well constitute public goods.[50] In the form of such "general" knowledge, knowledge is easily accessible and can be widely used; the cost of acquisition should be relatively small, or even zero.

In this case, the use by one agent does not preclude its use by another agent (excludability), and there is no competition when it comes to its use; it is difficult, if not impossible, for the creator of the claim, for example, to preclude others from using it (rivalry). That is, if A sells such information/knowledge to B, it is unlikely that B will enjoy the exclusive use of the information purchased. It is also unlikely that A and B will compete for access to the general stock of knowledge. All of this implies, in turn, that it is most difficult to assert one's property right to knowledge that one claims to have discovered. It is, for example, very difficult to detect that the knowledge has been used and claim that the use has generated certain benefits or profits. It is even more difficult to argue that because of the use of knowledge, a person or an organization has suffered a loss (Easterbrook, 1982).

In addition, the material base in which information is inscribed, and which restricts the noncompetitive consumption or nonexcludability of knowledge, affects the kinds of possible relations and transactions involving knowledge/information. For economists, the attributes of nonrivalous consumption and the nonexcludability of knowledge/information are critical features that make knowledge a prototypical example of a (global or local) public good (Samuelson, 1954)—or, if at least some of the profits of knowledge can be appropriated, using trade secrets or patents for example, an *impure* public good. The inability to appropriate or command most of the returns from knowledge is presumably a general disincentive to the private sector, and therefore to the private fabrication and supply of knowledge. Given these special characteristics of knowledge, the World Bank (1999: 17) reiterates the conventional premise of neoclassical economic discourse that "public action is sometimes required to provide the right incentive for its creation and dissemination by the private sector, as well as to directly create and disseminate knowledge when the market fails to provide enough."

However, not only in the context of the creation and dissemination of knowledge as a public good is it necessary for public policy to assume a role in providing incentives and resources to make such goods available; public policy can also attempt to assume a role controlling and regulating general knowledge that is a more or less pure public good, and that therefore "easily" circulates and is widely accessible. Obviously, public policy directed at the governance of knowledge as a pure public good is a most difficult task.

The notion that knowledge (or information) is self-protecting summons a very different perspective on knowledge and knowledge policies. The idea that knowledge is self-protecting involves a supply-and-demand argument, as Kitch (1980: 711–715) outlines.

On the supply side, the point would be that knowledge is difficult to steal, or that no one would have an interest in stealing knowledge because it is difficult to profit thereby. As envisioned here, the difficulty of acquiring or benefiting from knowledge is not meant to refer to the more or less straightforward case of property rights affixed to knowledge—as is the case for patents or copyright—which may deter the unproblematic dissemination of knowledge and the ability of competitors, for example, to profit from such knowledge. Knowledge is difficult to transmit, as anyone knows who is in the business of trying to transmit knowledge where success is measured against the successful communication of knowledge. This argument should be familiar to a teacher, for example, whose students fail to grasp most of what has been taught, or to an author who has the suspicion that his readers do not comprehend his argument. The most common notion appealed to in order to make the case that knowledge is hardly akin to a public good and therefore does not travel well is of course the notion of the "tacitness" of knowledge properties, as first explicated by Michael Polanyi (1958, 1977). The "stickiness" of knowledge (von Hippel, 1994) surely increases with the ways in which knowledge is organized.[51] Moreover, on the supply side, the self-protection of knowledge, if it could be observed, would be associated with exigencies that require the command of *scarce cognitive competencies*—the extent to which knowledge is *embedded* in specific sociotechnical contexts or knowledge infrastructures (such as the ability to learn how to learn; see Stiglitz, 1987) that are not freely mobile or easily reconstituted, or the ability to effectively control *access* to such knowledge.[52]

On the demand side, self-protective features of knowledge could be related to a high depreciation rate of knowledge. A high depreciation rate means that knowledge, once it is acquired, has become worthless in relation to the cost of acquisition and to future benefits that may be derived from it. Moreover, in the case of some forms of knowledge at least, the proprietary nature of such knowledge, not unlike a famous painting, can be easily identified by others and is therefore worthless except to its lawful owner. The exigencies that make it difficult to steal knowledge also protect it from theft, since the thief may have difficulty establishing the necessary competence to offer any credible warranty of its efficacy and authenticity. Finally, the value of knowledge is related to its scarcity. Any dissemination, or the anticipation of dissemination, of knowledge may reduce its value and therefore deter the incentive to obtain such knowledge. Such a depreciation of the value of knowledge occurs with greater likelihood among actors who compete in the same market or context. One can accelerate the depreciation of knowledge and information if one acts according to it and encourages others to do so. In short, a high depreciation rate means, "By the time someone steals the information it is worthless, which in turn means there is no incentive to steal it" (Kitch, 1980: 714).

These exigencies may in turn be self-protecting, indicating that knowledge is embedded in a "network" of cultural and structural attributes that affect the ease of its mobility and migration. The idea that knowledge is self-protecting, or can be "serviced" or protected in such a fashion that travel is bound to be difficult (e.g., avoiding its organization in written form), has implications for knowledge policies. If a stringent case can be made for the existence of self-protecting features of knowledge, then knowledge policies would have to be precisely directed toward those who happen to have within their sphere of influence the kind of knowledge deemed to be in need of regulation. No additional measures would have to be put into place, since the dissemination of knowledge is unlikely.[53]

But rising voices, especially in the developing world, that see efforts by Western commercial interests to appropriate (traditional) public knowledge for private gain as a form of the theft of such knowledge, would obviously oppose the notion that knowledge cannot be stolen and cannot be privatized easily. Vandana Shiva (2001: 284–285) for example defines "biopiracy" as "based on a false claim of creativity. It involves the appropriation of the cumulative, collective creativity of traditional societies and projects the theft as an 'innovation.'" The appropriation and translation of public knowledge in traditional societies into forms of knowledge protected by patents signal that knowledge—although in this case devalued by treating it as a form of indigenous, even invisible knowledge—can move, can be transported into different social contexts, while the original context is unable to protect its migration.

Knowledge Becomes Superfluous

There is another consideration that should be mentioned at least briefly, for it too implies that knowledge politics becomes unnecessary or superfluous.[54] Knowledge as a resource cannot be depleted (one can use Max Weber's ideas over and over again, and they will not be depleted, as a scarce resource would be). Knowledge is therefore not subject to Garrett Hardin's famous "tragedy of the commons"—but it may become superfluous. I am referring to the possibility that knowledge may become redundant as it is replaced by knowledge that supercedes earlier capacities to act. The volume of knowledge available already consists of many forms of knowledge that have become obsolete in light of more effective forms of knowledge, for example, in the fields of transportation and medicine.[55] Indeed, it is noteworthy how quickly intensively discussed and highly contested debates over aspects of knowledge politics can recede into the background or disappear from public attention altogether. Such a change in the visibility of an issue may be the result of many factors, including successful regulatory politics which removes the matter from the agenda, or the ability of proponents of the use of specific knowledge and techniques to persuade opponents that their fears about the impact are misplaced.[56]

While the obsolescence of knowledge would not by definition require any further intervention in order to regulate and control its use, a kind of passive knowledge politics, which relies on the likelihood that knowledge is bound to become obsolete, is hardly an effective form of knowledge politics. In addition, one might anticipate a kind of planned obsolescence of knowledge, accomplished by way of agreements or social arrangements that voluntarily or by law rule out the utilization of specific capacities to act—for example, an agreement that outlaws the use of certain weapons in warfare. However, a planned strategy employed to insure that knowledge becomes unnecessary represents only another definition of knowledge politics. Reliance on the inevitable "death" of knowledge is hardly a strategy that suggests itself in an era in which the ramifications of novel capacities to act are enormous.

My discussion of the nature of knowledge as a capacity to act and of knowledge as a self-realizing or self-protecting phenomenon, obviously has varied implications for the governance of knowledge. The discussion raises the general question of the importance of intellectual content and institutional factors involved in the realization of knowledge, and therefore the possibility, and possible methods, of regulating knowledge in society. In a way, this question renews the much-rehearsed issue of the power of ideas, and what exactly accounts for the power of ideas.

One matter quite clearly emerges in the context of an examination of the power of knowledge in relation to the very possibility of knowledge politics, perhaps in an even more stringent sense, in the context of a democratically organized knowledge politics—that is, the suggestion that such a field of political activity is irrelevant, superfluous, and a waste of everybody's energies if the control and the benefits of new knowledge (especially scientific knowledge) are almost "naturally" captured by and at the disposal of the powerful in society, be they powerful experts, highly rational social organizations, or simply the power elite in society. The assertion or the fear that this is in fact the case is a thesis that is far from unusual (e.g., Hayek, [1945] 1948). I will now turn to these questions. First, I will address the question of what attributes of knowledge, if any, can generally be seen to facilitate its practical implementation, and, second, I will briefly reopen the issue of the alleged symmetry between knowledge and power.

The Power of Ideas

> The fact that science contributes to the social life-process as a productive power and a means of production in no way legitimates a pragmatist theory of knowledge.
>
> *Max Horkheimer,* Critical Theory: Selected Essays

The difference to which Max Horkheimer pointed in his 1932 essay in the inaugural issue of the *Zeitschrift für Sozialforschung* favored a clear separation between the utility and the truth of knowledge. This distinction is one of the traditional cleavages in philosophical reflections about the attributes of knowledge that make ideas powerful in practice. The year 1932 was, of course, a sensitive one, and Horkheimer's insistence that economic and political interests should not determine what is true or not echoes and renews societal and political struggles about the role of science in society.

Science and the ideas that emerge from the scientific community are not the handmaidens of power, nor should they be deprived of their proper autonomy. In defending the autonomy of science, and perhaps the social immunity of scientists that comes with it, Horkheimer ([1932] 1972: 4) also insisted that this does not lead to a separation between theory and action. In the following section, I will inquire into the relation between theory and action, referring to a theoretical treatise with apparently immense practical consequences that appeared only a few years after Horkheimer's essay, namely Keynes' *General Theory*.

This work remains rather controversial, as far as any assessment of its practical impact on the course of economic development of capitalist societies in the thirties, in subsequent decades, or even today is concerned. This, of course, also makes the work attractive. Keynes' (1936: 383–384) book closes with the following, now almost classic, observations:

> The ideas of economists and political philosophers, both when they are right and when they are wrong, are more powerful than is commonly understood. Indeed the world is ruled by little else. Practical men, who believe themselves to be quite exempt

from any intellectual influences, are usually the slaves of some defunct economist. Madmen in authority, who hear voices in the air, are distilling their frenzy from some academic scribbler of a few years back. I am sure that the power of vested interests is vastly exaggerated compared with the gradual encroachment of ideas. Not, indeed, immediately, but after a certain interval; for in the field of economic and political philosophy there are not many who are influenced by new theories after they are twenty-five or thirty years of age, so that the ideas which civil servants and politicians and even agitators apply to current events are not likely to be the newest. But, soon or late, it is ideas, not vested interests, which are dangerous for good or evil.

Hidden in these sentences is not only a prophetic anticipation of the practical fate of the ideas of his *General Theory,* but also undoubtedly a biting rhetorical attack against classical economic theory, which is the major critical subject of his work. For Keynes, Karl Marx is one of the major representatives of classical theory. But at the same time, Keynes seems to argue—and this would appear of direct relevance to the topic at hand—that the potential *practical influence* of social science knowledge is propelled by the "ideas" produced by social science. The ambivalent term "ideas" was probably chosen quite deliberately by Keynes. It seems to signify, among other things, that the practical consequences of ideas (or, for that matter, their lack of practical relevance) depends less than many social scientists are convinced on their contribution to the discussion and informed decision about the *means* (that is, the instruments) of social action—assuming that such a designation and differentiation from sociopolitical purposes is sensible at all. The intriguing question raised by Keynes' closing remarks in the *General Theory,* however, is this: Was he trying to generate, in this manner, a measure of self-encouragement? And is Keynes generally correct when it comes to emphasizing the political and practical influence of economic *ideas,* including his own?

Opposing Keynes' conviction of the importance of economic ideas in society is, of course, a broad alliance of theoretical perspectives that emphasize the decisive influence of vested and organized interests on the course of many societies (e.g., Olson, 1982), or simply the derivative (and perhaps even subservient) role of ideas in economic and political struggles. Keynes' general assertion of the societal role of ideas raises many difficult questions which cannot be systematically addressed in this context[57]—for example, under what precise conditions is the influence of economic or other systematically developed ideas politically significant and stronger than well-organized vested interests, or what paths do such ideas have to travel in order to be responsible for major social transformations. His observation also creates a theoretical problem concerning the role of intellectual forces in different sociohistorical epochs. I will concentrate on this issue, and not on the question of the dependence of the power of ideas on the "quality" of their understanding of actual (economic) affairs (cf. Olson, 1990: 92–94).

Mancur Olson (1990: 107) concludes his brief survey of the practical efficacy of Keynesian economic ideas by suggesting that Britain may have been a leader in producing economic ideas, but "over the course of the century [has] fallen well behind comparable countries in its level of per capita income. An explanation of the British disease in terms of organized interests, on the other hand, fits the facts in Britain as in most other places quite well ... Though advances in economic knowledge may on some occasions ... be translated into superior policies through popular ideology, there is no strong or regular tendency for this to happen." The conclusion Olson reaches about the attributes ideas have to have in order to be successful in practice is, of course, dependent on the purposes and functions he chooses as the criteria that ideas are supposed to live up to. The purposes may extend to rather broad functions or to much more specific goals. A more general criterion for judging the practical efficacy of ideas could be, for example, the extent to which economic policies inspired by Keynesian conceptions contributed to the very survival of the capitalist system. A less general measure of their practical efficacy could, on the other hand, refer to the contribution of Keynesian economic policies to national unemployment rates (cf. Stehr, 1992a).

Although Keynes already signals in the title of his *General Theory* that he aspires to formulate a general theory of employment, interest, and money, his approach does not constitute such a general theoretical model as one might therefore imagine, especially when judged against widely supported and rather demanding methodological ideals about object-adequate social science knowledge. That is, Keynes fails to enumerate and examine, as explanatory factors, the intricate interrelation among the innumerable attributes and processes of economic and other variables, any and all of which all may affect the rate of employment, the value of money, and the interest rate. And one could surmise that the progress in knowledge represented by Keynes' ideas, compared to a neoclassical economic understanding of the dynamics of the modern economy, would surely have to be linked to a significant degree to a much more faithful, that is, more elaborate and comprehensive analysis of economic processes than that actually found in the *General Theory*. The disappointment, given such standards of adequate knowledge and advances in knowledge over time, could not be greater. Keynes' general theory of employment, money, and interest, above all, is rather parsimonious when it comes to identifying relevant theoretical dimensions for reflection and inquiry. His theory refers to only a few attributes of economic action. As a matter of fact, for my purposes, Keynes' theory can even be summarized merely by indicating that his theory represents, for the most part, the discovery of the importance of investment decisions for the level of employment in the national economy. His theory is therefore about as far removed as possible from attending to or capturing what Seymour M. Lipset ([1979] 1985: 340), for one, describes as the precondition for the power of ideas, namely the ability to reflect the "total system behavior" of a major social phenomenon. On the contrary, Keynes' theory appears to be an intellectual "throwback" to the fallacies of classical social science theorizing, with its abundance of limited factor theories.

The observation that Keynes restricted his theorizing to only a few dimensions of economic action may be a first hint that the paucity of factors is actually a precondition for the practical efficacy of his ideas. Such a conclusion is strengthened by two observations. One observation is that of Collingridge and Reeve, who point out that there is in fact the distinct possibility that access to impressive amounts of information and knowledge can be quite "dysfunctional" in practical decision-making processes. Their comment is intended to combat the prevailing view of certain qualities of rationality—in particular, the thesis that the rationality of political decisions somehow improves, in an almost linear manner, with the quantity of information available to the actors. Collingridge and Reeve (1986: 5) state, "It is simply not the case that a good decision can only be made once the uncertainties surrounding it have been reduced by gathering as much relevant information as possible. On the contrary, policy decisions may be made quite happily with the very scantiest information."

"If we seek a science of that which is in the process of becoming, of practice and for practice," Karl Mannheim ([1929] 1936: 152–153) stipulates in *Ideology and Utopia,* in an essay concerned with the foundations of political knowledge or a science of politics, "we can realize it only by discovering a new framework in which this kind of knowledge can find adequate expression." In accordance with Mannheim's observations, a theory of the pragmatic transformation of social science knowledge as a capacity for action should be governed by the elementary insight that all social action is bound to specific situations and affected by local constraints. How local they may in fact be is an empirical question. In addition, it can be assumed that such local situational constraints and conditions may be interpreted by the relevant actors as either open—that is, in some way subject to their control and manipulation (used nonpejoratively here)—or they may be apprehended as fixed, that is, largely beyond their control. Since the constraints that issue from a given social context are both subjective and objective constraints, the notion that constraints may be apprehended either as open to action or as more or less unalterable should not be interpreted to mean that the apprehension of pertinent constraints of action is merely a subjective matter and an idiosyncratic component of social action. The fundamental questions of the attributes of knowledge, the demand for knowledge, and the assessment of the adequacy or relevance of (additional) knowledge produced in one context but employed in another, can now be formulated to pertain to the relation between knowledge and the local conditions of action.

The transformation of knowledge for action into knowledge in action requires that theoretical knowledge take on features which constitute the conditions for practical knowledge as a special type of knowledge. This means that theoretical knowledge has to be reattached to the social context; that is, its relations to situational interests, purposes, and world-views, from which it had been detached for the purposes of theoretical reflection, have to be re-established (Mannheim, [1929] 1936: 170).

Despite the fact that only a few pertinent attributes of economic action appear to have been examined and taken into consideration by Keynes in his *General Theory,* vigorous voices could be heard almost immediately after its publication—and certainly a chorus of voices in later years—praising Keynes' theory and insisting that it might well have very important practical implications and benefits for the economic affairs of a nation. The practical success of Keynes' ideas is the result of his ability to couple successfully his theoretical notions to conditions of action that could be influenced and changed in directions desired by the actors of the day.[58]

The second basic question related to the coupling of power and knowledge is the question of why we speak of a close association between the exercise of power in society and knowledge, as is frequently done in critical observations about the social role of scientific and technical knowledge. In response to this question, several not necessarily unrelated answers can be found. One set of answers stresses the largely autonomous attributes of scientific and technical knowledge that assure its immense influence in society. The second set of answers emphasizes societal processes which assure that the fruits and the benefits of science accrue mainly to the powerful in society. I will in turn describe and critically examine each of these sets of answers by pointing to major representatives of each of these perspectives.

Knowledge and Power

> Today political power asserts itself through its power over the machine process and over the technical organization of the apparatus ... Validated by the accomplishments of science and technology, justified by its growing productivity, the status quo defies all transcendence.
>
> *Herbert Marcuse,* One-Dimensional Man

Although scientists and engineers are rarely in power themselves, it was not long ago that Herbert Marcuse, to much acclaim, portrayed science and technology as one of the essential repressive assets of governments in advanced and advancing industrial societies. He describes science and technology as critical resources of the state, whose control allows the administration to maintain and secure its rule in an almost uncontested fashion (also Eulau, 1973). Science and technology are seen as effective assets, not only for the maintenance of the political status quo, but also, by implication, for the absence of economic, political, and intellectual freedom in advanced societies. Marcuse's diagnosis evidently implies that whatever power scientific and technological rationality directly or indirectly generates, that power and authority is fairly easily and readily monopolized by the state or the powerful corporate agents of society.

One way to understand the attributes by which knowledge is seen to be controlled, even monopolized, and its gains—following the Matthew principle—primarily allocated to the affluent and powerful, is to examine the literature which informs us that precisely such outcomes are *built into* the very logic of scientific and technological development. These attributes endow science and technology with political reason. What exactly is it, in the view of the critics of the asymmetrical outcomes of the use of science and technology, that gives technological and scientific knowledge such potency and discriminatory power, and assures that knowledge easily attaches to power and cements regimes of social inequality? And, one may ask, what kinds of *mundane encounters* with modern science and technology may have prompted, or at least reinforced, the critics' theoretical conceptions of science and technology as a resource only of the powerful? Typical encounters with science and technology in everyday life must have left their marks, strengthening otherwise rather abstract reflections about modern technical artifacts and scientific knowledge. I will suggest that these essential and affirming encounters are experiences with "frozen" or arrested technical artifacts and knowledge forms.

My aim is not an exegesis of the epistemological or theoretical ancestry of such views. I presuppose that the critique of modernity, insofar as it touches upon the rationality of science and technology, represents a form of civilizational critique that has accompanied the emergence of modern societies from the beginning (see Ravetz, 1977). The critics of modern civilization flatly reject the claim that science and technology, as celebrated by its proponents, are socially and politically neutral. As Marcuse (1964: 166) pointedly asserts: "Science, *by virtue of its own method* and concepts, has projected and promoted a universe in which the domination of nature has remained linked to the domination of man." For illustrative purposes, I refer in some detail to two representative philosophical and sociological critiques of the interrelations between the social and intellectual fabric of society, knowledge, and technology—the analyses of modern science and technology by Herbert Marcuse and Helmut Schelsky.[59]

Marcuse's views of the role of modern science and technology gained considerable public resonance with the publication in 1964 of his *One-Dimensional Man,* subtitled *Studies in the Ideology of Advanced Industrial Society.* However, Marcuse's conception of the social nature and the social implications of science and technology may be traced back to his own earlier writings on the subject (e.g., Marcuse, 1941) and those of both Theodore Adorno and Max Horkheimer in the early 1940s.

The proponents of critical theory, in effect, abandon Marx for Weber on the issue of the emancipatory potential of modern reason. Marcuse observed at the time, "National Socialism is a striking example of the ways in which a highly rationalized and mechanized economy with the utmost efficiency in production can operate in the interest of totalitarian oppression and continued scarcity. The Third Reich is indeed a form of 'technocracy'" (Marcuse, 1941: 414). In the case of National Socialism, politics is still a decisive force; yet technical knowledge is already seen as an attachment of power and as an indispensable instrument of political control and oppression.

A quarter of a century later, Marcuse assailed the scientific mind and the transformation of knowledge into a form of scientific-technical rationality that perverted the project of emancipation and led to the human domination of nature. Marcuse (1964: 146) argued that such outcomes are inherent in science, that "scientific-technical rationality and manipulation are welded together into new forms of social control," resulting in a kind of epistemic enslavement of modern individuals. Modern people become incapable of seeing and dealing with the world in any other manner, hence their entrapment.

The technical presumption of science becomes a political presumption and so has consequences for human social organization, because the transformation of nature, according to the logic of technology, also involves changes in the social relations of individuals. Whatever claims may be made on behalf of the essential political neutrality and potential of technology, Marcuse (1964: 154) stresses emphatically, even against Marx, that a technology which has become the *universal* form of material production, "circumscribes an entire culture; it projects a historical totality—a 'world.'" In other words, the relation and respective implication of science and its technical application, and of the nature of the society that is thereby created, can in the final analysis only be viewed as an intimate connection that operates under the same logic. Technological reason and its universals, namely the discipline and control of production resulting in regimentation, the pursuit of narrow goals—or specialization—and the absolute uniformity of regimented and specialized labor or standardization, are bound to predominate throughout society.[60]

The same inherent force, the *rationality of domination,* soon propels the universes of scientific and ordinary discourse. All sectors of society, all social activities, and all subjectivities are brought under the control of technical forms of discourse. The domination of nature and society go hand in hand. Science and society become reflections of the logic of technical rationality. Marcuse (1964: 158) therefore concludes that the "scientific method which led to the ever-more-effective domination of nature thus came to provide the pure concepts as well as the instrumentalities for the ever-more-effective domination of man by man *through* the domination of nature . . . Today domination perpetuates and extends itself not only through technology but *as* technology, and the latter provides the great legitimation of the expanding political power, which absorbs all spheres of culture."[61] The resulting lack of freedom and autonomy appears neither as irrational nor as the result of political forces, but rather as a "rational" submission to the technical necessities of existence. In the final instance, therefore, instrumental reason becomes ubiquitous and turns life in society into a "totalitarian" existence. As in Schelsky's scientific civilization, the sphere of the political becomes the sphere of the technical ("the incessant dynamic of technical progress has become permeated with political content" [Marcuse, 1964: 159]), and rationality becomes irrationality. The state becomes merely an expression of the technical base and is depoliticized. Social change will be arrested for the most part, especially by virtue of the power and primacy of the society's administrative apparatus, and this containment of social transformations is perhaps the most singular achievement of advanced industrial society.

Marcuse's analysis of scientific rationality is highly abstract and representative of a fatalistic philosophy of history. Mainly, however, it lacks congruence with social reality, especially with the ways in which—and the extent to which—many modern individuals experience spheres of autonomy and responsibility. He provides no persuasive examples of how technological means are turned into means of social control and domination—for example, how the telephone, printing, or television invariably become instruments of domination. The reluctance of dictators to promote modern telephone systems in the early part of this century would indicate that they feared its subversive possibilities. To this very day, differences in economic and demographic factors do not satisfactorily account for the large disparities in the dissemination of the telephone in state socialist and capitalist societies after the Second World War (cf. Buchner, 1988). But even more to the point is Alain Touraine's ([1992] 1995: 159) observation that Marcuse's theory of modern society lacks reality congruence: "The image of a totally unified society, in which there is a perfect correspondence between technology, firms, the State, and the behavior of consumers and even citizens could not be further removed from observable reality." The theoretical assimilation of progress in domination with progress in science and technology fails simple affirmative tests in practice in advanced societies.

Helmut Schelsky's thesis that advanced industrial society is evolving into "scientific civilization" was first expounded by him in a lecture in 1961 entitled "Humans in scientific civilization."[62] For Schelsky, *modern* technology represents not merely an adaptive capacity to the constraints of nature, but a reconstruction of nature by society, and therefore of society. In the context of modern technology, humans no longer confront nature with the assistance of organs aided, improved, and developed in their capacity by technology, but on the basis of a "detour" via the brain, or the application of theoretical knowledge in practical contexts. The outcome, using the language Schelsky ([1961] 1965: 16) employs, is an "artificial" nature as well as an "artificial" change in humankind itself. The result is therefore a "re-construction and re-creation of man . . . in his corporal, psychological, and social existence" (Schelsky, [1961] 1965: 16). We produce, as Schelsky ([1961] 1965: 17) observes, "the scientific civilization not only as technology but necessarily also in a much broader sense ... as 'society' and as 'soul.'"

Modern technology changes the relations of humans to nature, to themselves, and to others. The result of these transformations is the "circulation of self-determined production" (Schelsky, [1961] 1965: 16), which represents the real foundation of scientific civilization. The self-regulated and self-propelled nature of this process, the constant production and reproduction, evolves into a self-steering process which does not appear to allow for any escape:

> Every technical problem and every technical solution invariably becomes also a social and psychological issue because the self-propelled nature of this process, created by man, confronts humans as a social and psychological dictate which in turn requires nothing but a technical solution, a solution planned and executed by man since this is the nature of the condition to be tackled (Schelsky, [1961] 1965: 16–17).

Modern technology constitutes a particular logic, and this logic necessarily becomes the dominant logic of human life. One of the significant consequences of such a conception of technology is that the traditional "logic" of technology reverses itself. That is, technology as a producer of mere means of human action becomes a producer of ends or meaning, or in other words, the "means" of action determine its ends and prefigure the direction of social change. Schelsky describes technology as an intellectual process that dissects various natural objects into their elementary parts in order to reassemble them according to the principle of least effort or maximum efficiency. The result of modern technological construction, therefore, is a novel product or process with *artificial* features—and, by analogy, an *artificial* human being.

Schelsky's and Marcuse's theories evidently converge. They share the thesis that there is the distinct danger that inherent, powerful attributes of science and technology in modern society will increasingly displace spontaneous social and political action and significantly reduce individual spheres of responsibility and autonomy, resulting, in the end, in the "death of the self."

Marcuse and Schelsky are by no means alone in their assessment of the trajectory of the social, political, and economic development of advanced industrialized societies. Nor are they alone in attributing the societal changes they describe to intrinsic and enslaving "laws" of science and technology. On the contrary, their observations and warnings resonate with a broad intellectual trend that actually began to take on its peculiar characteristic in the 1950s, when social theorists first noted distinctive and presumably irreversible trends in industry and production. The genealogy of Schelsky's and Marcuse's fears about the impact of modern science and technology is of course much longer. I will refer to Max Weber, but could list many more observers who have expressed concerns about the fateful consequences of science and technology in the age of modernity. Marcuse's and Schelsky's diagnoses resonate closely with Max Weber's analysis of the modern age as a demystification of the world, resulting from the growing rationalization of social relations through science and technology. Weber emphasizes the painful tension between rational, empirical knowledge and the meaning systems found in the lifeworld. Moreover, Weber's intellectual "grandchildren" often share an "Exodus impulse," namely the attempt "to explode the fatalistically closed 'steel-hard casing' of the demystified world" (Bolz, 1989: 7). Schelsky and Marcuse therefore also make use, although for the most part implicitly, of a long established (romantic) intellectual tradition, both radical and conservative, which launched a highly critical and skeptical analysis of the impact of technology and science on culture and social relations.

An earlier generation of social scientists asserted a tendency in industry toward increasing technological progress, manifesting itself in the rapid mechanization or *automation* of production. The increased automation, as Marcuse (1964: 35) observed, is inherent in technological progress itself and enormously enlarges the output of commodities, yet it does not, as many observers then noted, make work more meaningful, demanding, or challenging. The result was summed up by David Riesman and his collaborators in *The Lonely Crowd* (1950): Industry was producing bored workers through simplified work routines, and the central meaning of life was increasingly shifting away from work toward a search for creative expressions in leisure activities.

Schelsky's and Marcuse's observations resonated with Bell's (1960) thesis about the end of ideology, as well as with Robert Lane's (1965) prediction that we were about to enter an age in which scientific knowledge would increasingly dislodge the political element from politics. By the same token, the futurists Herman Kahn and B. Bruce-Briggs (1972: 8–29) in the early 1970s discerned multiple trends within modern society that had been widely noticed by "macro-historians"; these included both the "centralization and concentration of economic and political power" and "innovative and manipulative social engineering." The growing rationality that comes with the rapid accumulation of scientific and technical knowledge, according to Kahn and Bruce-Briggs, was increasingly applied to "social, political, cultural, and economic worlds" (Kahn and Bruce-Briggs, 1972: 9). Although this trend would not necessarily accelerate, the desirability of social engineering was widely supported, and was an "almost universal belief among the educated" (Kahn and Bruce-Briggs, 1972: 29).

More recently, in the wake of September 11, 2001, and the Iraq war, expressions about the enormous destructive and almost independent power of scientific and technological knowledge have been renewed, indicating that they are held responsible for the excessive tempo with which social relations are changing:

> There is far too much change around, not too little. Whole ways of life are wiped out almost overnight. Men and women must scramble frantically to acquire new skills or be thrown on the scapheap. Technology becomes monstrous in its infancy, and monstrously swollen corporations threaten to implode. All that is solid—banks, pension schemes, anti-arms treaties, obese newspaper magnates—melts into the air. Human identities are shucked off, tried on for size, tilted at a roguish angle, and flamboyantly paraded along the catwalks of social life (Eagleton, 2003: 164).

The influence of ideological and, more generally, of political factors on scientific and technical developments remains unanalyzed, however. This suggests that the conventional central theoretical categories employed in the analysis of modern society, partly inherited by present-day social science from the past century—such as class and economy, as well as such notions as capitalism and socialism—have lost their crucial role in social theory (e.g., Aron, [1966] 1968; Bell, 1969). In the 1960s, observers became increasingly convinced that the distinction between capitalist and state socialist economic orders was becoming obsolete. At the same time, however, confidence in the power and uniqueness of scientific knowledge remained strong. Raymond Aron ([1962] 1967: 42) embraced and highlighted these assumptions in his theory of "progressive" industrial society. At the same time, questions about the motor of "social change" or the centrality of the economic system for societal transformations were raised anew. It was at this time that theorists began to advance the thesis that technology and science, rather than the economy, provide the real motor of societal change in modern social systems (cf. Parsons, 1970: 619).

More generally, however, Schelsky's and Marcuse's accounts of the social and political force of modern science and technology suffer from an unintended, but nonetheless misplaced, confidence in the practical efficacy of scientific reasoning and quantification. Knowledge and technology are for the most part treated as a black box. The concern with technical artifacts is primarily functionalist. The major questions posed concern the psychological, social, and political consequences of objects in the sphere of social relations. What exactly confers such power on objects is never examined. Marcuse and Schelsky presuppose an image of science and technology that then gives them reason to despair. One perceived consequence of technology and science—the extent to which the world of objects begins to dominate the world of subjects—paradoxically rests on the acceptance by both Marcuse and Schelsky of the positivist image of science as a most efficient, rational enterprise that produces highly useful devices and knowledge claims. As a result, we must return to our initial question: What nourishes such a view of science and technology, in spite of Marcuse's and Schelsky's otherwise deep misgivings about such a science and such efficient technical objects?

At this point, we must take cognizance of some phenomenological analyses of everyday experience and common-sense understanding of science, especially regarding technical matters, which are not further investigated by Marcuse and Schelsky, even though they serve as the starting point and affirmation of their observations. The primary experience in everyday contact with technology is the *finished* product; the everyday experience of technology is not rooted in an understanding of the conception and fabrication. In short, the decisions that constitute the nearly always invisible "technical code" of a matter, and that codetermine the ways of using such technologies in everyday contexts, are not manifest to the user.

Feenberg (1995: 4) has provided us with a fruitful explication of the concept of the technical code: The technical code refers to those attributes of an object that

> reflect the hegemonic values and beliefs that prevail in the design process. Such codes are usually invisible because, like culture itself, they appear self-evident. For example, tools and workplaces are designed for adult hands and heights not because workers are necessarily adults, but because our society expelled children from the work process at a certain point in history with design consequences we now take for granted. Technical codes also include the basic definition of many technical objects insofar as they become universal, culturally accepted features of daily life. The telephone, the automobile, the refrigerator, and a hundred other everyday devices have clear and unambiguous definitions in the dominant culture.

While the technical code of an object originates or is provided in the context of its production, it is not yet decided how ultimately to handle an object—in the context of its use—as if it were natural. For this, the "cultural code" is a further requirement, since it contributes to the decision of which possibilities for use are connected with an object. Technical and cultural codes may overlap, but they can also diverge. Ultimately, the cultural code can also change. In any case, technical and cultural codes more or less definitively limit the imaginative possibilities for use, and have as a consequence the fact that everyday experiences with objects are primarily "successful" experiences. And this counters the disappointments that naturally also continually occur, while nonetheless probably basically confirming the confidence in the predetermined technical and cultural process of the object. The technical and cultural codes endow the object with a specific process or even a purpose that it will fulfill. The codes stabilize usage. Objects confer certainty. The degree of security that allows these coded processes to be reproduced again and again is then associated primarily with an image of reliability—although the goals that can be realized with this reliability can be of various different kinds. In any case, in the process an emotional connection with the object takes form. This certainty, security, and reliability in principle in everyday dealings with technical objects at the same time induces, according to my thesis, a high degree of confidence in the efficiency of objects. The fact that connected with this efficiency there might at the same time be a feeling of helplessness, or of the "power of objects over us," is understandable. The limited technical and cultural code of an object—especially if "the radical constraints on possible integration of objects are in the interest of ... powerful individuals or groups" (Joerges, [1979] 1996: 25)—obstructs alternative possibilities for use and confirms one's helplessness in handling objects. This is, to be sure, nothing other than a reification of the dominant code.

A phenomenology of technology underlines some general observations by Alain Touraine ([1992] 1995: 148–149) about the actual role of technology in a society that is increasingly based on technology:

> We live in a society in which means have been completely divorced from ends. Far from determining or absorbing ends, the same means can be used for both good and evil ends, for both reducing inequality and exterminating minorities. The increasingly dense networks of technologies and signs in which we now live, and which orient and govern the ways in which we behave, by no means imprison us in a technological world and by no means destroy social actors. They impose neither a logic of efficacy and production nor a logic of control and reproduction. The image of technocracy triumphant is pathetically inadequate if we contrast it with the increase in consumption, the rise of nationalisms and the might of transnational companies.

Finally, it is worth noting in this context that some of the most defining technical inventions of past centuries—for example, the invention of printing and the subsequent enlargement of literacy among formerly illiterate populations—did not, contrary to the image Schelsky and Marcuse provide, easily attach to the powers of the day, maintaining and even enhancing the authority and the power of the churches. In fact, the ability of the churches to control and monopolize information and knowledge actually declined, contributing to their persistent loss of influence in society and the secularization, democratization, and differentiation of societies.

There is a family resemblance of the first and the second set of answers to the assertion that power and knowledge are closely allied, even twin forces. I now turn to the second set of answers that stress not inherent, built-in attributes of knowledge acquired in the course of its construction, but rather processes that are situated in specific social arrangements outside of the scientific community.

The Disappearance of Human Agency

In an early postwar essay on the social role and impact of technology, Helmut Schelsky (1954: 26–27) held not only modern technology, but also excessive functional differentiation, responsible for what he regarded as a serious decline in, or even the prospect of the eventual disappearance of, individual human agency. On the institutional plane, he observed profound transformations as well. Two decades later, the American political scientist Hans Morgenthau (1972: 73) observed a growing concentration in the hands of an elite that could not claim to be democratically legitimated. He depicted the concentration of power in the hands of a few as both the outcome of scientific and technological developments and nourished by it:

The modern scientific age has had three major effects. Within the government, power has shifted from democratically responsible officials to certain technological elites, military and scientific, which are not democratically responsible. In consequence, popular participation in, and control over, the affairs of government have drastically decreased.

Present-day social theorists typically write in a similar mode, although the claims that there is a growing threat to self-determination and an increasing moral indifference appear to have largely vanished. For example, references to elite conspiratorial motives, such as the calculated defense of vested economic interest, the fusion of military and political institutions, or the conflictual division into opposing social classes, had not been heard for two decades; yet, before and after the Iraq war, some of these sentiments have been voiced again.

Reiteration of such threats to human agency has declined. Yet reference to such phenomena and structures has partly been replaced by allusions to more ambiguous, at times even invisible, threats and risks, for example the presumed disappearance of privacy. Today it is more likely that concern will be with largely self-evolving or self-propelling processes, and with unintended and unanticipated consequences of the social incorporation of digital computers. As the communication and information "revolution" was just getting under way, Gouldner (1976: 240), along with many other social theorists, diagnosed and took it for granted that "the power of the state apparatus has increased greatly" as a function of that technological development. The enlargement of state power aided by modern technologies in particular was grounded "in the prior development of the bureaucratic organization form that stressed instrumental behavior, formal rationality, and scientific, expert administration" (Gouldner, 1976: 240).

Although, as Gouldner (1976: 241) also notes, the "rational-scientific elements of bureaucratic organization remain encased within and limited by nonrational, nonscientific political and economic interests," computerization, mechanized retrieval and control of information, and electronic communications systems measurably enhance the efficiency of the apparatus and extend its reach of social control.

Among prominent manifestations of such self-propelling processes and risks are the notions of an unintended concentration of social activities, the threat of extremely efficacious surveillance, centralized decentralization, the destruction of privacy, and the widespread enforcement of ever-greater regulations of human conduct. In an effort to substantiate the threat of increasing social regulation, rationalization, and concentration in present-day life, observers tend to dissent from those formerly predominant theoretical perspectives that emphasized differentiation, division, and fragmentation, for such outcomes would appear to run counter to effective and centralized social control based on new knowledge and novel technical devices.

Even more recently, combining arguments taken from Foucault and Braverman, it has been suggested that the rapid deployment of information technology for control purposes and the extension of even more flexible forms of surveillance into the market sphere have contributed decisively to the acceleration of a long-term historical trend of increasingly *centralizing power.* Taylorism is more than a mere factory management doctrine; in fact, what we are witnessing in modern society is a movement from Taylorism to Social Taylorism (Webster and Robins, 1993:243).

The pursuit of regulated integration and diminishing spheres of self-governed contexts of autonomy of individual actors in advanced societies have been orchestrated by state and corporate groups in order to extend and solidify their own power:

> Drawing in and extending into once exempted activities, corporate capitalism and state agencies typically have achieved greater management of social relationships, have increasingly 'scripted' roles and encounters, at the same time as they have advanced their criteria as those most appropriate for conducting affairs. This process should be seen as the rationalization of control in pursuit of particular interests (Robins and Webster, 1989: 34; also Webster and Robins, 1986).

The result is continuation of "insufficient participation, insufficient integration, and unattainable, abstract requirements" (Narr, [1979] 1985: 41). Forms of control and domination, recently through the mobilization of information and communication resources, "operate in terms of longer periodicity" (Webster and Robins, 1989: 325).

But what exactly has enabled state agencies and corporations to effectively rationalize and extend their efficient social manipulation to ordinary everyday activities? How is it possible for a repressive apparatus to make use, even with apparent ease, of the technological innovations in the "information sector"? Finally, who can avoid the iron grip of this manipulation, concentration, and regulation, and expose their dangers? And how is this possible?

Robins and Webster (1988; 1989) assign a special ability to the state and to corporations to systematically gather, store, scrutinize, and disseminate information for purposes of control. Surveillance by way of new information and communication technologies is, in their view, the crucial ingredient for disciplining workers and citizens. It is feared that computer-based surveillance may turn the office, for example, into a sweatshop. In the most draconian scenario, every move in every minute of the workday is monitored. In the end, these technologies reinvent and reinforce conditions akin to the panopticon advocated by Jeremy Bentham in 1791 as a control device (cf. Foucault, 1977).[63]

But the precise reasons for the ability of the state and the large corporations to collaborate efficiently and to almost wholly control the development of technical and scientific knowledge remain somewhat obscure. Despite the unprecedented growth of the volume of information and the channels of communication, in the end they diminish the individual's role in democratic participation; they intensify isolation, threaten individual privacy, heighten the sense of individual helplessness, and erode the differentiation between private and public spheres of life.

Even social theorists who generally display a sensible and consistent skepticism toward any built-in, self-propelled logic of technological development tend to voice the fear that new technological regimes might be mainly used as instruments of repression, centralization, and regulation. "Technological choices are first and foremost political ones," Alain Touraine ([1984] 1988: 107–108) observes, but he is nevertheless convinced that the "elaboration of information-producing and information-managing apparatuses results in most areas in a concentration of power. Such a concentration has been under way for quite some time in the industrial realm; it has advanced even further now, but the concentration of decision-making power has become even more pronounced in areas where it had limited importance until recently."

Moral Indifference, Power, and Science

The powerful images contained in warnings of the moral indifference inherent in modern life, or of a diminution of individual human agency and the ability of corporate actors to effectively intervene on their own behalf, are potentially linked to a particular conception of science and technology. Regulation, restriction, surveillance, and concentration are seen as the direct outcomes of scientific and technological developments. In this view, the powerful inner logic of these developments creates a self-propelling superstructure within and outside of science.[64] Science itself (as well as its application) becomes a technical process without politics and ethics. Resignation or resentment appear to be the only appropriate responses in the face of the overwhelming and irresistible force of the developments set in motion by science and technology.

However, if analysis of the state apparatus—as a major player among modern control agencies—is linked to the functions of surveillance, registration, and collection of information, the inevitable result is a reductionist perspective that collapses all state activity into a single ahistorical purpose. Of course, surveillance activities by the state and other modern institutions are by no means negligible. But the state and other organizations do many things. They do not merely collect and monopolize information or knowledge. This view both overestimates the practical efficacy of the state, which typically also functions as a producer of knowledge and information, and underestimates the wide range of functions it actually performs. It would be equally mistaken, in light of the persistence of pressing public and private problems, to assign such unquestioned efficacy to scientific knowledge and technical artifacts.[65]

The main issue, in my view, is exactly the opposite problem. My concern is the extent to which science and technology, combined with their growing societal importance, represent a source of uncertainty in and for modern society, and, in combination with the sociostructural transformation of modern into what I have termed fragile societies (Stehr, 2001), produce essential obstacles to controlling and regulating the new knowledge that issues from the scientific community.

In the following two sections, I will attempt to examine some of the motives and methods of governing knowledge in modern societies. It will emerge that we are confronted with a most complicated and complex field of political activity and that we must challenge the erroneous view that monopolizing and controlling new knowledge and technical artifacts is a rather straightforward process in pluralistic societies.

Notes

1. My translation. The English translation published by MIT Press is in parts rather poor.

2. Cf. the critique of the superficiality of the thesis of the unity of civilization by Arnold Toynbee (1946: 36–41).

3. E.g., Malinowski (1955) and Machlup (1984, 1981, 1962).

4. One classical social theorist who examined the relation between ethical conduct and knowing, and concluded that there was unquestionably a positive association, was Max Weber. In an essay discussing the particularisms advocated by Eduard Meyer, for example, Weber ([1905] 1949: 124–125) observed that it is not in irrational conduct that any "freedom of human will" manifests itself: "We associate the highest measure of an empirical 'feeling of freedom' with those actions which we are conscious of performing *rationally*—i.e., in the absence of physical and psychic 'coercion,' emotional 'affects,' and 'accidental' disturbances of the clarity of judgment—in which we pursue a clearly per- ceived end by 'means' which are the most adequate in accordance with empirical *rules*" (slightly modified translation).

5. This does not imply that *individuals* do not possess knowledge. Knowledge repre- sents participation in the cultural affairs of society. And this suggests that knowledge can- not be reduced to individual acts (see Gilbert, 1989: 252–253).

6. If a social collectivity *treats* knowledge *in toto* as a pure public or collective good, which means that its enjoyment cannot be denied to anyone, or that its use is open to all *insiders* (assuming that there are legitimate ways of excluding outsiders), it would only be *logical* to infer that knowledge politics would be not necessary or required (see Cerny, 1999: 95–102). Indeed, it is often neoclassical economic discourse and commercial inter- ests that dominate the discussion about public goods (see Ostrom and Ostrom, 1977). In this instance, arguments are advanced that justify regulations designed to insure that infor- mation or knowledge mimics the commodity features of tangible goods. From a normative or political point of view, public goods are those goods that citizens and its representative institutions believe *ought* to be treated as collective property (see also the latter section that deals with the "self-protection of knowledge"). As a matter of fact, however, knowledge not only has properties that resemble public goods but also has attributes that ally it to commodities with rivalry and excludability of typical economic goods.

7. Speaking (of course) from the vantage point of a system theoretical position, Niklas Luhmann ([1981] 1987:57) argues that differentiated and largely autonomous social sys- tems cannot in principle control their own growth; as a result, there are no scientific rea- sons why science should not continue to grow and produce more and more knowledge claims. Luhmann concedes, however that the growth of systems may be limited, for ex- ample, due to a lack of resources supplied by other systems.

8. It is of interest to note that the discussions of the completion of science to which I have referred—though prompted by the suspicion that a given trend cannot be extended indefinitely into the future but must be subject to reversals or deceleration, or must reach some finality—make no reference to the stratified nature of global scientific activity, the likelihood that advantages now enjoyed in one region of the world are not fixed and the fact that the center of scientific activity may undergo some kind of significant shift. The disin- terest in shifts in the distribution of the production of scientific knowledge is presumably the result of the conviction that scientific knowledge is universally valid and that location is irrelevant to the question of the exhaustion of questions to be solved.

9. John Horgan (1996: 16–17, 273–274) has a somewhat ambivalent view on this

issue. On the one hand, he refers to applied science as continuing for a long time, but, on the other hand, he also describes applied science as rapidly approaching its limits.

10. The demystification of science by science has led to the call for a philosophy of research, since research is all that science cannot be. Research produces controversies and is permitted to do so. Science is supposed to end disputes. Science distances itself from society, research becomes involved (see Latour, 1998).

11. The position of Silvio Funtowicz and Jerome Ravetz on the origins and the persistence of uncertainty in science constitutes a different vantage point. Funtowicz and Ravetz (1990:7) consider the issue to be a novel problem for science and locate the origins of uncertainty outside of science, as they observe that the scientific community is confronted with a set of unique substantive problems that are responsible for injecting uncertainty into the work of scientists: "Amidst all the great progress in scientific theory and in technological development, ... [we] are confronted by a new class of environmental challenges and threats. Among these are hazardous wastes, the greenhouse effect, and ozone depletion. These give rise to problems of a different sort from those of traditional science, either in the laboratory, classroom, or industry. Science was previously understood as achieving ever greater certainty in our knowledge and control of the natural world; now it is seen as coping with increasing uncertainties in these urgent environmental issues."

12. An example from climate research may illustrate the point. Few scientists today doubt that the global temperature has risen during the last century. It is also the case that agreement on future climate developments is less widespread, as is the consensus on the forces that contribute to climatic changes. And the uncertainties that can be observed among climate scientists actually appear to be rising, despite intensified research efforts in the last few decades. This observation of the growth of uncertainty applies not only to global changes but to regional transformations as well. A study carried out by Chris E. Forest (2002) and colleagues was unable to reach a firm answer on the decisive question of the notion of climate sensitivity (that is, what would be the response of climatic conditions to a doubling of CO_2 emissions into the atmosphere). The researchers of the study by Forest arrived at an estimate of climate sensitivity between 1.4 and 7.7 degrees Celsius, while the International Panel on Climate Change, in a kind of compromise, agreed on values between 1.5 and 4.5 degrees Celsius. The probability that actual climate sensitivity might fall outside the limits set by the IPCC is judged by Forest and his colleagues to be in the range of 30 percent. In other words, the uncertainty regarding the decisive measure of climate forecasts is still considerable; it may even have increased in the wake of growing efforts to arrive at such an estimate.

13. The German term describing knowledge as a generalized capacity to act would be *Handlungsvermögen*. The verb *vermögen* signals "to be able to do," while the noun *Vermögen*, in this context, is best translated as "capacity" (rather than "fortune"). Georg Simmel ([1907]1989:276), in his discussion of money as a generalized code, uses the word *Vermögen* to describe the fact that money is more than merely a medium of exchange and to emphasize that his definition of money thereby transcends a mere functional understanding of its social capacities.

14. As a result, the societal legitimacy of any support for scientific research and also the legitimacy of scientific knowledge itself in society is mostly a function of the *use value* of science. In the forefront of most discussions in society about science is the utility of the knowledge generated in science and therefore the capacity of science to construct or alter the conditions of the life world (cf. Tenbruck, 1969:63).

15. Etymologically, however, power refers to ability, and to "make a difference" would be among the most basic definitions of the concept of "ability." In that sense, and therefore

not in the sense in which power is usually deployed in discussions about power in social relations, namely as power exercised to accomplish something or as power over someone, the basic definition of power as ability resonates with the notion of knowledge as capacity (compare Dyrberg, 1997: 88–99).

16. The idea that knowledge is a model for reality that illuminates, discloses, and transforms, but also displaces reality, resonates with Albert Borgmann's (1999:1) conception of the "recipe" (or plans, scores, and constitutions) as a "model of *information for reality.*"

17. That knowledge is *becoming* is reflected in a fundamental change in metaphysics from an ontology that stresses being to an ontology of becoming.

18. The conception of knowledge advanced here resonates with Ludwig von Mises' (1922: 14) *sociological* definition of *property,* for von Mises suggests that as a sociological category, "property represents the capacity to determine the use of economic goods." The ownership of knowledge, and thus the power to dispose of knowledge, is as a rule not exclusive. This exclusivity, however, is required by jurisprudence as the definition of property or of the institution of ownership. Formal law, as is well-known, recognizes owners and proprietors; in particular, it recognizes individuals who ought to possess, but do not possess. In the eyes of the legal system, property is indivisible. It is also of no importance what concrete material or immaterial "things" are at issue. Likewise, the sociological significance of knowledge lies primarily in the actual ability to dispose of knowledge as capacity for action.

19. It is relevant here to refer to the social role of knowledge generated by the natural sciences and the humanities, the social and cultural sciences. For Niklas Luhmann ([1981] 1987:55), for example, the social role of natural science occurs via the effect such knowledge has on *action* and, through action, on *experience.* For the humanities, exactly the opposite is the case: the influence of cultural knowledge takes place via experience (experiencing) and only through experiencing, on action. (For an account of the difference between action and experience in Luhmann's work, see Luhmann, 1979). Whether or not one follows Luhmann's distinction and the reasons he adduces justifying the difference between acting and experiencing, the idea that knowledge represents a capacity for action is implicit in Luhmann's difference.

20. Based on the basic idea that knowledge constitutes a capacity for action, one can, of course, develop distinctive categories or forms of knowledge depending on the enabling *function* knowledge may be seen to fulfill. I believe Lyotard's ([1979] 1984: 6) attempt to differentiate—in analogy to the categorical distinction between expenditures for consumption and investment—"payment knowledge" from "investment knowledge" constitutes an example of such a functional differentiation of more or less distinctive forms of knowledge.

21. Luhmann's ([1992] 1998: 67) observations about the conditions for the possibility of decision-making perhaps allow for an even broader use of knowledge. Decision-making "is possible only if and insofar as what will happen is uncertain." Assuming or depending upon whether one assumes that the future is most uncertain, the deployment of knowledge in decisions to be made may extend to many more social contexts, even those that are otherwise characterized by nothing but routine attributes and habitual conduct.

22. From an "interactionist" perspective, organizations or any other social structures constitute "negotiated orders" (Strauss et al., 1964; 1978). However, this cannot mean that any and every aspect of the social reality of an organization is continuously available or accessible to every member for negotiation. Only particular, limited aspects of the organizational structure are available for disposition, and only with respect to these contingent features of social action can members mobilize knowledge in order to design and plan

social conduct with a view to realizing collective practical tasks (cf. also George H. Mead's [1964: 555] concept of "reflexive action").

23. Similar conceptions may be found in Friedrich Hayek's 1945 essay, "The use of knowledge in society," which is in fact a treatise in praise of decentralization, the importance of knowledge of local circumstances for action, and the price system as an agency that communicates information and constitutes the answer to the question of coordinating local knowledges. Hayek ([1945] 1948: 82) emphasizes that "as long as things continue as before, or at least as they were expected to, there arise no new problems requiring a decision, no need to form a new plan."

24. A recent definition of knowledge by an economist who tries to raise various conceptual issues about the measurement and incorporation of knowledge into economic theory resembles, in part at least, the definition of knowledge as a capacity for action: "I define knowledge in terms of potentially observable behavior, as the ability of an individual or group of individuals to undertake, or to instruct or otherwise induce others to undertake, procedures resulting in predictable transformations of material objects" (Howitt, [1996] 1998: 99). Aside from the somewhat cumbersome nature of the definition, its restriction to the manipulation of *material objects* is a drawback, as is the essentially black box of "procedures" and "observable behavior." Finally, Howitt appears, at least at the conceptual level, to conflate knowledge with action.

25. As Peter Drucker speculates in a description of the "next society" (*Economist*, November 1, 2001). The essay conflates information and knowledge.

26. It is worth noting that Peter Drucker (1969: 269) sees the economic benefits of knowledge in a "knowledge economy" as extending to all forms of knowledge and to an equal degree. What counts, he adds, is the applicability of knowledge, not whether it is "old or new." What is relevant in the social system of the economy is "the imagination and skill of whoever applies it, rather than the sophistication or newness of the information." My assertion, in contrast, is that it is meaningful to distinguish between the stock of knowledge at hand and marginal additions to knowledge. The process of the fabrication, implementation, and return of each is not identical.

27. Peter Drucker (1993: 184) observes, however, that the initial economic advantages gained by the application of (new) knowledge become permanent and irreversible. What this implies, according to Drucker, is that imperfect competition becomes a constitutive element of the economy. Knowledge can be disseminated or sold without leaving the context from which it is disseminated or sold. The edge that remains is perhaps best described as an advantage based on cumulative learning.

28. As Laurence Tribe (1972: 66) has noted, seeking a psychological rationale for the striking appeal of technocratic scenarios, especially in the early 1960s, perhaps "passion was simply learning to pose as reason."

29. It is of course possible, and by no means unusual, to formulate general assertions about the changing reputation and power of experts—the extent to which the public extends a taken-for-granted measure of trust and is therefore willing to suspend doubt in the judgments of experts. However, the evolving response of the public and of different segments of the public is quite a complex and complicated matter. Response patterns to expert knowledge not only depend on the issue at hand, but are also conditional on a host of psychological, political, and ideological considerations, including the volume of knowledge at hand among those who are forced to define their role as that of laypersons. The often-expressed optimism (or for that matter, fear) regarding the efficacy of experts as political advisers is countered and affected by phases of distinct skepticism and disillusionment regarding their role in politics and government in modern society (cf. Jasanoff, 1990:

9–12). Also, the power exercised by experts, in light of the growing phenomenon of counter-experts and the fundamental contestability of scientific knowledge claims, is by no means extensive and influential, as important theories of modern society assert, but in actual fact quite fragile and limited. Despite the revisable nature of expert knowledge, influential theoretical perspectives tend mainly to emphasize, as Reed (1996: 574) well describes it, the constraining role of experts, and therefore to emphasize "the strategic contribution that experts and expertise make to the much more sophisticated and pervasive systems of organizational surveillance and control crystallizing in (post) modern societies" (see also Castells, 1989; Lash and Urry, 1994; Webster, 1995).

30. Recent studies of innovation processes have shown how important the close coupling of social networks is for the transfer of knowledge, as well as for the ultimate success of innovations in economic contexts. The studies indicate that the traffic of *people* within and among firms, for example, is crucial to the transfer process of knowledge (e.g., DeBressoon and Amesse, 1991; Freeman, 1991; Callon, 1992; Faulkner, Senker, and Velho, 1995).

31. The identification and distinction of different attributes of knowledge is an important task for the purposes of any classification of knowledge, for example, in efforts to identify and judge intellectual innovations or an empirical work that aims at the reconstruction of the social history of knowledge (Burke, 2000). Yet our brains process any input we perceive, be it classified as knowledge or information.

32. Debra Amidon (1997:17), who promotes the notion of knowledge management in a knowledge economy, claims that "*knowledge* is information with meaning" and "*information* is data with context." These concepts, in addition, "when applied to any community … refer to the sum total of experience and learning that reside within an individual, group, enterprise, or nation." Similarly, in a recent essay that attempts to describe "successful knowledge management projects," one finds the following definition: "Knowledge is information combined with experience, context, interpretation, and reflection" (Davenport, DeLong and Beers, 1998: 43). I doubt that such highly ambivalent notions move us much beyond treating information and knowledge as black boxes, or beyond the dilemma of conflating information and knowledge.

33. Bell (1973: 175), in addition, offers an "operational" definition of knowledge when he indicates that knowledge "is that which is objectively known, an intellectual property, attached to a name or group of names and certified by copyright or some other form of social recognition."

34. A perhaps somewhat underdeveloped critique of Bell's definition of the term "information" may be found in a recent publication by Schiller (1997: 106–109). In any event, Schiller emphasizes the positivistic usage of Bell's concept of information. The positivistic usage implies, first and foremost, that Bell decides to eliminate any reference to social or cultural contexts within which information is generated or deployed.

35. The terms "tacit knowledge" and "local knowledge" find increasing usage in the social sciences, but their definition is essentially contested. Compare the extensive documentation of the different usages of these terms in science studies by Cambrosio and Keating, 1998.

36. It is mainly for this reason that Blackler (1995: 1022) suggests knowledge is "embrained" (dependent on conceptual skills and cognitive abilities), "encultured" (dependent on processes of achieving mutual understanding), "embedded" (dependent on systematic routines), "embodied" (dependent on action), and "encoded" (dependent on signs and symbols)—that is, located in brains, dialogue, and symbols. Needless to say, such a conception of knowledge makes it a most complex phenomenon, one that is not sufficiently described by pointing to a couple of constitutive attributes.

37. If I am not mistaken, the description of the resource that information typically conveys and that is explicated here resonates with Gregory Bateson's (1972: 482) definition of information as "news of a difference." Elsewhere, Bateson (1972: 381) indicates that information is that which "*excludes* certain alternatives." That is, according to classical information theory, as Bruner (1990: 4) also stresses, "a message is informative if it reduces certain alternatives." Pre-existing codes allow for the reduction of possible alternative choices. However, by defining information as pertaining to "any difference which makes a difference in some later event," Bateson moves the idea of information, it seems to me, closer to the notion of knowledge as a capacity for action. Niklas Luhmann's (1997a: 198) central conceptual platform (see Bechmann and Stehr, 2001) allows him to follow Bateson's definition of information as a difference that makes a difference, inasmuch as the "news"—which could be an increase in the population or a change in climatic conditions—alerts a system and thereby triggers new system conditions.

38. In a study of the diffusion of business computer technology, Attewell (1992: 6) emphasizes that "implementing a complex new technology requires both individual and organizational learning. Individual learning involves the distillation of an individual's experiences regarding a technology into understandings that may be viewed as personal skills and knowledge. Organizational learning is built out of this individual learning of members of an organization, but it is distinctive. The organization learns only insofar as individual insights and skills become embodied in organizational routines, practices, and beliefs that outlast the presence of the originating individual."

39. Borgmann (1999: 1–2), in his delineation of information and types of information, also emphasizes the signaling function of information. In addition, he differentiates between "natural" or immediate, "cultural," and "technological" information. The acquisition, the nature of the embeddedness in specific contexts (for example, technical or cultural artifacts such as maps of the transmission), as well as the transmission of the information play a role in assigning information to a particular category. For the time being, these types of information, which emerged in different historical periods, continue to co-exist in modern society. However, Borgmann (1999: 2) is skeptical that the co-existence will last: "Today the three kinds of information are layered over one another in one place, grind against each other in a second place, and are heaved and folded up in a third. But clearly technological information is the most prominent layer of the contemporary cultural landscape, and increasingly it is more of a flood than a layer, a deluge that threatens to erode, suspend, and dissolve its predecessors."

40. Richard Dawkins, "The word made flesh," *Guardian,* December 27, 2001.

41. A more extensive critical exposition of the ideas of two prominent proponents of technological determinism, Herbert Marcuse and Helmut Schelsky, may be found in a subsequent section of this study entitled "Knowledge Hierarchies and Monopolies."

42. As Habermas ([1969] 1970: 87) explains, "technological development ... follows a logic that corresponds to the structure of purposive-rational action regulated by its own results, which is in fact the structure of *work*. Realizing this, it is impossible to envisage how, as long as the organization of human nature does not change and as long as therefore as we have to achieve self-preservation through social labour and with the aid of means that substitute for work, we could renounce technology, more particularly *our* technology, in favor of a qualitatively different one."

43. Compare the much more skeptical and hesitant stance that Georg Simmel ([1911/12] 1968: 44) takes toward the knowledge explosion or the incessant enlargement of the objective culture: "The infinitely growing supply of objectified spirit places demands before the subject, creates desires in him, throws him into total relationships from whose

impact he cannot withdraw, although he cannot master their principal content. Thus, the typically problematic situation of modern man comes into being: his sense of being surrounded by an innumerable number of cultural elements which are neither meaningless to him nor, in the final analysis, meaningful. In their mass they depress him, since he is not capable of assimilating them all, nor can he simply reject them, since after all, they do belong *potentially* within the sphere of his cultural development."

44. For an analysis of the elective borrowing and blending of the rhetoric of sociobiology and its semantic relations to population genetics, molecular genetics, and biometrical genetics, see Howe and Lyne, 1992.

45. Economists do not speak with one voice when it comes to the apparent ease with which information and knowledge can be communicated and appropriated. For example, Teece (1977) and Pavitt (1987) are far less certain than many other economists who have reflected on this issue that the costs and benefits of transmitting information are uniformly low. However, the proposition that the issue of appropriability of the economic benefits that accrue from knowledge can be addressed by creating property rights to knowledge (reward for invention) becomes the principal justification for the legal enactment of intellectual property rights (Dam, 1994).

46. An important further noneconomic point of view that remains largely underexposed in the examination of knowledge as a good—compared to the dominant reference to the legal properties of scientific discoveries—is that of the *divisibility* and the possibilities for *distributing* knowledge. In contrast to money, knowledge is in many respects akin to goods that are not divisible. Conflicts involving nondivisible goods have the character of either-or conflicts that are difficult to solve. Divisible goods more or less imply conflicts that tend to be solved more easily (Hirschman, 1994: 213). Nondivisible goods, moreover, are very difficult to distribute, for example, according to the principle of equality. An equitable distribution is extremely difficult to achieve, not only because knowledge cannot be dismantled into an infinite number of pieces, but also because every transaction that has as its goal a more equitable distribution demands both time and preconditions that cannot simply be provided by decree. Georg Simmel ([1900] 1907: 439–440) must have had the fragile relations between principles of justice and the distribution of knowledge in mind when he stressed, "The apparent equality with which educational materials are available to everyone interested in them is, in reality, a sheer mockery. The same is true for other freedoms accorded by liberal doctrines which, though they certainly do not hamper the individual from gaining goods of any kind, do however disregard the fact that only those already privileged in some way or another have the possibility of acquiring them. For just as the substance of education—in spite of, or because of its general availability—can ultimately be acquired only through individual activity, so it gives rise to the most intangible and thus the most unassailable aristocracy, to a distinction between high and low which can be abolished neither (as can socioeconomic differences) by a decree or a revolution, nor by the good will of those concerned."

47. The legal framework and the sanctioning of legal intervention into competitive markets by economists come into play precisely because knowledge is seen as a commodity that is both nonrival and nonexcludable, as will be discussed shortly. Thus, the point would be that legal intervention in the market would be necessary to make knowledge a saleable commodity.

48. Callon (1992: 73) defines techno-economic networks as a "coordinated set of heterogeneous actors—for instance, public laboratories, centers for technical research, companies, financial organizations, users, and the government—who participate collectively in the conception, development, production, and distribution or diffusion of procedures for producing goods and services, some of which give rise to market transactions."

49. Starbuck's (1992: 716) definition of a knowledge-intensive firm resonates with these observations about the function of incremental knowledge, since he stresses "exceptional and valuable expertise," not the possession of knowledge per se, as constitutive of knowledge-intensive firms: "If one defines knowledge broadly to encompass what everybody knows, every firm can appear knowledge-intensive." These broad designations, however, do not as yet represent operational measures of incremental knowledge or exceptional expertise.

50. These characteristics of knowledge allow for a decoupling of the "cost" of the fabrication of the knowledge from the benefits that accrue to those who use it. As a result, the nonrival and the nonexcludable attributes of knowledge constitute a disincentive to invest in the production of knowledge (see Dosi, 1996: 83). Geroski (1994: 94–100) discusses various strategies that might be instrumental in overcoming the appropriability problem of incremental knowledge (also Dam, 1994). For a critique of the notion that enhanced restrictions on the use of (new) knowledge rather than the free flow of information are incentives for innovation and research efforts, see Dempsey, 1999; and, for a critical discussion of the role of the patent profession in developing the patent system, see Drahos and Braithwaite, 2002:43–48.

51. These features of knowledge are enabling when it comes to the protection of knowledge. As Kitch (1980: 712), for example, suggests, "managers can avoid increasing the ease with which information can be transmitted by resisting the temptation to assemble the information in organized written form."

52. If one assumes that knowledges travels as part of the baggage of actors then arguments that knowledge is protected as the result of its "stickiness" or tacitness is weakened by the possible migration of research and engineering personnel able to carry critical tacit knowledge to a competitor or to another country.

53. In the context of economic discourse, arguments about the "tacitness" of knowledge or its levels of appropriability and excludability—higher than often assumed—are employed to make the case *for* state subsidies for research and development. Economists maintain that tacitness of knowledge is actually crucial for innovation. Defenders of government support for science summon the idea of the tacitness of knowledge to make their case: Since the economic benefits of new knowledge are only available "locally," it is important to strongly support research and development activities to gain national competitive advantages (for example, see Cowan, David and Forey, 1999; Kay, 1999). In an even more restricted sense of "local," knowledge is seen as embedded in highly local contexts; for example, it is specific "to each industry, region, and firm and consequently costly to use elsewhere" (Antonelli, 1999: 244).

54. I am grateful to Walter Schindler for suggestions that led to this discussion.

55. A more recent example of knowledge that may quickly become redundant or obsolete as the result of "advances" in knowledge, and therefore no longer requires extensive regulation, comes from the contested issue of stem cell research and therapy. The discovery of versatile—much more versatile than previously imagined—adult stem cells may contribute to the obsolescence of embryonic stem cells in research and therapy (see "Scientists herald a versatile adult cell," *New York Times,* January 25, 2000). In a report for the U.S. president on the ethics of stem cell research issued by the National Bioethics Advisory Commission (1999: ii), one encounters the much more cautionary conclusion that research on adult stem cells should proceed because there are no legal and ethical restrictions. However, "because important biological differences exist between embryonic and adult stem cells, they should not be considered an alternative to ES [embryonic stem cells] or EH [embryonic germ cells] cell research."

56. Susan Wright (1986b) describes the emergence of a consensus among molecular biologists in the 1970s on the minimal potential hazards of recombinant DNA technology. The organized defense of recombinant DNA work by molecular biologists contributed much to appeasing both the government and the public and was instrumental in avoiding external regulation.

57. What makes the analysis of the social role of ideas even more complicated is the distinct possibility that the kind of practical influence ideas have may also occur in the form of "productive" counter-images and metaphors, which tend to bolster the attractiveness and legitimacy of opposing ideas. For example, Keynes' support for state intervention in economic affairs may be influential in formulating economic policies that prevent such intervention by strengthening market forces. But then, even post-Keynesian economic policies may be indebted to post-Keynesian macroeconomic ideas.

58. A more comprehensive statement on the reasons for the power of Keynes' ideas may be found in Stehr, 1992.

59. A more extensive description and analysis of both Schelsky's and Marcuse's critiques of the excessive power of modern science and technology in society may be found in Stehr, 1994: 203–221.

60. The decisive outcome of these developments is that the workers are incapable of acquiring a critical view of the repressive social order. A kind of "masterly enslavement" is pervasive throughout society, affecting all individuals at all levels of production.

61. Theodor W. Adorno's ([1966] 1973: 320) image of the extension of the rule of nature to a rule of humans by humans is similar. Adorno warns that the "unity of the control over nature, progressing to that over man and finally to that over men's inner nature" is one of the threatening dangers of the present age.

62. It is by no means an accident that Helmut Schelsky should prefer the category of scientific *civilization*. The term itself carries a latent critique of and resentment toward a society subjected to (rational) scientific civilizational processes, for as Spengler (1938: 256–257) has stressed, civilization "is a *costume,* a sum of external ways of life."

63. As Webster and Robins (1986: 346) suggest, information technology control is the "same dissemination of power and control, but freed from the architectural constraints of Bentham's stone and brick prototype. On the basis of the 'information revolution,' not just the prison or the factory, but the social totality, comes to function as the hierarchical and disciplinary panoptic machine."

64. While not all proponents of the notion that centralized control and regulation are dangers in modern society might subscribe to the image of science developed by Arnold Gehlen (1949: 12), they nonetheless express quite well a particular epistemological view of the almost limitless societal powers of science and technology. In natural science research, it is not the individual scientist who "poses" the problems, Gehlen writes, "nor does he 'decide' to apply the discoveries, as the layman imagines. The determination of problems follows from what has already been discovered and from the logic of the experiment; the control of outcomes already is part of experimental knowledge. The decision to apply a discovery is unnecessary; it is taken on behalf of the scientist by the object he studies. The process of knowing is an inherently technical process. The relation between science, technical application, and industrial exploitation constitutes an automated and ethically indifferent superstructure. A radical departure can only be imagined if it commences at the extremes of the process, that is, at the starting point (the desire to know) or at the completion of the process (the desire to consume). In each case, asceticism, if it is present at all, would signal a new epoch."

65. Attewell (1987) studied the role of computer technology in surveillance activities in the office of a large medical insurance company; he did not find that computers per se create sweatshop conditions in the workplace. Management not only had tools of surveillance in the past that allowed them to tell who was, in their opinion, a good worker, but the volume of information needed for many management purposes actually was limited. Aside from the resistance massive surveillance creates, the nature of the treatment of clerical workers is much more dependent on the organizational context and environment of the firm, including the balance of the demand and supply of workers.

Chapter 2

The Governance of Knowledge

> Religion has existed since before the dawn of history, while science has existed for at most four centuries; but when science has become old and venerable it will control our lives as much as religion has ever done.
>
> *Bertrand Russell,* Marriage and Morals

Most contemporary contributions to the analysis of the social role of science agree with Bertrand Russell's eighty-year-old prediction of the powerful, controlling influence of scientific knowledge in society. My basic contention is therefore increasingly commonplace in the analysis of modern societies: *ideas,* when compared to other social forces, such as sociostructural or demographic transformations, or to natural impacts on society—for example, climate change or extreme weather—make an important difference when it comes to the course of their history. The difference they make is not constant, nor is the importance of incremental ideas homogenous. I have already examined why incremental knowledge carries such societal significance in modern societies (see the section "Additional Knowledge"; also Stehr, 1994, 2002).

It is my theoretical intention to bring a critical and enriched conceptual perspective to bear on the practical dilemmas that face modern societies, institutions, and citizens as they discuss and determine the practical uses of novel knowledge—or, for that matter, as society contemplates and chooses to permit only limited access to the forms of knowledge; or even decides to refrain altogether from applying newly gained capacities for action or models for reality. The main, but certainly not the only, source of new knowledge and novel technical artifacts *within* science and technology will likely be the fields of biological research and computer science.

71

The form of knowledge politics of primary interest in this study aims on the one hand to preempt, *outside* the boundaries of the scientific community, the practical deployment of novel knowledge claims. In the context of knowledge politics in modern societies, it will likely be the norm, rather than the exception, that the initiative for political action will originate with scientists, who detect problems well before they become political issues. Efforts to regulate knowledge may allow, for example, the possibility of attaching certain attributes such as proprietary restrictions to knowledge,[1] or of restricting access to and limiting the international transfer of knowledge and information,[2] or even of prohibiting certain procedures— for example, gene therapy to alter the human germline.

On the other hand, however, as I have already stressed, knowledge policies need not be based invariably on motives and interests that aim at restriction and rely on command and control. There is no reason why knowledge politics could not be concerned with ways to enlarge the options and capacities with which novel knowledge claims and technical artifacts are deployed in society.[3]

As a matter of fact, there are bound to be incessant struggles among contending interests between these two basic options in the face of new capacities to act. The emerging conflicts will invoke references to the most basic constitutional norms of democratic societies, such as freedom of speech and related basic rights enshrined in the Constitution as well as more recently instituted political principles—especially in the field of environmental policies and regulation, such as the ecological concept of sustainable development and the precautionary principle. Knowledge politics in contemporary societies refers also to issues that are inevitably characterized by a considerable interdependency of problems across national boundaries. A discussion of knowledge politics therefore has to incorporate the question of policies, rules, and restrictions that are contemplated, generated, and implemented beyond the limits of the nation-state.

As I have indicated, in this particular context I am referring to knowledge politics as preemptive regulatory efforts, external to science, which may include measures whose goal is the self-regulation of actors to secure the restrictive use of new knowledge in society. Steve Fuller (1988) has also adopted the notion of "knowledge policy." However, he uses the concept to advocate a philosophy of science perspective that attempts, in contrast to more traditional reflections on rationality, to construct a normative perspective on how best to institutionalize the production, dissemination, and criticism of knowledge within the institution of the scientific community.[4]

On the surface, the foundations of knowledge politics may be quite straightforward; for example, a policy might utilize a conventionally modernist cost-benefit analysis as a "rational" tool kit, offering techniques and principles of problem-solving to assist in relevant decision-making processes. A cost-benefit analysis concerning the introduction of technological innovations would involve, as Radnitzky (1986: 115), for instance, suggests, "predictions about the likely consequences of the use or the abstention from use of the particular piece of technology and evaluations of these consequences made from extrascientific, evaluative standpoints." Needless to say, the advice to employ a cost-benefit analysis is the only easy part in the process of cost-benefit analysis in problem-solving. Reference to unintended and unexpected consequences or to inevitable conflicts—including contested (if often unwitting) cultural points of reference (cf. LaFleur, 1992) in the valuation of the costs and benefits that may flow from an implementation of novel technologies—begins to highlight some of the nearly insurmountable problems of a societal cost-benefit analysis. "Negative" effects are simply ignored or, as the term "unintended consequences" already signals, these "second-order" effects are difficult to anticipate or conceptualize. Radnitzky is therefore resigned to the dilemma that the consequences of introducing a new technology can be properly evaluated only with hindsight, if at all.

Nonetheless, part and parcel of an examination of the practice of knowledge politics is, of course, a critical analysis not only of the anticipated consequences or missed opportunities that, proponents or opponents argue, come with the implementation of new capacities to act—but also of the nature of the narratives invoked to "calculate" and calibrate promises and threats of new capacities to act. What considerations flow into such discourse? Is it the impact on moral convictions, the environment, the political system, the workplace, individual rights and civil liberties, or collective goals and convictions? In the context of discourse about the likely consequences of novel scientific ideas and technical artifacts, one will often include references to past social, economic, and political contexts that serve as anchors in deliberations and in the defense of judgments of the anticipated impact of such devices and capacities. This is most prominently the case, for example, in the field of genetic engineering, where discussions make frequent reference to the practice of eugenics in many countries, but especially in the Nazi era.[5] Invoking the practice of eugenics by the Nazis is then connected to the warning that history might repeat itself (Watson, 1990: 46; Wright, 1990: 27; Duster, 1990; Paul, 1992). Hilary Rose (1995: 169), for example, bemoans the complacency with which the risk of a new eugenicism sustained by the new genetics has been dismissed, because there are "more than traces of eugenics scattered around the HGP [human genome project] literature."

The mere reference to possible dilemmas, conflicts of interest, and past experiences associated with the anticipated use of new knowledge already signals that knowledge can be apprehended as inopportune, repugnant, and dangerous, perhaps as a catastrophic peril to human welfare, and as an (essentially contestable) indication that other cultural "values" are much superior to the "progressive" and unrestricted unlocking of the secrets of nature and society by science. Robert Sinsheimer (1978: 24), for example, offers the cautionary observation that there are inherent dangers to human welfare in scientific advances into *new* territories "uncharted by experiment and unencompassed by theory [where we] must rely wholly upon our faith in the resilience of nature." More specifically, the danger could be that new knowledge might "displace some key element of our protective environment and thereby collapse our ecological niche" (also Moravec, 1999; Joy, 2000).

As at least some molecular biologists and biotechnology companies claim, biomedical discoveries and advances in genetics and neurosciences are on the verge of delivering powerful techniques for the general enhancement of human performance (see Roco and Bainbridge, 2002), as well as the possibility of "genetic profiling" or "genetic redlining" of individuals, which could be deployed throughout their lives in medical settings, the insurance industry, by the police, the courts, the workplace, and the educational system—defining, or perhaps ascribing, "normality," access, responsibilities, benefits, and punishments (Nelkin and Tancredi, 1989: 159–176). It is only too evident that the kind of social control that may be exercised using genetic profiling has significant implications for such citizenship rights as the right to privacy and nondiscrimination in all of the settings I have listed. On the other hand, it is equally evident that arguments in favor of such profiling will be advanced in the same settings on behalf of efficiency, transparency, equity, competence, predictability, cost control, safety, the fight against terrorism, and so on. More generally, those who advance causes in favor of regulating knowledge will have to contend with arguments about "the suffering and environmental damage that will be caused by holding back innovation."[6]

The narratives in advertising, media, science-fiction literature, and movies that accompany or make possible assessments of the merits or the dangers of developments anticipated from the deployment of new knowledge are themselves subject to strategies that invoke powerful forms of discourse. For example, reflections and political or legal decisions about the impact of biomedical innovations may be couched primarily in terms that refer, or better, defer to a kind of fixed or true *nature of human nature,* and to the extent to which that nature may be violated by new capacities of human reproduction. Indeed, the most far-reaching concept of the nature of human nature that may be invoked in the context of such narratives is the notion that there is no fixed human nature.

Elsewhere, for example, in the movie *Gattica* (1997), genetic enhancement is harnessed for profit, reflecting capitalism's ruthless remaking of the world in its search for financial gain. Reflections about the potential consequences of biomedical innovations may, on the other hand, be based on a "denaturalized" perspective of human existence that would stress, in this instance, not the "mechanics" of reproduction, but the importance of the nature of socialization for the identity of humans and the malleability of seemingly fixed anchors for human values. Such anchors for human values, it turns out, are under human control.

But how *emotionally* charged the emerging conflicts over new capacities to act, especially in the field of biomedical innovation, are bound to be can be gleaned from the uncompromising positions taken by influential individuals and corporate actors in the initial debate over the prospect and likely consequences of expanding knowledge in human reproduction, for example. In this instance, reference to "rational" modes of discourse and coping is replaced by emotionally charged terms from science fiction, religious discourse, and reference to dark episodes in human history. Leon Kass, a bioethicist from the University of Chicago and designated chair of the Council on Bioethics of the U.S. government, doubts that we can "give proper rational voice" to the horrors he anticipates once human cloning is practiced. He warns that human cloning offers us (at best) the "dehumanized rationality of Brave New World." "Repulsive" and "revolting," among other words, best describe many aspects of human cloning, which include according to Kass, the prospects of mass production of human beings, with large clones of look-alikes, compromised in their individuality; the idea of father-son or mother-daughter twins; the bizarre prospects of a woman giving birth to a genetic copy of herself, her spouse, or even her deceased father or mother; the creation of homologous organ transplantation; the narcissism of those who would clone themselves, the arrogance of others who think they know who deserves to be cloned or which genotypes any child-to-be should be thrilled to receive; the Frankensteinian hubris to create human life and increasingly to control its destiny; man playing at being God.[7]

In this context one also has to be sensitive to the frailty of prognostications and predictions about future developments of science, complex technologies, and the anticipated consequences of such discoveries and inventions. Predictive discourse about future accomplishments of science and technology is simply littered with failures to anticipate inventions actually made and discoveries never realized, at least not until this day.[8] While professional associations of scientists (most recently, the American Association for the Advancement of Science, 2003), ethical committees, the media, and political bodies, as well as many scholars, continue to debate whether human cloning ought to be permitted and how it might be regulated, reproductive scientists contest the very possibility of human cloning (Simerly et al., 2003).[9]

Under the general heading of the "Governance of Knowledge," I plan to discuss a broad set of issues, including motives, methods, and institutional possibilities for arriving at collective decisions that are new, and yet refer back to intentions and practices that are by no means novel.[10] Knowledge politics and knowledge policies—the control and regulation of the social, cultural, and economic use of (not only newly added) knowledge, and therefore of the kind of impact knowledge and technical artifacts have on the social fabric that deploys rules and sanctions—have always been a part of the modern "regulatory" apparatus of societies, social institutions, and organizations, and are widely accepted as part of "doing business" (e.g., Burke, 2000:116–148). However, there has been an explosion in the volume of regulation and the range of activities to which they apply since the 1970s. Environmental policy is such a growing field of government regulation in recent decades. Moreover, the approaches to regulation and the scope and coverage of regulation, as well as the regulatory standards and regulatory apparatus—for example, in the form of regulatory jurisdiction, implementation, enforcement, sanctions, and supervision—vary considerably from country to country.[11]

As I have stressed, however, a great diversity of social activities have been subject to state-imposed control and command for decades and even centuries.[12] New technological developments have always induced the need to regulate their use. But the rules and norms that were formulated *followed* the implementation of new technologies and the discovery of problems related to them. Even the more recent field of environmental policy and regulation aims for the most part at fixing existing and unanticipated externalities. In many instances, environmental regulatory measures now in force were directly linked to very visible and often local environmental problems. For example, the enactment of the 1956 Clean Air Act in the United Kingdom was the immediate response of policymakers to growing pressure from the public in the wake of the "killer smog" of 1952, held responsible for the deaths of thirty-eight hundred Londoners (Elsom, 1995; Albrecht and Gobbin, 2001).

Similarly, intervention by the state into economic affairs—often not so much imposed as demanded (Stigler, 1971; Posner, 1974; Becker, 1983)—has a long history, with persistent practices of control and command in one or another of the following dimensions: price, discount, rebate, rate of return, entry, exit, the rate of output, and the conditions of service (within specific industries). Generally these measures are directed to a range of industries and enterprises, the methods of production, the attributes of products and services, the conditions of sale and employment, the disclosure of information, and the nature of the environmental impact of goods. The majority of regulatory efforts in economic production, exchange, and consumption include "environmental protection, health and safety (encompassing transportation and occupation aspects), land use and building codes, consumer protection, 'fairness' regulation (principally in the area of human rights), and what we have called 'nation-building' regulation, which is peculiar to Canada (i.e., content requirements in broadcasting, foreign ownership, and official language legislation)" (Nemetz, Stanbury, and Thompson, 1986). The economic theory of regulation asserts that economic actors seek regulation to respond to existing problems, for example, the "lack of protection" of their industry, and demand from political actors the imposition of regulations that offer protection from national or foreign competitors.

The impact of regulation on individual economic actors or market forces varies, of course, from firm to firm, from industry to industry, from consumer to producer, and from service sector to service sector. Emission controls have hardly any direct impact on financial institutions, but the impact on such resource extraction industries as mining may be quite significant. Regulatory techniques involve legislation of rules and prescriptions, which spell out regulatory measures in some specificity and are enforced by government inspectors and investigators. In the field of environmental policies both nationally and internationally (Frank, 1997), regulatory efforts are of more recent origin; but the last third of the twentieth century has seen a spectacular rise in regulations and international treaties designed to protect the environment (Frank, Hironaka, and Schofer, 2000).

The innovation that brought about state regulatory practices, at least in the United States, was the steam engine (Burke, [1966] 1972). While most Americans initially greeted steam power with enthusiasm, tragic accidents, especially the growing frequency of disastrous boiler explosions on boats, alarmed the public. In 1851, a total of 407 casualties were attributed to boiler explosions. However, no government agency existed to investigate these accidents, and the legal responsibilities and liabilities of the manufactures of the steam engines were in their infancy. It was assumed that the enlightened self-interest of the entrepreneurs was a sufficient vehicle to safeguard public welfare. Prevailing public conviction therefore mitigated against government regulations. But once the death toll from boiler explosions mounted, opinions changed about intervening in private enterprise. In the case of the steam boiler explosions, John G. Burke ([1966] 1972) has traced the influence of knowledgeable members of society who investigated the accidents, and who from the outset were firmly in favor of government intervention and regulation, in bringing about legislation that controlled the deployment of steam boilers. The change in attitudes toward regulation took a few decades to evolve, and a law enacted by the U.S. Congress in 1852 had the desired preventive effect.

When it comes to past efforts specifically to target and control *knowledge,* one need only refer to the notorious attempt in the 1920s to outlaw the teaching of Darwinian principles in schools in the state of Tennessee, or to efforts in totalitarian societies to establish "German physics" or "the heritability of acquired characteristics," as in the case of Lysenkoism (Lecourt, 1977; Medvedev, 1971).

More recently there have been more or less urgent appeals demanding that knowledge already well into circulation be regulated, and proposals have been advanced as to how this can best be done. The vote of the Kansas Board of Education to delete virtually any mention of evolution from the state's science curriculum is one contemporary example of the continuing, but ultimately unsuccessful, efforts of creationists in Kansas to ban mention not only of biological evolution, but also of the big bang theory, from the curricular guidelines of schools in the United States.[13] The members of the Kansas Board lost their seats in the next election, and their successors reversed the earlier decision.[14]

Past strategies and instruments designed to control, regulate, and counter knowledge have for the most part been *reactive* responses by institutions such as regulatory agencies, laws, the courts, and social movements. The regulations and controls put in place by reactive strategies respond to scientific knowledge and technical devices that are already well-developed, be it in the intellectual marketplace or in the marketplace for commodities. The social consequences and the intellectual impacts of knowledge that is in place are already evident.

Moreover, early reactive responses of state regulatory agencies were supposed to be benevolent, rather than restrictive, interventions into the affairs of the citizen, at least in nineteenth-century America (see Burke, [1966] 1972: 94). Regulatory practices now in place for the most part have proceeded on the premise that the issue is not *whether* we should use our knowledge and technological capacities, but *how* we should use them. Regulative politics in the past followed the lead of technical developments. Rules and norms were formulated after problems appeared. As Jürgen Habermas (2001: 47) therefore underlines, normative adaptation follows implementation: "The social changes that are induced in the fields of production and exchange, communication and transportation, military and health were in the lead." Reactive knowledge politics of course are closely linked to and based on convictions about the nature of nature, for example, the idea that the environment was "somehow self-cleansing and self-restoring and that the pollutants of nature and other interruptions by industry were only marginally problematic and finally unimportant" (Tiger, 2002:26). The atomic age and individuals such as Rachel Carson exposed such convictions about the harmlessness of much of human action as a somewhat frail belief.

The knowledge politics now in demand includes responses to novel knowledge and to technical inventions whose impacts are unclear, far more contested, and difficult to gauge. The arguments, the motives, the concerns, the narratives, and the objections that will govern future knowledge politics which attempts to regulate new capacities to act therefore are not necessarily related to real existing problems. As Joseph Schumpeter ([1942] 1962: 144) underlined in 1942 in his pessimistic vision of the future of capitalism: "It is an error to believe that political attack arises primarily from grievance and that it can be turned by justification." It does not take reference to existing threats; anticipated threats can equally well generate political disputes and action. The impacts of new capacities to act have to be foreseen, and anticipatory controls have to be put into place. Interventions now in demand clearly opt for strategies that are restrictive rather than benevolent. It is no longer taken for granted, for example, that inventions are the motor of change, or that norms and rules governing their use will only subsequently have to be devised.

To take an example that is less well-known but that centers more directly on the issues I want to examine in this study: In the 1930s, in an analysis of the societal role of technology that reiterated his earlier critique of and distance from modern technology (Sombart, 1911; Grundmann and Stehr, 2001), Werner Sombart (1934: 266) called for the creation of a *Kulturrat,* or Cultural Affairs Commission, whose mandate would be to decide whether "an invention should be discarded, passed on to a museum, or ... realized in practice" (also Lenger, 1996: 366–377). Engineers were supposed to have an advisory role in the commission. Sombart's choice of the name of the commission is not accidental, but rather programmatic. The term "cultural" refers, of course, to the difference between mere civilization and culture—implying that the difference between the civilizational and the cultural sphere is not symmetrical but hierarchical. Although threatened by civilizational developments, culture is superior and is in charge of determining the fate of purely civilizational products. Sombart's aims for the realization of cultural policies were deeply embedded in ideologies of the merits of mere civilizational accomplishments, designed to regulate new technological inventions. But have new knowledge and new technical capacities ever been relegated to a "museum," and therefore not utilized?

A debate that has yet to engage the general public concerns the technical means now in place to alter through gene therapy the human germline—that is, a person's sperm or eggs. Corrective genes injected into the sperm of a patient would become heritable and pass on to future offspring. Experimental work to do this, if only inadvertently, is underway. The biotechnology company Avigen Inc. of Alameda, California, is attempting to insert a corrective gene into the liver of patients with hemophilia B, the less common of two forms of hemophilia. The idea, of course, is to prevent the patient's disease from occurring. However, the company has discovered the presence of the gene's vector in a patient's seminal fluid. A vector is a disabled virus deployed by gene therapeutic procedures to carry the corrective gene into human cells. The discovery of the vector in the seminal fluid could amount to an alteration of the germline, even though it might prevent hemophilia from recurring in the next generations. But gene therapy that alters the human germline is considered a threshold that should not be crossed, in the opinion of some scientists and regulators. As a matter of fact, gene therapy is closely monitored by the U.S. Food and Drug Administration and the National Institutes of Health in the

United States. In this case, the company halted the experiment. Avigen Inc. claims that there is no evidence that the vector has found its way into the sperm of the patient. Upon being consulted, the Recombinant DNA Advisory Committee, the NIH panel that oversees gene therapy issues, recommended that the trials at Avigen Inc. be continued. The panel's recommendation was accepted by the Food and Drug Administration. The trial's patient will be required to use a condom.

The dilemma in this case is self-evident, as are the difficulties in gaining information that might be crucial in regulating gene therapy knowledge. Unless one is convinced that any treatment that may lead to an alteration of the human germline should be outlawed from the outset, the regulation of gene therapy knowledge requires one to weigh the risks associated with inadvertently modifying the human germline against the benefits that come with the possibility of a gene-thrifty treatment for hemophilia. But determining whether the latter is indeed possible seems to require, for the time being at least, that the experiment be carried forward. If, however, the treatment turns out to live up to its promise—and also alters the human germline—pressure for approval of the techniques, and against their prohibition, will undoubtedly be strong.[15]

It may be a contentious issue whether normative demands for the social control of new scientific knowledge are a peculiar feature of modern politics, and therefore of constraints faced primarily by *modern* science. Dror (1968: 3–4) is inclined to argue, in an examination of public policy, that "it is modern science that has made the relationship between knowledge and social action a radical problem," and that the "conscious calculation of social direction must therefore replace the automatic and semi-spontaneous adjustment of society to new knowledge that generally sufficed in the past."

The suspicion that the prompt utilization of scientific knowledge is not always an indication of and basis for social progress has been advanced numerous times. Doubts about the societal benefits of an unrestricted growth of science and its practical applications grew between the wars during the last century. Spengler's massive *Decline of the West* (first published in 1918) was a primary expression and source of the disillusionment with science. The observation—and the concern— that science constituted not only the solution for a host of contemporary social problems (unemployment, overproduction, poverty, and war), but also one of their codetermining causes, became much more common. Today reference would more likely be to pollution, nuclear contamination, and mass destruction.

In this context, voices can be heard both in the present and the past: for example, the English Bishop of Ripon, in a sermon before the 1927 meeting of the British Association for the Advancement of Science, not only demanded a social assessment of research results and their impact but also pleaded for a moratorium on further scientific work:

> Dare I even suggest, at the risk of being lynched by some of my hearers, that the sum of human happiness outside scientific circles would not necessarily be reduced if for ten years every physical and chemical laboratory were closed and the patient and resourceful energy in them transferred to recovering the lost art of getting on together

and finding the formula for making both ends meet in the scale of human life.[16]

By the same token, various forms of knowledge traditions, such as religious knowledge, professional knowledge, and everyday knowledge, have been entangled in struggles and efforts of interested groups aiming to control knowledge by regulating the flow and the utilization of new knowledge.[17] At the same time, clashes between competing knowledge traditions, for example in the field of health care, have been accompanied by demands to regulate rival and contending knowledge claims. However, I will try to distinguish between the entrenched, existing political economy of knowledge and what I consider to be new forms of regulating, policing, and controlling additional knowledge—especially knowledge emanating from biotechnology and computer science, which appears to be very much unlike knowledge already subject to regulatory schemes.

I will try to delineate in greater detail in later sections the kinds of knowledge policies that are of interest in this context, as well as the practical difficulties such policies are bound to encounter. The depiction of the knowledge-guiding interests of this inquiry also requires that from time to time I refer to what are evidently multiple legal, economic, political, or moral ways of regulating information and knowledge, but which do not immediately fall within the self-defined limits of the study. For example, concerns about expanding the (legal as well as technical) means of controlling access to information, be it for proprietary or moral purposes, are not of immediate interest in the examination of the governance of knowledge in this study, because the control of access to information is really an age-old phenomenon that does not impinge on the use of such information by many actors. This is not to say that the control of access to information and knowledge is without various deleterious (or even beneficial) social, political, or economic consequences. It is important, in short, to describe in specific terms what is meant by the governance of knowledge, although it is at times difficult precisely to fix the boundaries.

Even in prehistory, elements of defensive knowledge policies might have been present, if only to affirm and assure the perpetuation of what by all accounts must have been fairly stable and robust cultural patterns. The impact on and control of technology has not only been a vital theme in economic, political, and social theory for at least two centuries, but also led to the formation of early social movements, as the following discussion shows.

On Machinery and Class Interests

The question of the impact of inventions and technical change on employment is, in economic discourse for example, part of the disciplinary tradition that periodically moves to the forefront of discussion. This has been the case since David Ricardo added a chapter entitled "On Machinery" to the third edition of his *Principles of Political Economy and Taxation* in 1823.

The years between the 1776 publication of Adam Smith's *Inquiry into the Nature and Cause of the Wealth of Nations* and Ricardo's discovery of structural unemployment as the result of machinery's impact on economic affairs half a century later witnessed the initial technical transformations of the textile industry, the first deployment of steam engines, and the introduction of machines in the production of iron. But many events occurred beyond this technical change of introducing machines into various contemporary industries.

Beginning in February of 1811, riots broke out in Nottinghamshire and adjoining counties against the introduction of a new wider frame in the cottage knitting industry. By April of the following year, close to one thousand knitting frames had been smashed. These activities spread and affected other industries in England. The Luddites, named for their celebrated leader Ned Ludd, whose early success caused considerable political alarm, provoked similar reactions elsewhere in England and thrust the issue of technological change and employment to the forefront of the day's agenda. The Luddites were skilled workers. Their protest was directed against what might today be called de-skilling. Today, the term "Luddites" has taken on a negative connotation, referring to a kind of mindless destruction of new technology and obscurantist opposition to technological change. But one might suggest that the Luddites opposed, in an almost rational fashion, a new technology that they perceived as destructive to their way of life and livelihood. Frame breaking became a capital offense in 1812. Many Luddites were prosecuted and received severe sentences, including the death penalty.

David Ricardo ([1821] 1973: 264) stated (after stressing that he had turned his interest to questions of political economy) that he had been convinced that "an application of machinery to any branch of production . . . was a general good," even when this was accompanied, at worst, by frictional unemployment. He went on to offer the cautious but plain observation that the "substitution of machinery for human labor is often very injurious to the interests of the class of laborers." Ricardo's observations corrected what by then he considered a mistake—namely, the conviction he had shared with other classical economists that the employment effects of technical advances would actually be beneficial to the workers. He had envisioned that there would be no reduction in wages or in employment: "I thought that no reduction of wages would take place because the capitalist would have the power of demanding and employing the same quantity of labor as before, although he might be under the necessity of employing it in the production of a new, or at any rate, of a different product" (Ricardo, [1821] 1973: 264). In line with equilibrium theory, he had anticipated that market forces would regulate employment. The market theoretically ensures that, ultimately, all those who desire it will be able to work. Temporary or frictional unemployment is unavoidable, but the market will heal structural unemployment.

Ricardo [1821] 1973: 269) indicated, somewhat to the shock of his readers, that he had been mistaken. The introduction of labor-saving machinery caused unemployment beyond a temporary or frictional displacement of jobs because of the lack of elasticity of wages. In other words, what Ricardo discovered was really structural unemployment. Structural unemployment refers to changes in the work environment that are not brief. It involves the obsolescence of skills or appropriate locations. Ricardo qualified his observations about the extent to which the laboring classes would be in distress and poverty by saying that in the medium or long term, compensatory mechanisms would assert themselves that would reabsorb those thrown out of work. However, overall, he insisted that the statements he made "will, I hope, lead to the inference that machinery should not be encouraged."

In his treatise *Knowledge is Power,* first published in 1855, Charles Knight related the story of the discovery of the fabrication of soda from salt at the beginning of 1800 in France and its realization in manufacturing in England beginning in 1820. The production of both soap and glass depended on soda as an alkaline ingredient. Before 1820, nearly all commercial soda was obtained from the ashes of seaweed, which were sold under the name of Spanish barilla and kelp. As soda prepared from salt was introduced, the price for soap and glass fell sharply. Knight (1856: 374) noted that the "manufacturers of kelp and barilla were in great measure deprived of employment ... but the compensation rendered by the employment of a greater number of laborers in manufacturing and exporting soda-ash, and in producing the increased amounts of glass and soap required, was not all. To manufacture soda from salt requires the employment of sulfuric acid and common salt. To produce sulfuric acid, sulfur and nitrate of soda was necessary. The new and increased demand for these articles gave an impetus to labor all over the world." And in speaking of the French chemist Le Blanc, who discovered the process, Knight (1856: 375) added, thus "we see how great a benefit to the world has resulted directly and indirectly, from the labors of a comparatively obscure chemist, working in his laboratory—labors, which at the time they were performed, were no doubt considered by the great majority of those cognizant of them as of no practical value."

The debate and the interest in the relation between employment and technical change receded into the background. It disappeared from the agenda of economics and politics in the wake of persistent economic expansion that lasted into the second decade of the next century. It was this experience, and more precisely the sixty-year time span prior to the First World War, that led Schumpeter ([1942] 1950: 69), for example, to conclude that there is no tendency "for the unemployment percentage to increase in the long run." For Schumpeter, the high levels of unemployment in the 1930s did not warrant an alteration of this conclusion. Frictional and therefore temporary unemployment is considered simply a fact of life of the capitalist system.

The Ascendancy of Knowledge Politics

> Wait until you see what we have in store for you. We will change your life toward the better. You should be grateful.
>
> *Carl Feldbaum*[18]

The politicians, scientists, critics, social movements, and individual citizens who are alarmed by and urgently demand control of research activities and the use of novel scientific knowledge are mobilized to issue such calls for legal or other action by effusive promises of the potential consequences of research efforts—most recently, of course, in the fields of biotechnology and computer science—which extend to planned radical interventions in and the reconstruction of nature, including (deficient) human nature. The American Museum of Natural History's exhibition, "The Genomic Revolution," pledges that "by the year 2020 it is highly possible that the average human life span will be increased by 50 percent; gene therapy will make most common surgery of today obsolete; and we will be able to genetically enhance our capacity for memory."[19]

However, the promised release from inherited afflictions, for example, does not find universal acclaim. The biochemist Erwin Chargaff, who has early and persistently criticized such aims as excessive and unacceptable, may be quoted as putting forward representative concerns. The frequent references to health in the promises issued by proponents of biotechnology research are a mere pretense, Chargaff argues: "Once science promises that it will reduce or even eliminate pain, the public pays attention. The genetic technocrats know that they are able to easily seduce the public because in the case of health and eternal life people are only too willing to enter into a pact with the devil."[20]

In the field of genetics and biotechnology, one therefore encounters radically opposed forms of discourse. On the one hand, there is a narrative that champions genetic engineering as a most promising contribution to agriculture (Brill, 1986; Wambugu, 1999) or human health, especially in the case of diseases that are fatal, as exemplified by Carl Feldbaum and other scientists. On the other hand, there is a narrative that sees genetics as a tool that is part of a "totalitarian conspiracy to rid the world of disabled people" (Shakespeare, 1999: 669).

Knowledge politics in the most general sense is an almost timeless phenomenon. There have always been attempts to assign specific cultural values to knowledge, and to regulate and control novel scientific knowledge. As a result, it is important to ask what accounts for the ascendancy of knowledge politics in this age.

Aside from the changing ways in which especially science-based knowledge is apprehended in modern societies—both inside and outside of the scientific community—and the extent to which, despite these image changes, we define our age in terms of its relation to knowledge, the economic, political, and societal importance of *knowledge policy* in this century escalates because:

(1) We are faced with *new forms of knowledge* (or new types of capacities to act) that both set off alarms and encourage broad sets of promises. The route from basic research to applied research to commercial application is in some fields of science, for instance molecular biology, a particularly short and direct one.[21] The difference between basic and applied research is diminishing. The identification of a gene presupposes a test for that particular gene. The transformation of knowledge is codetermined by an increasing specialization in science and a massive infusion of private and public funds in support of particular research fields. The limits of what is feasible in practice are decisively displaced. Knowledge itself is transformed. Knowledge now emerging is more powerful in shifting or destroying the boundaries of the possible; for example, the techniques of genetic engineering make DNA subject to direct human access and control.[22] The bio-utopian future, as it is

promised, amounts to control of the biological destiny of mankind. With the emancipation from "their genetic straightjackets and the constraints of Nature, people will find a new kind of freedom—a freedom to overcome disease and hunger, to have an improved standard of health and, of course, to live longer" (Hindmarsh, Lawrence, and Norton, 1998: 5).

(2) As the result of the *speed* with which the *volume* of the available stock of knowledge grows, the opportunities for *contacts* with knowledge multiply. As a matter of fact, the very definition of and concern with the speed of cultural evolution refer to the presence and accelerated appearance of incremental knowledge.

(3) The rapid increase of knowledge multiplies, by definition, our *capacities to act,* for knowledge represents capacities of action or models for reality that considerably enlarge our options for changing social realities. The economic, political, and social centrality of knowledge grows. For the political system, constantly on the lookout for political topics, new scientific knowledge constitutes problems that have to be dealt with politically. The enlarged capacities to act bring about an increase in concerns about the various effects of new knowledge, as well as access to it and its control, distribution, benefits, and costs (see Horowitz, 1985). Nothing appears to be impossible anymore. The prevailing public sentiments about the benefits and costs associated with our enlarged ability to alter the environment and society are changing.

(4) Although every past technical invention and scientific breakthrough has produced *responses* of exhilaration, as well as deep concern and dire predictions about its social or psychological impact, there is a tendency to shift, when it comes to the assessment of the role of science and technology in society, from a willingness to engage in posteriori cleanup to efforts to reduce or even prevent harmful effects. But questions such as, "How can we possibly use it?" invariably compete, at least in the field of medical inventions, with questions such as, "How could we not?" The rapidity with which incremental knowledge is produced has not only increased the awareness that knowledge becomes the motor of social change, but has also heightened the sense of alarm, risk, and *uncertainty* that are seen to be associated with the transformative capacity of knowledge. Similarly, an element of outright hostility may even be one of the visible responses from the general public—for example, with respect to the heightened tempo of scientific and technological "progress" and its anticipated effects. During periods of accelerated social change, demands for planning, regulating, and policing the forces of change always grow as well. Rapid social change generated by knowledge is no exception to the rule.

(5) Efforts to regulate and control incremental knowledge cannot be uncoupled from *time and place.* As a matter of fact, the importance of the context and the boundaries of the context within which efforts may be launched to control knowledge immediately point to one of the dilemmas knowledge policy inevitably faces, even in a world that is supposedly shrinking as the result of the forces of globalization—namely the limits of control, legitimacy, and authority to police knowledge across contingent boundaries and borders.[23]

(6) Finally, the extensive industrial, military, and medical applications of science in the last century account for the kind of esteem it widely enjoys among the

citizens and institutions in modern society. Scientism, or technocratic perspectives that deny the possibility of alternative decisions about the use of science and technology, takes the repute of science to the extreme. The *authority of science* is virtually impossible to doubt. However, the taken-for-granted social standing science and scientific knowledge enjoy in modern societies—for example, as rather neutral, value-fee, instrumental agencies—has never been without its detractors. Increasingly, scientism is under scrutiny. Widespread scrutiny of science and technology, dating at least from the decade of the 1960s, and concerns voiced then about the environmental impacts of science-based products, allow for the possibility of proposing and justifying limits to the deployment of novel scientific knowledge in society.

New knowledge is not evenly distributed, homogeneous, freely available, nonpartisan, beneficial for all, nor even isomorphic with human progress. But neither is new knowledge necessarily harmful, monopolistic, elite-ruled, easily subject to censorship, or antithetical to constructive social change.

Despite the unanticipated consequences, and the difficulties of controlling or limiting the impact of technology on social relations or the ways in which novel knowledge affects the future of humankind, modern societies are caught in a kind of Faustian bargain, as they can only rely on their evolving knowledge to understand what kind of work knowledge performs. The regulation and control of new scientific knowledge and novel technical devices, and therefore of knowledge politics, will in many instances be through science-based policy. Knowledge politics will be a risky business. The observation that we are witnessing a growing dependence of governance on scientific knowledge, and a growing need to govern scientific knowledge, can only hint at the dilemmas at issue. The formation of regulatory regimes, in the forms of legislation, guidelines, appeals, voluntary codes, and compliance systems in the field of knowledge, will have to reply on specific science input even more than other regulations imposed by government. Whether knowledge politics and decision-making can, in addition, also rely on other mechanisms and inputs—for example, signals that markets and voters impose—will have to be seen.

The restrained optimism still expressed by Langdon Winner (1977) therefore sounds like a faint echo from the past, when knowledge was primarily seen as the key to unlocking the secrets of the universe, and not as the becoming of a world:

> Modern people have filled the world with the most remarkable array of contrivances and innovations. If it now happens that these worlds cannot be fundamentally reconsidered and reconstructed, humankind faces a woefully permanent bondage to the power of its own inventions. But if it is still thinkable to dismantle, to learn and start again, there is the prospect of liberation. Perhaps means can be found to rid the human world of our self-made afflictions.

Yet many professional observers, as manifest in a number of recent publications (Smith, 1994; Garfinkel and Russel, 2001; Rosen, 2000; Whitaker, 1999), and the public in general, as indicated by survey findings, are alarmed about the erosion of privacy as the result of new surveillance devices and information-gathering technologies which they see deployed everywhere in society.[24] They will hardly be satisfied with mere affirmations that it could be otherwise, that there is limited privacy anyway, that devices that protect one's privacy are equally effective, and therefore that privacy concerns and information technologies are not at odds.[25]

The investigation carried out in this study and its premises may be questioned on a number of important counts. First, as indicated already, there is the intuitive and undefeatable argument that the governance of knowledge is hardly a novel process. The point is not that the regulation of knowledge is new. Attention to the messy empirical details of social, economic, and political reality, however, indicates that the volume and the importance of knowledge regulation has increased, and will further increase, immensely. Second, the social consequences of innovations, discoveries, and new capacities to act generally continue to occur mostly in an "indirect" fashion (see Barber, 1952: 272–273). Social changes are, as it were, not even attributed to new ideas. If an attribution is made, such a connection is erroneous, because prior "infrastructural" changes account for the impact (e.g. Bowker, 1994). Third, knowledge policies are futile because knowledge is, for example, either self-realizing or self-protective.

I will try to demonstrate in the sections to follow that the reservations I have just enumerated are not warranted.

Regulating Knowledge

Public concern and fear of the ethical, social, economic, or environmental implications of the development of *new* scientific knowledge—for example, the implications of genetic engineering—have taken a variety of forms. The individuals, groups, and movements that have entered the debate or engaged in action range from labor unions, indigenous people, trade organizations, and environmentalists, to political parties, consumer groups, farmer associations, religious organizations, and globalization critics (see Phelps, 1998). While direct action is still the exception, it is by no means absent, as the following examples demonstrate.

Early one morning in late July of 1999, Lord Melchett, the head of Greenpeace in Britain, was detained for questioning by the police after he and about thirty Greenpeace members raided a field of genetically modified maize near Norfolk. The protest came to an abrupt end after the farmer called the police and they arrested the protesters. According to the *Times* (July 27, 1999), the raid left government trials of seed crops that had been genetically modified in disarray. The farm on which the protest took place was one of seven test sites damaged or destroyed within months. The protest by Greenpeace followed a recommendation by the Association of Local Governments to its 170 members in England and Wales to phase out genetically manipulated foods (or GM foods) until they had been proven safe. A number of councils followed the recommendation. Major food manufacturers, supermarket chains, and fast-food chains in Britain had already announced that they would not carry any products that contained genetically modified ingredients.

A poll in the summer of 1999 found that 79 percent of the British public agreed that GM crop testing should be stopped. The response to experimental crop sites seen in England in 1999 has not been confined to that country. In the summer of 2003, more than half of all experimental fields with genetically modified crops in France were destroyed, prompting fifteen hundred French scientists to sign a petition demanding an end to the destruction.[26]

In the U.K., the nationwide "GM Nation?" debate in 2003 found that most individuals who took part in the public consultations were not only cautious, suspicious, or outright hostile to GM crops, but also expressed a strong and wide degree of suspicion about the motives, intentions, and actions of those involved in decisions about genetic modification, especially the government and multinational corporations. The attitude of the European Union and the European Parliament was less strict. In July of 2003, the European Parliament passed legislation that replaced a ban on *new* biotech foods which had been in place since 1998 in response to consumer concerns. The new rules allow genetically modified products if they are clearly labeled. At present, only a few countries can be said to embrace transgenic foodstuffs.

In Canada and the United States genetic modification of foodstuffs has hardly been questioned by the public. Whether public responses in North America are the result of a lack of information among consumers or related to positive statements by politicians and widespread trust in the regulatory apparatus of the FDA remains a controversial issue (see Arntzen et al., 2003). A major political and trade battle on this front between North America and Europe is likely. However, strong responses and reactions are not confined to advanced societies. In India, a group of farmers in September of 2003 wrecked a research station in Bangalore run by Monsanto, the U.S. firm with a monopoly on the sale of genetically modified cotton seeds in six of India's states that permit them.[27] On the other hand, Cuba has an active agricultural biotechnology research program, and forced by circumstances, the technocratic elite of the country will hardly resist employing genetically modified seeds. In still other countries, the controversial issue is not so much whether or not to allow and market GM crops but rather whether transgenic plants should be based on nationally produced seeds or imports from foreign multinational corporations (see Aldhous, 2003: 655).

In January of 1999, the *Daily Telegraph* (January 22, 1999, p. 9) reported that the British Medical Association warned, in a report entitled "Biotechnology Weapons and Humanity," that rapid advances in genetics would "soon transform biological weapons into potent tools of ethnic cleansing and terrorism." The British Medical Association urged that the regulations of the 1972 International Biological and Toxic Weapons Convention be tightened and improved, anticipating the possibility of genetic warfare, which is a practical possibility today.

In Switzerland, the so-called "genetic protection initiative" (a petition for a referendum "for the protection of life and the environment from genetic manipulation") was clearly rejected in a June 1998 plebiscite in all the cantons, to the great "relief of the pharmaceutical industry" (*Neue Zürcher Zeitung,* June 8, 1998).[28] With a voter turnout of 40.6 percent, 66.6 percent of voters opposed the petition, which according to its advocates would have declared Switzerland to be a great, unified "genetic protection area." The petition demanded, among other things, changes to the Swiss constitution forbidding the production, purchase, and sale of genetically modified animals; the release of genetically modified organisms into the environment; and the granting of patents for genetically modified animals and plants. The fact that all of my examples of recent attempts to regulate the application of knowledge deal with genetic research—and the list could easily be extended—is, of course, a result of both the hopes and fears, or even nightmares, that have lately been prompted by this one rapidly growing branch of research in molecular biology.[29]

In democratically organized societies, it is a legitimate role for political discourse and action, as well as civil society, to contribute to and take part in decisions that affect the ways in which scientific knowledge and possible technological artifacts are used in society. But in highly differentiated modern societies, single and collective actors are also forced to suspend judgment. In order to get on with the mundane task of living, one has to delegate authority and judgments. For to conceive of a world in which such delegation did not occur, one has to imagine a simple society in which everyone knows what everyone else knows that may be relevant to knowledge politics. Thus, citizens of modern societies, even knowledgeable citizens, cannot escape the dilemma of not only having the right to be involved in decisions about the utilization of new knowledge, but also having to delegate cognitive authority to experts, counselors, and advisors. Stephen Turner (2001: 144) therefore posits, "Some facts need to be taken for granted in order for there to be a genuine political discussion, and some of the work of establishing the facts is, properly, delegated to experts. ... But granting them cognitive authority is not the same as granting them some sort of absolute and unquestionable power over us."

It may well be that I exaggerate the political, economic, and societal importance of the emergent field of the regulation and control of knowledge. I do not mean merely that other issues may displace knowledge policies on the agenda of important and contentious fields of polemical activity, but rather that I acknowledge that there may be limits to knowledge politics which will reduce the requirement to engage in the regulation and control of knowledge.

For example, there may be distinct limits to the capacity of societies to "absorb" new knowledge and the uncertainties and problems it creates. These limits to the absorption of such knowledge would constitute the unplanned knowledge policies of a society.[30] It is easy to raise this question, but more difficult to pose answers. What would these limits look like? Are they a matter of social organization, for example, imposed by a political regime, and/or are they the outcome of limiting natural endowments? The question, focusing as it does on an uncertain future, is impossible to answer. At the other extreme, perhaps, one might argue that knowledge is self-realizing. I will return to this assertion. Suffice it to say at this point that knowledge policies would surely be futile if knowledge is self-realizing, in the sense that what is known is also bound to be utilized in practice. Any effort to plan, control, or restrict usage is bound to fail, since knowledge inexorably rises toward realization. In this case, submission can be the only response.

However, I am not convinced that the governance of knowledge is unnecessary, either because as a collectivity we will soon exhaust our ability to absorb and deploy new knowledge, or because knowledge automatically realizes itself. Neither mere submission nor limits to what can be absorbed appear to be meaningful knowledge policies, assuming such responses should be seen as policies in the first place.

As I observed in the introduction, the claim cannot be sustained that either the idea of controlling knowledge or efforts to control knowledge in general, and additional knowledge in particular, are entirely new. But that there is and that there will be a consequential shift in knowledge politics in modern society is what is at issue here. In the past, observers have largely been impressed by the enigma of biased social change. For whatever reasons, in the case of the trajectory of earlier societies, the instrumental or even logical priority of the material culture was beyond question. Observers took it for granted that the evolution in material culture (or the substructure of society) not only constitutes a readily discernable and valid inference about historical sequences, but also triggers forms of "maladjustments" to which attention ought to turn first and foremost.

The material culture is seen as much more malleable and less persistent than the structure of social arrangements, worldviews, "folkways" and beliefs, or the non-material culture. David Landes (2000: 2) perhaps exaggerates, but expresses the same observation in strong terms: Culture, "in the sense of the inner values and attitudes that guide a population, frighten[s] scholars. It has a sulfuric odor of race and inheritance, an air of immutability." Although cultural elements may be changing with accelerated speed, material culture adds new elements or inventions at an even faster pace; it expands and diffuses with greater and greater swiftness.[31] Since the movement in the growth of different cultural elements along an exponential curve is less than "satisfactorily" coordinated, both in specific places and across locations, the focus becomes the lagging adjustments in dynamic societies with unequal rates of change, cultural inertia, or "cultural lag" (Ogburn, [1922] 1950: 200–212); patterns of "disorganization"; and the societal benefits of "the integration of cultural patterns" (Ogburn and Nimkoff, 1947: 592).

For William F. Ogburn, the pace and desirability of changes in those cultural elements that advance more rapidly is not at issue; as a matter of fact, the exponential principle suggests that knowledge is bound to accumulate at a growing rate. In short, efforts to suppress and control changes in the "precipitating" cultural variables are not what matters, nor can they be contained.[32]

It is surely without contention that knowledge which emerges from the scientific community is not risk-free, and can even be dangerous. The dangers, the risks, the apprehended damages, and the costs may be intended, or they may be the unexpected by-products of research. Concerns about the harm, the unequal distribution of the benefits and opportunities, or the uncertainties for society generated by new knowledge are far from exceptional. It is only prudent to reflect on these matters.

During the early postwar decades of rapid economic growth in the last century, the application of scientific and technical knowledge in developed societies was not necessarily unanimously and uncritically advocated, to be sure, but there was a considerable degree of silent assent. Increased knowledge of society and nature, as well as the rapid deployment of new technologies, were once again widely hailed—as was the case at the dawn of modern science in the seventeenth century—as desirable progress and an enhancement of the human condition. Voices doubting the benefits of increased knowledge for the human condition became fainter and fainter. Science and technology were seen to have almost self-healing qualities. The problems science creates, it is also able to solve, was a commonly held optimistic view.

We are about to enter a new, transitional era. Science and technology are not perceived as the key for "considerable relief from our troubles" (Leibniz, 1951: 584), but rather as the root cause of trouble. But such misgivings about the human benefits of science and technology are not new. It is therefore necessary to examine both the origins and the novelties of the emerging doubts about the role of scientific and technological "progress." I believe that we can be somewhat confident that we are not witnessing a mere repetition of the most recent concerns with conditions that were attributed to science and technology.

Such headlines of recent times as "We know too much," "Homo Xerox," "Now everything can be manufactured," "Fertility ethics authority approves sex selection," "Insurers insist on genetic testing," "Clone's cells turn back aging process," and "How much genetic self-knowledge is good for us?" or keywords from ever more vehement disputes, such as "We dare not make use of everything we know," are part of the background and the environment of the current increasingly urgent demands for the regulation and control of knowledge in modern societies. In analogy to the much asserted but little analyzed alleged "information overload" in modern society (see Bowles, 2000),[33] one could refer to these concerns and demands for control as a perceived "knowledge overload."

The discussion and formulation of the novel moral principle of the "right to ignorance" of an *individual,* as advanced by Hans Jonas (1974: 161–163), is clearly germane in the context of a discussion of the political and ethical dilemmas generated by the dynamics with which knowledge grows (for example, the freedom of the individual to submit or not to submit to a gene-based diagnostic test). Jonas' moral principle that ignorance can be bliss (Berlin, [1998] 2002: 22) will be opposed by equally formidable ethical demands that insist on a "right to know," especially at the *collective* level or from a "macro" perspective (cf. Stiglitz, 1999; Sen, 1981). In everyday life, sentiments that support the virtue of not knowing find expression in such sayings as "what I don't know can't hurt me" or "where ignorance is bliss, it is folly to be wise."[34] James Watson (as cited by Brave, 2001: 4), in strict contrast, insists that "the biggest ethical problem we have is not using our knowledge ... people not having the guts to go ahead and try and help someone." However, at the center of the emerging controversies about the growth of biomedical knowledge, for example, is not what in the past was known as "things we should not know" collectively (see Shattuck, 1996: 302–313). Explicit knowledge politics commences once new capacities for action have been discovered.

Science and technology controversies concerned with the things we know open a window, as it were, on modern struggles over meaning and morality, economic benefits and damages, as well as on the emerging and shifting locations of social power and control in knowledge societies.

The new political field that I identify as "knowledge politics" is certainly not immediately connected with the often-described ambivalent sense of crisis in modern societies, based on the over- and/or mass production of knowledge. The tension between the extent of knowledge production in advanced societies and the limited capability of the individual person to assimilate the huge amount of knowledge available was already described by Georg Simmel ([1907] 1989) a hundred years ago, in a theory of the current age in the final chapter of his *Philosophy of Money*. The tragedy of culture manifests itself in the cleavage between objective culture made independent and the obstinacy of subjective culture. The problem of policing knowledge is not related to the production of knowledge in total—even if it is related to overproduction, however that may be defined—but rather to the range of incremental knowledge, which is conceived as being capable of changing reality.

The main, but by no means only, societal role and relevance of scientific knowledge is a pragmatic one in a world that is to a large extent driven by knowledge. Knowledge is the basis of our way of life. In the context of knowledge politics, another question will therefore be of considerable significance: the question of whether human curiosity poses a threat to that way of life.

The social control of knowledge I plan to examine refers, in the first place, to the regulation of anticipated uses and consequences of incremental knowledge. It is important to emphasize the governance of novel knowledge, rather than the control of knowledge per se, inasmuch as the former is what constitutes the *new* field of political activity. The differentiation between existing and perhaps widespread formal and informal efforts to control knowledge (for example, the knowledge or information embodied in human capital by firms and other social organizations, such as universities)[35] is necessary in order to reasonably delimit the range of my inquiry.

The concern raised by Paul David (2000), for example, that "ill-considered government support for expanding legal means of controlling access to information for the purpose of extracting economic rent is resulting in the 'over-fencing of the knowledge commons' in science and engineering" is, for a number of reasons, not a central part of the issues I wish to examine in this study.

The control purposes to which David refers are conventional codes that demand the protection of certain information from being used by competitors or adversaries. The codes refer to measures that examine access and control to information as property and as a contractual matter, for example. They are an extension of well-known disputes surrounding rights to information. Moreover, whether or not access is closely restricted, open, or even encouraged does not speak to the question of whether or not such knowledge should be utilized at all. Presumably it allows use by those who are permitted access.

More specifically, my concern is the shift in the aims of control from regulating and policing normality or identity (Foucault) to the growing concern in knowledge societies with efforts to police novelty and differences.[36] Moreover, the attempted control and regulation of novelty is based on codes or steering mechanisms that have not been extensively invoked in the modern era for the purposes of judging knowledge claims. New actors are bound to appear on the scene, while traditional political forces are transformed in the course of struggles that pertain to the social control of new technical capacities, novel processes, and products.

As I have indicated, the examples that come to mind, and that have captured the attention of the media and the public recently, are numerous and growing.[37] For example, the United Nations, provoked by advances in ocean exploration, is drafting a treaty that attempts to regulate marine archeology and commercial efforts to hunt for and reclaim lost cultural treasures—and therefore the knowledge about ancient civilizations, such as the empire of the Phoenicians, that may come with their discovery (*New York Times*, October 12, 1998). Transgenic Pets, a small company in Syracuse, has announced that it is developing a genetically modified cat which will not cause allergies (*New York Times*, June 27, 2001). Other companies are trying to clone pets. On an even grander scale, transgenic human engineering (for instance, genetically modified crops that contain human genes or cow-human pre-embryos) is now an energetically discussed theme in bioethics journals (e.g., Robert and Baylis, 2003). Such chimeras will generate strong public protests and objections that are bound to grow as these capacities to engage in transgenic human engineering are realized.

It is perhaps self-evident to anticipate that "knowing" will be seen in knowledge societies as a domain in urgent need of policing, and as a site to study the functioning of power in modern society.[38] Inasmuch as the widespread dissemination of knowledge increases the fragility of modern societies (Stehr, 2000a), efforts designed to control knowledge may be interpreted as strategic attempts to intervene and reduce or manage that fragility. Whether such attempts are likely to be successful is therefore an important issue. In modern societies, knowledge becomes a *model for reality,* a system for action, rather than the key that reliably unlocks the mysteries of nature and society, or a social institution that is widely perceived as issuing truths.[39] Nature and society have themselves become the laboratory and the site of thought experiments.

But the issue of the control of knowledge becomes significant for another reason as well. Insofar as knowledge, especially "additional" knowledge, assumes growing importance within the economic system and becomes subject to economic interests, efforts to control, restrict, or privatize its use will grow as well. A prominent example comes from genetic research, in particular the Human Genome Project. In light of the intensive competition among hundreds of researchers worldwide in the Human Genome Project, concerns have intensified that findings which might "alter the world economy" will be monopolized, at last temporarily, if they can be protected by patents or other forms of intervention by the state. And since it is not only knowledge about genes that may turn into a valuable raw material, the fear of a progressive privatization of science grows.

In addition, the growth of research activities in nonacademic settings not only affects the knowledge that is produced, it also raises questions about the regulation of new capacities for action generated in "private" settings, and the extent to which the discovery of (intended and unintended) impacts and their control is left to the producing organizations. The "authors" of additional capacities for action will certainly advance claims that self-regulation is not only best and most efficient, but also complies with widely accepted ethical standards.

With the ascendancy of knowledge in modern society, there will also evolve new dilemmas, discontinuities, and conflicts in the interrelations among established social institutions that at one time appeared to be self-sufficient, self-governing, and immune to the intervention of codes, world-views, and artifacts apprehended as system-specific accomplishments (e.g. Luhmann, 1988). Social change and innovation made possible by the enlargement of knowledge reconstitutes social institutions. For example, as Rosenberg (1999: 30) notes, the modern health-care system is marked, on the one hand, by a "boundless faith in the power of the laboratory and the market, on the other by a failure to anticipate and respond to the human implications of technical and institutional innovation." These dilemmas grow directly out of the extension of knowledge-based solutions to existing imperatives and problems in institutions; in the health-care field, these problems and imperatives are sickness, disability, and death.[40]

Finally, demands to cope with the growth of knowledge refer to the attendant extension of capacities to act. Actors increasingly find themselves in situations in which the need for novel decisions emerges, and with them, of course, newly apprehended dangers and risks. The potential openness, and not the self-evident traditional closure, of situations calls for the regulation and policing of knowledge, it seems, now that knowledge allows new possibilities to "manipulate" elements of a situation that in the past had been apprehended as beyond the control of all participants. The role and the prominence of references to fate, nature, or the design of some higher being that symbolize the closure of conditions of action lose their relevance. What was seen as forever beyond the control of everyone now becomes—initially in the thought experiments of a few individuals, at least—subject to control and manipulation. And what was in the past seen as an exceptional moral dilemma, or the need to arrive at a decision in an extreme situation or under rare circumstances, now becomes increasingly common.

Knowledge as a Weapon[41]

> Knowledge, more than ever before, is power. ... The information advantage [of the United States] can strengthen the intellectual link between U.S. foreign policy and military power and offer new ways of maintaining leadership in alliances and ad hoc coalitions.
> *Joseph S. Nye and William A. Owens, "America's information edge"*

It would be mistaken to conclude, given the prominence that developments in molecular biology and computer science have had in recent public debates about the social impact of science and technology, that the issue of knowledge politics is either confined to these fields or is a wholly civilian matter. As Joseph S. Nye, former chairman of the U.S. National Intelligence Council, and William A. Owens, former vice-chairman of the U.S. Joint Chiefs of Staff (in the Clinton Administration), make plain, knowledge politics extends to military uses. But knowledge politics in its military version extends to fields other than biotechnology and information warfare; it could include, as the following excursus shows, the field of meteorology as well.

At the recent Fifth German Climate Conference in Hamburg in 2000, a climate scientist and I gave a joint paper on man-made climate disasters that have threatened man in historic times. After we had spoken, a participant approached us and told us about research carried out by the U.S. Air Force. The findings were reported back in 1996 but have since been generally ignored. The research paper is available at www.au.af.mil/au/2025/ on the Web. All past climate catastrophes caused by man pale in comparison to the study's findings, which are only a taste of things to come in the next quarter century. He who controls the weather, controls the world.

In 1977, the UN General Assembly adopted a resolution prohibiting the hostile use of environmental modification techniques. The resulting convention (ENMOD, Convention on the Prohibition of Military or Any Other Hostile Use of Environmental Modification Technique) committed the signatories—which include the United States—to refrain from any military or other hostile use of weather modification that could result in widespread, long-lasting, or severe effects on the economy and society. In the 1996 study, seven military officers considered how the weather might be used as a weapon. Their task was to ensure that the United States would remain the dominant power in aviation and space travel in the year 2025. The study suggested that America's airborne military forces could "own" and control the weather. This would promote the development of new technology, and that technology would provide the "warriors of the future" with undreamt-of resources for controlling the course of military conflicts, the study concluded.

The byword here is weather modification, in the sense of increasing or decreasing the intensity of natural phenomena. Taken to an extreme, this could include creating entirely new weather phenomena (made-to-order weather) and manipulation of the global climate.

But because of the probable conflict with the ENMOD convention, the study concentrated on influencing weather processes in geographic areas only up to two thousand square kilometers (eight hundred square miles). What is at stake becomes clear when the authors talk of a dilemma akin to the one faced by the pioneers of nuclear research. They stress that only those who are prepared to capitulate strategically could want to renounce the military use of weather modification.

But what are the technologies that will give those who control them in the next thirty years the means for planning weather and actually creating weather patterns? Weather control techniques—some already exist—can be improved in four ways: by using complex nonlinear modeling systems, by increasing computing capacity, by improving data collection and transmission, and by the creation of a globally operative military weather network. Specific operations to curtail an opponent's operating ability and improve one's own could include manipulation of precipitation, storms, and fog, but could also involve controlling the ionosphere to guarantee dominance of worldwide communication. The research paper did not speak of controlling temperature.

The report explained how military encounters could be decided through weather manipulation. It cited the following example: It is the year 2025 and a South American drug cartel has purchased hundreds of Russian and Chinese fighter planes. So far, the drug barons have been able to protect their production facilities from every attack. The cartel controls the skies and is able to launch ten of its own planes for each American fighter. It also has a sophisticated French air defense system. Despite all this, the American military wants to engage the enemy.

The Air Force meteorologists are to play a crucial role. They point out that there is a thunderstorm nearly every afternoon in the equatorial regions of South America. The U.S. Secret Service knows that the cartel pilots are reluctant to fly in or near thunderstorms. So the weather force support element is tasked not only to forecast storm paths, but also to trigger or intensify thunderstorms over critical target areas. And as U.S. fighters fly in any type of weather, they are able to snatch control of the skies from the enemy. Moreover, it is likely the Air Force will routinely use unmanned drones to manipulate the weather by 2025.

These operations will be supported by highly developed, sophisticated technologies for data collection, weather forecasting, and weather manipulation. The unmanned craft can spread cirrus clouds over areas of military deployment. Not only does this deprive people on the ground of a clear view, it also prevents them from using their infrared equipment properly. While microwave heaters create local zones of destructive interference to restrict the use of radar-controlled equipment, the naturally occurring thunderstorm is artificially intensified. It is all part of the game plan. The weather force support element watches the complete operation and reports another—by now routine—successful deployment of the weather weapon.

It is therefore not only possible, but highly likely that such systematic weather modification will become a potent, accurate, and globally available weapon of war. It could be used in all conceivable conflicts. Weather is not only everywhere; it is at the same time the most implacable enemy of the ruled and of the rulers, as this report illustrates. In the future, the weather may be a party to conflict.

Systematic attempts to influence the weather by technical means have existed for a considerable time. However, these efforts have not been particularly successful so far—for example, attempts to control precipitation in arid areas or during droughts. Rainmaking is certainly possible in certain situations. But these situations are rare and not easy to control, given the complexity of weather systems. The authors of the U.S. Air Force research paper were clearly aware of these facts. Thus, they speak of significant and rapid progress in our understanding of the variables that affect weather. They are certain that by 2025, it should be possible to identify and parameterize all important weather factors. The authors also say that there must be quick and meaningful technical progress, so that micrometeorology can develop into a discipline that is technically sound and practical. As things now stand, implementing the report's ideas appears utopian and expensive. Furthermore, that implementation could be hindered if opponents initiated contrary processes.

The major significance of the weather for the living conditions of a rapidly growing world population could, however, also cause appropriate resources to be provided for research into improving our knowledge of the weather. Summing up: It is likely that by 2025, man will have taken the step from scenario planning to effective weather modification. The military uses of this knowledge are obvious.

The report of the U.S. Air Force raises the general and urgent issue of the control and regulation of new knowledge. Should we be able to utilize new knowledge produced by micrometeorology? Who should apply such knowledge, and for what goals? And how can one possibly manage and control the uses of new knowledge?

The Social Regulation of Inquiry

> It is the first time that science has produced results that require an immediate intervention by government. Of course, science has produced results before which were of great importance directly or indirectly. And there have been scientific processes that required some minor policing measures by the government.
>
> *Von Neumann*[42]

In testimony before the U.S. Special Senate Committee on Atomic Energy on January 31, 1946, John von Neumann pleaded with the senators to enact strict government regulations on scientific research in the atomic energy area. Indeed, the Senate went on to enact the Atomic Energy Act of 1946. The stringent regulations are still in effect. There can be no question that both the scientific community and the public welcomed the social regulation of scientific inquiry, and therefore of the laboratories of atomic scientists, as manifested in the Atomic Energy Act.[43]

To mention a more recent plea that also comes from an eminent scientist for the social regulation of inquiry, and not merely the application of scientific knowledge, one could refer to the following example: Should we attempt to contact intelligent extraterrestrial "aliens"? What would happen to earthbound science if an extraterrestrial civilization already knew all the answers? As Robert Sinsheimer (1976a) warns us, and as we know from our own history, the experience of a collision of a less advanced with a more advanced civilization can be shattering. Humans ought to fabricate their own knowledge. Aside from the fear that an extraterrestrial invasion of knowledge might preempt the thrill of our own homegrown search for new knowledge, Sinsheimer's cautionary note implies the more general policy suggestion that we ought to impose limits on scientific inquiry itself.[44]

In other words, demands for *science and technology policies* that do not merely concentrate on the distribution of research funds and therefore monetary issues have something of a tradition in the relationship between science and society, at least since the end of World War Two (Nelkin, 1977). Scientific research that is heavily dependent on an expensive infrastructure and large sums of external funding is, of course, almost automatically subject to considerable leverage exercised by private or public funding agencies. However, calls for science policies that amount to a societal regulation of original scientific inquiry, as issued from time to time by politicians as well as scientists, are mainly justified by a perceived lack of desired results designed to deal with urgent social problems of the day, and by the motive to reach specific political goals, rather than any demands to forego a search for "forbidden" knowledge. In times of crisis, such demands to pursue specific substantive goals multiply. In other instances, scientists have freely offered their services in support of the politics and the power structures of the day (for example, German race and rocket scientists). In the future, it is likely that regulatory efforts aimed at limiting scientific research will be launched more often. And social regulation will attempt to restrict inquiry based on the anticipated "deleterious" consequences of applications of knowledge generated by scientific research not as yet undertaken.

One question that must be examined in the face of demands for the regulation of scientific findings has to do with the problem (which is not merely a new problem) of the extent of the social independence of science—its origins, its foundation, and its development—as well as the demand, which under certain circumstances opposes such independence, for some kind of control over scientific development, the communication of scientific findings, and/or the consequences of scientific knowledge, whether through a kind of voluntary self-control by scientists or by means of externally implemented measures.

The type of control over science that is chiefly of interest here is therefore not related to the (primary) social control of scientific findings—that is, to forms of control that arise from the existence of such social constructs as the "scientific community" itself. I will turn attention to the system-specific regulation of knowledge in the next section. Robert K. Merton, in one of the most influential treatments of this topic, has attempted to describe the peculiar form of primary or system-immanent social control in the modern scientific community by drawing attention to the existence of a number of special social norms that regulate social relations among scientists. The presence of a particular social convention, such as the demand for unimpeded access of all scientists to all research findings—which simultaneously means a ban on any form of secrecy or selective communication of scientific results—represents, no matter what attitude one takes to the concrete rules of conduct, a form of social control that influences or regulates, for example, the possible content, extent, goals, and methods of communication. In summary, only a limited palette of possibilities from a multitude of other possibilities in the relevant context can be realized. In terms of primary social control, it is therefore a matter of control taken for granted by scientists and of a form of constraint on their social and intellectual life that is largely regarded as legitimate and necessary. Whenever the control and/or the freedom of science are under discussion, this taken-for-granted social control cannot be at issue. This control, which certainly must vary in its extent and manner and in the degree to which it is accepted, is, if you like, one of the indispensable resources of the social cohesion or solidarity of any institution, and thus of the scientific community as well.

Against the background of system-specific social control within science, therefore, those discussions that lead to a revision or extension of the already existing forms of control in the scientific community are of interest. With mounting efforts outside of science to regulate new knowledge produced by science, the nature of social control within science is bound to be affected and changed. I do not mean to refer merely to what constitutes a kind of anticipatory regulation of research efforts, and the informal or formal acceptance of zones that constitute investigatory matters and methods that are off limits, for instance, in the form of ethical certification requirements. In fact, what can and likely may increasingly occur is a convergence or mixture of regulatory practices.

Appended to the U.S. Human Genome Project is an NIH/DOE Committee to Evaluate the Ethical, Legal, and Social Implications Program of the Human Genome Project (ELSI). The committee has a short but contested history. The National Institutes of Health (NIH) has proposed to attach ELSI units to its other institutes and research endeavors (Murray, 2000). Such a program, though peer-review based (but not in the usual sense, since assessments of research proposals are interdisciplinary), represents at least an enlargement of traditional system-specific mechanisms of social control in science, if not, in this instance, an intrusion of the state and the public into the regulation of the development of knowledge and the obviously difficult anticipatory judgments about its social implications. Such committees also raise the general question of the role of democratic order and the influence civic society ought to have on the ways in which the results of scientific research are deployed, if at all.

I will begin my discussion of more recent developments with a case typical for the 1970s. In this case, an attempt was made to point to and control the risks associated with laboratory research involving recombinant DNA. At this time, a discussion of the possible broader social and ecological consequences of genetic research was not part of the debate to regulate scientific inquiry. But first I will explain the context that is relevant to the case. Just as atomic scientists had done in 1945, scientists engaged in recombinant DNA research in 1973 first alerted the general public and public officials to the social implications of their work. The possibility of genetic manipulation using recombinant DNA techniques had been demonstrated a year earlier (see Wright, 1986a: 310–315). The scientists warned of the hazards that might unintentionally arise from the new techniques, and worried about the dangers that might result from its use. The scientists also proposed measures to devise laboratory procedures to protect the health and safety of the researchers, the general public, and the environment. In February 1975, an international conference on recombinant DNA was convened at the Asilomar (California) conference center. The Assembly of Life Sciences, the National Research Council, and the National Academy of Sciences sponsored the conference. The agenda of the conference focused on risk in terms of the potential injury to health of biotechnology research of the day. The Asilomar Conference recommended containment standards for recombinant DNA research. The dominant theme that emerged from the meeting was caution. Even earlier, in July of 1974, a panel of the National Institutes of Health recommended a voluntary moratorium of certain types of gene-splicing research. The recommended suspension of certain types of gene-splicing research alerted the press; hazards and benefits of recombinant DNA research were widely discussed (Krimsky, 1982: 13–23; Nelkin, 2001a).

In mid-July of 1976, the City Council of Cambridge, Massachusetts, after public hearings, enacted a three-month moratorium on recombinant DNA research in the city (Goodell, 1979), upon recommendation of a committee appointed by the mayor of the city, Alfred Vellucci. The mayor made it clear that he had to be concerned about activities that might be injurious to the health of the citizens of Cambridge. Following the advice of its own Cambridge Experimentation Review Board, City Council passed an ordinance on February 7, 1977, concerned with DNA research.

The Cambridge Experimentation Review Board, whose members were all non-scientists, "investigated" the intention and potential consequences of a decision by Harvard University to remodel one of its laboratories into a laboratory for recombinant DNA research. The board met twice weekly for more than four months. About a quarter of the time was used to question opponents and proponents of recombinant DNA research. The original discussion of recombinant DNA research in Cambridge did not involve objections to intentionally produced research results and technologies, but rather referred to the possibility of an unintended, accidental production of pathogenic organisms that might be immune to available antibiotics and therefore constitute a serious public health risk.

The experiment of the city council of Cambridge to select nonexperts for the Cambridge Experimentation Review Board, who then had to enter into a dialogue with scientists, represents a remarkable maneuver that was quite successful, according to the testimony of its chair, despite the expectations of the specialists. Dan Hayes (Dutton, 1988: 320) reports, for example, that all the recommendations the commission made in its final report, "including some sophisticated measures overlooked or avoided by NIH officials and experts, came from members of the citizens' group itself, not from its scientific advisors."

The ordinance established conditions for the conduct of scientific research involving recombinant DNA within the city limits of Cambridge.[45] A series of further recommendations, addressed to higher-placed political agencies, were added relating to the role and responsibilities of the agencies in monitoring DNA research and safeguarding the staff and the public from potential hazards. The legislation followed six months of at times bitterly disputed public hearings into the biohazards of DNA research (see Mendelsohn, 1978; Goodell, 1979).

The Cambridge mayor at the time expressed the essence of the anxieties that prompted the action of the city government:

> They don't even know what's going to eventually come out of this experimentation. It could be anything, contamination, infection, something that could crawl out of the laboratory ... that cannot be controlled by the scientists that created it ... [We must] control all these experiments and all these things coming out of the sardine cans and tuna fish cans and even the milk you drink ... I don't like to be contaminated (cited in Nelkin, 1978a: 24).

My interpretation of what has been called the "social assessment of science" in the wake of the Cambridge ordinance on recombinant DNA is that its manifest concerns are most immediately with qualms about the uncertainties of research activities, about methods deployed in the search for new knowledge, and about the possibility of accidental but harmful discoveries in the course of such research.

The editors of a volume of proceedings of a conference held in 1978 at the science study unit of the University of Bielefeld point out that the social assessment of science is not a new phenomenon. Indeed, research efforts in science and in technology have from the beginning been the subject of political and cultural concerns and scrutiny. What was new about the "social assessment of science" in the late seventies was the intensity of the *"public involvement* in questions of the *potential dangers of research* and in the value conflicts of *research"* (Mendelsohn, Nelkin and Weingart, 1978: 1; emphasis added). A more appropriate term for what was at stake and for what was practiced in Cambridge would have been the social assessment of the *research process.*

On the basis of an enumeration of scientific activity and research that has been subjected to social assessment, Mendelsohn and Weingart (1978: 9) conclude that the "focal point of the assessment process is not the end of scientific activity—the potential product or use of knowledge and technique—as has been the case so far and is also typical for technology assessment. Instead, assessment efforts have been directed at the very process of problem definition and conceptual design as in the cases of heredity and intelligence and XYY chromosome research." If the scientific community is forced to participate in a social assessment of research, issues pertaining to external participation and control that may be exercised over the research process itself will invariably become part of the deliberations.[46]

The Cambridge City Council intervention and regulation has been among the more dramatic and widely discussed external interventions in the research process of science in recent decades. Earlier and less contested interventions occurred in medicine, in particular in the field of therapeutic experimentation with human subjects (cf. Reiss, 1979; Swazey, 1978; Swazey and Fox, 1970). In March 1997, in the wake of the success of Scottish scientists in cloning a sheep, President Bill Clinton, responding to what he called the "troubling prospect" of cloning human beings, temporarily banned the use of all federal funds for such experiments. CNN (March 4, 1997) quotes the president saying, "Any discovery that touches upon human creation is not simply a matter of scientific inquiry. It is a matter of morality and spirituality as well." Equally fundamental is the question of the legal authority to curtail scientific inquiry rather than to merely support scientific activity. In the United States, as in other countries, the question becomes whether the Constitution allows for limitation in the pursuit of knowledge in science. The argument will of course be made that the right to pursue knowledge is by analogy protected by the constitutionally guaranteed rights to freedom of speech and the press (see Green [1977] 1979: 140). The possible boundaries to the right of free scientific inquiry are therefore identical with the limits to freedom of speech, if any. Here the difference between speech and action is highly relevant. Scientists have (unlimited) freedom of speech but must be prepared to accept limits on what they can act out, especially given the impact of their action on others. As Harold P. Green ([1977] 1979: 140) therefore concludes, where scientific research "involves experimentation with human or animal subjects or where it impinges upon the community, it would clearly become subject to regulation."

Making a distinction between public concerns about or support for research and the involvement of society in deliberations about the uses of new knowledge is sensible from the point of view of analyzing the governance of knowledge, as one should not easily forget; but the distinction is also difficult to sustain, since science policies and what I have called knowledge policies interact in practice and are often conflated. Although science and knowledge policies are both future-oriented, the functional relations differ, as I have already emphasized.

Broadly defined, policy for science is concerned with the political, legal, administrative, and ethical control of the social process of science in general and the *fabrication* of new knowledge and techniques in particular. The regulation of scientific inquiry and the research process becomes a branch of science policy (see Dworkin, 1996: 147–163). Knowledge policies refer to the societal regulation of *new* knowledge generated in science. In that sense and only in that sense, science and knowledge policies are symmetrical. That is also why all those past and present public and political efforts to *promote* science and technology in society are not part of what I define as knowledge policies. If the aim happens to be to limit scientific inquiry, then anticipated deleterious consequences of inquiry itself are part of science policy measures, while anticipated deleterious consequences of the practical implementation of knowledge generated by inquiry becomes part of knowledge policies. In other words, using more traditional terminology, science policy is about "progress in science," and knowledge policy is about "progress in society." The understanding of obstacles to progress in science, and therefore effective science policies, mainly requires a theory of science. The analysis of obstacles to progress in society requires a theory of society.

In addition, the distinction between science and knowledge policy is sensible because the convergence of science and knowledge policies varies, at least in degree, in different historical eras and in different societies, signaling distinct stages in the relation between science and society—the autonomy science enjoys or the dependence of the scientific community in relation to varying institutional arrangements with which it must coexist. Public intervention in and scrutiny of the research process, or of the fabrication of knowledge itself (when defined as pure or basic research, for example), since it is seen as a threat to the freedom of inquiry in science and self-government of the scientific community (cf. Nelkin, 1978b: 191–194), has less legitimacy than the social control or accountability of applied science and technology assigned to groups of individuals other than the peers of scientists and engineers.[47] As James Watson is quoted, tersely saying in the context of the heated discussion about the pitfalls of recombinant DNA research, "All I can say is that we want to go on with what we are doing, and I don't think we are crazy" (cited in Morrison, 1978: ix). Science policies are, though by no means exclusively, more about science than are knowledge policies. Knowledge policies are more political. The responses to science and knowledge policies by scientists, the public, and the political and economic system are bound to differ from country to country.

And not unlike the conceptual distinction between "science in policy" and "policy for science," first introduced by Harvey Brooks (1964) in the mid-sixties, the field of political activity called "knowledge policies" will have a strong component of "scientific knowledge in policy." The notion of scientific knowledge in policy decisions about the regulation of knowledge merely emphasizes the point that such debates and decisions do not occur in isolation from the scientific community, but rather include considerable input from scientists as expert advisors. What is new and different from "science in policy" in the past is that the scientists themselves are more likely, intentionally or unintentionally, to originate the debate about the need for knowledge policies.

The extent to which current broad trends in science policy amount to more than common fiscal policies is, of course, a contested matter. In the case of U.S. science policy, Michael Crow (2001), who advocates science policies that link outcomes closely to societal needs, suggests that there are only marginal elements of U.S. science policy which couple that policy to sociopolitical purposes. Science policy that tries to incorporate considerations of societal outcomes into the national research agenda does so on a very small and marginalized basis—for example, in the case of the human dimensions component of the U.S. Global Change Research Program, and parts of the Human Genome Project that deal with its ethical, legal, and social implications.

The social regulation of science-in-progress and of scientific inquiry not yet even undertaken is a highly difficult and perhaps impossible project, which furthermore has the unintended consequence of reducing the authority of science as an asset to politics. There can be no question that the anticipated risks and dangers possibly connected to the use of research results still in the making are not only a most uncertain attribution, but also have to be located in a distant future. Nonetheless, it is likely that efforts to control the research process externally will increase in frequency and be subject to contested public discussion and debate. The observation that the future is without a political lobby no longer applies in such a general sense. The way in which debates over the apprehended impact of as yet nonexistent capacities to act are successfully coupled to values and value conflicts will to a large extent determine whether political responses and sanctions can be mobilized.

Perhaps the most significant barrier to extensive external social-control mechanisms on science-in-progress is the size and organization of the scientific enterprise today, as well as its competitive and international texture.[48] The politics of science must not be conflated with the politics of society. The politics of knowledge cannot simply be reduced to political power, and science generates many kinds of knowledge, not only knowledge that is essentially political and therefore of immediate practical use.

The conviction that external management, planning, and control of the *fabrication* of knowledge *in detail* is not merely desirable, but possible, is in any event based on the mistaken premise that one is able to anticipate or predict the practical outcome of basic research and that one is able to encourage or forbid such work.

The Social Control of Knowledge in Science

> All efforts to halt, to slow or at least in a prophylactic sense to control a progress that is unrelenting, are bound to tie up useful resources that can be better deployed in order to channel the consequences of progress in a direction desirable to us.
>
> *Heinrich Rohrer*[49]

I interpret this assertion by the physicist Rohrer as a plea to empower the scientific community to follow the lead of theoretical curiosity (*curiositas*) wherever it may lead.[50] Scientists ought to be free to ask any kind of question and assert anything that is methodologically sound.[51] The scientific community (system) tries to avoid societal control and steering, and is interested only in an environment offering conducive conditions for scientific work (cf. Luhmann, [1981] 1987: 54).

Rohrer does not claim that there exists a kind of pre-existing harmony between science and social aims. But whatever the need to regulate science may be, it is best organized at another point. Rohrer declares that regulation of the *use* made of science not only is possible, but also allows societies to channel science in useful directions.

In yet another sense, the social control of knowledge claims in knowledge-rich and knowledge-based social systems is not a novel phenomenon. What makes science unique among social systems, for example, is the way in which and the extent to which the social task of maintaining the "quality of the products" of science is accomplished "with so little difficulty that the problem of quality control has received no more than passing mention in any systematic discussion of science" (Ravetz, 1971: 273). Assessment of "quality" is constitutive of much of the work done in science. More generally, it is the system-specific ethos of science or the "territorial morals of the scientific realm" that regulate knowledge claims (Jonas, [1976] 1979: 33). While the assessment of the adequacy of knowledge claims within science is taken for granted, discourse about the responsibility for examining the potential dangers and risks of scientific activity is left by science to special occasions and circumstances. But implicit in some claims that science is itself best suited to police the adequacy of knowledge is the assumption or hope that the social benefits of knowledge that survive rigorous, institutionalized challenges within science also exceed the risks and hazards associated with its practical use. What is good for science is good for society. But what may be good enough for science may not be good enough for certain organizations.

For Karl Popper, as is well known, the willingness to submit ideas to critical scrutiny and commitment, and not to accept knowledge claims at face value, constitutes the demarcation criterion between science and other social systems, including social systems driven by ideas. Whether or not such a demarcation criterion linked to the motives of individual scientists and institutional norms allows us to distinguish in an unambivalent manner between science and other increasingly knowledge-based social institutions is not at issue in this context. Nor do I intend to inquire into the functions of quality control, how the standards of quality control may be elaborated, the precise mechanisms and enforcement of the social control of knowledge in science, whether these processes are effective in weeding out "shoddy science," or how science may be stratified with respect to the policing of knowledge. Much has been written about these matters in recent years. Quality control in present-day science is clearly no longer as invisible and taken for granted as in the past. However, a more extensive discussion of the internal control mechanisms of science is accompanied by skepticism about the efficacy of self-policing, and therefore by demands that control within the scientific community must become a strictly formalized undertaking. In a society that is itself knowledge-based, the problem of the social control of knowledge both within and outside of science inevitably becomes a central social and political problem.

Knowledge Politics

In December of 1984 the veterinary surgeon David Bee was called to the Pitsham Farm on the South Downs, West Sussex, by its owner Peter Stent, in order to attend to a cow that was evidently quite ill. The cow was arching its back and moving its head in the air from side to side, and it was pathetically thin. Peter Stent and his vet had no idea what was wrong with the cow, which later became famous as "cow 133."[52] They did not know that bovine spongiform encephalopathy (BSE) existed. Cow 133 was the first reported case of BSE. The cow eventually developed head tremors and uncoordination. It died in February of 1985. By the end of April that year, six cows at Pitsham Farm had died.

David Bee contacted the British government's Central Veterinary Laboratory (CVL). The pathologists of the laboratory in September of 1985 issued a report after they had studied the brain and other organs of a cow from Pitsham Farm. They diagnosed "moderate spongiform encephalopathy acute." During the following year, as more evidence emerged, questions arose about how to deal with this information. Dr. William Watson, the director of the CVL, and Dr. Brian Shreeve, the director of research, received a memo from the head of the pathology department, David Bradley, which read in part:

> If the disease turns out to be bovine scrapie, it would have severe repercussions for the export trade and possibly also for humans if for example it was discovered that humans with spongiform encephalopathies had close association with cattle. It is for this reason that I have classified this document confidential. At present I would recommend that we play it low key.

Plans to make the initial findings and subsequent information available were also cancelled. University researchers and outside research institutes were blocked from obtaining the information (see "Madness," *Observer,* October 29, 2000). A memorandum of the CVL director leaves no doubt as to why such a restrictive policy of regulating new knowledge was implemented.

Nonetheless, it is necessary to clarify briefly the concept of the social regulation of knowledge. One should be able to distinguish among different purposes or aims of regulatory activities: for example, what exactly prompts regulation, what classes of future results of novel knowledge are anticipated, and what consequences do these results appear to promote, or with what are they in conflict? What types of proposals are made for regulation, and what exactly do they attempt to regulate? In the past, some of the most intense public reactions to new scientific knowledge have been occasioned not so much by the impact of technological practices and artifacts that may be possible as the result of new scientific development, but rather in response to apprehended conflicts of novel scientific ideas and perspectives with widely held convictions, such as the nature of the human being (see Graham, 1978).

Further, one needs to identify the actors (as well as the institutional settings in which they are embedded) that attempt to regulate or to intervene in the regulation process, the instruments that are deployed, and the anticipated outcomes of regulatory policies, be they based on economic, legal, or fiscal incentives, or moral pressures. Not unlike other "jurisdictional" conflicts among social institutions, demands for knowledge policies will be seen by some as best left to "private citizens," or to self-interested decisions taken under competitive conditions in the market place; some will ascribe a larger or lesser role to the state, and still others will opt for measures of self-regulation by the scientific community. But regulation is by no means identical only with prohibitions, suppression, or disincentives. Regulation can also occur in the form of encouraging desirable or best practices.

Conscious efforts to police knowledge are not new. The incorporation of the Ptolemaic system into the theological teachings of the Catholic Church, the vigorous objections raised by the spiritual leaders of the Reformation against Galileo's ideas, and the suppression and censure of Galileo's work by the Catholic Church are prominent early examples from the history of science that involve the policing of knowledge itself. The stance church leaders took and the debate they began continues to resonate with contemporary conflicts about the "nature of human nature." Efforts to control the proliferation of knowledge about weapons of mass destruction constitute examples of modern knowledge politics designed to restrict, through legal and political means, access to capacities to act that could have catastrophic consequences. Yet any conscious attempt to regulate and control knowledge apparently encompasses, at the same time, forms of knowledge as well as their application, even in the case of modern warfare.

The ongoing struggle in some parts of the United States, for example, to ban the teaching of evolution in schools, is a relevant contemporary case in point. I have already referred to the Kansas Board of Education's 1999 decision to remove evolution from the state's science curriculum, and to similar controversies over teaching the big bang theory in American schools.[53]

Paul Feyerabend believes, obviously based on different considerations, that decisions about curricula in public schools should be made by democratically constituted committees. As Feyerabend (1978: 87) demands, "If the taxpayers of California want their state universities to teach Voodoo, folk medicine, rain dance ceremonies, then this is what the universities will have to teach."[54] Expert opinion will "of course be taken into consideration, but experts will not have the last word. The last word is the decision of democratically constituted committees, and in these committees laymen have the upper hand" (Feyerabend, 1978: 87). In Feyerabend's view, the legitimacy and the necessity of democratically constituted committees that rule over truth and expert opinion are simply a question of the civil rights of citizens and the exercise of these rights in a free society, which means living according to their traditions. And among these traditions could well be convictions of the truth of the biblical creation. The participation of laymen in basic decisions about knowledge policies is therefore, if one follows Feyerabend's program, an urgent requirement.[55]

In the summer of 2000, the decision by the Kansas Board of Education became the hottest issue in Kansas politics, "with unprecedented attention and spending in the campaigns for board seats" (*Associated Press*, July 26, 2000). It was the first time that voters in Kansas had a chance to decide whether the individuals who supported the new curriculum standards should retain their positions on the board. The Republican proponents of the new science standards that de-emphasized evolution in Kansas were defeated in their party's primaries. (*Associated Press*, August 2, 2000).

But as the Kansas example also appears to demonstrate, most of the efforts undertaken from time to time in different societies to regulate and police the possible ideological and cultural effects of science have not been overly successful in the long run, or across diverse settings.[56] In addition, there is a distinctive shift in the kinds of concerns and consequences that may prompt efforts directed toward the regulation of knowledge.

In the last couple of decades, there has been a noticeable change in public and political debate about the social consequences of science and technology. These concerns and debates now revolve around insecurity, fears of risks, and, more and more often, around the kind of uncertainty generated by science and the impact science and technology may have on individuals and society (see the section on dangers, risks, and chances in Bechmann and Stehr, 2000). A transformation in public and political sentiments[57] in favor of policing knowledge would signal a basic change in the legitimacy of science.[58] In particular, it would mark a shift away from a preoccupation with the "ideological" or cultural implications of basic knowledge claims generated by science and possible conflicts with established world views, and toward an increasing preoccupation with the practical application and consequences of science.

But aside from the increasing realization that science fabricates risks and uncertainty, the shift in public attitudes away from the once widely taken-for-granted conviction that advances in science and technology invariably produce social benefits may also be associated with changes in the kinds of scientific knowledge now increasingly fabricated. Many biotechnologies, for example, represent techniques and capacities for action whose social implications outside the laboratory are immediately evident. There is a greater awareness, and more instant evidence, of what the potential impact may be than was the case for forms of scientific knowledge generated in the past. In this instance, therefore, the issue of the alleged knowledge and comprehension gap between science and the public is less relevant.

What I have in mind when I speak of knowledge politics is perhaps best described as an attempt to directly control or regulate the immediate use or anticipated consequences of *incremental* or novel knowledge.[59]

The now widely discussed public demystification of experts and the nature of expertise (e.g., Barnes, 1999) may be seen not only as a prime example of a fundamental change in the nature of the relations between knowledge-based occupations and clients, consumers, patients, students, trainees, customers, etc., but also as a profound transformation in the public image of scientific knowledge. This change considerably enlarges the number and range of individuals who relinquish their traditionally subordinate role in such expert/client relations as recipients of advice that rests on an a priori suspension of doubt.

Helen Lopata (1976: 437) has described the process I have in mind as the "sophistication and the rebelliousness of the client" in contexts in which expert knowledge is dispensed. Lopata notes that several social changes are responsible for the difficulty in monopolizing knowledge—by the professions for instance—and for the refusal of consumers and clients to remain passive and conforming recipients of expert advice. There is, first of all, the very increase in the volume of knowledge-based occupations, which reduces the ability to strictly enforce and control the boundaries and the nature of discourse and increases the fragmentation of fields of expertise. The fragmentation of expertise becomes public knowledge. Whether or not consensus within different scientific fields was ever unchallenged is not at issue. What is at issue is the publicly visible breakdown of consensus among, say, biologists with respect to the social consequences of genetic engineering.[60] A visible breakdown of consensus triggers and sustains public concern. It activates embarrassment and humiliation among experts who are not expected to make mistakes and yet do so, and moreover in public. It also undermines the taken-for-granted faith in meritocracy. Second, the astuteness and cognitive skills of the public increase. New organizations and pressure groups emerge, reinforcing the decline in the authority of experts. What at one time appeared to be a highly technical and esoteric field of discourse opens up to public debate, scrutiny, and regulation (see Nelkin, 1975; 1992).

I am using "regulation" and "regulatory regime" as terms that signify efforts toward a "planned" rather than unrestricted or spontaneous use of new knowledge. My use of the concept of "regulation" resonates with the way in which Steinmetz (1993) uses the term to analyze the regulation of the emergence of the welfare state in Imperial Germany. This concept is quite distanced from the economic literature on regulating the practices of capital accumulation (e.g., Jessop, 1990), because that approach tends to rely on an overdetermined image of the ultimate efficacy of regulation practices.

Regulation aims, for example, "to reduce the potential harmful effects" of such knowledge, or to enhance the potential capacities of such knowledge that deserve exploitation. This is in contrast to, say, the world of contemporary economic discourse, in which arguments about regulatory regimes primarily advocate a lowering of barriers (interferences) to capital as well as trade flow, preferably on a global scale (on the notion of regulation, see Mitnick, 1980). In economics, the case is therefore often made that markets should discipline other social institutions; for example, that states ought to conform to markets' needs. In the case of Marxist-inspired perspectives, regulation theories are concerned with the ways in which principally the state deploys regulatory practices to sustain and nourish capitalist accumulation (Jessop, 1990). In this context, I inquire into the desire and ability of social institutions to discipline knowledge. And in this instance, the state is not necessarily the principal agency of regulation.

Efforts to regulate and police knowledge are typically undertaken and/or initiated, as well as legitimated, outside the boundaries of the scientific community (naturally with repercussions for the production of knowledge within the science system). For the purposes at hand, "regulating" refers, in the most general sense, to the conscious, strategic use of political and legal power, economic resources, and cultural authority, to shape—whatever the specific objective—the utilization of scientific-technical knowledge. It involves a complex set of mainly formal ventures designed to encourage, restrict, shape, or banish knowledge claims and set standards for their use through the exertion of pressure, the creation of institutions, and the deployment of norms and beliefs to make certain that knowledge evolves along a desired path and has only sanctioned consequences.

The source of the standards chosen to police knowledge, the regulatory procedures put in place, and the intellectual systems legitimizing the cultural dismissal of certain uses of knowledge typically also do not originate in science and technology itself, although scientists may be called upon as experts in ensuing legal and political struggles to assess norms that may be put in place. For example, in the face of demands to preserve and defend the nature of human nature in response to developments in scientific and technical capacities to alter the status quo of human reproduction, scientific "notions of nature do not provide us with unambiguous standards of naturalness to which we can appeal for normative orientation" (van den Daele, 1992: 549). Since scientific notions of naturalness allow for the construction of a range of possible natures, regulatory efforts advancing the cause of abstaining from practical steps intervening in human nature have to appeal to moral claims and political action that may or may not succeed in arresting human nature. The anchoring of standards and justifications outside of science does not mean that individuals who are scientists may not be found among those who vigorously support attempts to regulate knowledge.

My list of the available measures to control knowledge may at first leave the impression that I include science and technology policies as primary examples of such efforts. Strategies designed to regulate knowledge are mostly responses to changed and novel knowledge, not vice versa. Science and technology policies aim to encourage the development of knowledge, but they generally do so in highly ambivalent and open-ended fashion. Many decades of experience demonstrate, furthermore, that it is difficult or even impossible to steer and control the dynamics of developments in science and technology by way of political standards (cf. van den Daele, 1992: 553–555).

In contrast to strategic efforts designed to plan and encourage future knowledge, attempts to "police" knowledge cover a much wider social field than science and technology policies, including more informal control processes. The controls that knowledge politics may impose could extend to the ways in which knowledge is disseminated, dispensed, made accessible, employed, and interpreted.

The ideal or typical concepts of research and knowledge policies and their separate strategic functions for the development of knowledge and its societal deployment may increasingly be blurred in knowledge societies, as the boundaries of science and society become more fluid and porous. Efforts to regulate knowledge will influence science policies, and science policies will have an impact on attempts to police knowledge.[61] Science policy has much to do with the political climate in a society—that is, perceived economic, environmental, and social needs— as well as the ability of the scientific community to respond effectively to such opportunities or to combat external demands (cf. Zuckerman, 1986).

Shifting boundaries between science and politics, for example, may be manifest in the process of the fabrication of knowledge; in particular, the emergence of cognitive closure, the formation of consensus, or the evolution of uncontested facts in scientific fields may increasingly incorporate nonscientific actors and nonsystemic groups. The more or less direct intervention in cognitive processes in science is perhaps most evident in the case of problem-oriented research, such as environmental research or risk and technology assessment. Some fields of medical research may serve as another example. In France, the involvement and support of patient groups for the treatment of muscular dystrophy has led to considerable investments by their organizations into molecular biology and human genome research (cf. Latour, 1998: 208).

Pre-Implantation Genetic Diagnosis

The technique of pre-implantation genetic diagnosis (P.G.D.) exemplifies quite well the idea that knowledge is a capacity to act, or that knowledge is a first step toward action. In assessing the potential results of realizing knowledge, we discover that knowledge is almost inseparable from its consequences. Efforts to regulate the practical outcomes of knowledge therefore amount to a control of the knowledge itself. In the case of advances in medical science, it is widely assumed that there is an almost immediate exploitation of significant advances in medical knowledge and technical devices (Mulkay, 1997; 1972). Thus, an examination of the technique of pre-implantation genetic diagnosis would appear to be a good case study for the practice of knowledge politics.

The cultures related to the birth of a child, especially the culture of the relevant medical knowledge, have been transformed radically as the result of new technical developments. The scientification of birth (Böhme, 1981) continues to evolve rapidly, most recently as a result of advances introduced by genetics (Steinberg, 1997). Medical science alerts interested individuals (patients) to the possibility that a far greater range of illnesses than was heretofore assumed may be inherited. The result of these developments is, among other things, reproductive genetics. On the surface it would appear that reproductive genetics is a biological term. If, however, one defines reproductive genetics, as Elizabeth Ettore (1999: 539) stresses, as the application of DNA-based techniques to the medical control and policing of human reproduction, then reproductive genetics is (also) a social scientific concept. One is confronted with sociocultural and sociopolitical processes that are instrumental in determining whether certain genetic techniques and tests are utilized. If the decision is to use such techniques and tests, the organization of prenatal test methods is embedded in social processes. The chosen organization administering the tests determines outcomes.

Without question, the reaction of individual patients is complex and highly differentiated, but the technique and the social organization of prenatal diagnosis that confronts pregnant women today is increasingly routinized and widely administered. What has crystallized into a routine test is—to list but a few of the important factors—the outcome of sweeping changes in biological knowledge, social policy agendas, multiple cultural and political contexts, economic interests, demographic trends, localized conceptions of what constitutes pregnancy, and, last but not least, the desires of the future mother.[62] A diagnosis carried out during pregnancy, and responses based on the result of the tests, are now also increasingly accepted.

The French geneticist Jerome Lejeune and the cardiologist Marthe Gauthier, as well as scientists in England who simultaneously made the same experimental observation, could hardly have anticipated in the spring of 1958 the medical and social consequences of their discovery that individuals with Down's syndrome have one chromosome less than is common. This discovery was embedded in highly differentiated national and regional conditions (Rapp, 2000: 32–34). The techniques of prenatal diagnostics continued to develop rapidly. The technique of pre-implantation genetic diagnosis can be applied not in a preventative sense, but rather as a therapeutic instrument. In the latter case, the procedure of pre-implantation genetic diagnosis does not, as in the earlier case, assist only the "patient" but also the family, especially the sister or brother.

The technique of pre-implantation genetic diagnosis enables in principle the "acquisition of a designer child." That the desired child does not have to be the result of the (perhaps exceptional) desire of parents to have a second, identical clone of another, already living, child may be shown with reference to the unusual illness "Fanconi anemia" (named after the Swiss medical scientist who discovered it).[63] The best chance to save a child who has Fanconi anemia is a bone marrow transplant from a genetically perfectly matched sibling. In the hope of producing just such a child suitable for a successful bone marrow transplant, parents of a Fanconi anemia child have in the past borne another child. With the help of the pre-implantation genetic diagnostic technique, parents no longer have to rely on an accidental match.[64] Once the media reported such an approach to procreation and the possibility of embryonal "genetic screening," concerns mounted among the public and other interested groups. Attributions such as "Frankenstein medicine," and concerned questions about the permissibility of "mining" a child created as a kind of repair kit or "spare parts depot," were raised almost immediately.

In the United States, as well as in many other countries, debates are under way over whether one should outlaw techniques that rely on embryonic research and disallow for the possibility of deploying capacities to act that may emerge from embryo stem cell research. In England, the state committee responsible for overseeing and regulating P.G.D., the Human Fertilisation and Embryology Authority, has recently agreed to permit such a procedure.[65]

The German Association of Physicians (*Bundesärztekammer*) (2000: A-525), in an introduction to a discussion paper about rules concerning P.G.D., plainly comments that the unique ethical conflicts of P.G.D. can be avoided if the "couples in question consciously decide not to have children or decide instead to follow the adoption route." But conversations with couples that carry a high genetic risk show that these alternatives are hardly ever endorsed by them. In the case of a therapeutic application of P.G.D., for example in the event of a Fanconi child, one is able to predict with great certainty that the parents will try everything possible and within their power to help the sick child. Is it necessary to impose limits on the use of

P.G.D., and do we have to accept such restrictions? Or is it, perhaps, already too late for effective restrictions?

The former German federal minister of health, Andrea Fischer, in a television interview that aired in August 2000, argued against the introduction of pre-imple-mentation diagnostics in Germany: "I can appreciate that the desire exists to use P.G.D. in an attempt to preclude a serious handicap. However, I would still submit that what appears to be reasonable from the point of view of the individual may profoundly change our society. The prospect that illness and handicap are seen as something that can be precluded from happening from the beginning is a develop-ment I personally find dangerous. And this explains why I will continue to advo-cate that P.G.D. should not be permitted in Germany."[66] While assisted reproduc-tion in the form of in vitro fertilization (IVF) is already a routine medical intervention in the case of fertility deficiencies,[67] and the examination of the fetus in the womb is also a routine procedure, since the 1980s pre-implementation genetic diagnosis represents a technique that allows the examination of the embryo for certain mono-chromosomal defects—such as cystic fibrosis or Duchenne muscular dystrophy—outside the womb. P.G.D. therefore represents a manifest knowledge advance. It allows for a discussion of some of the practical problems and dilemmas that knowl-edge politics incurs. The diagnostic results of the P.G.D. procedure determine or codetermine the decision taken by the parents whether to implant or refrain from implanting the embryo. It would evidently have to be a significant genetic defect of the embryo, leading to an illness of the individual, that would influence the decision to forego implantation. The immediate responsibility for the decision to implant or forego implantation falls on the shoulders of the patient and the attend-ing physicians.

Outlawing P.G.D. can only mean that a "sick" embryo may be implanted and at a later stage aborted, along with the risk that such an abortion might have for the mother. The implementation of the P.G.D technique may also mean that the num-ber of abortions granted on medical grounds can be reduced. A prohibition of P.G.D. would imply that the number of embryos not utilized for pregnancy would be low-ered. The utilization of pre-implantation diagnostics could indicate that embryos not implanted do not enjoy the protection granted to unborn life. Outlawing P.G.D. implies that parents are not permitted to take advantage of the benefits for them associated with the technique. That there are such advantages cannot be questioned; but whether the disadvantages, judged from whatever platform and by whatever group of individuals, compensate for the advantages is, of course, an essentially contested matter. Finally, applying the pre-implantation diagnostic technique in-curs costs, and therefore raises the question of who should be responsible for such costs. Should it be the individuals who gain, or the collectivity, whose gain may be less evident?

Headlines such as "the new eugenics," "humans ordered made to measure," and "the dream of the perfect child" made evident that the prospects and the consequences of P.G.D. can be immediately grasped. Perhaps this explains why the German Asso-ciation of Physicians (2000: A-525) claims in its P.G.D. discussion paper—without even hinting, however, how this might be accomplished in practice—that society has to determine on the basis of a public debate "whether and to what extent the pre-implantation diagnostic technique should be implemented in Germany."

According to the Ministry of Health, P.G.D. is forbidden in Germany.[68] The view of the ministry makes reference to the German law pertaining to the treatment of embryos (*Embryonenschutzgesetz*).[69] Put more precisely, the German prohibition of P.G.D. is based on analogous reasoning using the embryo protection law of December 13, 1990. The law protecting embryos considers pluripotent cells extracted from an embryo as equivalent to an embryo. Pre-implantation diagnosis requires that one extract such a cell from the embryo for testing purposes. The remaining cell can develop after implantation without deficiencies. The extracted cells could in principle, in the proper environment, develop further and be implanted as well, evolving into, as the law puts it, an individual. In such a case, the original embryo and the embryo that develops from the extracted cell have identical genetic information.

Dangers, Risks, and Opportunities

The governance of knowledge will invariably reignite the issues of risks and dangers in the new context of knowledge politics. Similarly, knowledge politics forces the issue of the difference between (conventional) individual responsibility and (postconventional) collective co-responsibility to the forefront of public debate and discussions. Ethical conduct in a world of growing (apprehended) risks and dangers will be a highly contentious topic of discussion that itself carries with it considerable risks and dangers. In examining knowledge politics, it is therefore of some utility to focus on the general question of social risks and dangers.[70]

In the last few years, there appears to have been some progress in our understanding of risks. Among the main results so far are: (1) the successful conceptual differentiation between the terms "risk" (or more precisely, the risk of decision) and "danger," and (2) the differentiation between self-estimates of risk and dangers and those of other agents. But aside from these insights, knowledge regarding the issue of constructing and communicating risks in modern society remains fragile. Given the nature of knowledge politics in modern society that I have sketched, it would appear that we could not expect significant advances to occur in our ability to generate robust knowledge about risks and dangers. Within the field of risk research, it is possible to discern, in addition to the agreement already mentioned, a number of further broad areas of consensus:

First, and in analogy to the knowledge concept I explicated earlier, vigorous academic debate within the field of risk research yields the conclusion that there is no *objective or disembedded concept of risk*. There is no definition of risk that is both universally accepted and radically distinct from an everyday, common-sense concept of risk. Instead, risk is seen as a social construct, which has varying significance and which can only be understood with reference to specific social contexts and purposes.

Second, it is now well understood that risk communication has created a new layer and structure of social conflict within modern society, which may be more socially and politically explosive than any of the older distributional conflicts of the welfare state. The emergence of knowledge politics as a new field of political activity adds to these sociopolitical difficulties. Generally accepted institutional-ized forms and techniques of regulation have yet to be established as a frame for risk communication in society.

Third, and significantly, there is a return of fundamental uncertainty in soci-ety—if it was ever absent from society—and the agency that produces such uncer-tainty is the scientific community. At the same time, there is now agreement that science and the political system have to come to terms and cope with the uncer-tainty produced by scientific knowledge claims. All of these features of knowl-edge, their institutional location, and the fragile linkages between social systems in modern society act as multipliers heightening the contentious nature of knowl-edge politics and the difficulties of regulative politics. Yet there can be hardly any doubt that the category of risk and the activities of risk assessment and risk com-munication will play a central role in knowledge politics. The risks pertain both to the risk of permission, or decisions permitting and encouraging the deployment of novel knowledge, and the risks of omission, or decisions that restrict or even fore-close the utilization of new technical devices and new knowledge.

Criticism of the formal concept of risk

Initially, risk research was dominated by the distinction between subjective and objective risk. Subjective risk was defined as the risk perceived by individuals. Objective risk was risk as determined by science and calculated in accordance with formal principles. The difference between subjective and objective risk was re-flected in debates over the risk formula. The goal of this research was to develop a universally valid measure of risk that could be used for comparative purposes—comparing the most widely differing types of risk. It was hoped that this approach to the calculation of risks would make possible a rational clarification of the ac-ceptability of different risks as a function of their probability and the seriousness of the resulting damage.

The core of the objective approach was a formula borrowed from the insurance industry, which defines risk (R) as the product of probability (P) and the scale of the damage (D). This formula is applicable where the probability of a disaster can be clearly stated and damage can be uniquely determined in quantitative terms. The formula $R = P \times D$ was supposed to provide a model for rational decisions, since it seemed to offer a possibility of putting different activities and potential damage into relationship with each other. Formalizing risk assessment appeared to allow the evalu-ation of different sources of risk in terms of a formal calculation, independent of personal, political, or economic interests. The elimination of qualitative differences along the damage dimension, and the removal of history and context from the time dimension through the probability calculation, is the price paid for a generally valid and universal measure of risk for estimating socially created risks.

One significant component of the risk-determining formula is therefore the scale of damage. But as one attempts to apply this measure of risk outside purely technical fields, the problem of nonquantifiable aspects of damage often arises. It was thought that "utility theory" might prove useful in achieving a quantification of risk. This approach seeks to move from individual preference structures to quantitative measures of risk on which the various aspects of utility and damage can be constructed. However, it proved to be impossible to find a uniform measure for utility and damage. Translating the most widely varying damage estimates into monetary terms led to rather arbitrary and highly contestable results.

The second component of the risk formula, the calculation of the probability of an event, takes us to the limits of what can objectively be known, for example, about a nuclear reactor core meltdown. Until an adequate number of empirical cases are available, we can only offer subjective probabilities, which on closer inspection prove to involve a considerable measure of wishful thinking and guesswork.

The emerging crisis in objective risk assessment research was based on two conclusions: first, it is impossible to develop a uniform, formal concept of risk; and second, the logic of the formula $R = P \times D$, borrowed from commercial discourse, was not accepted in the public realm, as discussions moved to the enormous potential risk from large-scale technological installations.

The critique of the formal concept of risk may be summed up by saying that in the course of highly contested public debate on the assessment of the consequences and potential impacts of new large-scale technologies, it quickly became evident that the transformation of risk elements into formal calculations, as with any approach to risk assessment, carried within it the potential for considerable social and political conflict.

Especially in the case of risks that do not involve individual options for action, but rather entail impacts on third parties, decisions on risks cannot separate the acceptability of damage to others from the formal calculation. This is particularly true when no clear statement can be made regarding the likely scale of damage. Discussions of social and environmental compatibility are inevitably normative discussions. In the case of pollution limits, for example, it is not possible to establish any *objective, incontestable* criterion for determining whether something is harmful or not. Instead, risk assessment, and discussions and determination of limits always represent the result of a dynamic process of debate and dispute, in which conflicting interests have to be accommodated.

Risks and dangers

These observations about the complexity of risk calculation remain at the surface of the problem of communicating risk, because behind these problems lurk fundamental societal changes that also impact the assessment of risks and risk communication. For with the development and implementation of new large-scale technologies and the recognition of an increasing number of irreversible impacts on the environment, a new element of social and political conflict has emerged, which separates decision-makers from those affected by their decisions.

As explicated by Niklas Luhmann ([1991] 1993: 22–23), the difference amounts to the distinction between *risk* and *danger.* Risks are situations where possible future damage can be attributed to an individual's own decision, while dangers relate to damage and hazards from external sources over which the affected individual has no control whatsoever. All *"dangers* against which we could insure ourselves are thereby transformed into *risks.* The risk lies in the decision to insure or not to insure" (Luhmann, [1992] 1998: 73). Risks are features of decisions; one cannot escape decisions, and every decision can produce unwelcome results. Risks refer to time differences, and to judgments before and after a loss. Although today all dangers of a technical or ecological nature are caused by deliberate actions and decisions made by knowledgeable agents—this is the essence of the thesis that modern society poses a danger for itself—the technological and ecological dangers are perceived by some as risks and by others as dangers, and people behave accordingly.

There are several reasons for this:

(1) The costs and benefits attributed to and associated with technical and ecological risks in fact may not correlate and do not simultaneously affect the same set of actors. As a result, a cost-benefit calculation no longer supplies relevant information for a decision.

(2) There is a basic disjuncture between those causing risks by decisions and those affected by the risks. This is due to the extensive functional differentiation within modern society. As the chains of action and impact have become longer, decisions and the consequences of decisions no longer coincide geographically, temporally, or socially.

(3) Technical and ecological hazards are *societal* or collective risks. For the individual actor, dangers, not unlike social norms, constitute constraints that are externally imposed rather than voluntarily accepted. Whether ecological risks are caused by the acts of many (such as the destruction of forests) or whether technical risks arise from the decisions of a few decision-makers, one thing is quite evident: individuals neither desired nor were able to share in the decision-making process under which the risks were accepted. Risks are events that occur without the individual's knowledge, assent, or direct involvement. Faced by this situation, the individual agent only has the choice between moving away from the danger, coming to terms with it—or protesting.

Technological and ecological hazards generate dissension with respect to a future constituted by different agents either as a risk or as a danger. The facts that uncertainty emerges as a hidden but common denominator, and that future states of affairs become the shared point of reference for agents on both sides of the divide, mean that there are no general, rational criteria that can be mobilized to resolve this conflict.

Uncertainty in society

Western societies are characterized by a historically unique level of private wealth and social security, supported by a highly effective social safety net. The life expectancy of the population is rising steadily. A comprehensive health care system either prevents plagues, epidemics, and many other illnesses, or sharply reduces their impact. Not only the danger of economic poverty and illness, but also many other common hazards have been curtailed. In a society that has not faced a serious threat of war for decades, it is remarkable that fear of the future has become a major public issue and a reason for protests against new technologies.

The interesting question that arises, therefore, is how the contentious language of risk has been able to gain so much ground in the public arena in modern society. We need to ask why the future has become an essentially contested matter, interpreted in terms of risk rather than progress. In response, there are at least three ongoing debates in society that deal with the issue of society's danger to itself; these debates may shed some light on the renewed public role of uncertainty.

(1) There is the question of the consequences of using complex advanced technologies. Whether rooted in physics, chemistry, or biology, these technologies have a high potential for devastating catastrophes. In the event of accidents or total failures, the damage is out of all proportion to the purposes of the technologies. What is more, existing mechanisms for compensation based on operator liability also fail, because the scale of damage is so huge that it is uninsurable. A characteristic of advanced technologies is that total control is not possible. Accidents can only be made more improbable, not ruled out altogether. If the vulnerability to catastrophe can only be contained but not eliminated, the technical problem of safety measures becomes a social problem of acceptance of possible man-made catastrophes.

(2) In the course of the risk debate it has emerged that a further dimension of uncertainty is generated socially. The discussion involves the growing discrepancy between the intentions and the consequences of technological actions. Through and with the help of genetic engineering, for example, humanity can now try to manipulate the conditions of its own evolution. But it is impossible, from our present vantage point, to forecast the scale of the associated social and cultural changes and the shifts in humanity's view of itself.

(3) A third type of uncertainty appears in the nonspectacular consequences of daily actions, that is, long-term ecological changes due to everyday acts and decisions. Whether these involve road transport, carbon dioxide production, clearing the tropical rain forests, or the massive use of detergents, the consequences of our behavior are the destruction of forests, possible climatic change, or the irreversible pollution of our ground water. Typical for dangers that result from everyday conduct in modern life are the long interval and the complex relationship between cause and effect. Some of the effects of this type of uncertainty can only be made evident by science, and the gap between actions, consequences, and causative agents is so great that it is impossible to establish a clear relationship between them. The very ambiguity of ecological damage and the globality of the consequences make prevention difficult.

What is common to all three areas of anthropogenically generated hazards is that no one can predict with certainty how great the danger really is. The modern issue of risk involves an "irresolvable ambivalence." Not only is uncertainty produced on a previously unknown scale, but all attempts to solve the possible problems make us even more aware of how fragile modern societies happen to be.

The language of risk and risk research must therefore reflect these new uncertainties in society, which take the form of a conscious perception of the future as contingent upon the present.

Seen in these terms, risk means that possible damage is *already attributed* or incorporated into decision-making attitudes, even though it is impossible to know the scale of the damage, or whether there will be damage at all. This ignorance, the unpredictability of a decision's consequences, becomes part of the decision-making process. The only certainty is that a decision must be made, leaving us with the dilemma of decision-making under conditions of great uncertainty. The expansion of the potential need for decisions in the absence of any readily agreed-upon metasocial rules, with the resulting pressure to choose options, have resulted in a society increasingly viewing its future in terms of risk.

Risks of decision

If we try to draw some conclusions from what has been said so far, the most striking observation is the lack of robust knowledge in the risk debate. Positive or negative consequences of decisions relating to technologies or ecological changes are associated with great uncertainty, so that ultimately there can be only more or less plausible opinions, scenarios, etc., regarding what to expect in the future. Because we sense uncertainty but would prefer to be certain, we turn to science. We turn to science with the persistent conviction of its superior rationality and as if we retained our formerly unimpaired confidence in its ability to manage, plan, and design the modern world, and in the feasibility of doing so. However, these convictions are seriously and increasingly impaired and undermined by the problem of risks—technical, social, and in terms of time.

Knowledge of risk is a precariously balanced, fragile entity based on a hypothetical approach. Trial and error processes, that is, stepwise adjustments of technical systems to the needs of concrete situations, are being replaced in many cases by scientifically developed, long-term planning and statistical risk analyses, which are only able to make theoretical assumptions and approximations regarding reality.

Practical experience and empirical research are increasingly being replaced by models, scenarios, and idealizations. Empirical knowledge is being pushed out by subjective probability calculation. The potential for damage is no longer determined by experience and by trial and error, but has to be intellectually anticipated. This is because tests cannot be made on an adequate scale, and observations or experiments cannot be repeated as often as desired—or even made at all.

In normative terms, science has lost its authority as a result of the conflict between experts. Sophisticated technological products are increasingly accompanied by a socially relevant syndrome combining mistrust and uncertainty, and containing the seeds of political conflict. Every new accident releases the built-up tensions

and causes public opinion to explode. Technological risk has become a focus for
social uncertainty and fears over the past twenty years. Belief in progress has itself
reached its limits, and tipped into mistrust of the main institutions of the scientific
and technical world.

The dethroning of the experts is only one result of this trend; another is the loss
of respect accorded to government decision-making procedures. The decline in
reliable knowledge based on experience, in favor of scientifically generated theoretical knowledge which can be revised at any time, threatens the credibility of
government decisions. Those authorized under our constitutional norms to make
decisions in the name of the general welfare depend on expert committees in form-
ing their opinions; those who have the knowledge to make the decisions are not
authorized to make such decisions. The result of this process is the loss of a clearly
defined structure of responsibilities, which makes it impossible to place responsibility clearly for poorly executed decisions.

In terms of time, scientific and technical progress leads to a backlog of demand
for knowledge, relative to the actual accumulation of knowledge. Given the manner in which technical progress is speeding up, constantly causing changes, all
decisions need more time due to the increased involvement of different bodies and
the need to incorporate more and more complex consequences. While this socially
necessary time is passing, the data that made a decision necessary are also changing. To get through and execute decisions, it is often necessary to ignore such data.
The decision is thus made on the basis of hypotheses. Marquard (1986) regards
this as a general feature of our technological culture—the expansion of the hypothetical.

For the onlooker, this leads to an erosion of trust in public decision-making
systems, because from the outside they can see the hypothetical for what it is and
attack it as such—a perspective which the decision-maker is denied.

Coping with the lack of robust knowledge becomes the decisive dimension in
decision-making. Because we cannot know the future, it becomes all the more
important how this lack of knowledge is dealt with in the public decision-making
process. That this situation is still relatively new is clear from the fact that there are
no developed theories for it, let alone emerging techniques or routines that are able
to handle these new uncertainties.

A modern risk theory must face the problems of how to organize learning processes in situations of fundamental uncertainty and how to make decisions under
conditions of uncertainty in highly organized social systems. More knowledge will
not assure a shift from risk to security. The opposite seems to be the case: "The
more we know, the better we know that we do not know, and the more elaborate
our risk awareness becomes. The more rationally we calculate and the more complex the calculations become, the more aspects come into view involving uncertainty about the future and thus risk" (Luhmann, [1991] 1993: 28).

The paradox with which we will have to cope in knowledge societies—that is in
societies that are increasingly human-made—is that the growing social, political,
and economic importance of knowledge goes hand in hand with a decline in our
ability to intervene in our affairs in ways so as to remove contingency, fortuitous

circumstances, surprises, misfortune and so on. And knowledge politics both exemplifies and heightens all of these dilemmas.

Technology Assessment

The notion of knowledge policies resonates, to some extent at least, with earlier efforts to publicly appraise and regulate technologies using the process called "technology assessment," a term that dates from the late 1960s. In this section, I therefore want to offer both a brief history and an appraisal of efforts to generate technology assessments, and ask about the lessons that might be learned for the emerging field of knowledge politics. The practices of technology assessment and the perception of its social functions have changed in the course of the last decades. I will refer to some key changes that have taken place, leading to the current emphasis on participatory activities in technology assessment efforts.

The relevant questions in this context include: what methodological devices and theoretical perspectives are used to anticipate the societal consequences of technological developments; whether in the final analysis, it is only possible to generate ex post facto judgments; how to deal with manifest conflicts of interest; how assessments about the societal, legal, economic, political, and psychological consequences of technological developments are brought into relation to each other; what institutions are responsible for technology assessment; how it is organized in practice and who takes part; what role the scientific community assumes; and what the impact of technology assessment efforts is. Are there cases or examples of the restrictive use, or the discovery of new options, of technological artifacts as the result of prior technology assessment?

In the United States, a public law was enacted in October 1972 that led to the creation of the Office of Technology Assessment in 1973. The legislation stipulates that "the basic function of the Office shall be to provide early indications of the beneficial and adverse impacts of the applications of technology and to develop other coordinant information that may assist Congress" (Ninety-Second Congress, October 13, 1972). It should be noted that this portrayal of the function of the new office takes both the beneficial and harmful impacts of new technologies into consideration. However, the closer we move toward the present time and the establishment of new but similar activities in other countries, the less one hears about beneficial effects of the phenomena that are supposed to be examined and regulated. Just a few years later, Smits, Leyten, and Hertog (1995: 279) therefore already referred to a tradition that had been firmly established within technology assessment efforts: "Technology assessment is concerned with the potential negative or undesired social and economic outcomes of technological development." After all, legislation and scholarly reflections respond to the nature of the political and cultural agendas of the day,[71] and these agendas increasingly gave way to much more skeptical and hesitant conceptions of the social impact of new technologies.

The *institutionalization* and professionalization of discursive fields such as medical ethics, science ethics, bioethics, and also technology assessment, is a recent development. As the U.S. legislation makes clear, tasks constitutive of these discursive fields are attempts to "cope," that is, to manage the anticipated impact of new developments in associated branches of the sciences and technology. However, this would only appear to be the manifest goal of technology assessment.

An examination of many of the activities that have taken and are taking place under the auspices of "technology assessment," especially the self-observation of these projects by scientists who are part of the technology assessment efforts, shows that there are links to the emerging field of knowledge politics, but that the differences are more impressive. The most immediate difference, it seems to me, is the basically affirmative attitude of technology assessment, at least in its early incarnation, as an instrument of (more informed) policy advice concerned with issues of technical change and innovation. The affirmative stance is evident in the following self-description of the functions of technology assessment: The introduction of technology assessment into the political process has as its purpose

> to support, on the one hand, a noticeable future robustness, compatibility with welfare considerations and acceptance of economic-technical innovation and, on the other hand, to point to social problems that may be solved more effectively with the aid of innovative sociotechnical solutions (Simonis, 1999: 13).

Based on such a professional self-assessment of the social function of technology assessment, this process becomes an instrument for the societal diffusion, or even acceptance, of social change induced by technological developments, or a kind of "social management of technology"—which does not intend nor aspire to cancel existing political and economic decision-making processes. Whether it is indeed possible to expedite, channel, and manage the social acceptance of technological innovation is another matter.

Exactly opposite expectations were also directed toward the technology assessment enterprise. Such expectations were based on the assumption that technology assessment efforts could amount to more than *reactions* to the impact of technologies. It was hoped that undesirable and unintended social consequences of the introduction of new technologies could be anticipated and managed, in the end. A report issued by the U.S. National Academy of Sciences therefore stipulates, "There should be limits on the extent to which any major technology is allowed to proliferate or to stagnate without the gathering of evidence on the possible harmful effects and on the relative merits of alternatives" (Brooks and Bowers, 1970: 15). The goals specified by the academy refer to a kind of underconsumption of technology, and a displacement in goals of technology policies away from a perspective that concentrates on the supply side and switches attention to factors on the demand or the consumer side (see Smits, Leyten, and Hertog, 1995; Schot and Rip, 1997).

In the early phases of the development of technology assessment, these efforts were seen to serve a dual purpose. Technology assessment was seen as a kind of corrective that could harness or steer the blind forces of science and technology development, which follow their own inherent logic,[72] and therefore make them more immediately subservient to the needs of individuals and society. Technology assessment was also perceived as a method that could effectively intervene in existing decision-making processes that are governed, for example, by the rules of the market or decentralized policymaking, in order to more directly manage the social consequences of technological development and make them accessible to explicit reflection. However, the kind of reflections that prevailed in technology assessment discourse in its early phase was still dominated by convictions that a scientific—that is, a more or less formal and objective—conception of technology assessment serving improved political decision-making was possible. A 1972 panel of the National Science Foundation expected technology assessment efforts to provide "a neutral and objective input into public decision-making" (as cited in Cambrosio and Limoges, 1991: 379). The groups or individuals involved in the process of technology assessment were seen to be restricted, for the most part, to expert scientists and policymakers. However, it was soon recognized that technology assessment as a new field of scientific activity was hard pressed to live up to its early heroic billing. Without explicitly repudiating its manifest goals, technology assessment soon engaged in efforts to better understand existing technologies, launched impact assessment studies, and attempted to better comprehend and respond to the nature of policymaking.

The emergence of technology assessment responds to an erosion in the once unquestioned and widespread faith in the civilizational accomplishment of new technical artifacts that appeared in the mid-1960s and early 1970s.[73] The carriers and proponents of the more skeptical stance toward science and technology in the latter part of the last century were, last but not least, new social movements. In the same vein, the earlier and then widely accepted best public policy toward technology development, namely support and encouragement of technological developments with as little intervention as possible, came under intense scrutiny. Affirmative views of the desirability of technological innovation gave way to concerns about multiple, especially adverse and undesirable, risks associated with technological trends—manifested in such phenomena as environmental pollution and deteriorating infrastructures—and ultimately, the need to supervise, channel, and control technological developments through closer external regulation, supposedly designed to achieve specific policy outcomes.

American scientists described the purposes of technology assessment efforts, even before the Office of Technology Assessment was established in 1973, as the analysis of how "such benefits [of technology] might be achieved with less injury to the society and the environment" (Brooks and Bowers, 1970: 14). But even such a goal, in the end, appears to imply the need for a deployment of even more technology, for "many of the problems that are identified as undesirable results of technological development can also be seen as the result of failure to develop or apply technologies that would have mitigated the undesired effects" (Brooks and Bowers, 1970: 14). Any successful regime of technology assessment might therefore be seen as a system that would enhance, rather than restrict, technological innovation.

The reference to the erosion of confidence in the benefits of new technology raises the question of whether harmful effects and social risks apprehended as the result of new technological developments are the outcome of any actual *use*; after all, technology is widely presented merely as a means, as an instrument, as exogenous, as neutral, and perhaps even as an autonomous force in society. If the answer to the question about the causes of specific dangers and risks associated with technology is that it is the kind of usage that generates such dangers, then the onus of technology assessment is on the user, and not on the innovative process, nor on the selection and specific articulation of technical artifacts, for example. The abstract differentiation of means (technology) and ends (politics) conceals the extent to which technological developments are driven by sociopolitical as well as socioeconomic considerations, and generally allows for "interpretive flexibility" (Pinch and Bijker, 1984).

In its more recent trajectory, and in response to disappointed expectations of the practical efficacy of technology assessment and demands by new social movements for participation, technology assessment efforts aim to incorporate various participatory activities (Carroll, 1971; Cambrosio and Limoges, 1991). The emphasis on broader public participation is supposed to eradicate what is widely apprehended as a legitimation deficit in the process of technology assessment. At the same time, technology assessment activities that are more inclusive are supposed to recognize the essentially contested nature of evaluation procedures of new technologies. After all, social change induced by technological development is bound to infringe on the interests of some social groups, while it is bound to benefit other groups or institutions. Assessment is now expected to benefit from more inclusive and joint efforts among a range of affected stakeholders. The new approach is exemplified by so-called consensus-developing conferences organized in Denmark, for example (Hamstra, 1995; Hennen, 1995). The procedure presumably aims for consensual policy outcomes, rather than regulatory practices designed to reach pre-established policy outcomes.

The practical influence and success of technology assessment, on the whole, can only be called marginal. Although the closure was primarily prompted by an agenda of fiscal restraints, a Republican Congress eliminated the U.S. Office of Technology Assessment in 1995 (Bimber, 1996).[74]

Knowledge Management

Aside from technology assessment, knowledge management, one of the most widely discussed managerial "instruments" in the 1990s, may appear to be a tool for knowledge politics.[75] In analogy to technology assessment, knowledge management is primarily designed, as far as I can see, to improve the efficient *use of existing resources.*

The emphasis in knowledge management is not directed toward the regulation or restriction of the use of knowledge, nor toward influencing the production of knowledge in corporations, universities, and public sector agencies.[76] The effort to manage knowledge is designed to assist in the administration of a company, for example, in which such a management tool has to be subsidiary in its function to the primary goal of the organization. For a company, this would mean that knowledge management has to facilitate the introduction of new processes and products, their improvement, and the speed with which they hit the market, in order to improve the economic success of the corporation. Knowledge management constitutes a form and development of what earlier, in management science, was known as organizational learning (Dierkes, 2001). Critics of the notion of knowledge management are therefore quick to ask questions about what exactly is novel about knowledge management. The same critics observe that there are many examples from past management approaches indicating that there always have been (or should have been) more or less well-elaborated efforts in various social organizations to manage their knowledge (Epstein 1998; Forey, 2001).

This skeptical attitude toward the assertion that there is anything new about knowledge management has some affinities to the critical question of the possible novelty of knowledge politics. Since the societal function—especially the role of knowledge in the economic system—changes, it is not surprising that the idea of knowledge management is intensively discussed, and various efforts are under way consciously to practice it. Apparently new problems are arising, which cannot be solved effectively using conventional approaches (such as personnel management and the administration of intellectual capital) that were often only latent practices in different social organizations. Moreover, knowledge is no longer treated as a black box. The literature that deals with knowledge management mainly addresses the question of how knowledge can be detected and *measured* and how knowledge resources can be *administered* effectively (OECD, 2000). Our knowledge about knowledge improves gradually; although the core of any knowledge management, namely knowledge, is likely still the Achilles' heel of any effort to "manage" it efficiently. Such caution applies, for example, to the issue of the general productivity of knowledge and the differential productivity of different types of knowledge (Stehr, 2002a). Knowledge is turned into a commodity. Efforts are under way to problematize and organize the production of knowledge. Access to and dissemination of knowledge and information are affected, improved, and transformed by new techniques. In other words, the societal function of knowledge changes rapidly, and therefore the need to organize the work of knowledge changes as well, and more explicitly. As a result, the apprehended necessity of developing new instruments of dealing consciously with knowledge grows. But the hopes that are typically extended toward the payoffs that may derive from knowledge management by far exceed robust knowledge about the benefits that may result from knowledge management in practice. There are few, if any, studies that ask empirical questions about the extent to which knowledge management principles generate sustainable gains for corporations and other organizations (Landry and Amara, 2001).

As I have indicated, to be effective the practice of knowledge management requires some understanding of different forms of knowledge—perhaps a way of identifying productive knowledge, a conception of the possibility of excavating tacit knowledge, and so on. Aside from the explication and recognition of different forms of knowledge, knowledge management also refers to the social organization of knowledge—its production, dissemination, and utilization. I will focus here on the issue of productive knowledge.

Given the diversity of knowledge, the range of ways in which knowledge is augmented and acquired, and, last but not least, the diversity of circumstances in which it may be attempted to be realized and/or given legitimacy,[77] it would indeed seem impossible to discover invariables—such as levels of "innovative opportunity" or degrees of "cumulativeness" (Dosi, 1996: 85)—that hold across different knowledge forms and that make knowledge productive inherently, permanently, and across contexts.[78] Indeed, this would seem to be a demand that can hardly be fulfilled, even if we tend to think of knowledge invariably—for instance, in comparison to ignorance—in the highest possible terms.

The skepticism expressed in these observations about the likely absence of intrinsic, permanent features of knowledge that assure its productivity/practicality already indicate that productive knowledge is also, like the very idea of productivity, a relational concept. Thus, if one defines knowledge as a capacity for action or as a model for reality, then productive knowledge refers to knowledge claims that are in fact capable of setting something in motion.[79]

Since it is impossible to overcome the basic uncertainty associated with any effort to utilize knowledge as a capacity for action, any economic calculation of the productivity of knowledge can only be carried out effectively ex post and not ex ante—that is, only once a context of application has been stabilized, but not before a context stabilizes. As a result, the economic analysis of productive knowledge becomes problematic; but because it becomes problematic, the sociology of knowledge is relevant for generating and augmenting knowledge that may turn out to be productive.

I would like to suggest that reflections about the conditions or constituents of productive knowledge have to start from the assumption that the productivity or adequacy (usefulness) of knowledge, produced in one context but employed in another context, can now be formulated to pertain to the *relation* between knowledge and the local conditions of action.

Within the context of application, constraints and conditions of action are apprehended as either open or beyond the control of relevant actors. Given such a differentiation of conditions of action, productive knowledge pertains to open conditions of action, which means that theoretical knowledge has to be reattached to the social context in general, and to those elements of the situation that are actionable in particular.

More precisely, knowledge acquires a productive or active role in the course of social action only under circumstances where such action does not follow purely stereotypical patterns (Max Weber) or is not strictly regulated in some other fashion. Knowledge assumes significance under conditions where social action is, for whatever reasons, based on a certain degree of freedom in the courses of action that can be chosen. Karl Mannheim ([1929] 1936: 102) defines, in much the same sense, the range of social conduct in which knowledge plays a role as restricted to spheres of social life that have not been routinized and regulated completely. For, as he observes, "Conduct, in the sense in which we use it, does not begin until we reach the area where rationalization has not yet penetrated, and where we are forced to make decisions in situations which have as yet not been subjected to regulation."

The question of the relation of theory to practice is thus restricted, for Mannheim, precisely to situations that offer a measure of discretion in social conduct, and that have not therefore been reduced to a corset of strictly ordered and predictable patterns of social action—although it cannot be ruled out that even under these circumstances, in situations which are repeated with routine regularity, elements of "irrationality" remain. Defiantly, knowledge is seen as inherently productive. I have argued, contrary to essentialist perspectives, that the utility of knowledge does not reside intrinsically in knowledge. Knowledge as a capacity for action is neither inherently self-protecting nor self-realizing, nor is knowledge immediately productive. Knowledge tends to be localized and its realization embedded in specific technical, institutional, regional, and industrial contexts. The productivity of knowledge, and hence knowledge management, is specific to industrial sectors, regions, and settings of firms.

The Societal Regulation of Knowledge

It seems highly likely that not only the state and major social institutions, but also social movements and groups of affected "laypersons," will organize and increasingly demand measures to regulate knowledge. In the past two decades, for example, AIDS research and the clinical treatment of AIDS in the United States has been marked "by a sustained lay invasion of the domain of scientific fact-making" (Epstein, 1996: 330; also Indyk and Rier, 1993), as well as by a struggle toward a "democratization" of medicine, breaking down some of the entrenched barriers between experts and laymen and between science and society.[80] The experience of AIDS research signals that efforts to control the application of knowledge—in this case, prominently, the aspects of who is to benefit, when, and for what "price"— have repercussions for the development of knowledge in academic science and for research and development in corporations (see also Rabinow, 1999; Epstein, 1991).

It is perhaps self-evident that the growing efforts to police knowledge signal that claims of the inevitability of a self-propelled domination of society by science are simply unsupportable. The specific issue I will therefore discuss is not what I consider almost beyond dispute—namely that the deployment of control and regulation measures will increasingly be aimed at knowledge—but rather the entirely unresolved issue of the likely efficacy and consequences of efforts to police knowledge. There is a yawning gulf between approaches that stress the ease with which knowledge is monopolized and controlled by an elite, and the very different perspective advanced here, which emphasizes the extent to which the expanded role of knowledge significantly diminishes the ability of either major societal institutions or small groups to harness without serious challenge the gains that result from the growth of knowledge.

During the evolution of industrial society, liberal democracies successively instituted increasingly elaborate legal frames pertaining to the social status and use of property and labor. Thus the freedom of economic actors to exercise power and authority by virtue of their individual or collective ownership over labor power or the means of production is increasingly constrained and circumscribed by a host of legal norms, as well as organizations and political programs that emerge around these factors. Ownership is restrained not only spontaneously by the market, for example, but also by the state. Deliberate and anticipatory legal constraints on the use of property and labor are not neutral. From the point of view of certain actors, especially those who feel impotent in acquiring ownership and in affecting the legal rules pertaining to its disposition, legal norms convey privileges; while they signal (natural) rights to those who control property and labor. Unequal access to ownership, and therefore any stratification of effective influence on the construction of the legal restraints and rights, is in turn typically—but not always exclusively—based on an unequal distribution of labor and property in industrial society, elements that are constitutive for its social and economic existence.

It is almost self-evident that *legal* efforts and legislation in knowledge societies will increasingly be directed toward ways of controlling the employment, and indirectly the development, of knowledge. I emphasize political and legislative efforts to control and direct the implementation of scientific knowledge rather than more tenuous forms of informal or spontaneous social control, because the latter are simply part and parcel of the conventional state of affairs in business and science, namely the standard selectivity with which knowledge develops and is protected and utilized.

Vigorous opposition to political ventures to limit the considerable autonomy of the modern scientific community, to restrict investment opportunities, and perhaps to limit market competition in order to control knowledge utilization, will be as common as was opposition to efforts to control the use of property, or to control the ways in which labor power might be utilized by the owners of the means of production.

Committees for Knowledge Affairs

> The sciences ... should be used in a district, a village, a city, a region in a way determined by the representatives of the citizens of this district, village, city or region.
>
> *Paul Feyerabend,* Erkenntnis für freie Menschen

Much of the contemporary discussion about the control and regulation of novel scientific knowledge takes place in an historical context. But concerted efforts and varied proposals to plan, manage, check, and enhance the utilization of discoveries and new ideas have predecessors that are worth examining. Concerns about the unintended and perhaps destructive consequences of science and technology have from time to time generated various strategies of regulation and control of new knowledge and technical inventions. I will discuss a number of radical strategies that are in many ways predecessors of the ethics commissions now in place in many countries. These efforts share the conviction that novel scientific knowledge can and should be managed.

First, I wish to refer to a suggestion already mentioned: the idea of a Committee for Knowledge Affairs, suggested by the sociologist and economist Werner Sombart

(Grundmann and Stehr, 2001). Sombart's idea can be found in his book *German Socialism* (1934). Although the author insisted that his monograph about German socialism was not a hastily conceived, journalistic treatise attending solely to the issues of the day, but rather a serious scientific study, the book nevertheless carried a title and comments responsive to the political developments of that time.[81] In his monograph, Sombart, among other political suggestions and proposals, recommended the establishment of a National Committee for Knowledge or Cultural Affairs (*Kulturrat*).

What was supposed to be the function of the Committee for Cultural Affairs? As Sombart (1934: 264–267) described it under the heading of "The Taming of Technology," a leading committee for cultural affairs should generally be charged with the task of ensuring that new knowledge and practices are not harmful to society. How this was supposed to be accomplished, in analogy to the patent office, was briefly outlined by Sombart (1930: 266): "Every invention has to be officially registered and investigated for its value." Permission to deploy would be granted by the committee, which would have among its members "engineers in an advisory capacity" (Sombart, 1930: 266). According to Sombart (1930: 266), the committee he proposed would determine whether an invention "is forbidden, assigned to a museum or can in fact be used in practice," and every invention would have to be checked for how it would be implemented. "The inventor will be paid a fee by the state based on the value of the invention independently of the commercial promise of the invention and whether or not the invention ends up in the museum or is utilized in society."

Sombart was determined to encourage state intervention and state regulation of inventions and knowledge in order to arrest, as he saw it, the chaotic, arbitrary, and self-serving process of technological scientific development. The chances that such a regulatory organ of new technical devices and new knowledge could be successful in practice, according to Sombart (1934: 262), would mainly be a function of the fact that technology is a civilizational feature of social action, divisible into many discrete parts. Moreover, in his view, technology was "culturally neutral, ethically indifferent and can be utilized for good or evil purposes."

The need to determine beforehand the purposes for which technology is utilized merely represents the idea that new technological devices constitute a *capacity* for action, as well as the conviction that human actors are in principle able first to experiment with inventions and new ideas, and, of course, the conviction that a Committee for Cultural Affairs ought be to be able to successfully enact any supervision of inventions. Sombart (1934: 262) stressed with great confidence that it is naive to think that everything that is possible and doable will in fact be done. If one wants to prevent discoveries and inventions from being utilized in practice, it is necessary that one be able to make prior judgments about the social impact, and that one be capable of resisting interest-driven pressures from industry, the military, or the health system. The modalities on which all of this might be based would be determined and implemented by the Committee on Cultural Affairs.

What prompted Sombart to call for the establishment of a Committee for Cultural Affairs was his general, persistent, and decided unease about the societal consequences of modern technology. And this was not a view about the "cultural" role of modern technology that Sombart first expressed in 1934. In his earlier social analysis, and also in his political statements about contemporary technology, Sombart already displayed quite an ambivalent relationship to modern technological features and practices.[82]

Half a century later, Paul Feyerabend (1978: 86–87)[83] demanded the establishment of committees made of "laypersons," or citizen initiatives organized according to basic democratic principles and operating according to transparent organizational principles, charged with arriving at fundamental decisions directed against the "truth" and the opinions of experts. Scientists should be supervised by citizens and citizen initiatives, and not by epistemology, theories of society, or political theories such as liberalism or Marxism that generate freedom (Feyerabend, 1980: 163). Feyerabend's plea for democratic participation in scientific matters was directed against the dangers for a free society that come with the unregulated dominance, ignorance, and one-sidedness of the sciences in modern societies.[84] Experts should be heard and listened to, but they should not have the last word. The last word belongs to citizen movements led by laypersons. Feyerabend was optimistic that the specialized knowledge of the experts would not prevail in citizen committees.

Institutions that are financed by taxpayers should also be directly controlled and regulated by the taxpaying public, as a widely accepted political premise in the United States stresses. In a democratic society, Feyerabend (1978: 86) emphasized, the "individual citizen has the right to read, write, to make propaganda for whatever strikes his fancy." Concretely, "duly elected committees of laymen must examine whether the theory of evolution is really as well-established as biologists want us to believe, whether being established in their sense settles the matter, and whether it should replace other views in schools" (Feyerabend, 1978: 96). Space and opportunities ought to be created for traditions that conflict with reigning scientific views. It is easily understood that Feyerabend's demands did not meet with a responsive echo in the scientific community. But his idea that perspectives and traditions other than those prevailing in science should be given a voice can be heard from time to time. One need hardly make special mention of the practical difficulties, also recognized by Feyerabend, of organizing democratic control of science and technology.

The origins and the impetus for Feyerabend's proposal, in contrast to Sombart's suggestions, are linked to epistemological convictions and their political implications. In the context of the epistemological idea, for example, that it is impossible to demonstrate convincingly, using methodological arguments, that scientific knowledge is a superior form of knowledge when compared to other intellectual traditions, it is important that different world views, opinions, and forms of knowledge are treated symmetrically. The equal treatment of different ideas is supposed to ensure that the authority of scientific knowledge in society—or the chauvinism of science, as Feyerabend labels it—is not cemented. The proposal Feyerabend advances for ways of negotiating democratically among competing ideas is not so much aimed at new scientific knowledge and technical devices as at ensuring a fair competition among contending perspectives. Intellectual traditions ought to have equal chances at gaining support in society. But Sombart's and Feyerabend's proposals share a deep-seated suspicion of specialists and experts. The populism of Feyerabend and Sombart is likely based on different everyday experiences with science and technology, and on distinct encounters with science in the context of the scientific community. However, their proposals for policing different intellectual traditions and new knowledge and new technical devices share utopian elements. It would be quite difficult to implement their proposals.

The assumptions that knowledge is among the most important productive forces, and that its economic significance continues to grow, are now widely accepted premises of most analyses of the modern economy. But this does not mean that we have made much headway in understanding some of the peculiar features of the social role of knowledge. Insights into these exceptional features are not a precondition for the growing practical success of knowledge. However, insights into some of the basic features of knowledge (as a capacity to act) may well be a requirement for ethics committees, biotechnology advisory boards, committees for cultural affairs, or whatever the designation and composition of such councils may be, in order to achieve more than mere promises about their capacity to channel, restrict, or police the application of new knowledge.

As I have already asked, does knowledge realize itself almost automatically? Is it even possible to influence the development of new technologies, let alone affect their use and application? Will matters simply evolve as they should? If this is indeed the case, then any efforts politically to plan and regulate new ideas and devices will be futile. Or is knowledge, perhaps, self-protecting? If so, one can only expect that the producers of a particular invention and a set of new ideas will be capable of controlling their invention and the new capacity to act. Only the inventors are free. If it comes to a decision as to whether we know too much, can we only decide between some kind of apologetic stance and fatalism? These questions, as we have seen, are not easy to answer.

The conditions Sombart already experienced as uncomfortable have not changed to this day; as he lamented, we are used to the fact that we are prepared to enact and practice everything we are capable of doing. Sombart called this expectation that we will practice everything we are capable of practicing a childish perspective, which had long been transcended by more "mature" societies. To overcome this immature point of view toward new discoveries, it will have to be possible in the future that an invention may be discarded and sent to the museum almost immediately after it is made. What could be accomplished if one followed such a resolve is quite evident, according to Sombart. Although Sombart could not have anticipated contemporary biotechnological invention, he apparently had a point of reference and action in mind that connects easily to present disputes and debates about knowledge politics.

If one were able to decide that a discovery should be relegated to the museum—many of today's inventions are very difficult to exhibit in the museums of the industrial age—this would have the advantage, according to Sombart, that one could be free in everyday life from the harm and miseries that might accompany the widespread application and use of a particular discovery. With his pleas to consign discoveries to a museum, of course, Sombart decided against the idea that knowledge automatically realizes itself, and he also passed judgment against the notion that knowledge is self-protecting. Accordingly, new knowledge and novel technical gadgets can be controlled in an anticipatory manner. But in order to avoid simple or even random decision procedures, one needs a calculus on the basis of which regulation can proceed. Sombart proposed such a decision-making calculus. The evaluation of new technologies and knowledge should be based, first and foremost, on the utilities they offer for society as a whole. But the interests of individuals should also be taken into account—obviously a very complicated and difficult task for any Committee of Cultural Affairs to live up to. Finally, Sombart could not avoid reference to past discoveries and knowledge that should have been exiled to a museum, had the kind of committee he demanded been in existence: the record player, radio, telephone, and zeppelin. How much more peaceful, Sombart lamented, would life have been if only someone had insisted on not acting on and disseminating these inventions.

Knowledge politics can be undemocratic. But knowledge politics, to use a well-worn cliché, is much too important to leave to the experts. This is also the conviction that Paul Feyerabend expresses. Feyerabend has no hesitation in arguing that knowledge politics ought to be organized according to democratic principles. In a democracy, knowledge politics has to be organized using plebiscitary features. The ultimate goal can only be—and this includes the functions of knowledge politics in a free society—a society in which "all traditions have equal rights and equal access to the centres of power" (Feyerabend, 1978: 106).

How knowledge politics is supposed to look can only be discussed in the context of some understanding of how a society in which we live ought to look. The chance and the uncertainty connected to discussion about the future course of society cannot be eliminated. Sombart recognized this as well. The purposes of the Committee for Cultural Affairs are part of the design, as Friedrich Pollock calls it in a review of Sombart's treatise, of a "peculiar" German socialism. A functioning Committee for Cultural Affairs is part of all those instruments that codetermine the course of society. The "guidelines for the decisions the Committee of Cultural Affairs has to arrive at" (Sombart, 1934: 267) can be derived from an overall plan that is drawn for the reconstitution for the entire society. Yet knowledge politics, however organized, cannot do without some basic insight into the nature of knowledge and its social role. But in this respect we are only at the beginning.

The Public and Science

For practical purposes, what exactly is, or could be, the role of the public in the field of knowledge politics? In democratic societies there can be no doubt that the role of the public in either pressing for or sanctioning knowledge policies is of considerable importance. The reference to the role of the public is also a useful reminder that the kinds of practical choices knowledge politics may represent—as it is both drafted and implemented—are embedded not only in dynamic political and economic contexts, but also in perhaps somewhat less dynamic sociocultural settings (Klitgaard, 1997). As a result, knowledge policies are conditioned by a complicated host of factors, of which the notion of the public is one of the useful metaphors.

More specifically, I want to examine some of the issues that have surfaced in recent years regarding the relationship between science and the public. Observations about this relationship range from the straightforwardly empirical to contested normative or political analyses of the role of the public in scientific matters—demands, for example, that "knowledge production should proceed only insofar as public involvement is possible" (Fuller, 1993: xviii)—to dismissive or discouraged comments on the ability or inability of the public to engage with modern science.

While Fuller would like to change the boundaries of knowledge politics and move it right into the center of the scientific community, observations of an apparent "loss of contact" (Holton, 1986: 92) between scientific knowledge and the larger public are more frequent in reflections about the interrelation between scientific knowledge and society at large. Large segments of the public have become disenfranchised, at least in the view of some members of the scientific community who pay attention to these matters. This loss of contact is not only the result of a growing cognitive distance between scientific and everyday knowledge,[85] it is also affected by the ever-increasing speed of knowledge expansion, the rapid deployment of knowledge as a productive capacity, and influential discourse about science that stresses its antipoetic, self-transforming features, which transform science into a system beyond the control of actors' values and intentions (see Touraine, [1995] 1997: 48).

However, one also needs to take into account that as a result of the nature of contemporary science, it takes an enormous amount of energy, resources, and good will by members of the public to acquire and observe relevant scientific information. In cases where their interests are at stake—for example, in hearings with experts on hand—it takes considerable effort for laymen to judge contending sources of scientific information and understanding, or to acquire an idea of what expert knowledge might be relevant, given their local circumstances and situational needs (Wynne, 1991). In other words, bridging the cognitive divide between science and the public is quite demanding of both sides and cannot be guaranteed to function at all, even under favorable circumstances such as an atmosphere of good will, or lack of pressure in terms of time and available resources.

This allegedly decaying cognitive proximity surely increases the political distance of nonscientists from science, for example, by restricting public reflection on both anticipated and unanticipated transformations of social, economic, and cultural relations resulting from the application of new scientific knowledge. There should be little doubt that such a state of cognitive distance and ambiguity, perhaps even suspicion, is bound to influence the public debate over knowledge politics, the willingness to participate in such debates, and the support of decisions that either restrict or enhance the potential utilization of new scientific knowledge.

The great majority of citizens in the developed world—or so it appears, at least, to those scientists who reflect on these matters—are bound to be excluded and disenfranchised when it comes to participation in such disputes and controversies. One should not commit the fallacy, moreover, of viewing the public understanding of science[86] as a mere mirror image of professional conceptions of science. The public conception of science among different groups and strata of society is not a passive construct, but rather a social accomplishment, and is therefore actively produced and influenced by a host of cultural factors, educational institutions, media discourses, and traditional everyday conceptions.[87] The self-conception scientists convey to the public is therefore only one element in the equation of the public understanding of science and its social consequences.

As late as the 1970s, confidence in the capacity of "disinterested" scientists to resolve public issues in the areas of space exploration, nuclear power, or food additive regulation, etc., was still considerable, and significantly exceeded confidence in other groups or agencies (cf. Miller, 1983: 90–93; Durant, Evans, and Thomas, 1989; Jasanoff, 1990: 12). The general decline in trust in the last two or three decades among the public of developed societies in science and technology as problem-solvers—a trust that had hitherto been a core element of modernity—has been documented by Inglehart (1995: 391). However, the observed loss in the esteem of science and scientists parallels a broad decline in public trust in authority figures and major social institutions generally. Whether the loss of esteem of science is associated with the identification of the scientific community with power structures in society, as Morrison (1978: vii), for example, suspects, is an empirical issue.

The scientific community shares responsibility for this diminishing intellectual proximity and loss of trust, since the preferred self-image of science as a consensual, even monolithic and monologic, enterprise is increasingly in conflict with both its public role and its own internal struggles over research priorities, as well as the generation and interpretation of data. However, on political and moral grounds many groups, constituencies, and institutions must be consulted before decisions are made about issues that affect the regulation of knowledge and, indirectly, the development of science and technology. It would be misleading to think that the distance from and the loss of contact with science, or the considerable scientific illiteracy in modern societies, is somehow a "potentially fatal flaw in the self-conception of the people today" (Holton, 1992: 105) or signals the possibility of a dramatic collapse in public support for science.

It is more accurate, perhaps, to speak of a state of precarious balance affecting the autonomy and dependence of science in modern society. A loss of close intellectual contact between science and the public, a lack of interest in science,[88] and a deficient scientific literacy is apparently perfectly compatible with both a diffuse support for science in modern society and an assent to legal and political efforts to control the impact of science and technology. It is also possible that a limited, superficial knowledge about scientific matters may be linked with an outspoken interest in science, especially medical science, as I will indicate.

The general expectations, hopes, and also concerns connected with science among the public, as far as these attitudes are reflected in recent survey findings (e.g., National Science Board, 2000: 8–13), continue to be quite positive. Favorable responses toward science can be observed especially in the United States, while attitudes in Japan and in the countries of the European Union are less approving. However, in all regions of the world just mentioned, there are sizeable minorities of the public that express considerable reservations about science (see statistical appendix).

From the point of view of rational choice theory, a consciously accepted stance of ignorance toward complicated and difficult questions that are troublesome to judge independently and that are linked to decisions based on contested scientific issues is actually a quite rational attitude to take. In contrast, Isaac Asimov (1983: 119) points out that the difference between public understanding and public ignorance of science, as construed in rational choice theory, also extends to the difference between respect and admiration for science on the one side, and hate and fear on the other side.

Rational choice theory expects that the average citizen determines on which issue to spend what amount of time in order to reach a decision. If one assumes that the probability of reaching a rational decision improves with the amount of time spent on reaching a decision, it would make sense to encourage the average citizen to allocate considerable time to decisions that affect the personal and societal impact of the practical application of new scientific knowledge and new technical devices. The actor cannot expect, however, that he will be able to draw disproportional personal benefits from the collective advantages that may flow from political decisions in the field of knowledge politics. The crucial majority of the gains will be benefits that accrue to the collectivity. The asymmetrical distribution of gains may mean, Mancur Olson (1990: 99) emphasizes, that "the individual citizen does not have an incentive to devote enough time to fact-finding and to thinking about what would be best for the country." It is only when one succeeds in persuading the large majority of the public to devote a considerable amount of time to decisions in the field of knowledge politics that a "just" distribution of the utility of rational decision-making might be possible. If the acquisition of information and knowledge about matters that require a high degree of scientific or technical comprehension is not of interest, either as the result of intrinsic concern with science, the outcome of ideological commitments, or professional curiosity, one must conclude—judging on the basis of the relation between competing benefits and costs involved—then most of the public has little incentive to engage at length and in detail in knowledge politics. As Olson (1990: 100) therefore underlines, "The typical citizen will usually find that his or her income and life chances will not be improved by the zealous study of public affairs or even a single collective good." In other words—and why should the issue of knowledge politics be an exception from the point of view of rational choice theory?—information about public affairs is for most actors a public good, and "the rational ignorance of the typical [citizen] … is an example of the logic of collective action" (Olson, 1990: 100).

The conclusions and the advice of rational choice theorists are in stark contrast to a perspective that is also concerned about the lack of scientific knowledge among the public, but that is even more worried about the interrelations between knowledge, democracy, social inequality, and the repression of certain segments of society.

As Durant, Evans, and Thomas (1989: 11), for example, suggest, many political decisions "involve science, and these can only be genuinely democratic if they arise out of informed public debate." Sandra Harding (1991: 33) reaches an analogous conclusion when she laments the lack of intellectual familiarity and involvement of the public with contemporary scientific culture and when she pleads for science to be communicated and taught like any other culture: "We live in a scientific culture; to be scientifically illiterate is simply to be illiterate—a condition of far too many women and men."

In yet another sense, however, the loss of cognitive contact is almost irrelevant, and yet highly controversial—for example, when "contact" is meant to refer to close cognitive proximity as a prerequisite of public participation in decisions affecting scientific and technological knowledge. Such an expectation is practically meaningless, because it almost requires public engagement in science-in-progress (cf. Collins, 1987: 691).

From the point of view of the scientific community, the lack of cognitive proximity to the general public has both advantages and disadvantages. The loss of contact between science and the public can perhaps explain, at least in part, why the scientific community, in view of its attractiveness and usefulness for corporations, the military, and the state, has been able to preserve a considerable degree of intellectual autonomy (cf. Gilbert and Mulkay, 1984). Such autonomy, however, is contingent on a host of factors within and without the scientific community. The loss of contact is a resource for the scientific community. It signals a symbolic detachment and independence that can be translated into an asset vis-à-vis the state and other societal agencies. Science becomes an authoritative voice in policy matters, or it represents, in ideological and material struggles with other political systems, the openness of society (cf. Mukerji, 1989: 190–203). But this cognitive distance also limits the immediate effectiveness of the "voice of science" in policy matters,[89] and extensive autonomy and independence of science may result in an excessive celebration of "normal" scientific activity and lead to a lack of innovativeness.

From the point of view of nonscientific institutions, the lack of intellectual proximity of the public to scientific knowledge in general, and research fronts in particular, also has both advantages and drawbacks. Selected disaffection with science and technology has always accompanied its development; strong demands and efforts to legislate selectivity in the ways knowledge is implemented and deployed can lead to even stronger disaffections with science, although such a response may be dismissed as part of an antiscience crusade or movement. But the term "antiscience" is vague and brings together a broad range of elements that typically "have in common only that they tend to annoy or threaten those who regard themselves as more enlightened" (Holton, 1992: 104).

But with the emergence of knowledge politics as a contentious field of political activity in advanced societies, the benefits and risks associated with the implementation of novel scientific knowledge will move into the center of public debate and negotiation. Thus, it is very likely that these disputes about the anticipated consequences of discoveries and inventions will form an important base for the development of changing relations between science and the public. Scientists will be forced in increasing numbers to move out of their laboratories and offices and engage in public discourse about the impact of their labor on social relations, forms of life, and our understanding of the former. By the same token, larger segments of the public will engage in debates about science and take advantage of new organizational platforms to become knowledgeable actors contributing to a renegotiation of the boundaries between science and the public domain.

That such an extension of the boundaries of the debate about the social role of science is not entirely new and has long been viewed with some suspicion shows in the exemplary debate that took place at the turn of the last century between the physician Rudolf Virchow and the biologist Rudolf Haeckel. I will briefly explain their dispute in the following section.

The Haeckel-Virchow Controversy

I begin with a lecture given by Rudolf Virchow in September 1877 at the fiftieth Convention of German Natural Scientists and Physicians in Munich, and the demands for the behavior of scientists expressed therein. The lecture is entitled, "The Freedom of Science in the Modern State." This address was Virchow's response to a talk given at the same meeting by Ernst Haeckel, with the title, "The Current Teachings on Development in Relation to Science as a Whole." In it Haeckel described the significance and consequences of "the doctrine of descent" (*Descendenzlehre*)—as it was then called—that is, the theory of evolution, which in his opinion ought to have been part of the lesson plan in all schools.

Regarding the opponents Virchow and Haeckel, perhaps the following brief biographical facts should be mentioned. Rudolf Virchow, physician and anthropologist, was born in 1821 and died at the age of 81 in Berlin. He studied and lived at the university there. In 1849 he became professor of anatomy in Würzburg, but returned in 1856 to the University of Berlin. Virchow was the founder of cellular pathology and advanced almost every aspect of pathological anatomy. Theories regarding inflammation, tumors, embolism and metastasis, tuberculosis, leukemia, diphtheria, etc., were either established or crucially influenced by Virchow. In 1892, fifteen years after his Munich lecture, Virchow, who had been a member of the Imperial German Parliament since 1880 as the founder of the Progressive Party, was elected to the Prussian Parliament. He exercised a decisive influence on the formation of hygiene laws and on social welfare. Politically he was counted among Bismarck's bitterest opponents.

Virchow, however, was not only a physician, but an archaeologist and ethnologist as well. He assisted Heinrich Schliemann, for example, during the excavation of Troy. Virchow was active in the field of physical anthropology, he developed the foundations of cellular pathology, he was instrumental in the creation of a number of medical journals, and he was active in the organization of hospitals and institutions of public health. In the 1880s, Virchow ([1885] 1922) took part in a heated debate about the prospects of acclimatization of white individuals to the climatic conditions of the tropical and subtropical regions, stimulated, of course, by colonization processes under way at the time. Virchow was convinced that any long-term acclimatization of an "alien race" to strange climatic conditions was an impossibility. Based on a variety of more or less well-documented empirical case studies in the contemporary medical and geographic literature, he argued that females, in particular, would find it impossible to adapt. In short, Virchow was one of the most important scientists of his time, and he combined these interests with intensive political activism.

Ernst Haeckel, born at Potsdam in 1834, was a student of Virchow's in Würzburg. He qualified in zoology and became a professor in this discipline in 1865 at the University of Jena, where he remained for forty-three years until 1909. Haeckel was arguably one of the most influential biologists of the late 1800s. He was one of the first scholars in the German-speaking world to endorse Darwin's teachings without reservation. Darwin went on record saying that Haeckel's enthusiastic sanction of his doctrine was crucial for his success in Germany. Haeckel's own research was particularly devoted to the lower forms of marine life. He was the first to draw up a genealogical tree showing the various relations among various types of animals and their common origin. Haeckel's most original contribution was the idea that embryological developments parallel evolutionary development, or that ontogeny reproduces phylogeny (Gould, 1977: 80–81). Haeckel, who died in 1919 at the age of 83, was not satisfied with applying evolutionary theory to zoological issues. He also applied an evolutionary perspective to both philosophical and religious questions. Haeckel was responsible for the introduction into scientific discourse in 1873 of the term "ecology."

Haeckel too was quite visible and influential in public life. The publication of his *Riddle of the Universe (Die Welträtsel)* in 1899, for example, was an enormous success, with more than 100,000 copies of the book sold in the first year of its publication. Haeckel attempted to develop an uncompromising materialist (monistic) worldview that nonetheless allowed for the possibility of atoms having souls and crystals having organic life. Both Haeckel and Virchow shared the strong enthusiasm of their age for taxonomy.

In his debate with Haeckel, Virchow placed the central thesis of his thoughts immediately at the beginning of his remarks; he was of the opinion that the very freedom science had won for itself in the 1870s, if interpreted too broadly by scientists, could trigger a curtailment of this freedom. He wanted to "warn that one ought not arbitrarily continue in just any speculation that may presently be spreading into many areas of science." This warning to the assembled scientists to be circumspect in public had its basis in the differentiation between factual, established, or accepted knowledge and comprehensive speculative ideas that precede the process of development of unalterable knowledge, but which lack the vital property of provability. Virchow argued that the communication of knowledge should be limited to the category of reliable knowledge; knowledge of this type had certain material and intellectual consequences for the "nation," in terms of production, for instance, but also in the lesson plans of the schools.

Virchow (1877: 8) stressed the "boundary between the speculative field of science and the actually acquired and fully determined field." Speculative knowledge should be held back until its "official" certification; then, certainly, it should be published without regard for the consequences. He continued: "There are a number of experiences in the natural sciences which demonstrate how long certain problems are outstanding before it is possible to find their real solution." As an example, he named the theory of *Contagium animatum,* which had appeared as far back as the Middle Ages; yet in the last third of the previous century it could still not be said that "all contagious or even all infectious diseases are caused by living organisms" (Virchow, 1877: 16). "Let us not forget," Virchow (1877: 22) warned his listeners, "that every time it occurs before the eyes of many, that a doctrine that seemed to be certain, well-founded, reliable, that seemed to make a claim to general validity, proves to be mistaken in its vital features or is felt in essential, major schools of thought to be arbitrary and despotic, a great many people lose their faith in science."

This was the reason for his urgently presented demand to strictly limit the public scientific discussion on the topic of the *organic history of development,* meaning of course Darwin's theory. An inappropriate generalization in the area of the theory of evolution would immediately be understood as competition to the creation thesis, thus endangering the freedom of science. Or, and this is a particularly interesting utterance of Virchow's, "Just imagine how the theory of descent appears today in the mind of a socialist!" (1877: 12). To this warning he added the ominous reference, "May the theory of descent not bring us all the terrors that similar theories have actually caused in our neighboring country" (Virchow, 1877: 12). By this, Virchow apparently meant to imply that the Paris Commune received its crucial political-intellectual impetus from the theory of evolution. Speaking in more concrete terms, Virchow conceded that the question of whether man has ancestors among the other vertebrates might indeed be an interesting scientific problem; nonetheless, from the point of view of over a hundred years ago, there was no sign of any fossil of lower human development. Thus he concluded, "We cannot teach, we cannot describe as scientifically demonstrated, that man is descended from the ape or from any other animal" (Virchow, 1877: 31). Consequently, it is important strictly to differentiate between what is taught and what is researched. The public's attention can be drawn to the problems to be researched, but these problems should "not be the subject of teaching without further research." When we teach, Virchow (1877: 29) concluded, "then we must keep to those rather small and yet already so great areas that we truly command." Not speculative knowledge, not knowledge that the problems exist, but only what Virchow (1877: 32) described as "objective, factual knowledge," may be communicated to the public. In other words, Virchow praised caution, self-restraint, and circumspection as especially worthy virtues of the scientist, to be sanctioned in the scientific community itself. If science did not conform to this norm, it would not only misuse, but also endanger, its power. "Let us resign ourselves," Virchow (1877: 29) continued, "that we shall always put forward even those problems that are most dear to us as mere problems, but then say over and over again: Do not take this for the established truth, be prepared to accept that it may change; only for the moment are we of the opinion, *it could be so.*" Only if scientists keep strictly to this ethos of "reasonable renunciation" (as one representative of the press put it) do they have a chance to hold their own against their opponents in society, the church, and politics.

The public reaction to Virchow's speech was varied and complex. Ernst Haeckel published a reply in the following year under the title, "Science and its Teaching are Free (Article 152 of the Constitution of the German Empire)." In this reply, Haeckel (1888: 3) stamped Virchow as an enemy of scientific freedom and asked rhetorically: How can "a Virchow of all people, under the banner of political liberalism, and wrapped in the mantle of rigorous science, resolutely combat the freedom of science and its teaching?" In short, Haeckel interpreted Virchow's request for the scientists' circumspection not as a defense of academic freedom, but rather as a demand for the abolition of academic freedom. A part of his rhetoric, however, was also the reproach of incompetence, for Haeckel charged that Virchow was ignorant of the most important principles of the theory of evolution and that he was therefore "incompetent" to pass judgment (Haeckel, 1888: 71). In other words, it can already be seen in this dispute that scientific knowledge is only seldom, if ever, free of room for interpretation; this leeway can be seen—in the view of science— as a precondition for the growth of scientific knowledge. From the perspective of external control and regulation of knowledge, these qualities are of course more likely to be serious obstacles, because they simply make more difficult the precise definition of that which is to be subject to control measures.

The vehemence with which Haeckel identified Virchow as an enemy of scientific freedom was directly related to his firm conviction of the scientific accuracy of the theory of evolution, particularly since the competing alternative theories, in his opinion, required an unambiguous decision between the scientific theory of natural development and religious faith in a supernatural creation of the species. The major part of Haeckel's response was therefore also a defense of the general theory of evolution and the reliability of the facts that speak for it.

The conflict of opinions regarding the scientific status of the theory of descent was therefore described by Haeckel (1888: 68) as follows: "The only difference in our opinions is merely this—that Virchow believes the theory of descent to be unproven and unprovable, whereas I consider it a fully proven and indispensable theory." This statement of Haeckel's was certainly not correct on one point. Virchow did indeed consider the theory of evolution as yet unproven, but he did not—as Haeckel assumed—deny the possibility that it might someday achieve this status. This fine distinction was obscured in the heat of polemics. Virchow was denounced by Haeckel as an open adherent of "creationism."

Haeckel then addressed the circumspection that Virchow demanded of scientists in their teaching and asked how compelling the border was that Virchow saw as existing between objective and subjective knowledge. Haeckel stressed categorically that there was no such demarcation, and that it would be more appropriate to conceive of human knowledge in general as *subjective* knowledge: "An objective science that consists of nothing but facts, without subjective theories, is simply inconceivable. . . . The subjective cognitive abilities of man can recognize the objective 'facts' of the external world only so far as his sensory organs and his brain in their individual development permit" (Haeckel, 1888: 52–53). Haeckel worked this thesis out in detail and attempted to establish its relevance in physics, chemistry, and other natural sciences. Anthropology (which Virchow, as Haeckel put it in his speech, "particularly goes in for at present") and ethnology, in contrast, were still largely dependent on speculative knowledge. This was also true for political science and philosophy. Haeckel (1888: 69) believed that for these reasons, but even more from considerations of principle, the conclusion of the debate with Virchow could only be: "Science has either complete freedom or it has none at all." And that was also true for the closely intertwined research and teaching in the sciences.

To Virchow's rather ambivalent reproach that the theory of evolution might be misused politically by the Social Democrats, Haeckel answered with reference to the contradiction between the theory of evolution and social democratic goals: "More clearly than any other scientific theory, it is the theory of descent which preaches that the equality of individuals for which socialism strives is an impossibility that is in irreconcilable contradiction with the actual ubiquitous and necessary inequality of individuals" (Haeckel, 1888: 72). In other words, sociopolitical measures cannot abolish the natural inequality among human beings. He wondered, of course, whether social democratic or socialist programs of any kind would have formulated demands of this sort. According to Haeckel, Darwinism could in any case be politically useful only for the aristocrat. Nonetheless, Haeckel's actual conclusion from Virchow's reference to the political consequences of scientific theory was the affirmation of the unambiguous differentiation of the function of science from politics or other social systems. He emphasized that the scientist "alone has the task of searching for truth, and of teaching what he has acknowledged as truth, without regard for the consequences that may be drawn, for instance, by the various parties of state and church" (Haeckel, 1888: 77).

Intellectual disputes and debates about the social implications of new knowledge, discoveries, and inventions are fascinating, especially if they are moved into the pubic domain and are affected in their development by the ways in which they resonate with the state of politics and the culture of a society at the time. However, knowledge politics is a new form of responding to and dealing with novel knowledge, in that society experiments with new ways and methods of embedding these disputes in domains outside of the scientific community.

Notes

1. In the strict sense of my conception of knowledge politics, copyright law, for example, is not a tool of the governance of new knowledge, since intellectual property rights pertain to knowledge and information that is already on the "market." Copyright and patent laws originally designed to provide incentive for innovation may well have become "bloated" in some countries, as Lessig (2001) argues in the case of the United States, but they were not designed to prevent ideas from reaching the marketplace. The enlargement of the reach of copyright laws—for example, by restricting the ways in which available intellectual products may be utilized—could prevent the production of new artifacts and ideas and slow the tempo with which novel products come to the market. The creation of new knowl-

edge thrives on existing knowledge. The pressure that is brought to bear on lawmakers and the courts to enlarge copyright proscriptions does not originate so much with the original authors, composers, or artists of a text, song, or picture, but with the secondary users, for example, publishing companies of various sorts.

2. For example, legislation that extends export controls on armaments from hardware to intangible goods is currently (2002) before the British Parliament. The aim of the *Export Control Bill,* as outlined in its introduction, is to "make provision enabling controls to be imposed on the exportation of goods, the transfer of technology, the provision of technical assistance overseas and activities connected with trade in controlled goods; and for connected purposes." As defined in the Export Control Bill, "'technology' means information (including information comprised in software)." While the bill is seen by the government as an additional weapon in its fight against international terrorism, critics view the proposed law as being so widely drawn that it would provide ministers with the power to review and suppress any scientific paper prior to its publication, and to license foreign students (not just at British universities, but students taught by U.K. nationals anywhere in the world); see Ashley Benigno, "Knowledge Transfer Controls and Academic Freedom," http://www.heise.de/tp/english/inhalt/te/12191/1.html.

3. Examinations of science and technology policies that aim to promote the utilization of new technological developments and scientific discoveries, including the transfer of new technologies from one area, such as space or military research, to the civilian sector, are plentiful (e.g., Berkowitz, 1970; Nelkin, 1977: 404–406). Similarly, studies of the recalcitrance of established patterns of social action against social change, and the resistance to innovation, are relevant to science and technology policies that hope to enlarge the options available for new technologies or knowledge (e.g., Schon, 1967).

4. For a critique of Fuller's project of social epistemology, see Rouse (1991).

5. Presumably, the raison d'etre of eugenics is the individual sacrifice in the alleged interest of a future collectivity. However, this hardly applies to the practice of eugenics by the Nazis. The Nazis practiced the sacrifice of individuals as determined by the "collectivity."

6. See Matt Ridley, "We've never had it so good—and it's all thanks to science," *Guardian,* April 3, 2003; and Ridley, 2003.

7. Leon R. Kass, testimony before the American Bioethics Advisory Commission (a body established by the American Life League to defend "the human being, his innate dignity, and his unique nature"), March 14, 1997 (see the website of the ABAC).

8. A useful, skeptical discussion of the possibilities and impediments of human "genetic enhancement"—in the context of fearful predictions or excessive promises made on behalf of such "procedures"—may be found in the testimony of Steven Pinker before the U.S. Biothethics Commission; see the transcript of the March 6, 2003, session: *www.bioethics.gov/transcripts/march03/session3.html.*

9. Many respected scientists maintain that human genetic *engineering* may never be practical and safe because most human traits as far as they are determined or codetermined by our genetic makeup are the result of the action of multiple genes. The action of multiple genes leads to a combinatorial explosion and therefore a vast array of relevant potential interactions (see also "Better babies? Why genetic enhancement is too unlikely to worry about," *Boston Globe,* June 1, 2003).

10. Hollingsworth and Lindberg (1985: 221–222) define the function of "governance" in the economic system as the solution to different types of contingent coordination problems faced by economic actors as well as in the relations between economy and environment. Coordination problems include the problems of setting the prices of commodities and services, the determination of the volume of production, the relation between workers

and management, the allocation of the factors of production, the conditions that govern competition, etc. The enumeration of these coordination activities makes it evident that governance refers in a most general sense to coordination and communication tasks that all social entities have to perform. For the most part, economists maintain that the institution of the self-adjusting market is the most efficient economic governance mechanism and that the market ought to be the norm for solutions to the coordination of communication and exchange. Other social scientists emphasize the importance of coordinating mechanisms alternative to the market (Hollingsworth and Boyer, 1997). Changes in governance regimes in the economic system are attributed to shifting economic transformations—for example, variations in the demand and price of production factors, the efficient composition of production factors, and matters that inhibit firms from operating efficiently (see Campbell and Lindberg, 1985).

11. Comparative studies dealing with environmental policies may be found in research carried out by Rabe and Lowry, 1999; Nivola, 1997; and Vogel, 1986.

12. Regulatory activities of the state that pertain to the environment are mostly of recent origin, but some legal provisions may be traced back as far as the fourteenth century—to efforts to control pollution in England (Brimblecombe, 1987: 90–122; Lowenthal, 1990: 121), and to game laws that originated in 1769 in the United States (Andrews, 1999).

13. See "Kansas votes to delete evolution from state's science curriculum," *New York Times,* national ed., August 12, 1999.

14. At present, aside from local school boards in the United States, the state of Alabama maintains its distinction as the only *state* in the United States where biology textbooks include a sticker on the cover, warning students that evolution is a "controversial theory" that they should approach critically ("Alabama retains disclaimer on evolution," *New York Times,* November 10, 2001). I will return to the matter of the Kansas Board of Education's decision in a later chapter.

15. A discussion of the gene therapy experiment by Avigen Inc. may be found in "Gene experiment comes close to crossing ethicist's line," *New York Times,* December 23, 2001. According to a report in the *Guardian* ("Pioneering gene treatment gives frail toddler a new lease on life," April 4, 2002), An "18–month-old boy has successfully undergone pioneering gene therapy to correct a potentially fatal bone marrow condition that left his frail body incapable of fighting infection. Rhys Evans, a toddler unaware of his place in British medical history, is the first recipient in this country of a treatment that scientists hope will pave the way for conquering a host of other diseases, from hemophilia to cancers and cystic fibrosis . . . Tests [had] ... revealed he was the victim of a faulty gene, called gamma c, believed to be responsible for a failure of the immune system."

16. Cited after John D. Bernal (1939: 2).

17. I am referring in particular to the now well-established social science analysis of the phenomenon of "professionalization" (see Derber, 1982; Freidson, 1983, 1994; Rueschemeyer, 1986), the emergence of knowledge-bearing elites (e.g., the intelligentsia; see Gouldner, 1979; Konrad and Szlenyi, 1979), the growing stratum of "experts" in modern societies (Bruce-Briggs, 1979; Stehr, 1992b), and the persistent function of everyday and indigenous knowledge even in the age of modernity (Dei, Hall, and Rosenberg, 2000).

18. Carl B. Feldbaum is the president of the Biotechnology Industry Organization (BIO), which has as its members 950 biotechnology companies in the United States and thirty-three other countries. The quote may be found in the opening address delivered by Feldbaum on the occasion of the "BIO 2001" convention in San Diego, California, in June 2001 (see "Es wäre unmenschlich, das Wissen zu verbieten," *Frankfurter Allgemeine Zeitung,* June 28, 2001, p. 48).

19. Cited in Jackie Stevens, "PR for the 'book of life,'" *Nation,* December 10, 2001. See also the analysis of "molecular metaphors" by Dorothy Nelkin (2001b) and her examination of the euphoric language of hope found in the media discussions of gene therapy (Nelkin, 2001a).

20. "Wohin mit dem Homunkulus," *Welt am Sonntag,* July 8, 2001, p. 37.

21. The field of molecular biology, the parent discipline of biotechnology, was until 1972 (when the possibility of genetic engineering by recombinant DNA techniques was discovered), almost without exception an academic field of research with few, if any, practical applications (see Wright, 1986a; Krimsky, 1995).

22. The reference to "techniques of genetic engineering" raises the question of whether the differences in the contents of science and technology, otherwise strictly defended (e.g. Pavitt, 1987), are in fact vanishing, and whether they are still relevant for an examination of knowledge politics. At least in some fields, such as molecular biology, biochemistry, and solid state physics, as some would observe (e.g., Dasgupta and David, 1986), the boundaries between science and technology are increasingly blurred. Pavitt (1987: 197) acknowledges that in the case of biotechnology patents and biomedical research, science and technology are very close. In other fields, technology largely builds on technology. In general, we are facing what might be called a moving target, and attempts to fix the boundaries between science and technology are bound to be surpassed by practical developments that will not be constrained by terminological debates.

23. I do not see the emergence of modern knowledge politics as evidence of a backlash against the dominance of "rationalist" thinking and discourse in science as well as mundane reasoning, and therefore as a resurgence of traditional thought, such as "magic, ritual, and superstition," in modern institutions.

24. The firm conviction that a decline of privacy in modern society is primarily a function of advancing *technology* as well as gains in the size and the complexity of social systems is a disparaging observation that has been raised various times in the past century (e.g., Rovere [1958] 1963: 68).

25. Current discussions of the threats to and erosion of privacy in modern societies tend to focus on the nature of the alleged violations (Scarf, 2001), the role of the state in surveillance (Margalit, 2001), the legal construction of privacy (Schauer, 2001), whether privacy is still possible in modern societies (e.g., Berman and Bruening, 2001), and, of course, on what massive invasions of privacy may mean for the individual citizen (Rosen, 2001). One aspect that tends to be neglected in current debates about the decline of privacy, but which in my view is quite significant, was raised by Heinrich Popitz (1968). It concerns the role of "imperfect" information about fellow human actors as a condition of social life; that is, as Popitz (1968: 6) stipulates, "reciprocal insights into each other's conduct is a condition for the possibility of social life only if such information remains *incomplete*" (emphasis added). And, one might add, incomplete and diverse information about other actors could well be a prerequisite for the possibility of social transformation.

26. "Scientists support modified crop tests," *International Herald Tribune,* September 18, 2003.

27. "Monsanto greenhouse destroyed," *Associated Press,* September 12, 2003.

28. An earlier referendum on biotechnology in Switzerland in May of 1992 that involved amendments to the constitution, formulated by the Federal Assembly, passed with a large majority of the votes cast. The amendments guarantee, on the one hand, the continued development of biotechnology and reproductive medicine, but on the other hand, they enact regulations that are supposed to prevent the misuse of biotechnical applications (Buchmann, 1995).

29. Since social scientists to this day rarely contribute points of view to the debate over the social implications of molecular genetics referring to *beneficial* aspects, an important exception should be noted, namely Novas and Rose's (2000) observation that modern genetics introduces new and active relations to oneself and one's future.

30. David Goslin (1985: 10–11) raises the issue of the limit of the capacity of *societies* to incorporate new knowledge, but acknowledges that it is impossible to answer such a question. Ian Hacking (1990), following Crombie (1961), on the other hand, refers to a *limited* set of tools available to scientists and other *individuals* to store and analyze *information*.

31. As a result, Ogburn and Nimkoff (1947: 529) refer to the *exponential principle* in the growth of culture, for the dynamics of the "growth" of culture are a function of the body of accumulated knowledge.

32. As Ogburn and Nimkoff (1947: 595–596) admit, "If the change in the variable precipitating changes in other variables could be foreseen and prevented, the maladjustment could be avoided. But such a course of action requires a high degree of planning and control. The truth and the seriousness of the lags due to prior changes in science is admitted when it is suggested that a moratorium on mechanical invention be declared until the lags of society have caught up; but so far the suggestion has not been acted upon."

33. In the United States, it was Vannevar Bush, an analog computer scientist and science policy advocate, who alerted the country in 1945 to the "dangers" of an information crisis in the form of information overload, and who triggered a debate about excessive dissemination of information or "overpublication" in science, for example.

34. Cf. Moore and Tumin (1949) on the "social functions" of "ignorance," Merton's (1957: 344) reference to "excessive knowledge," or the essay by Popitz (1968) on the social functions of the essential limits in access to information—total transparency—about other individuals. See also Smithson (1985), who points out that early discussions of ignorance were often based on an absolutist epistemology. Ignorance is socially constructed.

35. As Kitch (1983: 684) explains, since 1800 in Anglo-American law no protection is granted to firms for the value of the human capital of its employees. However, these provisions "displaced an earlier legal regime, centered on the Statute of Laborers of 1492, which significantly restricted the free movement of labor." Voluntary contractual arrangements that would amount to postemployment restraints can be used, of course, to protect the knowledge assets of a firm, as far as these tend to be embedded in human capital. U.S. courts have applied "strict standards of reasonableness to these contracts and have upheld them only in the case of employees who possess secret technical information or who have customer contact responsibility" (Kitch, 1983: 685). On the other hand, in some cases, such as those of entertainment executives or professional athletes, restraints are commonly accepted and enforced.

36. Historians of technology, in their analysis of modern control systems, their origins and justifications, stress that the belief that it is "possible to extend the scale and scope of control to maximize the material and social benefits of human labor for all members of society dates from the Enlightenment" (Levin, 2000: 13). In other words, it is argued, the major goals of modern technological control systems as a master theme in the history of industrial society aim for coordinated systems that aid in generating and sustaining economic prosperity (see Beniger, 1986).

37. Dorothy Nelkin (1995: 447–456) has published an informative typology of public controversies in which the scientific community was embroiled in recent years in the United States.

38. Steve Fuller (1993: 377) advances a similar assertion, as far as I can see. He indicates that "in the world of tomorrow, breakthroughs in the natural sciences are regarded as

triumphs of applied sociology and political economy, rather than of, say theoretical physics, chemistry, or biology." It is better understood that the implementation of a specific knowledge claim can alter the social fabric of society, and the anticipated transformation is no longer seen as mainly beneficial.

39. A prominent scientific field that represents a possible exception to the idea that scientific knowledge is a model for reality is cosmology. As Hans Jonas (1979: 36), for example, observes, "The expanding universe, the evolution of galaxies, the big bang and black holes—these are matters for knowing only and for no possible doing on our part." Perhaps cosmology is a scientific field of inquiry that ought to be located within the humanities, inasmuch as its practicality may be found in the intellectual realm. The "practicality" of cosmology for society is that of a source of metaphors, images, and figures.

40. A further example of the emerging relations among social institutions and the breakdown of what once may well have been strong boundaries between social systems is discussed in Chapter 4 of this book. It examines the growing significance of ethical considerations and reference points in the context of economic decision-making both by consumers and producers that amount, as I will observe, to a "moralization of the market."

41. An earlier version of this section appeared November 8, 2000, in the *Frankfurter Allgemeine Zeitung,* p. 67.

42. John von Neumann, Hearing before the Senate Special Committee on Atomic Energy, Seventy-Ninth Congress, Second Session, 206, p. 1717 (as cited in Green, [1978] 1979: 115).

43. The same political discussion about the "moral" status of nuclear science prompted John Dewey ([1927] 1954: 231), in his afterword written in July of 1946 to *The Public and Its Problems,* to warn that there are those who employ the evils (of the physical sciences) "that are apparent as a ground for the subjection of science to what they take to be moral ideals and standards ... The net outcome of their position, were it adopted, would not be the subordination of science to ideal moral aims ... but the production of political despotism with all the moral evils which attend that mode of social organization."

44. Another example of a restriction of research activities imposed by external regulation and encouraged by scientists concerns the case of the emerging technology of laser enrichment of uranium, as demanded by the physicist Barry Casper in 1977. There was still time, he argued, to stop and consider whether laser enrichment should be developed. A moratorium on such research would obviously not occur if the decision was left exclusively to those promoting the technology. Although laser isotope separation was not the only avenue to nuclear proliferation, laser-enriched uranium offered a new and dangerous path to the proliferation of nuclear weapons by making possible small clandestine facilities for the production of nuclear bombs (Casper, 1977). In the wake of the discovery of the technique of in vitro fertilization (IVF) in Britain, to mention a further case, a vigorous public debate ensued about scientific research on human IVF embryos. Even though such research ultimately received parliamentary approval, it came close to being banned by law. The embryo research that was sanctioned, however, was subject to strict control (Mulkay, 1997).

45. The constitutional legal scholar Harold Green ([1977] 1997: 141) points out that he has no doubt that the Cambridge City Council had the right to impose restrictions: "A city's prohibition against recombinant DNA molecule experiments within city limits does not violate any constitutionally protected right of scientific inquiry where the city may rationally—even though perhaps not reasonably—have believed that such experiments might endanger the health and the safety of the public."

46. As Dorothy Nelkin (1978b: 193) has pointed out, negotiations, as an exchange of conditional promises and threats, are affected by mutually valued resources that the parties

bring to the negotiation process. The interaction between science policies and the demand for knowledge policies becomes evident in such negotiations as public ambivalence—declining trust and growing concerns about the risks and dangers associated with the consequences of new knowledge—devalues the resource that science—in the form of the desirable results of research—is able to bring to the table.

47. In this respect, social and natural scientists are often in unusually strong agreement. Take, for example, the vigorous stipulation by Robert S. Lynd (1939: 249) in his classic treatise *Knowledge for What?* Lynd warns that "social science cannot perform its function if the culture constrains it at certain points in ways foreign to the spirit of science; and at all points where such constraints limit the free use of intelligence to pose problems, to analyze all relevant aspects of them, or to draw conclusions, it is necessary for social science to work directly to remove the causes of the obstacles."

48. The enlargement of the scientific community into an international or even global community is becoming a focus of reflection and research in science studies (e.g., Schott, 1988; 1993).

49. Heinrich Rohrer, "Nanotechnik—Versprechen und Ängste. Soll man den technischen Fortschritt wegen seiner möglichen Folgen aufhalten?" *Neue Zürcher Zeitung,* October 13, 2001. Rohrer was the recipient of the Nobel Prize for Physics in 1986 (jointly with Gerd Binnig) for their discovery of the scanning tunneling microscope.

50. See Hans Blumenberg's ([1966] 1983: 229–453) enlightening and extensive discussion of the nature and transformation of theoretical curiosity. In its most recent incarnation, "curiosity cannot produce from itself any criterion for its restriction" (Blumenberg, ([1966] 1983: 411).

51. Rohrer's plea in favor of science pursued for its own sake, free of outside intervention and regulation, echoes among other disputes the debates between Michael Polanyi ([1946] 1964) and J.D. Bernal (1939) and their followers prior to World War Two about the necessity for "social guidance to the progress of science" (see Rose and Appignanesi, 1986) or the desirability of the self-governance of science. The debate continues. The appeal that scientific research ought to be linked "more closely to the societal results that we want to achieve" (Crow, 2001) is heard both from within the scientific community and the political system, as well as the claim that judgments about scientific conduct should fall solely under the jurisdiction of the scientific community.

52. See David Bee's testimony to the U.K. BSE Inquiry: http://www.bse.org.uk/transcripts/tr980310c.pdf

53. The current American president is on record as supporting "equal time" for creationism or, as its followers prefer, creation science and Darwinian ideas in U.S. school curricula. The term "creation science" is not only designed to benefit from whatever prestige and deference science enjoys but is also intended to preempt any charge that religious ideas might enter the public school curriculum and thereby run up against the constitutional prohibition on established religion in public schools.

54. Paul Feyerabend's philosophical views on the nature of science in general, and his ideas about democratizing the use of scientific knowledge, have not gone without vigorous opposition from scientists. The physicists Theocharis and Psimopoulos (1987: 596), for example, in a commentary in *Nature,* identify Feyerabend as the "worst enemy of science" and as the Salvador Dali of academic philosophy. One suspects that Feyerabend would have liked both compliments.

55. When it comes to the relation between the public and science in advanced societies, Steven Shapin (1992) advocates a probably more realistic, more pragmatic, and more effective approach that is not based, as far as I can see, on the premise that all cognitive

traditions are equal in democratic societies. Shapin suggests that the public ought to be enlightened about science-in-the-making, enabling them to achieve a more informed understanding of the nature of scientific knowledge claims.

56. The regulation or stratification of access to knowledge and information is nonetheless a constitutive component of everyday life. The world of adults, for example, is differentiated from that of children. These stratified worlds go hand in hand with the ability to impede, or even to obstruct, children's access to certain forms of knowledge. The quotidian forms of regulating access to knowledge are not under discussion here. The American Civil Liberties Union contests, in the name of seven libraries, eight librarians, and nine Internet sites, the constitutionality of the "Children's Internet Protection Act" (the text of the CIPA may be found at: http://www.ala.org/cipa/Law.PDF). According to the CIPA, libraries will not receive any federal funds after 2002 unless they have installed measures to keep minors from accessing Internet pages that are "harmful" to minors. Two previous laws designed to protect children from pornography on the Internet have already been declared unconstitutional.

57. Contemplating the increase in legal and administrative constraints placed on the autonomy of inquiry in science and the annoying change in political attitudes to scientists, Don Price (1978: 75) laments that in the United States "members of Congress now tend to look on them as just another selfish pressure group, and not as the wizards of perpetual progress."

58. Whether public willingness to support the field of knowledge politics will intensify in spite of, or because of, what some scientists have labeled a "comprehension gap" among the population at large, or whether this disposition will have any significance at all, remains to be seen. In a lead article, the English Sunday paper the *Observer* (February 21, 1999, p. 28) describes the perceived wide comprehension gap as follows: "Between the scientific upper class, the latter-day Leonardos trekking into the brain or sketching the universe, and the majority of voters and politicians in all Western democracies, there is now a deep comprehension gap." But it should not be overlooked that such a comprehension deficit or knowledge gap exists, of course, among members of the scientific community as well. Given the growing division of labor among or fragmentation within and among scientific disciplines and research fields, it is as likely that a top scientist will display a considerable comprehension deficit with respect to neighboring, let alone more distant disciplines, as it is that a layperson will display a similar knowledge gap (Moffat, 1993).

59. A shift toward concerns with the externalities of science does not mean that contested efforts to regulate the conduct of "scientific inquiry" (see Wulff, 1979) or, for that matter, attempts to manage or plan scientific research (e.g., van den Daele, Krohn and Weingart, 1979) will disappear. On the contrary, issues of ethics, accountability, and conflict, as they relate to the genesis and execution of inquiry, will of course remain highly significant. At the same time, discussions about the conduct of inquiry will be affected by anticipated outcomes of research (cf. also the following section on the social assessment of science).

60. The public challenge by Erwin Chargaff in 1975 and 1976 to guidelines for recombinant DNA research developed by the research community without external intervention may have been instrumental in bringing public attention to the discussion of biohazards among biologists (see Chargaff, 1975; 1976).

61. In an essay analyzing the contending forces that affect the allocation of support for the fabrication of social science knowledge in the U.S. National Science Foundation, Larsen (1985: 14) observes that "*the expected uses of social science knowledge* have in a variety of ways led to effective control of opportunities to extend that knowledge" (emphasis added).

62. The decisions taken by the female (the consumer of medical care) and her expectations of the heath care system, the hospitals, and the physicians in light of available techniques to determine the risks associated with pregnancy are major factors in the diffusion, acceptance, and routinized use of such techniques, as legal decisions in the United States demonstrate in which women have successfully sued for damages because of the absence of amniocentesis, for example (Cowan, 1993). In Europe, the influence of the legal system in this context is much less important and relevant. In some regions of the world, the gender of the embryo counts among the risks of pregnancy that are determined with the help of ultrasonic examinations and amniocentesis. Female embryos are aborted.

63. Fanconi anemia is a rare disease; it is inherited and shows up in children aged 4 to 12. The probability that the relevant gene is inherited from both parents varies for different ethnic groups. Under the term "familial, infantile pernicious-like anemia," Fanconi first described a fatal disorder in three brothers, characterized by pancytopenia, bone marrow hypoplasia, and congenital anomalies. The disorder is characterized by a variable clinical picture consisting of pancytopenia, skeletal abnormalities, neurological and endocrine disorders, chromosomal instability, and a heightened risk of leukemia and other cancers. The only "curative" therapy to date has been bone marrow transplantation.

64. An extensive documentation of the case in question may be found in the *New York Times Magazine* of July 1, 2001 ("The made-to-order savior: Producing a perfect baby sibling").

65. The extent to which these issues already are highly contested public issues can be gleaned from the support in the United States for embryo stem cell research by individual states, foundations, hospitals, universities, and companies despite the restriction the federal government issued in 2001 limiting the federal monies available for embryonic stem cell research ("Broad movement is backing embryo stem cell research," *New York Times,* March 16, 2003).

66. See www.zdf.de/ratgeber/aktuell/monalisa/39501/index.html.

67. A quarter of a century ago, Louise Brown became famous as the first human conceived outside the body. Today, she is alive and well and working as a nursery school aide in England. In the United States, approximately 1 percent of all live births in 2000 were born as the result of IVF ("At 25, in vitro fertilization has come of age," *International Herald Tribune,* July 17, 2003).

68. In 1944 three American geneticists (Avery, MacLeod, and McCarty) discovered the location of cellular genetic information storage: deoxyribonucleic acid (DNA). Nine years later Watson, Crick, and Wilkins announced a model of the helical nature of DNA structure. The DNA strand in a human cell is not all in one piece. In time, cell biologists discovered forty-six DNA pieces, then named chromosomes. Each normal human cell has a complete set of twenty-three pairs of chromosomes (one chromosome of each pair derived from the female parent, one from the male parent). In the course of human sexual reproduction a female egg cell (oocyte) fuses with a male sperm (spermatocyte). These specialized cells contain only one set of chromosomes to ensure a constant number of chromosomes in succeeding generations and to facilitate genetic recombination. The newly formed cell is called a zygote and starts to divide itself: first from one to two cells (after thirty hours), then to four cells (after forty to fifty hours). The eight-cell stage is called the morula, and the eight cells are called blastomeres. Experiments have shown that each of these blastomeres, once removed from the morula, still has the capability to develop into a normal embryo (thus creating an identical twin). More important for genetic engineering, removal of one of the blastomeres does not endanger the development of the original organism. In later developmental stages, each cell takes over specialized functions, and removal

leads to the development of an incomplete (mostly nonfunctional) organism. The zygote continues to divide itself while traveling down the Fallopian tube and reaches the uterus after about six days (by then consisting of over one hundred single cells).

69. The first child born in France after the application of the P.G.D. technique was born at the end of the year 2000; see *Die Zeit,* May 23, 2001, "Nah am britischen Vorbild. Ein Gespräch mit dem Pariser Gynäkologen René Frydman über die französische Biopolitik." Within the countries of the European Union, the technique of pre-implantation diagnosis is permitted in ten of the fifteen member countries: Finland, Sweden, Denmark, United Kingdom, Belgium, France, Spain, Italy, and Greece. The technique is illegal in Austria, Ireland, Luxembourg, Germany, and Portugal—as well as Switzerland.

70. I have adapted the following discussion of risks and dangers from a lecture, "The communication of risks and the risks of communicating scientific knowledge," written jointly with Gotthard Bechmann and presented first to the Ninth Annual Meeting of the Society of Environmental Toxicology and Chemistry (Europe), Leipzig, May 1999. I am grateful for Gotthard Bechmann's permission to use part of the lecture in this study.

71. It is not necessary, at least in retrospect, to dismiss technology assessment as a handmaiden of capitalist society and a wholly ideological enterprise to prop up the faltering legitimacy of that very regime (cf. Wynne, 1975: 111–112). This assigns too much credit to what turns out to be a rather mundane, optimistic, and in practice rather ineffective rhetoric about systemic ability to regulate and control social processes in modern society, under whatever auspices.

72. In the context of such discussions, the development of technology is seen as a largely exogenous process driven by inherent necessities of technical and scientific development. (For a critique of such views, see Holt, 1977.)

73. The 1970 panel of the U.S. National Academy of Sciences that investigated the desirability of a national "Technology Assessment Board" and the possibilities of technology assessment coupled their inquiry into the basic assumption that the "advances of technology have yielded benefits that on the whole vastly outweigh the injuries they have caused" (Brooks and Bowers, 1970: 13).

74. Efforts are currently under way, however, to resurrect the Office of Technology Assessment. Rep. Rush Holt (R-NJ) introduced such a bill on June 13, 2001. (The text of the bill to reestablish the Office of Technology Assessment may be found at http://thomas.loc.gov/cgi-bin/bdquery/z?d107: h.r.02148.)

75. The considerable interest in and the productive hopes for value added from the practice of knowledge management has led to the establishment of knowledge management offices in many enterprises and public sector organizations, as well as the creation of the "knowledge management officer."

76. There can be little doubt that the production and reproduction (for example, the dissemination) of knowledge are subject to processes and capacities that are largely symmetrical, assuring that comparable "constraints" affect both the fabrication and the replication of knowledge. Thus, in the context of studies of the notion of knowledge management, it is appropriate to ask, as Steve Fuller (2001) does, what influence efforts in the field of knowledge management in corporations have on the fabrication of knowledge in that organization (see also Stigler, 1980: 640–641). But it may nevertheless be sensible to suggest that the production and the dissemination of knowledge are separable; there are, for example, certain discontinuities in the production and reproduction of knowledge. Among these discontinuities are not only the kind of intellectual capital that has to be mobilized, or the different occupations roles and functions assigned, but also the temporal frame (if innovations are considered) or the special difficulties that any reproduction of knowledge may

present (see the section on the "Self-Protection of Knowledge" in Ch. 1). Moreover, the ethics of employing what one knows (for example, a physician who knows how to treat a particular disease being required to use this knowledge) and the ethics of rejecting the application of what one knows can be sensibly separated.

77. Although I will not explicate the idea in detail, I should emphasize that productive knowledge claims also resonate with social and cultural peculiarities—not only because productive knowledge may originate among the social and cultural sciences, where issues of legitimacy appear to be a self-evident matter, but also in the case of knowledge fabricated by the natural sciences. In the case of the natural sciences, the context of augmenting knowledge prior to use, for example, is both affected by social assumptions, such as the needs of potential users, and subsequently subjected to moral and ethical considerations. In addition, the legitimacy of knowledge includes, as Irwin and Wynne (1996: 214), for example, observe, its "accessibility and accountability, whether it implies empowerment or disempowerment of social actors, and its consistency or otherwise with relevant cultural idioms."

78. In a knowledge-based economy, the advantages that may be gained from *additional* productive knowledge are narrower than in the economy of industrial society, where the cycle that begins with invention and ends in obsolescence took years, at times even decades to complete; this cycle now takes months, weeks, or even days.

79. The concept of knowledge as a capacity for action signals that the operative difference is not between knowledge and non-knowledge but rather between knowledge and action knowledge. Action knowledge is equivalent to productive knowledge (see Stehr, 1992a).

80. Epstein (1996: 346) concludes, assessing the impact of the interventions by uncredentialed participants in biomedical research and in AIDS care, that "the impact of the AIDS movement on biomedical institutions in the United States has been impressive and conspicuous ... [and] it has rapidly become something of a cliché to say that the doctor-patient relationship will never be the same in the wake of AIDS."

81. Despite these qualifications, Werner Sombart (1934: xii) leaves hardly any doubt that his sympathies are with the new National Socialist regime: He emphasizes, for example, that he relies in his monograph on a unified approach to social problems of his day and that this perspective betrays the world view of National Socialism. He stresses at the same time that one should not be misled and count on the practical ineffectiveness of theoretical reflections. Those who reject the practical usefulness of theoretical reflections underestimate the power of ideas. It is likely no accident, moreover, that Sombart's proposal for a commission on cultural affairs was made at the outset of the Nazi era. It is safe to assume that Sombart was convinced that his idea of a regulative introduction or a state-sponsored prohibition of new technical developments would find a favorable response from Nazi politicians.

82. In an emotionally charged address to the city council of Breslau, Germany, which received notice well beyond the boundaries of the city, Sombart, who was a member of council (first elected in 1896) and a professor at the University of Breslau, argued vehemently against an extension of the streetcar system into the middle-class suburbs of the city. His speech to the city council is of interest because his address reflects and is based on his fundamental critique of modern technology and against an extension of the mass-culture features of modern urban life: "For wherever we might have a lovely square in Breslau, let there also be a restaurant, often with noise; with concerts morning, noon, and night; with a double concerto; even with American swings, dice-booths, carousels and the barrel-organs that go with them; as if one wanted to set [Hamburg's] St. Pauli down in Uhlenhorst, [Vienna's] Prater in the Ringstraße or [Berlin's] Hasenheide in the Tiergarten" (as cited in Lenger, 1994: 59). The reference to the American origin of some of the fair attractions,

found in a subordinate clause of the sentence, is an early indication of the still virulent objection to the global diffusion and dominance of elements of American culture and its technological artifacts. The newspapers of the day quickly discovered that Sombart's opposition was not merely intellectual and political but also interest-based, since his residence was located in that part of the city destined for the extension of the streetcar system.

83. I am using both the English and the German editions of Paul Feyerabend's essay, "Science in a free society" and "Erkenntnis für freie Menschen" because the German text, published later than the English edition, is not a merely a translation of the English version (see Feyerabend, 1980: 7).

84. The need for Feyerabend's demand for democratically organized control is not so much, as he observes, due to the lack of knowledge or the cognitive distance of the average citizen from science, but rather the result of the outright arrogance of scientists. Feyerabend does not trust scientists, or for that matter any other elites in society; he trusts the sensibilities of the average citizen, and insists that in democratic societies they have the right and the responsibility to exercise control over the affairs of the state, including the control of research, education, health care, the prisons and so on (Feyerabend, 1980: 163).

85. The mounting distance between the public and science and the growing fear of science that goes hand-in-hand with such estrangement is, according to Susan Greenfield, the outcome of "jargon and methodology" used by scientists that "more than ever, are raising the wall between the cognoscenti and Everyone Else" ("A new kind of literacy," *Guardian*, April 10, 2003).

86. For a discussion of the essential ambivalence of this term, see Durant, Hansen, and Bauer, 1996.

87. Such a conception of an active public understanding of science resonates with a conception of the "public" as a distinct communication system that comprises speakers, media, and audiences (Neidhardt, 1993), where "lay discourses" are *not* reflections or responses to expert discourses "as perceived through education, the media, the use of artifacts and participation in technological procedures" (Kyrtisis, Koulaidis, and Kouzelis, 1998: 5).

88. A more differentiated examination of the nature of the public's interest in science indicates that the concern with medical science issues occupies a special position. For obvious reasons, the comparative interest of the public in research findings in the field of health and illness is significant, as is the social status granted to the field of medicine (Durant, Evans, and Thomas, 1992). The association of the prospects for genetic therapy with questions of health and illness should also account for the widespread favorable response of the public in different countries to the use of genetic therapy, at least in the early 1990s (e.g., Macer, 1992), as well as the large number of successful popular books that celebrate the promise of the human genome project for medicine (e.g., Wingerson, 1990; Bishop and Waldholz, 1990; Davis, 1991). Similarly, the mass media allocate considerable time and space to issues in medical science. As a result, the public image of medical science is a major source and basis for the general public understanding and image of science in modern societies.

89. Chandra Mukerji (1989: 197) describes the trade-off: "What reassures scientists the most when they face the power of the voice of science and their powerlessness to use the voice in the public arena is the idea of their autonomy. Scientists are not, in the end, politicians, and they suffer political defeats better than the loss of face among their peers. As long as they can conduct research with which they can advance science [both science itself and their positions in it], they can feel potent. But the cost is that scientists cultivate an expertise that empowers someone else."

Chapter 3

Rules, Regulations, and Restrictions

> The empires of the future are the empires of the mind.
>
> *Winston Churchill*[1]

Some may well consider it a paradox that modern society increasingly relies on knowledge, yet is on the verge of investing a lot of its resources into the control of knowledge. Other observers may see developments directed toward the governance of knowledge simply as an extension, and perhaps an enlargement, of the modes of governance that take the form of regulative politics and that have accompanied the evolution of modern society. Indeed, in the course of the development of industrial society, liberal democracies have increasingly institutionalized legal norms that govern the status of labor and property and that limit and determine ever more precisely the ways in which both productive factors can be employed by their owners.

For example, the liberty of individual economic actors to enhance their power on the basis of their individual or collective ownership of the means of production or their labor power is extensively curtailed through many state regulations and self-administered controls. The ability of the owner of the means of production is "spontaneously" constrained not only by market forces, but also by policies of the state, norms of the legal system, and organizations situated within the context of these productive forces. The social control of ownership is not necessarily neutral, because the legal restrictions on ownership do not merely refer to constraints; in the eyes of the nonowners they also mainly involve limitations on the privileges associated with property. The uneven access to the policymaking process of legal norms pertaining to property and labor, and therefore the stratification of the ways of influencing this process, rest on the unequal distribution of the means of production in industrial society. The elaborate legal apparatus surrounding property and labor symbolizes and reflects the unique societal importance of the particular means of production in industrial societies.

The experiences of industrial societies allow for the prognosis that policymaking and legal norm-setting in knowledge societies will turn their attention more and more toward the regulation and control of new knowledge, and, indirectly, the fabrication of knowledge. I stress the control of knowledge by means of legal norms, not only through informal sanctions or self-regulatory measures that are already constitutive of the everyday system of social control of the science system and its societal regulation. Organized opposition to political measures to control and restrict both the use of knowledge and the autonomy of science will be as formidable as the opposition to legal restrictions on the unencumbered use of property in the past, or against laws that aimed to regulate the deployment of labor by the owners of the means of production. But who is to arrive at decisions that affect the use of knowledge in society, and how? Knowledge politics is not a matter of ethics that could be left to ethics committees, but rather of the ways in which collective issues are decided and how these decisions are managed and implemented in democratic societies.

In the context of this section, I therefore want to discuss the possible social and political practices on the basis of which rules and restrictions for the utilization of new knowledge and technical devices could be first articulated, then negotiated and constructed. How can societies best organize the governance of knowledge? Given the embeddedness of such activities, motives, and methods in specific social, political,[2] cultural,[3] and economic contexts,[4] such a discussion is necessarily limited to broader sketches of work-in-progress in efforts to regulate knowledge, to decide the manner in which governance is or can be organized, and to resolve the objections that may typically be voiced against the control of knowledge. In addition, I will refer in more detail to the specific case of bioethics, or the control of the human genome.

I assume, as does Harold Green (1976: 171) in his discussion of law in the area of genetic control, that the courts, for a variety of reasons, will contribute little to resolutions of the question of the governance of knowledge, at least in the Anglo-Saxon world. For example, courts are not well equipped to generate and establish public-policy controls; judges are experts in referring to past values and decisions, but the governance of knowledge initially involves reference to the future; and the enactment of controls is, of course, a legislative function.

Work-in-Progress, or the Development of Social Controls

> In a democracy, the public must be the ultimate arbiter of decisions that affect it, but it is unrealistic and impractical to appeal every issue—especially complex, technically oriented issues—to a public process.
>
> *Harvey Brooks*[5]

The social control and regulation of scientific knowledge that has moved from the state of being-in-progress to some form of completion, and that is implemented outside of the scientific community, is already quite extensive. But despite the enlargement of regulative politics involving science and technology, the dispute over who has a right to participate and is capable of participating in regulation remains a contested issue.

In all modern societies, we now find elaborate drug regulations and corresponding agencies that register, test, control, or permit pharmaceutical substances to enter the market as legalized drugs. Until a few decades ago, decisions about the production and marketing of chemicals as drugs were typically made by corporations, individual pharmacists, or physicians (cf. Bodewitz et al., 1987). As scientific knowledge is "applied," it becomes embedded in social contexts external to science. As a part of such embeddedness, knowledge is subject to the kinds of (latent) control mechanisms and social constraints found in and constitutive for these contexts. It simply cannot escape the selectivity that issues from such external contexts, even if only in efforts designed to generate trust toward a certain artifact or solution offered by novel knowledge.

The whole area of national and international intellectual property and copyright protection is another arena in which legislation to control the deployment of scientific and technical knowledge is already extensive. In many ways, such controls date back at least to the 1883 Paris Convention for patents and related industrial matters and to the 1886 Berne Convention for copyrights. The acceleration in the speed with which inventions reach the market, their shortened economic life-span, and the extent to which recent inventions—for example in the field of microelectronics—and the organization of production, medical treatments, and biotechnology, are difficult to protect from copying efforts, will increase pressures to enact further protective legislation (cf. Vaitsos, 1989).

In social theory, the institutions generating knowledge and the institutions contemplating and executing political action were once regarded as existing in entirely unrelated domains. At the beginning of the twentieth century, the dilemma of the indispensable separation of science and politics found perhaps its most influential expression in Max Weber's essays ([1921] 1948: 77–128; [1922] 1948: 129–156) on science and politics as a vocation. Today, the intellectual foundations that allowed Weber to legitimize the fundamental division between the practices of knowledge and politics have fallen into disrepute. Confidence in the impartiality, instrumentality, and political neutrality of science has been thoroughly eroded. Reference to the politics of knowledge therefore no longer constitutes a violation of the norms of scientific action and the essentially means-like attributes of scientific knowledge. Science is deeply implicated in social action, and political agendas hold sway over science. It appears that the difference between science and political processes has become redundant.

Precisely how dependent or interdependent science and politics should be is a matter of ongoing debate and empirical analysis. But the widespread disenchantment with science and the extensive material dependence of the scientific community on the state do not justify the equally unrealistic proposition that the boundaries between politics and science have altogether vanished. Science remains embedded in particular political realities, and as long as it is situated in a form of civil and political society free of totalitarian strains, scientific activity tends to benefit. By the same token, as long as traffic across the boundaries of science remains widely unimpeded and subject to negotiation, both science and society gain.

Inasmuch as knowledge becomes the constitutive principle of modern society, the production, distribution, and especially the application of knowledge can avoid political struggles and conflicts less than ever. The distribution and implementation (and with it the fabrication) of knowledge increasingly become domains of explicit legislation and targets of political and economic decisions. Such a development is inevitable, because "as the institutions of knowledge lay claim to public resources, some public claim on these institutions" and their results is unavoidable (Bell, 1968: 238). Even more significant is that, as the importance of knowledge as a central societal resource increases, its social, economic, and political consequences for social relations grow rapidly, together with demands to regulate the specific utilization of and access to knowledge.

The dissemination and application of knowledge do not occur in the imaginary world of perfect, unimpeded competition and equality of opportunity. As a result, a politics of knowledge must confront the consequences of the social distribution of knowledge, especially the stratified access to and utilization of knowledge. It remains an open question, for example, to what extent the dispossession of knowledge generates social conflicts, and in what specific ways such struggles manifest themselves. Daniel Bell (1964: 49) warned several decades ago that right-wing extremism may "benefit" from any exclusion of social groups from access to and the acquisition of technical expertise.

However, such predictions of intellectual, social, and economic gaps in the distribution of knowledge overestimate the extent to which knowledge and its use can in fact be controlled. It will be increasingly difficult to control knowledge, in spite of the many efforts that will undoubtedly be made. Efforts to control knowledge encounter contradictions. Sustaining economic growth, for example, requires an expansion of knowledge. And knowledge that expands rapidly is difficult to control. The expansion of knowledge enlarges the segment of knowledge-based occupations. Knowledge expansion and knowledge dissemination rely on conditions that are themselves inimical to control. Nonetheless, as I have observed, the typically expressed fear that an inevitable outcome of such developments is the greater ease with which knowledge (and information) can be monopolized and effectively employed for repressive (even totalitarian) purposes, or even as a tool of maintaining the benign status quo, had been a widely accepted premise in discussions of the social control of knowledge, even before Orwell's classic book on the subject. What exactly nourishes this point of view? What is the basis for the widespread conviction that knowledge and technical artifacts are relatively easy to control and that access to knowledge can be easily denied?

Regulatory Practices

In the meantime, the literature that reports on modern techno-scientific law and regulations by public agencies has grown greatly in recent decades, reflecting the

growing efforts to police the consequences of science and technology. Most studies of regulatory practices employ the case-study method, presenting a kind of
biography of the case that takes the form of storytelling. The case is disclosed as a
series of events in specific settings with specific actors. The observations the story
makes, of course, depend on the commitments the observer brings to the scene.
Martin and Richards (1995) present a typology of approaches found in the *analysis*
of techno-scientific *controversies*. They categorize controversy analyses as "positivist," "group-politics," "constructivist," and "social-structural." However, few
actual cases strictly conform to any one of the four types. Martin and Richards
therefore propose integrated approaches for future analyses. Turner (2001) points
to the power of the narrative components that underlie and affect the disputes that
are examined. The (hidden) narrative elements or logic that engage the attention of
the audience, that persuade the readers and that enable the listener tacitly to accept
the story as meaningful and as a confirmation of world views, are even more powerful attributes than the "analytical" approach chosen by the observer. Turner (2001:
477) argues even more strongly that the "narrative choices dictate the political and
moral arguments implicit" in accounts. Presumably, this applies to both the stories
found in the settings that are studied and the story about the stories told by the
observer.

The actors engaged in knowledge politics often tend to find themselves cast in
one of two opposing camps. The camps do not always present a united front. First,
there are the proponents, whose motivation appears at times to be mainly interest-
based—for example, when the pharmaceutical industry favors licensing Bovine
Somatotropin (BST or recombinant rBST), a synthesized protein hormone which
increases milk production by as much as 40 percent in adult cattle.[6] Then there are
the opponents—in the case just cited, major environmental groups, animal welfare
and consumer groups, as well as other social movements—who for broader and
more complex reasons oppose the use of the hormone by dairy farmers. In December 1994, the ministers of agriculture of the European Union imposed a moratorium on the use of BST until 1999 (Ashford, 1996).

Also among the corporate actors who are bound to play an influential role in the
formation of knowledge politics are the media. The publication and presentation
of new scientific knowledge by the media, and their reconstruction and assessment
of the ensuing political debates and conflicts that grow up around new findings,
will have an important impact on generating interest in knowledge policies, their
formulation, and their implementation.

Bioethics or Governing the Genome

The belief that the Human Genome Project is more than merely an attempt to
break the human genetic code is widespread. In a nutshell, the conviction is that
the Human Genome Project is "the vision of biopower in the information age"
(Kay, 2000: 327). One of the obvious and, as some see it, perhaps inconsequential
ways of framing and coping with new knowledge and technical artifacts with the

aim to regulate and police them is to call on and defer to ethics. As a result, "ethical debates have become so central in recent years to social and cultural theory that they can no longer be ignored" by social scientists (Lash, 1996: 75), although ethics, as it turns out, is very well able to bypass the potential contributions of social scientists. Ethics and the knowledge it is supposed to assess are historically variable, socially shaped, dynamic, and essentially contested. There is no widely acceptable ethical platform from which biomedical innovation may be governed. Bioethicists have, of course, recognized the dilemma, posed in this fashion: "How to reconcile the clearly immense differences in the social and personal realities of moral life with the need to apply a universal standard to those fragments of experience that can foster not only comparison and evaluation but also action" (Kleinman, 1999: 70). But the fact that some of the issues in bioethics have become so well known that they are by now almost clichés does not mean that advice generated by "councils on bioethics" is not urgently in demand and seen as a source of publicly contesting ways of dealing with advances in cloning technology, for example.

The context sensitivity of knowledge politics that is reflected in bioethics is considerable, as can be shown by referring to but a few examples set in recent years of bioethical practices, advice, and bodies. The settings within which bioethics evolves and is practiced differ greatly from country to country. Needless to say, this creates immense dilemmas and potential lines of conflict; for instance, how is it possible to enhance patient autonomy while legally restricting the use of certain procedures? Or for that matter, how can the economic interests of the medical-industrial complex and the moral concerns of physicians and patients be brought into line? Nonetheless, the turn to ethics is one of the main responses to the problem of the governance of knowledge, especially biomedical knowledge, which justifies speaking of the "governance of the genome" in this context. In the field of medical science, these developments, most prominently in the United States, have stimulated the institutionalization of the field of bioethical discourse, and have led to the emergence of a new profession, the "bioethicist."

Whether we are, in fact, witnessing a convergence in the settings within which health care is delivered is a contentious issue. For example, are we seeing, as a result of the increasing use of new scientific knowledge and technical developments, an evolution in the "physician-patient relationships from a somewhat paternalistic, personal relationship imbued with (at least some) trust, toward a rights-based, but also more impersonal and adversarial (but accountable) relationship between 'strangers'" (Benatar, 1997: 399)? If a convergence of typical settings within which health care is delivered does occur in modern societies, then the context sensitivity of the emerging field of bioethics might indeed be somewhat reduced, but not eliminated. Efforts to develop global bioethics initiatives are just beginning.

The case of bioethics—a recent field of discourse with distinctly American roots in the late 1960s and early 1970s—is important for a number of reasons (see Spallone et al., 2000: 196–203). It is possible to observe how an academic and practical domain of expertise, intended to respond to and regulate novel knowledge, is justified (e.g., are there universal goods that can be called upon?), develops context-specific accounts and practices (e.g., what issues are ethical issues, and is the individual and/or the collectivity the main referent?), manages to operate in a given environment and does so in response to the contingencies (e.g., boundaries between domains) that it encounters. Moreover, it is possible to observe what bioethics manages to accomplish given the goals of its domain of discourse. For example, is bioethics less of a brake on the deployment of new medical knowledge than it is a "cheerleader" or facilitator of the progress of medical techniques, encouraging their moral acceptability? Finally, what are some of the specific intellectual tools of inquiry (from the social sciences, from ethical theory, from law, from political philosophy) that bioethics deploys?

The *practice* of bioethics tends to concentrate on what health researchers call health care at the point of delivery, and most of all on "exotic new medical technologies and how they might affect our lives. It has paid considerable attention to the doctor-patient relationship and how changes in the health care system affect it" (Daniels, Kennedy, and Kawachi, 1999: 216).[7]

As a result, bioethics has with few exceptions stayed away from the social determinants and the processes that influence health "upstream," away from the medical system itself. Whether bioethics ought to focus more on the social determinants of health as well as the system of medical care is itself a normative issue. At the same time, the concentration of bioethics on acute issues (illnesses) also reflects the choices that the medical system and society have made when it comes to judgments about the relative importance of different short-term or long-term social and ideological purposes, and the processes that impact the incidence of illness and the ways of assuring or realizing greater public health.[8]

Expert Control

The regulation and control of knowledge based on the democratic participation of citizens, at the extreme in the form of plebiscites, is considered to be an absurd form of control by members of the scientific community who have publicly offered views on this matter in recent years (Kemeny, 1980; Brooks, 1984; Levitt and Gross, 1994). The kind of control that is advocated most often is regulation by experts, and the distinction between the capacities of experts and laypersons, in the case of specialized knowledge and competencies, is seen to be definite if not obvious. Moreover, members of the public, in the context of arguments favoring expert control, are seen as not having sufficient time and patience to understand contestable, technical issues in detail in order to make intelligent choices (Brooks, 1984: 46). However, the distinction between technical knowledge and nontechnical knowledge is foremost, and presumably extends not only to the social control of research but surely also to the regulation of the use of novel scientific knowledge and technical artifacts. After all, how are laypersons able to assess the nature of the risks associated with the implementation of new capacities to act—for example, those brought about by new biotechnology products? It appears obvious to both politicians and the public, apparently, that the management of knowledge politics and the organization and articulation of decisions ought to be delegated to experts, and that the judgment of experts should play a decisive role in the policy advice. As matter of fact, many, if not most, of the regulatory agencies that have been established in recent years in many countries are in fact variants of a form of control and regulation exercised by experts.[9] This is the case, for example, for the Food and Drug Administration (FDA) in the United States. The FDA approves drugs for marketing by judging their safety and efficacy.

However, another common distinction—namely, the distinction between instrumental knowledge and the goals of social action, or between what is rational and reasonable—suggests that the role of experts can be quite restricted. The role of expert or technical knowledge is void of meaning, and is therefore void of any help in decisions about goals that might be pursued with the aid of instrumental knowledge.

Participatory Control

Is it necessary or inevitable that one is forced to generate regulative decisions, requiring highly specialized competencies in the field of knowledge politics, without democratic practice and participation? Do we even have to assume that there is a linear trade-off between the (scientific-technical) complexity of an issue and the chances for democratic participation in knowledge politics (Rossini and Porter, 1984)?

The practice of regulatory politics in many countries, be it in efforts to determine permissible limits of hazardous substances, the location of large-scale technical plants, or the recycling of dangerous materials, indicates that the participation of laypersons is becoming more and more taken for granted. The reasons advanced for technocratic procedures and solutions in such cases have been successfully criticized. The change in the prevailing political conceptions of participation also applies to regulative politics, which in principle excludes citizens from codetermination. The potential impacts, hazards, and risks of knowledge politics are so severe for the individual that one cannot imagine an alternative to a scenario that extends democratic participation and control. However, the normative demand for participatory knowledge politics does not solve the issue of effective ways of organizing participation of laypersons. The organizational frame chosen for participatory politics is decisive when it comes to its legitimacy, the participatory opportunities, the learning possibilities of participants (Laird, 1993), how meaningful participation is judged to be generally, the kinds of results that can be achieved, and the external assessment and image participatory regulative politics may achieve.

During the course of the last couple of decades a new understanding of science and technology has emerged. The forces at work that accomplished the new understanding consisted, at the macro level so to speak, of vigorous public debates and controversies about the social role of science and technology, ranging from the disputes over nuclear power, the ecological impact of human activities, and the way major infectious diseases are treated to, most recently, the advent of biotechnology and biotechnology products.

The other force at work consisted of science and technology studies that have transformed our understanding of science and technology at the micro level. Both

debates strengthened the view that it could be otherwise—that society is not necessarily trapped by a kind of immanent logic of either the development or the application of science and technology. These changes include a demystification of the
idea still at the forefront of Marcuse's and Schelsky's analysis of the social role of
technology and science—namely, that the unequal distribution of social influence
on the ways in which science and technology are utilized in society is virtually
impossible to fundamentally alter. In addition, there has been a growing realization that the production of knowledge in science is not, as Norbert Elias preferred
to describe it, highly object-centered and driven toward neutrality, in the sense that
knowledge conforms to reality. In many ways, these developments are preconditions for the possibility of a more democratic, participatory intervention or control
of the production of scientific knowledge and technical capacities and their use in
society.

But many of the apprehended obstacles to a productive democratic involvement
in science and technology matters by nonexperts have not, therefore, diminished
or disappeared (Kleinman, 1998). Foremost among these hurdles is, of course, the
assertion that laypersons are unable to grasp the technical language, the subtle
cultural context, and complex methods of science. Aside from the intellectual obstacles, other hurdles frequently mentioned include more mundane reasons that
are by no means insignificant. The ability to engage in participatory control of the
use of knowledge in society can also be much affected by a lack of disposable
elementary resources (time, finances), not to mention a lack of concern, interest, or
perseverance. Material, motivational, and intellectual resources, of course, favor
interested groups and organizations, who have claims on the benefits of new knowledge and technical devices. Similarly, politically and economically influential groups
still retain many of the advantages they had in the past when it comes to science
policies, their preparation, and execution. Future knowledge politics will hardly be
an exception. However, many efforts and developments are in place that may undermine such traditions in policy formulation and policymaking.

It is necessary to distinguish between forms of democratic cooperation and
codetermination in decisions about science and technology, since the nature of the
design of democratic participation affects not only the possible outcomes and their
relevance to policy decisions, but also the kinds of topics that might be deliberated
upon; the legitimacy, timeliness, and practicality of decisions reached under the
auspices of broad participation; and the willingness to take part in such decisions.
Obviously, a great variety of issues can be considered under the general heading of
forms of participation in decision-making that affect science and technology matters.

One recent organizational innovation that should be noted in this context is the
so-called *consensus conference,* first introduced, in the form I will describe, in the
late 1980s by the Danish Board of Technology, a parliamentary body charged with
the task of assessing technologies.[10] Consensus conferences are designed to stimu-
late participatory and intelligent debate on technological issues. In the case of the
Danish conferences (Grundahl, 1995; Klüver, 1995), the purpose is to advise legislators, but not to dictate public policy. Conferences have been held on a range of

topics: food irradiation, air pollution, human infertility, sustainable agriculture, genetic engineering, and the future of the private car. In the meantime, other countries and associations have designed consensus conferences on a range of topics (see Joss and Durant, 1995)

Once a topic has been chosen, a consensus conference is organized by a steering committee in the form of a multi-day public forum (after a carefully planned program of reading and discussion among members) with active participation of ten to fifteen volunteer laypersons and a corresponding number of experts, chosen on the basis of questions generated by the nonexperts. The experts play, formally at least, only an advisory role in the process of the consensus conferences. The conference culminates in written, final reports that are widely publicized.

Observers of consensus conferences have noted that the "lay panel reports can be incisive and impassioned as well, especially in comparison with the circumspection and dry language that is conventional in expert policy analyses" (Sclove, 1996: 27). Given the initial experiences with consensus conferences, such reports can be both timely and responsive to urgent public issues. The relatively short time needed to organize such conferences allows for the possibility of responding to new knowledge and techniques prior to their introduction. The wide media coverage given to the reports of the consensus conferences enhances public knowledge and finds resonance among legislators.

Understanding of the function of consensus conferences is bound to vary depending on the interests at stake for different groups and individuals. Some see the conferences as a useful tool "of gaining public support for 'difficult' decisions in science and technology" (European Chemical Industry Council),[11] while others see them as an opportunity to enhance democratic control in the process of assessing and regulating technology and science (Nelkin and Pollak, 1975; Fiorino, 1990). It is self-evident that consensus conferences will only make a decisive difference in the context of knowledge politics if the outcomes of such deliberations are binding for regulative policies.

Hybrid Control Mechanisms

One of the potentially more effective and legitimate modes of organizing advice for policymaking; for mediating between the public, science, and politics; and for the construction of regulatory standards and sanctions, as a number of recent studies to which I will refer have shown (Cash, 2001; Miller 2001), has been the creation of "intermediary bodies"—"boundary organizations" in general and "hybrid associations" or "hybrid management" in particular.[12] Boundary constructs are mutually constraining associations situated in-between social systems, which draw on members of different systems, include substantive elements as well as material artifacts, and cooperate with different systems, for example, the political system and the scientific community, by providing resources and objects that can be deployed on both side of the divide.[13]

The functions of "boundary-transgressing" organizational forms responsible for knowledge politics should be based on or linked to the kinds of interactions that generally prevail in the relations between science and society. It is important to emphasize again in this context that our understanding of science and of the relations that typically obtain between the social system of science and other social systems has been significantly reconfigured. The idea that science (especially natural science) deals with the definite, philosophy and the social sciences with the unprovable, and politics with the moral, an idea hardly contested just half a century ago, can no longer be seriously maintained. Today, partly in a revisionist mood, social and natural scientists deal mainly in the conjectural. Moreover, in many of the widely accepted social models of science, especially in functionalist approaches—for example, those of Max Weber, Michael Polanyi, and Niklas Luhmann, or in Latour's idea of modernity as a purification ritual—the separation and distinctiveness of the scientific community as against the political system stood out not only as a reality-confirming observation, but also as a necessity for the growth of robust scientific knowledge. Today, we increasingly find well-elaborated views and systematic reflections about science in a world in which politics and science are closing in on each other and more and more depend on each other (see Porter, 1995; Jasanoff, 1996; Grundmann and Stehr, 2002).[14] At the same time, these linkages are less and less immediate or direct and more and more mediated by specialized associations, set at the intersections of social institutions. Hybrid associations contribute in significant ways to the fuzziness of established cultural and structural differences of social institutions. Hybrid organizations enlarge the chances that system-specific cultures can be translated, and they increase the likelihood of the articulation of practical knowledge.

The issue of the instrumentality of scientific knowledge for political purposes, which has preoccupied many discussions about the social utility of science, is increasingly displaced by the question of the "scientification" of political activities. The scientification of political activities not only means that political conflicts take on some of the characteristics of scientific controversies, but mainly that the substance of political contests and debates is codetermined by issues that are generated in the scientific community as issues needing political attention and decision. As a matter of fact, the number of contentious political issues in modern societies that have been recruited from science is growing. The reference to a scientification of the political agenda refers, for example, to the uptake of the science of climate change in historical times by the political system. After all, the discovery of the climate change issue did not happen in the political system, in everyday life, or in other societal institutions, but rather is a problem for society first detected in the scientific community.

The separation and the distance between science and politics does not vanish altogether; it remains in place despite the growing uptake of problems that are discovered and generated by science for the political system, as political problems that need to be solved. The persistent separation ensures that issues discovered by science do not automatically become political issues. The uptake is a complicated, stratified process that is affected by particular conditions of action, as well as by opportunistic considerations. Among the relevant actors are scientists. The actual connections and linkages between science and politics, and the influence scientists may have in this instance, have to be connected to concrete cases, such as climate change.

Among the attributes of scientific knowledge produced for practical purposes, as I have emphasized, are uncertainty, multiplicity, and contingency. In the case of each of these attributes, now more readily acknowledged, one is confronted with the question of whether these features of knowledge are a new attribute, largely absent from our understanding of science just a few decades ago, because contemporary society and therefore science is faced with a set of novel problems—for example, in the field of environmental issues—that did not exist in this manner half a century ago (Funtowicz and Ravetz, 1990: 7).

My assumption is that the uncertainty produced by science is not the outcome of novel problems confronted by science, although such problems are undoubtedly prominent on the agenda of the scientific community, but rather that uncertainty is a much older problem, already present in science a century and more ago. However, it was much easier to overlook or even repress the presence and importance of uncertainty until a few years ago. Uncertainty was less visible. A hundred years ago, the social function of science was less significant for society and for politics. Fertilizers and paints were the first major examples of the application of science. Many further examples followed, especially after the end of World War Two. It is possible to observe in a more restricted sense, therefore, that the visibility of the uncertainty that issues from science is made more evident with the emergence of "new" problems confronted by science.[15] When scientists are asked to assess uncertainties and risks, more is required than just a routine yes/no response. Rather, knowledge is demanded that often transcends specialized knowledge. Scientists who are willing to meet the demanding challenge of such a public assessment of risks and dangers are bound to have a significant public role and political influence. But as a result of these developments in the relations between science and politics, new opportunities and prospects loom for workable knowledge politics—that is, a type of knowledge politics that does not rely exclusively on experts nor demand that it be based on a radical, plebiscitary form of democratic decision-making.

The Limits of Knowledge Politics

Aside from the different methods and the difficulties of organizing knowledge politics, I now want to turn to what are essentially specific arguments and perspectives about the practicality of initiating and implementing knowledge politics measures, which one is bound to encounter in discussions about the prospects of regulating knowledge in society. Those who will advocate deferring decisions, using extreme caution in initiating regulative knowledge politics, careful examinations of possibly foregone benefits, studies on comparative advantages, and so on will not question that knowledge politics is possible in principle. The arguments I want to review will, of course, claim to espouse responsibility and avoidance of errors in judging new knowledge and take other high moral grounds. At the same time, the positions about the limits of knowledge politics I will introduce tend to have a kind

of universal applicability. But they will strongly interact and blend with one another as they are injected into debates about the merits of novel knowledge and
technologies in the context of the issues of the day.

Among the arguments that one is likely to encounter in debates about knowledge politics, and which are designed to defer, to deflect, and possibly to defeat
efforts to impose regulations and sanctions, are: "It is too early." "It is only in the
application of new knowledge that the consequences become evident." "We are not
alone." "We cannot afford to live without it." And, last but not least, "It is too late."
I will discuss each of these points in turn.

In addition, the limits of knowledge politics also pertain to the restrained ability
of science and politics to carry out practical experiments with new knowledge in
order to ascertain in a more reliable manner, for example, what the specific social
consequences of new technologies or scientific knowledge may be. Past regulative
policies could in some measure at least rely on the possibility of trial runs, limited
experiments, or voluntary restrictions. Or they simply responded once it became
evident that the introduction of new technical devices produced unintended as well
as harmful effects.

In the case of novel knowledge in some of the emerging fields of scientific
knowledge (for example, in the case of gene transfer methods), such experimentation appears to be an instrument that is in principle not available. Trials are not
available because even a single application or a restricted experiment in terms of
location or species could have irreversible consequences or might spread without
the ability of the experimenters to arrest the diffusion of the impact induced by the
experiment. This may well be the case, for example, with genetically altered crop
plants engineered for herbicide tolerance and weeds, which may cross-breed, resulting in the transfer of the herbicide resistance to the weeds. Moreover, those
who strongly fear the harmful consequences of such experiments will hardly be
prepared to endorse a trial run and await a more precise calculation of the social
costs of the introduction of new devices and techniques.

It is too early

Among those who are concerned about the implications of pending knowledge
policies, one argument will invariably surface—namely, the suggestion that it is
too early to contemplate and enact restrictions on the use of novel knowledge and
technical devices. Richard Dawkins,[16] for example, describes the possibility that
we will soon be able to reconstruct our ancestors through genetic engineering. A
sophisticated comparison of the human genome with that of the chimpanzee might
enable us to remake the genome of our common ancestor who lived in Africa some
six million years ago. Dawkins goes on to say that such a prospect might well
horrify rather than excite us at the present time, but "we are not living in 2050
[when such a project could be realized]. Things will seem different then."

The risks and dangers, as well as the *kinds* of risks and dangers associated with
the implementation of novel scientific knowledge and new technical devices may
indeed only become visible in the distant future. Indeed, impacts in many instances

operate slowly, encircled by uncertainty, and become transparent only after considerable time. And our ability to even sense, let alone measure, impacts often develops equally slowly. Knowing that impact assessment is difficult to foresee and complicated to measure provides ammunition and discursive advantages to those preferring to focus instead on the perceived benefits. It is possible, therefore, that arguments pointing to the possibility of future preventive measures, or even adaptation, gain in contested debates about the impact of new capacities to act.

The benefits might presumably become visible earlier and more clearly. At least, the advocates of the benefits and the lobby for gains resulting from implementation will likely have a stronger voice than those who warn of distant and uncertain dangers and risks. The argument that it is too early and that the benefits outweigh distant risks that are difficult to assess, in the first instance, is of course countered by a powerful counter-position, which points to the chance of irreversible impacts, such as the loss of the nature of human nature, however it may have been circumscribed. Or, how much can an ecological system be transformed before the damage reaches a point of no return? Unfortunately, uncertainty prevails strongly in this instance as well; as Lowenthal (1990: 128), for example, observes, "Whether or not a process is irreversible is unknown at its inception and usually in doubt when preventive measures are applied."

It is only in the application of new knowledge that the consequences become evident

The contention that it is too early to enact rules for the use of new knowledge is, of course, closely related to the argument that it is only possible to judge the risks and the benefits of the application of new technologies and knowledge after they have been realized in practice. And, as some of the examples of past knowledge and technology politics have shown—for example, the way the U.S. government controlled the deployment of steam boilers in the nineteenth century well after their widespread practical use—it is very difficult to anticipate potentially deleterious consequences of the use of new technical devices. The proponents of new technologies, at least in the initial phases of their introduction, have a distinct advantage in promoting their application by emphasizing the novel opportunities and benefits they see arising from their implementation. Moreover, if new products and processes are introduced into institutions or in aid of widely shared goals—for example, in the field of medicine—those who have an interest in the deployment of new capacities to act have an enormous advantage in presenting their conceptions and in gaining support for implementation.

We cannot afford to live without it

If by governance one still invokes, as is often done with great conviction today, what was its traditional concern—namely the "art of exercising power in the form, and according to the model, of the economy" (Foucault, [1978] 2000: 207)—then the argument that we really cannot afford to live without the benefits that may come from the application and utilization of new knowledge will be heard with great vigor, in one of its many variants, in public debates about knowledge politics. Aside from the argument that the potential, *direct* benefits outweigh the risks of the application of new technologies, one might encounter the view that related developments that are bound to follow from applications of the technology in question are bound to have considerable utility in the future. For example, in a report entitled "Genomics and World Health," the World Health Organization (WHO) recently encouraged developing countries not to uncouple themselves—despite their pressing, immediate health needs—from supporting genomics research in their own countries because of the promise of genetic research in combating diseases prominently found in the Third World.[17]

It is too late

Every development of new technologies and novel capacities to act, it could be argued, passes through a stage when decisions about future applications become crucial. The decision to go ahead depends on a set of factors, often narrow in scope and limited to technical feasibility and economic payoff, or even more narrowly based on special interests. Once the development has reached a certain momentum, it then quickly appears to be impossible to halt further development and application. In such a context, the argument that "it is too late" to halt or restrict the utilization easily comes into play.

We are not alone

An effective restriction of the implementation of new capacities to act requires, in the final analysis, a knowledge politics that is global in scale. On the one hand, in many instances, the ability to implement new scientific knowledge will not be limited in terms of space and time. The intellectual and material resources that might be required, and the ability to control as well as manage the circumstances of action, will not always be restricted to a particular political or economic entity. Voluntary or unilateral restrictions and action taken against the use of new capacities to act might of course be seen and be supported as heroic, moral, or even expedient.

The argument "we are not alone" will be equally forceful, if not more so, in decisions about specific courses of action taken in the field of knowledge politics. The view that we are not alone not only pertains to the potential economic disadvantages of uncoupling a village, a city, a region, or a country from developments and changes associated with new ideas, but may also imply the loss of future influence on the ways in which technological regimes, for example, develop. In short, the cautionary position, as some will see it, of considering that we are not alone in deciding about the application of new knowledge will be as powerful an argument in future debates in knowledge politics as are the other positions I have briefly enumerated.

Summing up, the limits to the governance of knowledge would appear to be formidable. Nonetheless, it is very likely that many different models of the governance of knowledge will emerge in different societies and transnational jurisdictions, and even on the global plane. The type of governance mechanism will respond to specific initial conditions and become institutionalized, and may well continue to persist even after the precipitating conditions have changed or disappeared altogether (Schmitter, 1997: 397). Moreover, the actors who will appear on the scene in struggles to argue for and against, and then establish rules and sanctions for the regulation of knowledge, will vary greatly, ranging from unitary to hybrid associations of capital, labor, and the professions, social movements, more or less stable networks of interested groups and organizations, alliances of political parties and private corporate actors, the churches, the media and individual scientists—to mention only a few of the possible actors who are bound to get involved. I now turn to such a case of "informal" knowledge politics, namely the "moralization of the markets."

The discussion of motives and methods of governing knowledge in modern societies in the previous two sections merges with the following chapter on the *Moralization of the Markets*. My examination of what I call the moralization of the markets has multiple purposes in the context of an analysis of knowledge politics. The moralization of the markets, or the gradual but growing transformation of the motives that govern market decisions by consumers, producers, and investors has the purpose of underscoring the observation that knowledge politics cannot be left to a state-centered analysis of the social control of knowledge. Market forces play a significant role. It is not only the state and legal apparatuses that have a central role in modern knowledge politics. Knowledge politics also result from what might be conceptualized as the unintended outcome of intentional (economic) action. Decisions of consumers and producers in the marketplace amount to a form of knowledge politics that is both highly significant and, at least initially, does not rely on a state-based regulatory system. State regulation may follow the marketplace.

Under the heading of the moralization of the markets, I will discuss the nature of economic exchange in market capitalism and refer to its transformation in a knowledge-based economy. I will discuss the "material" basis for a change of the motive structure of market decisions and refer for this purpose to the unique historical experience of advanced societies. Nothing in the history of the industrialized countries in Western Europe and North America resembles their experience between 1950 and 1985. By the end of that period, the perpetual possibility of serious economic hardship that had earlier always hovered over the lives of three-quarters of the population now menaced only about one-fifth of it. Although absolute poverty still existed in even the richest countries, the material standard of living for most people improved almost without interruption and often very rapidly for thirty-five years. Above all else, these are the marks of the uniqueness of the experience. The immense change in the existential conditions of millions of people provides one, perhaps the most important, foundation for the moralization of the markets in advanced societies.

At the center of the following section then are observations mainly about the market of consumer goods and the constitution of the *use value* of goods and services. The existential and then symbolic constitution of the value of goods and services are increasingly codetermined or even displaced by the ethical value of a product or service, which then constitutes the use value in the marketplace. The new values displace more "rational" or economic motives of decision-making in the marketplace. These transformations of the moral basis of economic conduct amount, as it were, to a form of highly consequential knowledge politics in modern societies.

Notes

1. Cited in Allee, 1997: 71.

2. Regulatory politics and regimes show significant variation not only over time but across political boundaries. For example, David Vogel (2003) has examined the evolution of consumer and environmental protection policies in Europe and the United States from the 1960s until the present time. He reports how the stringency of such regulations has changed over time on both continents. While consumer and environmental policies were more stringent, innovative, and comprehensive in the United States than in Europe until around 1990, regulatory standards since then have become more stringent in Europe than in the United States.

3. Even before knowledge politics moves to the level of regulatory efforts, it will have to reckon with diverse public attitudes toward the utilization of novel techniques and capacities. For example, the prospect of sex-selection for nonmedical reasons in human reproduction elicits very different responses from the public in Great Britain and Germany. Participants in a randomized telephone survey in the United Kingdom and Germany were asked whether they "would like to take advantage of a technology such as MicroSort to select the sex of their children." In order to enable the respondents to make a more informed response, they were told what the technology involves. For reasons that are unclear, compared to the Germans, the "British are much more receptive to the idea of employing reproductive technology to select the sex of their prospective children" (Dahl, Hinsch, Beutel, and Brosig, 2003: 2238). The ethical or normative discussion of sex selection is a highly contested matter; the recent report of the President's Council on Biothethics entitled "Beyond Therapy: Biotechnology and the Pursuit of Happiness" (2003) has little to say in favor of permitting sex selection and prefers the rule of "chance."

4. Comparative studies of regulative politics, regulatory organizations, policy advice, the role of experts, the legal system, the role of social movements, and the interaction between science and politics in Western democracies all show the varied nature of regulatory regimes, arrangements, and sanctions, the diversity of conceptions of what constitutes good science, and the contested usage that is made of scientific knowledge by governments (e.g., Jasanoff, 1986, 1995).

5. Brooks, 1984: 49.

6. The hormone BSE is produced "naturally" by dairy cows; another version is produced by the pharmaceutical industry through splicing together pieces of bovine DNA. The pharmaceutical industry claims that in terms of molecular chemistry, the two hormones are identical. Deploying the same term for both hormones, of course, is advantageous for industry (Ashford, 1996: 128).

7. One of the leading definitions of the field of bioethics, in line with the restrictive designation of its purposes, therefore stresses in an even more constraining fashion that

bioethics "has as its main task the determination, so far as that is possible, of what is right and wrong, good and bad, about the scientific developments and technological developments of biomedicine" (Callahan, 1999: 276). After the first meeting of his newly appointed Council on Bioethics, President George W. Bush received the council members in the White House, and is quoted as saying about the primary purposes of the council that the panel should help ordinary people "come to grips with how medicine and science interface" with "the dignity of life, and the notion that life is—you know, that there is a Creator" (see "Bush's advisers on ethics discuss human cloning," *New York Times,* January 18, 2002).

8. The notion that scientific medicine and the health care system are responsible for our health blinds us, as Daniels, Kennedy, and Kawachi (1999: 244) observe, "to the socio-economic inequality as a source of inequity in the realization of opportunity for health across populations."

9. As Langdon Winner (1992: 349) has observed, the separation (rather than the convergence) of politics and technology, and the decoupling of citizens' roles from decisions about technical practice, is linked to distinctive philosophical traditions, one ancient and one more modern. In classical Greek philosophy the decoupling of ordinary citizens was linked to the difference between the practical arts and knowledge. In modern philosophy the separation is transcended. Pessimism about technology is replaced by an affirmative endorsement, yet the separation between political and technical contexts is preserved: "Citizens are strongly encouraged to become involved in improving modern material culture, but only in the market or other highly privatized settings. There is no moral community or public space in which technological issues are topics for deliberation, debate, and shared action."

10. The idea of the consensus conference can be traced to the "consensus development conferences" developed by the U.S. National Institutes of Health, originally in response to congressional concerns about the rapid increase in health-care costs. The conferences were designed to evaluate "available scientific information and resolve safety and efficacy issues related to biomedical technology." The NIH conferences rely primarily on expert members. The first consensus development conference was held in September 1997 and dealt with breast cancer screening. Since then more than a hundred conferences have been conducted. The concept of the consensus development conferences can, in turn, be traced to the idea of the "science court," which was expected to enable scientists, using court-like adversarial procedures, to reach agreement behind closed doors on controversial issues (see Jørgensen, 1995: 17).

11. The quote is from a report of a member of the European Chemical Industry Council who took part in a consensus conference organized by the Commission of the European Union in Belgium in December of 1992. The topic of the conference was "Science, technology, and community cohesion" (www.cefic.be/position/St/pp_st01.htm). The author of the report suggests that the "use of consensus conferences could be envisaged as a means to gain broad public understanding and acceptance of industry positions," and he does so in light of the experience of the industry that the "general public is not only ignorant about the chemical industry but also mistrusts what it says and does."

12. One of the early conceptions of mediating associations that resonates with the more recent concept of boundary organizations (Guston, 2000) is Lammers' (1974: 132) notion of "missionary institutions" that promote science in society. For a discussion of the nature of the term and the growing number of domains in which the concept of "hybrid" plays a part, see Nederveen Pieterse, 2001.

13. In the context of a case study of a body of the UN Framework Convention on Climate Change, Clark Miller (2001: 480) defines hybrid associations at the interface of

politics and science as "social constructs that contain both scientific and political elements, often sufficiently intertwined to render separation a practical impossibility. They can include conceptual and material artifacts (e.g., the climate system or a nuclear power plant), techniques or practices (e.g., methods for attributing greenhouse gas emissions to particular countries), or organizations (e.g., the SBSTA [Subsidiary Body for Scientific and Technological Advice] or the Intergovernmental Panel on Climate Change)."

14. My observations have deliberately been cast in an ambivalent fashion. It is, of course, necessary to specify in greater detail what is meant by a "drawing together" of social systems. An important segment of contemporary social theorists would object in principle to the idea that scientific knowledge is capable of readily moving across the boundaries that separate science from other social systems, and would be able to operate successfully in systems other than the science system. For example, if one follows Niklas Luhmann's differentiation perspective, systems are operatively closed. Systems are unable to "export" inputs into other social systems (for a more extensive discussion see Bechmann and Stehr, 2002). Recent work in science studies assumes that science is in the process of structural changes that are rewriting the traditional disciplinary boundaries and the boundaries between science and nonscience (Gibbons et al., 1994; also Guston, 1999; Jasanoff 1995; van den Daele, Krohn, and Weingart 1979; Weingart 1981). The changes in the boundary regime between science and nonscience have consequences for the kind of knowledge produced by science (compare Nowotny, Scott, and Gibbons, 2001).

15. A better understanding of the reasons for the uncertainty of scientific knowledge is mainly relevant for an answer to the question of whether in principle such uncertainty can or even should be overcome. But such work is not immediately relevant for reflections about the relations between science and politics and how the political system copes with uncertain knowledge.

16. Richard Dawkins, "The word made flesh," *Guardian*, December 27, 2001.

17. See "Don't shun genetic research, WHO advises poor lands," *New York Times*, May 1, 2000.

Chapter 4

The Moralization of the Market

In the spring of 1999, Terry Wolf planted half of his central Illinois farm with genetically modified (GM) soya seeds, and they gave him, he says, an edge in the never-ending battle with weeds. This year, he'll plant one of the hi-tech beans. But as Wolf and other farmers across the state prepare for spring planting, many are turning away from GM for the first time since the crops stormed the market in 1995.[1]

The belief that the economic significance of biotechnology as a "technology of the future" (OECD, 1988) will exceed that of the Internet, as Lester Thurow, for example, maintains,[2] is just as strong or as fragile a prediction as the assertion that the management of biotechnology will never fall outside corporate control (Kloppenburg and Burrows, 2001: 104). As the title of this section indicates, I want to address the interaction between knowledge and the marketplace in modern economies, using the case of biotechnology products as my empirical referent. More specifically, the referent is new biotechnological *food products* (GM foods) already in the marketplace and typically competing with products using different production processes, which the consumer indeed envisions and comprehends as substitute products.

Evaluating biotechnology is a most difficult task. The arguments range from the assertion at one extreme that genetically modified food will "save the planet" (Rauch, 2003) to its opposite—that biotechnology may actually destroy the earth (Rees, 2003). The general public must find the critical assessment of biotechnology prospects, promises, and projects a very arduous chore. Perceptions of biotechnology are differently embedded in different societies (see Fleising, 1999: 98–100). A differentiation between assessing biotechnology as a general idea and evaluating

171

specific biotechnology products is also advisable because consumers appear to be ready (for the time being at least, as I would emphasize) to assess biotechnology products within the field of medicine more favorably.[3] Public discourse about such potential biotechnological pharmaceuticals therefore differs significantly from public discourse about GM food products (see Conrad, 1999; Brüggemann and Jungermann, 1998). One needs to distinguish here between "promised" biotechnology products—mainly in the field of medical genetics, where discourse is virtually controlled by its proponents—and products that are already competing in the marketplace. But there is no guarantee that discourse about medical genetics will continue along the same path.[4]

Moreover, the terminology in biotechnology is quite fluid. Terms are used interchangeably, and there is a vigorous contest to gain domination in the meanings assigned to various concepts, such as genetics, genetic manipulation, agricultural genetics, genetic engineering, genetic modification, and new biotechnology. The coupling to existing collective representations in debates about biotechnological products and procedures is significant. It matters, for example, whether one initially assigns biotechnology products to a field such as "disease, health, and medicine" or to "food" and discusses them accordingly, although the two domains are clearly related. Moreover, in early statements by scientists and industry representatives from biotechnology firms dealing with the impact of genetic engineering on agriculture, the figure of the consumer, at least as an active agent, did not appear to any significant extent (cf. Brill, 1986).

The focus I have chosen also indicates that I do not, in this context, care to discuss the ethics, the politics, the legal ramifications, or the need to enlighten the consumer more aggressively about what are seen by some as small[5] and by others as dangerous risks relative to the potential gains of deploying biotech products and processes in the marketplace.[6] Moreover, my focal point is limited, since I will concentrate on the effects of GM food in Europe and North America, but not the developing world. However, by implication my argument addresses why discourse is typically as restricted as it is (see also Lewontin, 2001). Finally, I do not intend to contribute to the theoretical debate over whether consumption has replaced production as the key to the intelligibility of modern societies (see Featherstone, 1991), or over the ways in which goods are culturally produced for the market (Miller and Rose, 1997).

The point I want to advance is that the current public controversies about genetic modifications of foods are a small but powerful pointer to more significant transformations of the modern market economy,[7] in which incremental knowledge that is basically contested, conjectural knowledge becomes the motor of the dynamics of the modern economy (see Stehr, 2000b). This in turn is one reason—perhaps it could be called the necessary condition—that allows for the possibility that the market is no longer merely a place where preferences are restricted to what is seen as the hallmark of pure "economic" reasoning—that is, a market in which all goods and services are priced according to their utility, and decisions taken by all market participants, and by institutions that modify market behavior,[8] operate according to the same code.

Max Weber ([1922] 1978: 636) described quite well the sober, distanced, and indirect personal relations that characterize the ideal-typical modern marketplace resulting from such an interest or utility-based orientation to the market:

> The market community as such is the most impersonal form of practical life into which humans can enter with one another. ... The reason for the impersonality of the market is its matter-of-factness, its orientation to the commodity and only to that. When the market is allowed to follow its own autonomous tendencies, its participants do not look toward the persons of each other but only toward the commodity; there are no obligations of brotherliness or reverence, and none of those spontaneous human relations that are sustained by personal unions.

Moreover, the change in the kinds of motives that more and more codetermine consumer decisions is accompanied by a shift in the center of gravity of the power of consumers, producers of, and investors in commodities and services. In the late sixties, John K. Galbraith ([1967] 1971) in *The New Industrial State,* for example, stressed both the need and the capacity of the producer to effectively rule consumer decisions. Everywhere Galbraith discovered and denounced "artificial accelerators" set in motion by producers to boost the demand for their products. The system imposed its own interests on the consumer as his or her interests and desires. As Jean Baudrillard ([1970] 2001: 42), writing at about the same time, approvingly observed, one must agree with Galbraith "in acknowledging that the liberty and the sovereignty of the consumer are nothing more than a mystification."

The assertion that the market increasingly allows for what might be called a "moralization" of economic decisions or, to put it differently, that steering functions of the market are no longer limited to purely economic reasoning,[9] runs counter to what many see as the iron logic of modernity—namely the functional differentiation of society, and the inescapable limits, as well as the collective (society-wide) power, of system-specific codes. The assertion that we are moving toward markets[10] where decisions of market participants are increasingly based on a moralization of economic action may be criticized on at least two further counts: (1) The economic system and economic action were really never all that detached from other social systems and forms of discourse. (2) More recently, the sustainable development debate, the demand for equal opportunities, health and safety regulations, and codetermination legislation have already gone a long way toward coupling economic action, assuming it operated more or less according to its own logic, to moral discourse and political purposes.

However, what I will describe here as the moralization of the market—without moralizing about an invasion of the market by moral considerations—or a de-commercialization of prices, I see primarily as an outcome of the dynamics of the economic system itself. I do not consider it the result, as some might suspect, of the successful intervention of social movements, the political and the legal system, or other societal forces—such as enlightened discourse about the profound paradoxes of modernity—that attempt, as they undeniably do, to impose their logic and their regulatory efforts on the marketplace. The moralization of market conduct is more than merely the presence of greater or lesser uncertainties and risks associated with human conduct. In addition, I want to sketch the societal processes under way in their broad outlines.[11] I do not attend to the complex details and contexts of different biotechnology applications, controversies, and prospects in different countries.

The perspective I want to advance requires that I first describe the logic of modernity as it manifests itself in the theoretical perspective of (societal) functional differentiation, that is, the centrifugal tendency inherent in all modern societies. A second and competing view relevant in this context suggests the opposite—namely, that economic rationality conquers and controls society. Although these views of the modern economy are diametrically opposed, they both testify to the inherent power and authority of economic reasoning. In the case of differentiation theory, the social system of the economy—first articulated as a political demand by the proponents of mercantilism—ought to be and in fact is self-sufficient: it administers its own affairs and does so on the basis of a logic or code that is uniquely its own. It follows that new developments within the economy must also submit to the same logic. In the case of the idea that we are faced not by a differentiation of social codes, but rather by an economization of society, it follows too that new biotechnological developments surrender to the logic of the market.

The Civilization of Capitalism[12]

> In capitalist reality as distinguished from its textbook picture, it is not (price) competition which counts but the competition from the new commodity, the new technology, the new source of supply, the new type of organization.
>
> *Joseph A. Schumpeter,* Capitalism, Socialism and Democracy

In response to the elementary question, "What is the economy?" or even, "What constitutes the modern economy?" there are two key features that are almost always mentioned as constitutive of economic conduct and that also happen to be of particular interest in this context. To cite Emil Lederer (1922: 18)—nothing, so it seems, is more straightforward than to enumerate the essential features of the economy.

It is, first, quite evident to us that the economic system differs from other social institutions, even though one is also forced to attend to economic issues in churches, in families, in city councils, and in universities. Economic activities as a distinct form of social conduct, in addition, satisfy (material) human needs; in other words, economics "examines that part of individual and social action which is most closely connected with the attainment and with the use of the material requisites of well-being" (Marshall, 1920: 1; also Sombart, [1916] 1921: 13).

Second, the governing professional images of economic activities imply that the economic conduct of producers and consumers, as well as market institutions, closely follows the rationality principle, generating the optimal gain with the smallest possible input. Since such profit/benefit ratios are not generated in isolation, the kind of social interactions and communications that typify "genuine" economic activities are those encountered within the boundaries of internal economic mar-kets,[13] where rational decisions and self-interested behavior are put into practice. In the context of this account, the consumer is, for the most part, a passive being. The consumer has to blindly follow and habitually execute the dominant code or logic of economic conduct.

In this respect there is a peculiar convergence between the modern consumer and cultural critics of modern consumption, such as Mills (1956), Packard (1960), and Marcuse (1968). In both cases, the traditional account of economics and the accounts of the cultural critic of the modern economy, the consumer does not re-ally act, but rather is acted upon, even manipulated by forces beyond her control. The view of the economy through the lens of orthodox economic discourse and cul-tural criticism has to accept the critique of the presence of a form of Taylorism in the field of consumption, since it excludes the main actor, the consumer, from the con-sumption process. Whether these images, even under different economic circumstances, resemble the conduct of many consumers and their decision-making patterns is doubtful. Marketing and advertising efforts were and are often consciously directed to consum-ers who make active choices (see Miller and Rose, 1997).

What is missing from these accounts is the fact that the economy is a dynamic system, and that the changes are accelerating. Moreover, the boundaries of the economic system may be much more porous than is implied in the account of the economy as a functional subsystem with its own unique logic and media of com-munication.[14] In particular, the motives, values, or preferences of at least some of the salient actors within the economic system may be much less restrictive than is implied in the predominant account (cf. Douglas and Isherwood, 1979: 56–70). In other words, using the Marxists' imagery, the nature of the cultural complement of the modern economy is perhaps changing as rapidly as its substructure. And the missing dynamic attributes may be related, as I will argue.

The changes I want to consider may, not only be linked, but may also lead to a reversal of the commonly assumed relationship between substructure and superstruc-ture. The much more complex or varied superstructure is not merely dependent, or a "cultural complement," as Schumpeter ([1942] 1962: 121) describes the derivative culture of capitalism; it is, rather, the motor of the transformation and the reason for the trajectory of the dynamism of capitalism. Market conditions and relations are altered by and respond to the contingencies of everyday life in modern, affluent society.

The Logic of Modernity

> The result of research should be truth and absolutely nothing further. A religion exhausts its meaning with the salvation that it brings to the soul. The economic product wishes to be economically perfect, and does not recognize for itself any other than the economic scale of values.
>
> *Georg Simmel,* The Conflict in Modern Culture and other Essays

The emergence of the economic order as a distinct social system in the first half of the nineteenth century, widely hailed as a moral accomplishment itself, is one of the hallmarks of modernity.[15] The economy was seen and comprehended in terms of its own laws and causalities. Political interventions should be limited, and should respect as well as nurture the unique contingencies of economic action. In contrast, the moral domain, at least in those days, was seen as the proper sphere of intervention, programs, and regulation by politicians and others, all designed to mold the character and conduct of moral subjects (cf. Rose, 1999, 101–107). What is noteworthy about these developments, aside from the particular understanding of the moral domain, is the strict separation of these spheres of conduct.

The most radical contemporary proponent of social differentiation as the logic of modernity is Niklas Luhmann (see Bechmann and Stehr, 2002). The perspective of functional differentiation favors dichotomies and exclusive logics of social action in differentiated social systems. Luhmann defines society as a system that operates on meaning, and therefore as a communicating system that is integrated on the basis of meaningful communication. Society reproduces itself on the basis of communication. Its unity is the autopoiesis of communication. In contrast to the societal system, subsystems also communicate with other subsystems that form part of their environment. The identity of subsystems is constituted on the basis of a differentiated principle or special code. In the case of the economy, according to Luhmann, this happens to be the principle of *payment* (and the opposite of the same code, namely nonpayment). Payments have exactly all the characteristics of autopoietic processes: "They are only possible on the basis of payments, and in the context of the recursive economic context of autopoiesis they have no other meaning but to assure payments" (Luhmann, 1988: 52). Payments (in the form of money and prices) reproduce the economy. These processes assure that the economic system is both a closed and an open system (in the sense of a future direction). The result of these reflections is to transform all economic categories that otherwise constitute core categories of economic discourse into derivatives of payment processes. However, this also implies that many elements that are usually considered to be part of the economic system are not part of Luhmann's discourse about the economy. This applies to resources—that is, to commodities and services for which payments are made—and to the psychological dispositions of actors, for example. These features or processes are part of the environment of the economic system. The economic subsystem, however, is the location in which communication about the elements takes place.

The realities of the economy are dramatically changing, and with them the classical as well as the radically modern perception of the economy. It is not only that national economies are inhabiting a much wider domain or space, commonly discussed under the heading of globalization, but also that the age of the "material" economy is giving way to the "symbolic" economy driven by the "immaterial" resource or "raw material"—knowledge.

The Knowledge-Based Economy

To an increasing degree, knowledge rather than labor or property is constitutive of economic and social activities. Knowledge is becoming the source of the possibil-

Table 4.1. The Knowledge-Based Economy, 1995/1996

	Investments in knowledge[a] compared to (physical investment) as percentage of 1995 GDP		Value-added of knowledge-based industries[b] as a percentage of the 1995/1996 business sector value-added
Italy	6.1	(18.0)	41.3
Japan	6.6	(28.5)	53.0
Australia	6.8	(22.6)	48.0
Germany[c]	7.1	(21.4)	58.6
OECD	7.9	(20.1)	50.9
European Union	8.0	(19.0)	48.4
United States	8.4	(16.9)	55.3
United Kingdom	8.5	(16.3)	51.5
France	10.2	(17.9)	50.0
Sweden	10.6	(14.6)	50.7
Canada	8.8	(16.9)	51.0

[a]Total investment in knowledge is calculated as the sum of R&D expenditures (minus equipment), public spending on education, and investment in software (minus household purchases of packaged software).

[b]The OECD includes all firms that are relatively intensive in their inputs of technology and/or human capital. From the service sector, communication firms, finance, insurance and business services, as well as "community, social, and personal services" are included.

[c]West Germany.

Source: OECD (1999: 114–115)

ity of economic growth and competitive advantage among firms and among entire societies and regions of the world. The developments in question allow us to speak of the transformation of modern industrial society into a *knowledge society*. Even more generally, the knowledge society represents a social and economic world in which more and more things are "made" to happen, rather than a social reality in which things simply "happen." (See table 4.1.)

It is therefore necessary to ask whether the economic principles and policies developed, tested, and adopted for the realities of the material economy are applicable to the new economic realities. In other words, the conditions that allow for the economic transformations under consideration also render traditional economic discourse (and policy derived from such premises) about economic affairs less practical and powerful. In particular, one has to ask whether the claims, assumptions, and principles now encountered in economic discourse have a bearing on the dynamics of the fabrication, distribution, and consumption of knowledge in economic processes.

I will point to only one salient attribute of knowledge that is of particular importance in this context: Unlike the conviction displayed in classical accounts of scientific knowledge, in many instances science is incapable of offering cognitive certainty. Science cannot offer definitive or even true statements (in the sense of proven causal chains) for practical purposes, but only more or less plausible and often contested assumptions, scenarios, and probabilities. Instead of being the source of reliable trustworthy knowledge, science thus becomes a source of uncertainty. And contrary to what rational scientific theories suggest, this problem cannot be comprehended or remedied by differentiating between "good" or "bad" science (or between pseudoscience and correct, i.e., proper, science). After all, who would be capable of doing this under conditions of uncertainty? Knowledge is essentially contested, and the standard areas of contestation around knowledge-based products in general and biotechnologies in particular are those of expertise, risk, responsibility, and regulation (cf. Gofton and Haimes, 1999: 2.7).

The translation of knowledge claims, or the "pragmatization" of scientific and technical knowledge, is the job performed by *experts,* counselors, and advisors, or, as some might say, knowledge workers who apply knowledge to knowledge. Counselors, advisers, and experts are needed to mediate between the complex distribution of changing knowledge and those who search for enabling knowledge. Ideas travel and are transferred as people's "baggage"—that is, knowledge is "encultured," "embrained," or "encoded"—whereas skills (in the sense of know-how or rules of thumb) are more firmly inscribed, embedded, or embodied in people, objects, and resources. Rather than seeing knowledge as something that is arrested and that is there, knowing should be seen as an activity, as something that people do. This active intervention is of particular relevance in the case of specialized scientific knowledge that is, as I have stressed, contestable and often de-pragmatized. A chain of interpretations, or the essential "openness" of knowledge claims, must come to an "end" in order to become relevant in practical contexts and therefore effective as a capacity of action. Experts in modern society largely perform this function of ending reflection, of reducing the openness and contestability of knowledge for the purpose of action. But what is new is not that knowledge-based work and workplaces which require such cognitive skills are emerging. Experts have always been around. The significant economic transition in general, and transformation of the labor market in particular, are to be found in the number and proportion of workplaces that require knowledge-based work and in the decline of workplaces that make or move things.

These developments represent, as I indicated earlier, what might be called the necessary conditions for the moralization of the market. I now turn to what I consider to be the primary sufficient condition for the transformation of the modern marketplace.

Affluence and Consumer Sovereignty

I look forward ... in days not so very remote, to the greatest change which has ever occurred in the material environment of life for human beings in the aggregate. ... The course of affairs will simply be that there will be ever larger and larger classes and groups of people from whom problems of economic necessity have been practically removed.

John Maynard Keynes, Collected Writings

Despite recurrent concerns about the performance of the economy—for example, the extent to which external, unanticipated events affect the global economy—I would like to point out that nothing in the history of the industrialized countries in Western Europe and North America resembles their experiences between 1950 and 1985. As Alan Milward (1992: 21) has stated:

> [B]y the end of this period, the perpetual possibility of serious economic hardship that had earlier always hovered over the lives of three-quarters of the population now menaced only about one-fifth of it. Although absolute poverty still existed in even the richest countries, the material standard of living for most people improved almost without interruption and often very rapidly for thirty-five years. Above all else, these are the marks of the uniqueness of the experience.

The emancipation of large segments of the population from economic vulnerability and subjugation, which Marx and Engels had not foreseen but which Keynes anticipated in the midst of the global slump in the late 1920s,[16] and which does not occur to the same extent and at a similar pace in all industrialized countries, provides the material foundation of new forms of inequality (see Stehr, 1999).

More concretely, what diminishes is the tightness of the linkage in the material dependence of many actors on their occupational status alone; and what increases is the relative material emancipation from the labor market, in the form of personal and household wealth. The economic wealth individual and households are able to mobilize takes the form of resources that are exchangeable at the marketplace. Wealth becomes a triggering device. The growth of individualism in modern society, as well as the moralization of the market, provides the cultural counterpart for the rise of affluence.[17]

Economic discourse today continues to be linked to the eighteenth-century definition of the *major* factors of production—namely, capital and labor, with their combinations and their consequences measured in monetary units. And to this day, in much of social science, consumption phenomena and practices tend to be seen as derivative of the core institutions of society, such as social class, the state, and culture, which are in turn shaped by production and employment.

However, if the focus on, and the implied equivalence and equilibrium between, production and consumption shift from work (in the narrow sense of the term) to *forms of life* of employees and households in modern society, then an analysis of the *consumption* side—especially in relation to total wealth and life expectancy—is more pertinent than the mere income of individuals or households.[18]

What a society makes still matters. But how it consumes what it makes increasingly matters more.[19] The growing degree of consumer sovereignty also affects the social organization of work and the ways in which products are generated through greater interactive contacts with consumers and clients. At least it changes the world of work for those who have to deal directly with the heightened self-confidence of the consumer in the marketplace (Frenkel, Korczynski, Shire, and Tam, 1999: 66–81) and for those charged with realizing and delivering inventions.

Biotechnological Processes and Products

Although the accidents of the atomic reactors at Chernobyl and Three Mile Island were both dramatic in the eyes of the public and had significant visible consequences, they did not produce comparable pressures on the political system to regulate or even prevent the use of certain technologies, as did the introduction of methods more recently to deploy genetically modified seeds in agriculture. Richard Lewontin (2001: 81) observes that we are faced with a historically unique public response toward a new technology, and that the response by the public is conspicuous despite the currently undisputed fact that "uncontained radioactivity has caused the sickness and death of very large numbers of people, while the dangers of genetically engineered food remain hypothetical." The uniqueness of the situation is also remarkable if one contemplates the considerable optimism of the biotechnology industry just a few years ago about their ability to master and control the public's response to biotechnology products. Only a decade ago, L. Christopher Plein (1991: 474) came to the conclusion that the public relations efforts of both the biotechnology industry and public officials assured that the image of "biotechnology has been transformed from one of danger and uncertainty to one of opportunity and familiarity." The positive image of biotechnology after opponents had linked it in the 1970s with environmental concerns was the result of a successful issue-defining campaign of the proponents of biotechnology, tying it to economic development.

But certain scientific findings that quickly migrated from the scientific community, carried and transformed by media discourse into the public consciousness, served as further catalysts (Conrad, 1997). In the case of genetically modified maize, the laboratory findings published in *Nature* by a group of Cornell entomologists in 1999 indicated that the monarch butterfly could be killed by a common form of GM maize. The findings attracted widespread attention. The researchers fed butterfly larvae with pollen from maize engineered with its own pesticide. After consuming the pollen for four days, 44 percent were dead. The findings triggered a widespread reaction that had the unanticipated consequence of mobilizing consumers for a moralization of the marketplace. Whether the laboratory conditions and findings could be generalized to "natural" conditions remained in doubt; experiments outside the laboratory found only limited effects. Given the lack of predators, some researchers even found that monarchs throve near or in GM maize fields.[20] More recent studies financed by the U.S. Department of Agriculture and biotechnology companies indicate that the impact of genetically engineered corn on monarch butterflies is negligible.[21] The new studies report that many of the monarch caterpillars did not die from ingesting contaminated pollen, but rather from ingesting other parts of the genetically modified plant mixed with the pollen. These findings will hardly appease the opponents of GM food, since the other parts of the plant may also be part of the diet of the monarch butterfly. However, the dispute is far from over.

The *products* we buy today are often pretty much the same as the ones that hung in our closets or found their way onto our tables a decade ago. However, the ways in which these products and new goods are produced have been radically altered.

They are, for example, the immediate outcome of new technical capacities to manipulate heredity. Biotechnological developments—and agricultural biotechnology in particular, as an object of publicly and commercially funded research now almost two decades old—are paradigmatic of the knowledge-intensive economy. It is true that in some countries, there are still modest pockets of nonbiotechnology. On the whole, however, according to a disputed claim by Buttel (1999: 1.2, emphasis added; cf. also Buttel, 2000a),[22] in "mainstream agricultural *research circles* across the globe, biotechnology (or 'genetic engineering') is largely the accepted approach." Humans, of course, at least since the beginnings of recorded history, have been selectively promoting or altering the genetic makeup of animals and plants—evolving over the centuries into the now "classical" methods of plant and animal breeding—ever since nature was domesticated by society.[23] That is why the history of domestication is the history of the social transformation of nature. What we are now capable of doing is injecting much greater precision into the process of genetically remaking heredity. At the same time, we have extended the limits of such manipulation far beyond the limits to which classical plant and animal breeding was confined. Now transgenic organisms can be fabricated. But the successes of modern research, and its success in moving its products to market based on new technical capacities for their fabrication, for making them acceptable, and for mastering the market represent very different stories.

There are a number of observations, arguments, and concerns that play a role in discussions about genetically modified foodstuffs. I will focus on the criticisms voiced in such debates. Among the faults that are identified by environmental groups, religious organizations, public interest groups, professional organizations, and scientists are first and foremost the (mainly unknown) health problems that may arise as the result of consuming genetically modified food (for example, allergies). Less relevant and significant to consumers and the everyday decisions they make are the following concerns and potential risks, all of which have been raised: the unintended impact/harm that genetically modified seeds and plants have on their environment, particularly other organisms (for example as the result of a gene transfer to nontarget species); the specific impact on developing countries; whether it is permissible to manipulate and manage the nature of nature; and, formulated in a highly ambivalent fashion, the societal, cultural, religious, and moral implications of an increasing application of GM crops (see Rissler and Mellon , 2000).

In discussing the moralization of the market in the case of biotechnology, it is useful to distinguish between *process* (generating products) and *product,* even though one of the characteristic features of the knowledge-intensive economy is the fusion of process and product. In the case of GM foods, however, it is the process that matters.

The moralization of the market occurs from the bottom up. It occurs in response to the products that appear in the market, and focuses on the processes on the basis of which the products are generated. The process is knowledge-based. But the inherent uncertainty and the endemic conflicts that surround knowledge systems, the lack of confidence or trust in expert opinions, the freedom of choice without guarantees, and the growing reflexive knowledgeability of consumers all make it highly likely that market decisions will not only be governed by risk aversion, but also by moral and ethical considerations.

Efforts that assist consumers in making "informed choices" are generally considered and advocated by regulators as the most rational (promising) approach for consumers in making market choices.[24] Under certain circumstances, information and education will not work.[25] One of the likely consequences of programs advocating informed choice could well be increased uncertainty about biotechnological products and processes. Consumer studies indicate that consumers respond to and resolve uncertainties, lack of confidence, and the complexity and volume of information in various ways, involving references to a complex set of values and social networks.[26] Thus, one of the unanticipated consequences of an extensive public information campaign in the case of biotechnology processes and products could well be a measurable shift in consumer trust away from pronouncements issued by governments, marketing agencies, and industry organizations, and toward activist groups—and in the end, an intensification of the moralization of the markets.

Conclusion

It is of some historical interest to note, if only for the purpose of contrast, that what I have described as the moralization of product consumption represents an era in the evolution of the economy far removed from the 1920s notion of "mass consumption," which could be engineered according to the principles of a kind of social Taylorism. What was needed, it was thought by Alfred P. Sloan, for example, was the scientific management of the needs, desires, and fantasies of the consumer (see Webster and Robins, 1989: 334–336). One outcome of these ideas was the immense growth of market research, advertising, and marketing. It is doubtful that traditional advertising and marketing tools will be very effective in an era of growing consumer independence and knowledgeability.

The reaction that can be observed on the supply side in response to the moralization of the markets takes the form of investments in firms and offices devoted to the issue of the "corporate citizenship" of their respective organizations. These corporate positions and actions are the functional equivalents of chairs in research ethics in the scientific community. Efforts designed to set up such units within corporations are expected, of course, to generate measurable economic benefits for the organizations. But these corporate developments are also a distinct indicator for the influence of changing consumer behavior and the growing power of the demand side.

The moralization of markets for products, or the de-commercialization of prices, does not imply that markets are collapsing, that competition is less efficient, that prices can no longer fulfill the function they perform in the economy, or that the freedom of consumers or producers is seriously undermined. But what it means is that, as a result of fundamental transformations in the economic system and society, the modern consumer's choice of products in the marketplace increasingly reflects considerations other than those of bare "utility." We have seen consumers making choices on the basis of such considerations at a growing pace; preferences expressed by choosing "fair" and "organic" products were only the beginning. Moral imperatives, it would appear, are surer guides to economic conduct than are utilitarian considerations.

The following section addresses the intermarriage between the now widely discussed issue of globalization and knowledge politics. I will trace the origins and explicate the notion of globalization—for example, the extent to which many of the discussions of globalization resonate with and grow out of an earlier conception about the convergence of modern societies into mass societies. The evolution of mass societies was seen last but not least as a process that forces individual societies to become almost indistinguishable from each other.

The same is true if one follows the strong imagery of the notion of globalization as portrayed in many accounts that see an incessant homogenization of the world and its forms of life if not already completed then definitely on the horizon. It would be more accurate to describe globalization processes as societal trends that are far from complete. But however critical one may be of accounts which insist that many of the major decisions about the course and the consequences of globalization have already been made, globalization will surely have an impact on knowledge politics as much as knowledge politics will have an impact on the course of globalization. Emerging complex technological systems that know no boundaries— an outcome anticipated in many images of globalization that are embedded in the social order and frames of social action—represent interactive material infrastructures and social settings that form contexts within which novel knowledge may be placed, or contexts with which knowledge politics not only has to deal but that may disempower knowledge regulation.

Notes

1. "Back to basics," *Guardian,* February 1, 2000.

2. As quoted in "Biotech fuelling latest revolution, economist says," *Globe and Mail,* November 24, 1999. A few years earlier, though in necessarily ambivalent terms, bioindustry analysts had made equally far-ranging predictions about the economic impact of biotechnology, for instance, that by the year 2025 between 70 and 80 percent of the global economy will have, at its base, some form of biotechnology (cited in Hindmarsh, Lawrence, and Norton, 1998: 3). Between 1979 and 1981 alone, a total of eighteen official reports in the industrialized world proclaimed that biotechnology would be the new technological basis for human civilization (see Bud, 1991). Fred Buttel (1989), however, comments that because biotechnology will be applied primarily in declining sectors of the economy, it is unlikely to be an epoch-making technology.

3. In a 1999 survey of public attitudes toward and understanding of science and technology conducted by the National Science Foundation, for example, more than 40 percent of respondents said that they are generally very interested in new scientific discoveries and in the use of new inventions and technologies. Only 10 percent reported no interest, while another 40 to 50 percent indicated they were moderately interested. However, two-thirds of the respondents reported that they were very interested in new medical discoveries. No

other science-related issue received such a high percentage of "very interested" responses (National Science Board, 2000: 8–4/8–5). Internationally comparative data show that the public in other countries is also primarily interested in new medical discoveries, among various scientific and other policy interests that could have been mentioned—although the times during which the surveys in question were carried out differ, which likely affected the responses that were obtained.

4. Compare "Financial ties in biomedicine get close look," *New York Times,* February 20, 2000.

5. Fred Hassan, the chief executive of Upjohn, the drug group, had rather bullish comments about the prospect of a merger between his company and Monsanto, the U.S. biotechnology company, although he admitted that an "education" campaign was needed to overcome the "PR problem" of the biotechnology industry. In January of 2000, however, Hassan offered to close a $600 million research program for genetically modified foods "in an attempt to pacify shareholders unhappy about its takeover of Monsanto" ("P&U offers to scrap $600m GM plan research," *Guardian,* February 1, 2000). The new, merged company would also, Hassan indicated, drop the Monsanto name. The company will be called Pharmacia if investors approve the merger.

6. Compare the article by Floyd Norris, "Public misinformed on genetically modified foods" (*New York Times,* December 17, 1999), in which he observes that companies such as Monsanto made a serious strategic error in not targeting or persuading the public instead of farmers and the Food and Drug Administration about the "evidently small risks" that offset the potential gains of genetically modified seeds.

7. Miguel Altieri (2001: 142) examines the impact of genetically engineered crops on agriculture in all parts of the world, as well as their alternatives in the form of a variety of agroecological approaches to farming that emphasize "biodiversity; recycling of nutrients; synergy among crops, animal, soils, and other biological components; as well as regeneration and conservation of resources." Such approaches are highly context-sensitive, rather than insensitive, as is the case for agroindustrial production methods that would include the widespread use of bioengineered crops.

8. The term "market behavior" is designed to signal that I also refer to consumer decisions and reasons for decisions in the marketplace when I employ the term "consumption." This usage of the term *consumption* differs from that advanced, for example, by Douglas and Isherwood (1979: 57; emphasis added) who refer to "consumption as a use of material possessions that is *beyond commerce* and free within the law."

9. The perhaps classical difference or counter-concept challenging the system-specific autonomy of the economic market are the terms *plan* or *state*. In the context of this paper I do not intend to address contentious market-plan-state relations.

10. A differentiation among markets and the corresponding social processes that determine prices and purchasing decisions based on the kind of actors typically found in these markets suggests for example the following ideal types: Labor markets, capital or financial markets, consumer markets, and industrial markets (cf. Swedberg, 1994: 274). My observations, given these distinctions, refer to consumer markets, in the first instance.

11. The assertion that the modern economic system is moving, based on endogenous developments, from a "production orientation" to a "consumption orientation" has indeed been advanced repeatedly in the last century, usually during periods of sustained economic growth. But these debates were entirely different from the economic transformations analyzed in this paper. Claims about the end of scarcity, the declining need of capitalism for asceticism, and the rise of virtues surrounding the act of consumption were heard in the United States in the 1920s and after World War Two. However, the discussion in each case

centered on the issue of *expanding* the volume of consumption and its cultural consequences. In the words of John K. Galbraith ([1967] 1971: 37), the "individual serves the
industrial system not by supplying it with savings and the resulting capital; he serves it by
consuming its products." A critique of these perspectives may be found in Martin, 1999. He
claims with justification that all versions of the consumption economy thesis are "based on
unwarranted exaggeration of theoretical trends, the over-generalization of empirical trends,
and a credulous treatment of interested parties' claims" [of advertisers for example] (Martin, 1999: 445). What did change in the course of the last century was the broad enrichment
of the consuming public that accelerated after World War Two. Discussions that centered
on the need to consume were soon followed by treatise after treatise informed by moral
indignation about consumerism. These works, castigating consumers as vulgar, greedy,
stupid, and insensitive, reinvoked Thorstein Veblen's scorn of conspicuous consumption
(see Douglas and Isherwood, 1979: vii-viii).

12. I have borrowed the title of this section from Joseph A. Schumpeter's *Capitalism,
Socialism and Democracy* ([1942] 1962). Schumpeter, although highly attuned to the evolutionary character of the capitalist system, is well-known for his pessimism about the
long-term dynamics of the capitalist economy. It is bound to fail because it becomes too
successful; it breaks "to pieces under the pressure of its own success" (Schumpeter,
[1942] 1962: 134). Both Marx and Schumpeter, in the end, underestimated the ability
of the capitalist system to evolve beyond its allegedly inherent limits. Schumpeter's
([1942] 1962: 125) title suggests something else, however—a thoroughly Marxian
notion that "all the features and achievements of modern civilization are, directly or indirectly, the products of the capitalist process." Modern society is not—to mention but one
alternative—politically constituted. The concept of society becomes economic. If one did
not care to accept Schumpeter's sweeping assertion, a more appropriate title of this section
would be "civilizing capitalism." A similar general premise about the seizure of control of
society and its institutions by capitalism surfaces in the context of critical theory and elsewhere in social theory. Most recently, this view finds expression in the idea of a colonization of the life-world by the systems of capitalism, bureaucracy, and law (Habermas, 1981,
1987).

13. In his suggestive system-theoretic perspective of economic activities, Niklas
Luhmann (1988: 94) defines the "market" as the system-internal *environment* of the economic subsystem. The economic system creates its own internal environment in order to
achieve reductions of complexity for the purpose of observing external environments, such
as the state, scientific and technological developments, or ecological transformations.

14. Traditional social thought champions centrality and unity. Aside from a strictly
system-theoretical perspective, the idea—as the title "The Civilization of Capitalism" already signals—that the logic or rational attitude of economic affairs would subjugate or
rationalize almost every form of life external to the economy has for the longest period
hardly been a contested assumption in social theory. While a system-theoretical perspective (Luhmann) resists assigning overall functional priority to any social system and the
exclusive logic that governs any subsystem, the much more common premise is that the
economy is the dominant social system in modern societies. Traffic that is seen to occur in
the opposite direction represents a controversial perspective, and the possibility that the
assumed rationalization of lifestyles, social institutions, ideas, etc., has been less than complete is also a contentious assertion.

15. The emergence of the market as a separate social institution is seen by prominent
economic historians as a benign or even benevolent development. Albert Hirschman, for
example, in his book *The Passions and the Interests* (1977), has asserted forcefully that the

pursuit of "interest" in the context of the evolving market was a vast improvement on the pursuit of "passion," since interest was governed by reason rather than unruly emotions. Not only radical opponents of market economies in the past, but also more liberal observers at the present time, take exactly the opposite position with respect to the consequences for the moral fabric of society: "The market contributes more to the erosion of our moral sense than any other modern social force" (Schwartz, 1999: 37).

16. In an essay entitled "Economic possibilities for our grandchildren," published in 1930, Keynes ([1930] 1984: 326–328) contemplates somewhat darkly such a future of plenty, for economic problems or "the struggle for existence, always has been hitherto the primary, most pressing problem of the human race.... If the economic problem is solved, mankind will be deprived of its traditional purpose. Will this be a benefit? If one believes at all in the real values of life, the prospect at least opens up the possibility of benefit. Yet I think with dread of the readjustment of the habits and instincts of the ordinary man, bred into him for countless generations, which he may be asked to discard within a few decades.... Thus for the first time since his creation man will be faced with his real, permanent problem—how to use his freedom from pressing economic cares, how to occupy the leisure which science and compound interest will have won for him, to live wisely and agreeably and well."

17. Alain Touraine ([1992] 1995: 207) captures the increased value of individualism in contemporary society and, in its wake, the rise of consumerism, as follows: "The modern world ... increasingly abounds with references to a Subject. That Subject is freedom, and the criterion of the good is the individual's ability to control his or her actions and situation, to see and experience modes of behavior as components in a personal life history, to see himself or herself as an actor. The Subject is an individual's will to act and to be recognised as an actor."

18. However, I am not suggesting that we are dealing with a plainly defined, fixed hierarchy of human needs in which cultural interests always take a back-seat role to material interests. Cultural interests exist at least side by side with material interests. Whether cultural interests come into conflict with material interests is a matter of historical contingency. Nor are the wealthy necessarily the only agents who are able to act according to moral concerns. The struggle between moral and material concerns and needs is a contingent one in which grounds shift; one of the ways in which the grounds shift is, as I indicate, linked to the general well-being of society. But even as cultural interests gain, material considerations do not simply vanish.

19. My observation about the role of consumption indicates that there evidently is an elective affinity to Pierre Bourdieu's (1984) examination of styles of consumption or consumption as competitive display, in his study *Distinction*. Consumption is more than the mere deployment of economic resources or the satisfaction of material welfare. Styles of consumption exhibit differential "cultural capital." The pageant of products is part of an unequal system of reputation and distinction (see also Friedman, 1994; Bauman, 1998).

20. Compare "Threat that never was," *Times,* December 14, 2000.

21. See "New research fuels debate over genetic food altering," *New York Times,* September 9, 2001.

22. According to Anthony Arundel (personal communication), the "'modest pockets of nonbiotechnology constitute 90 percent of the research effort by European seed firms today and an estimated 85 percent in 2002. Buttel has apparently fallen hook, line, and sinker for the continual propaganda from the biotechnology government-industry complex about the economic and technical importance of biotechnology." See also Arundel, 2000.

23. Lewontin (2001: 81) refers to the case of corn and relates that these often ancient modifications of nature are not only very different from the "natural," ancient ancestors, "but in many cases are the opposite of the organisms from which they were derived. The compact size of maize with large kernels adhering tightly to the cob is very useful in a grain that needs to be gathered and stored for long periods, but a plant with such a seed head would soon disappear in nature because it could not disperse its seed" (also Stich, 1982).

24. The source of the standards chosen to police knowledge, the regulatory procedures put in place, and the intellectual systems legitimizing the cultural dismissal of certain uses of knowledge typically also do not necessarily originate in science and technology itself. For example, in the face of demands to preserve and defend the nature of human nature (in response to developments in scientific and technical capacities to alter the status quo of human reproduction), scientific "notions of nature do not provide us with unambiguous standards of naturalness to which we can appeal for normative orientation" (van den Daele, 1992: 549). Since scientific notions of naturalness allow for the construction of a range of possible natures, regulation efforts advancing the cause of abstaining from practical steps intervening into human nature have to appeal to mundane moral claims and generate political action that may or may not succeed in arresting human nature. The anchoring of standards and justifications outside of science does not mean that individuals who are scientists may not be found among those who vigorously support attempts to regulate knowledge in certain specific ways.

25. A German study (Gath and Alvensleben, 1997) concurs that the "possibilities of influencing the acceptance of GM foods by information are limited ... the widespread opinion that the acceptance of GM food is primarily an information and education problem ... has to be questioned."

26. I have to leave open another, perhaps even more fascinating issue that addresses the relationships between active citizens and governance in modern society. Rose (1999: 166) refers to a symbiosis between sovereign citizens and forms of modern government when he observes that "advanced liberal forms of government ... rest, in new ways, upon the activation of the powers of the citizen." And the new, active role of the citizen includes the citizen as a consumer who becomes an active agent, not just active in the dynamics of markets exchanging products, but also "in the regulation of professional expertise" (Rose, 1999: 166) or symbolic properties.

Chapter 5

Globalization and Knowledge Politics

Investments in education and research are widely seen as a key to development and economic growth (e.g., World Bank, 1999). That there has in fact been a huge worldwide expansion of scientific research since World War Two is quite evident. This is not to say that there is a common, global view of scientific practice, or uniform conceptions about its social role, or equality in the volume of research across nations. Nor is it the case that knowledge "infrastructures" are distributed evenly.[1] However, the scientific community is not primarily differentiated along ethnic, regional, or national lines, but into disciplines, research areas, and problem areas. The spread of a particular model of the culture of scientific practice around the world is considerable, as is the extent to which scientific knowledge, produced somewhere in the world, crosses boundaries (although by no means effortlessly) and serves as a basis for national policy decisions and social transformations. Science is widely seen as relevant not merely for economic growth. Science acts as an authoritative institution addressing a wide variety of policy-relevant issues in the fields of health care, the environment, defense, human rights, social inequality, and social security (Schofer, 1999; Schofer, Ramirez and Meyer, 2000).

The global penetration of the culture of science that would appear to allow for the uptake of scientific knowledge in many regions and places of the world, and the authority of science that supports such an uptake, raise the question of knowledge politics in an age of the global presence of science and technology. The question the global diffusion of the culture of science raises is whether knowledge politics, especially in its *constraining* intentions, can function only as a global knowledge policy regime. The question of whether knowledge politics in its *option and opportunity creating function* must also rely on global arrangements is perhaps another issue, as I will try to show.[2]

A case in point of prohibitions in one country being undercut by moving the use of the forbidden technique to another where such procedures may not violate regulations is the recent use of a novel, experimental human fertilization technique by a team of scientists in China, who were advised by U.S. scientists. U.S. scientists developed the technique but were concerned that their work might infringe on U.S. regulations and offered it to their Chinese colleagues.

The technique, called human nuclear transfer, was outlawed in Britain amid fears that it might lead to human cloning. It involves the creation of a pregnancy that would produce children with three genetic parents. The first transfer in China took place in 2002. China has since instituted a ban. Scientists working in the field of reproductive medicine claim that human nuclear transfer could assist women with poor-quality eggs, for example, where the embryo ceases to develop in an early stage of pregnancy. The process involves removing the nucleus that contains all the genetic material from the unhealthy egg and transferring it into the shell of a donor egg from which all the genetic material has been removed. In most cases, nuclear transfer creates an embryo that has the genetic characteristics of two mothers and a father.[3] As the case demonstrates, the ability and the ease with which one is able to transfer knowledge as a capacity to act and techniques across borders that constitute the boundaries of legal entities makes the practice of knowledge politics a most difficult political field.

But first I would like to anchor my discussion about the relationship between knowledge politics and globalization in the context of some of the important issues in the globalization debate and its intellectual predecessors. One of the relevant recent theoretical precursors of the globalization thesis is the contention that modern societies are mass societies.

Mass Societies

The contested and widely discussed mass society thesis during the postwar years (Kornhauser, 1959) was linked to particular ideological commitments and also to specific cultural and political experiences, perceived and presented as fundamental predicaments of modern civilization. These perspectives offer simplified images of the allegedly highly efficacious, inescapable nature of modernity, especially of the social and psychological consequences of modern science and technology. However, they also exemplify the more complex thesis, indebted to the theory of evolution and applied to the development of human societies, that a decreasing variation over time is one of the clearly predictable features of stable systems and of social evolution.

This thesis has resurfaced more recently within the context of discussions about the globalization of social and economic action. Globalization, in this sense, and in the sense in which it will be criticized here, refers first and foremost to the more or less one-dimensional social, cultural, and economic processes by which the "peoples of the world are incorporated into a single world society, a global society" (Albrow, 1990: 9; Meyer, Boli, Thomas, and Ramirez, 1997).

However, crucial questions about the structures, limits of, and closures to the penetration of globalization and its conditions often do not get asked, in light of rather global assertions about the convergence of modern life-worlds (Cooper, 2001). Therefore, at this point in time, much more to the point is the observation that a great majority of the world's people do not have the means (property or knowledge) to participate in the economic globalization process (De Soto, 2000).

The alleged triumph of globalization is at once oversold and underestimated. Social, cultural, and economic globalization, the kinds of processes social scientists consider to be their unique referent and to which I will in the main turn, often tends to be oversold, especially by its critics, as an almost irresistible force. Universalistic processes linked to natural processes—for example, the universalism of the genetic code of humans as well as organisms not too distant from humans such as yeast, E. coli, or insects—may have implications for sociocultural and socioeconomic globalization processes that we are virtually unable to remotely anticipate. The boundaries between disciplines, and therefore the nature of the discussion of globalization and the nature of its major determining forces, will likely be reconstituted in the discussion of globalization as a result of the social consequences that emanate from developments in the physical sciences, especially in biology, genetics, and computer science.[4]

Setting aside the assumption of an incessant convergence of economic and especially financial markets that is shared among both critics and proponents of globalization, and which therefore gains in significance as an attribute of the globalization process, it is the global spread of information and the rapid diffusion of scientific knowledge across all boundaries and contexts that strengthens the contention of the globalization of the modern world. The assertion of the global and globalizing impact of information and knowledge already highlights the relationship of knowledge politics and globalization that should be discussed in this section. Among the specific questions that arise in this context is, of course, whether existing or emerging international and national institutions are capable of regulating the transnational migration of novel knowledge and those interests that desire its unencumbered realization.

One of the suspicions that surround demands for the political system of the nation-state to regulate new knowledge, for example, is that what some have called "ethics dumping" is bound to occur—namely, that nations will vigorously compete for comparative benefits, and that the logic of regulation will be driven by considerations of retaining or gaining competitive advantages with respect to the location of production sites, or the place where certain services may be offered.

The Globalization of the World

The hope that one cosmopolitan order, or the fear that a single world society is emerging, has animated the comparative analysis of societies in the postwar era under diverse headings. Taken together, these perspectives continue for the most part to stipulate that a convergence or even a unification of societies will be a reality. But this would not be a regression toward the mean. The social, cultural, and economic convergence of different societies occurs in terms of the most advanced societies.

In a number of present-day theoretical analyses, the concept of globalization, although by no means a self-contained concept or perspective, appears to be little more than a convenient substitute and extension for what used to be given various labels: the inevitable master process of rationalization (homogenization and standardization),[5] especially in the form of standards of rational economic practice; or later, the even more widely discussed perspective of the modernization and convergence of social relations around the world (cf. Inkeles, 1998); or more negatively, the unmasking of the enlightenment as a form of *mass* deception under the rule of capitalist market relations (cf. Robinson, 1996: 15). In all instances, reference is to a process that is the result not of some kind of mechanical law—for example, in the field of economic relations—but to globalization as a political or social creation. By the same token, in all of these perspectives there is a leading socioeconomic and sociopolitical agent, operating in its own interest and trying to universalize particular practices.

The same cautionary note applies, as one should be aware, to discourse about the alleged specter or the anticipated fruits of globalism or mass society. Such prescriptive discourse, be it affirmative or critical, serves as ideological armor in contemporary political debates and struggles.[6] Indeed, the affinity to discussions of mass society phenomena and their ideological thrust was particularly evident in the early literature on globalization, which exhibited (and continues to exhibit in some countries) a heightened sensibility about the dangers of a cultural imperialism that would result in the obliteration of ethnic, regional, and national cultural differences in the face of a seductive onslaught by American culture.

I refer here, for example, to the pessimistic diagnosis of the prospect of culture as mass culture in Horkheimer and Adorno's *Dialectic of Enlightenment* ([1944] 1972: 121). Their diagnosis resonates with many current analyses of the media:

> Under monopoly all mass culture is identical, and the lines of its artificial framework begin to show through. The people at the top are no longer so interested in concealing monopoly; as its violence becomes more open, so its power grows. Movies and radio need no longer pretend to be art. The truth [that] they are just businesses is made into an ideology in order to justify the rubbish they deliberately produce. They call themselves industries; and when their directors' incomes are published, any doubt about the social utility of the finished product is removed.

However, even in the case of the observed global concentration of cultural products and lifestyles across the globe (see Guerlain, 1997), we need to make distinctions. Recent analyses of the acceleration of the globalization process, that is, discussions in the social sciences that explicitly occur under the heading of "globalization" since the second half of the 1980s, and that do not examine globalization as mere ideology, can be divided into observations that deal with three different consequences of globalization and that have different notions about what may constitute the motor of globalization: (1) *economic* (and perhaps political as well as technological) consequences; (2) *cultural* consequences (including the internationalization of knowledge, information, and communicative capacities); and (3) *ecological* consequences, that is, the impact on the environment of increasingly global lifestyles and of the machinery that generates and sustains these.

The reality, the interpenetration, and the impact of economic and ecological globalization, as well as the internationalization of knowledge and information (Petit and Soete, 1999: 171–175), are practically uncontested in the literature.[7] In discussions of the enabling forces that drive globalization and the politics of the globalization of national economic systems, the least controversial are the globalization of financial markets or transactions; the internationalization of production (see Held, 1995: 127–134), as well as the continuous decrease in transportation costs (relative to costs of production); the rise of political issues in the wake of global economic developments that have a global nature (Luhmann, 1997b: 67); the increasing globalization of regulatory regimes, for example in the field of prescription drugs (Drahos and Braithwaite, 2001); and perhaps the global technological convergence along the path of specific economic-technical regimes and the logic of increasing returns. (cf. Nelson and Wright, 1992). A much more contested thesis is the observation that the "world market ... has the effect of creating the conditions of domination and brutally confronting the agents and the enterprises previously enclosed within national limits to the competition of the most efficient and powerful productive forces and means of production" (Birdie, 2001: 2).

The emergence of a global market that deals in symbolic, rather than conventional, commodities is one of the important outcomes of these developments. Another recent general economic trend that is difficult to overlook after the virtual disappearance of centrally planned economies is the move toward market-driven forces and policies that enhance the establishment of economic markets, including the liberalization of trade in commodities. However, even though such developments, and in particular economic processes, appear to penetrate virtually all national and regional systems, they are not simply one-way streets.

One of the exceptions to the virtually uncontested economic globalization thesis is Hirst and Thompson's (1992, 1996, 1997) analysis of a steady development of internationalization. Hirst and Thompson counter the globalization arguments by pointing to the persistent strong national linkages and embeddedness of multinational corporations and the concentration of various economic exchange processes in only a few regions of the world.[8] Moreover, on the basis of a comparison of relative trends in trade, migration, and capital flows, the present globalized world is less integrated than was the case in the early decades of the twentieth century (see Hirst and Thompson, 1996: 26–27; also Stehr, 1992a: 101–106). Such skepticism, however, competes with alarming assertions on the left of the political spectrum about the world war of capitalist globalization (cp. Robinson, 1996: 13).

The claims pro and contra globalization are only contradictory contentions at first glance. Even economic discourse rarely maintains that most relevant global economic processes are moving in only one direction and converge in a process akin to the speed and formation of traffic in a one-way street. It is true that the classical claims found in development theory of the 1950s have been amended. For example, the contention that the cause for economic backwardness is the result of only a slow diffusion and adoption of modern technologies and scientific knowledge in some regions of the world is no longer accepted as a valid observation about the stratification of global economic well-being. Multinational corporations are now present in almost all parts of the world. However, the presence of multinational corporations and their know-how in many countries has not produced a convergence of economic conditions, nor the production of knowledge-intensive goods and services in all regions of the globe. High-tech and science-based production is still concentrated in territories and countries characterized by an exceptional knowledge and technology infrastructure (Storper, 1996).

If one means to suggest that economic globalizing processes imply a noticeable *assimilation* of wealth, income, or conditions of production across the world, then the critique of the strong version of the globalization thesis that Hirst and Thompson, for example, offer is well taken. If one means to suggest that globalization implies an extension and continuation of a *concentration* of economic wealth and political power, as has been the case in the past, then the critics of globalization are correct that, despite specialization and an extensive global division of labor, one is able to discern a concentration of economic influence and its sociopolitical consequences.

Market economies evolved at different times and in different places within contexts of different national laws and policy styles, cultures and social structures, constitutions and policies. Whether these diverse patterns are bound to surrender to a common, global logic of capitalist production and exchange is therefore a contentious assertion. Some bet that they will (Strange, 1997: 182), while others are more skeptical and expect that robust multinational, national, or regional diversities will persist (cf. Crouch and Streeck, 1997). And nation-states differ enormously in scale; some national governments retain significant areas of discretion in economic policies (see Cable, 1995: 38–40).[9]

Even today, economic transformations cannot easily be uncoupled from cultural and political contingencies and traditions. The loss of sovereignty of effective national economic and fiscal policy implementation is typically accompanied by countervailing internal forces that impact international trade relations, for example, and therefore represent national, regional, and even local cultural and political effects *on* global commercial relations. Existing disciplinary divisions within the social sciences contribute to masking the significance of the interdependence of cultural, political, and economic forces, while fascination with the swift appearance, relentless immediacy, and apparent strength of global processes leads us to dismiss much too early, in my view, the recalcitrance of "national" realities.

In present-day public debates over the growing pressures on national economies to remain competitive and lower trade barriers to access from abroad, the positions articulated typically range from claims that any resistance to or uncoupling from actual economic developments is futile and would result in unacceptably high costs, all the way to the opposite claim that resistance to these developments is not only necessary but also politically feasible and legally possible. In many of these public debates—exemplifying the speedy global dissemination of the concept of "globalization"—economic, political, and cultural considerations are freely mixed, and arguments in favor of or in opposition to globalization rarely follow the convenient disciplinary divisions still influential in social science discourse. Disputes that involve the cultural impact and consequences of globalization remain the most intense and bitter controversies, however. This is not surprising, since what is at stake here, according to most participants, are the perceived dangers of a homogenization and standardization of life-worlds, popular culture, and esthetics—and therefore the eventual disappearance of the diversity of cultures around the globe.

While it may well be theoretically true that decreasing variation is associated with a greater stability of social systems,[10] the premise ought to be examined carefully in order to determine whether our age is *in fact* an age of decreasing variation. It could well be that the growth of knowledge and its rapid dissemination across the world leads to greater variation, that it supports a larger variety of lifestyles, patterns of conduct, world views, and living conditions.[11] The perspective of postmodernism is fundamentally opposed to the claim that there is a tendency toward global homogenization. The implosion of modernity, or fragmentation rather than uniformity, is seen as the new driving force, at least in the realm of culture.

My own perspective on the effects of globalization, however, is not a postmodern one. I also do not accept any rigid dichotomy between local (or regional) and global phenomena, according to which every characteristic of the social sphere must either take on strictly local attributes or eliminate them altogether in the wake of the effects of globalization. As long as the local/global axis is dichotomized in such a rigid and *asymmetrical* manner, the theoretical and empirical dilemma will be that political, social, and economic processes have to be categorized under the heading either of global attributes or of authentic local circumstances that bear at best only a superficial resemblance to phenomena alleged to be global in scope. As a result, a prohibition against a "synchronism of the incommensurable" (Max Frisch) or the "noncontemporaneity of the contemporaneous" (Wilhelm Pinder) must be strictly observed (also Mannheim, [1928] 1993: 358). To follow such prohibitions is to miss out on significant societal processes that result from struggles between local and global phenomena, or that constitute emerging social structures, cultural processes, or political developments which succeed in joining these forces in novel ways. Accordingly, globalization is not a stern developmental process that leads to (a kind of uniform) globality as its end. Globalization is the substance of globality itself, in the form of the multiple social, cultural, and economic transformations under way in many sectors and regions of society and across societies (cf. Bauman, 2001: 138).

Cultural manifestations are never created *ex nihilo* and strictly in accordance with either local or global reference (Tomlinson, 1999). But it is also unrealistic to expect that forms of knowledge disappear altogether in the wake of the effects of globalization, leaving no trace (cf. Stehr, 1991), or that well-established patterns of social conduct vanish without signs of lasting influence.[12] With globalization and fragmentation proceeding concurrently, global as well as particularistic political developments generate and heighten conflicts (cf. Schmidt, 1995)—for example, between claims of universal human rights and particularistic identities based on language, religion, nationality, race, and ethnicity (see Benhabib, 1999). Indeed, images of political opportunities that result from extending the boundaries of governance beyond the nation-state, as well as ominous threats that issue from the same developments for the nation-state appear to coexist side by side in many accounts of the political implications of globalization.

In a spirit strongly affected by the rationalization or the modernization thesis, many observers have prematurely asserted the fragility and even the obsolescence of traditions, belief systems, and worldviews. The assumption that certain "irrational" convictions are manifestations of the "childhood of the human race" (Bell, 1990: 45), and thus inherently brittle functions that can easily be replaced by "rational" doctrines, is not supported by social and cultural reality (cf. Snow and Machalek, 1982).

In the case of the worldwide exposure to the mass media and the nature of its impact, Appadurai (1996:21) argues that the "consumption of the mass media worldwide provokes resistance, irony, selectivity, and, in general, *agency.*" On the basis of internationally comparative survey data for the 1981–1998 period, Inglehart and Baker (2000) report that national cultures and values are of course transformed over time, though in "path-dependent" rather than convergent ways, as is suggested by the idea of a global culture as an outcome of the globalization process.

Generally speaking, the interest in globalization processes is most intense among ecologists; somewhat less so among economists, but still considerable; and perhaps least vigorous among sociologists. In the *social sciences,* the substantive focus during the past decade or longer has been on the globalization of economic processes and cultural practices as a new phase in world history. Contemporary sociologists and anthropologists tend to stress, as generations of sociologists before them did, the importance of diverse cultural forces and artifacts that are the motor of and subject to globalization, in addition to political and economic processes (see Robertson, 1990; 1992; Friedman, 1995; Kilminster, 1997). The global scope of ecological processes is rarely a matter of controversy. Environmentalists generally concur that the planet is approaching its carrying capacity, and that "the extension to the rest of the globe of rates of consumption and production characteristic of industrialized countries is simply not feasible" (Robinson and Tinker, 1997). Projections of an extension of modernization processes into the future that point to a series of global catastrophes are common, but are also seen by some as the precondition for a reconciliation of reason and globalization processes, since it is only as a result of such insights into the consequences of human actions that it may be possible to alter present economic practices and trends (for example, Richter, 1992: 192–204).

A secondary focus within the core social sciences, at least, has been the problem of global environmental risks. The cultural, economic, and ecological trajectories of globalization are, of course, interconnected. Yet discourse concerning these interrelationships tends to be sporadic and fragmentary. Economists, sociologists, and ecologists typically insist upon their own perspective as the theoretical anchorage of any common framework. The obstacles preventing a common frame of reference remain formidable and are strongly linked to the entrenched intellectual division of labor within social science (cf. Robinson and Tinker, 1997).

I want to focus my subsequent analysis on the significance of globalization for knowledge politics, keeping the contentious background of the inquiry into globalization processes in mind. Future political activities in the field of knowledge politics undoubtedly will have to contend with globalization. A difference that may advance an analysis of the relation between globalization and knowledge politics is the distinction in the intended function of the governance of knowledge, to which I have already referred a number of times. The distinction in the function of knowledge politics concerns either attempts to enlarge options and opportunities for the use of novel knowledge or the efforts to restrict and control its utilization. It may sound unconvincing upon first sight, but my contention will be that efforts to police knowledge on a global scale will be more successful than will be attempts to expand its worldwide opportunities and options.

New knowledge may do more than intrude upon world views and convictions, and therefore become the target of political efforts to control its practical use. This knowledge may also infringe on the economic interests of corporations or may be seen to generate asymmetrical benefits. I will start with an examination of efforts to enhance the options for new knowledge beyond the boundaries of their initial discovery and production, and concentrate in this instance on economic contexts within which there are attempts to realize such novel opportunities.

Economic Development and Knowledge Politics

When it comes to the economic affluence of a nation and the ability of a country's economy to improve the standard of living of its citizens and compete internationally, social scientists are in unusual agreement that productivity "in the long run is almost everything" (Krugman, 1994: 13). Manuel Castells (1996: 80), throughout his extensive study of modern society as a network society, seconds this observation and concludes that "productivity is the source of the wealth of nations."

Not only shifts in standards of living follow from changes in productivity performance. Less immediately related noneconomic transformations in response to unequal national productivity gains occur as well, including major changes in the balance of global power relations. The prosperity and competitiveness of a country depend, in short, on the productivity with which it uses its human, capital, and natural resources. In the past, the prosperity of a nation was largely seen as a function of its ability to command natural resources. Today, comparative advantages go to the country with advantages in "human capital" or, more generally, knowledge resources. Michael Porter (2000: 17) puts it as follows: "Comparative advantage has given way as the basis of wealth to *competitive* advantage residing in superior productivity in assembling resources to create valuable products and services."

The question is therefore not only what impact, if any, regional knowledge policies have on the competitive state of a set of countries such as the EU, but also whether *transnational* attempts at the governance of knowledge, also in the sense of enlarging options and opportunities for the uses of novel knowledge, can have much of an impact on the economic performance of countries.

At this point we need to recall, first, our definition of knowledge as a capacity for action. Second, the definition of knowledge as a capacity for action signals that its utilization depends on the nature of the socioeconomic context within which knowledge is supposed to set something in motion. How dependent the realization of knowledge on the local conditions of action may turn out to be depends on a variety of factors (cf. Hayek, [1945] 1948). Prime among the factors that may facilitate or hamper the realization of models of reality is the degree to which this (1) requires or is dependent on control over the conditions of action, and (2) how standardized or routinized the local conditions of action have to be.

What turn out to be "cosmopolitan" cognitive representations—that is, easily reproducible models of reality in many, perhaps even somewhat distinct, circumstances—are knowledge claims (or, better, information)[13] that either rely for their realization on minimal institutional, cultural (including legal and economic) infrastructures, or that are dependent on routinized knowledge infrastructures which can be found in many geographical locations or that can easily migrate.

By the same token, models of reality that require considerable degrees of control over the local circumstances of action—because they are dependent for their realization on extensive and complex convention-bound infrastructures (rationalities) or nonroutinized social contexts—are "local" (noncosmopolitan) cognitive representations.[14] Certain institutional arrangements and rationalities are *not* the outcome of the diffusion of knowledge, but rather are among the important preconditions for its diffusion beyond its points of origin.

One might expect that the force of the economic globalization process, the extent to which corporations produce globally, for example, must be accompanied by a rapid global diffusion of knowledge and production technologies. At least one might anticipate that local institutional conditions such as bureaucratic structures would quickly be displaced by more universal best practices, implemented by managers and professionals with the necessary skills acquired as the result of training based on standardized curricula. However, this is not the case (Zysman, 1994). Multinational corporations often have their own culture. Economic analysis shows that technologically sophisticated activities tend to be concentrated in countries with an equally advanced scientific and knowledge infrastructure. The "core technology and knowledge-intensive outputs of the world economy continue to be produced in relatively few places on the globe, and they are traded. The wealthy countries manifest increasing specialization in spite of their similar income levels" (Storper, 1996: 262; also Dosi, Pavitt, and Soete, 1990). Core areas of economic productivity around the globe are core areas because of the uniqueness of the local conditions, including setting-specific social and cognitive skills (cf. Asanuma, 1989),[15] which cannot be easily transported and transplanted into other geographical locations. Moreover, multinational corporations tend to keep their most important growth-enhancing technological activities in or near their home bases (Patel and Pavitt, 1991). The specificity of local conditions which assure that knowledge can be realized may not hamper the migration of knowledge per se, but it limits the conversion of capacities for action. Some of the required infrastructures may be highly localized, others regional or national. The knowledge-intensive economy is localized, and the production of technology is far from globalized (Porter, 1990).[16]

Effective knowledge policies designed to expand options of capacities for action, for example, in terms of location or spatial contexts, may be comparatively successful if they center on cosmopolitan knowledge, and the ease and low costs with which cosmopolitan knowledge may travel and be transferred. In economic terms, such knowledge likely involves highly standardized and routinized activity in manufacturing and services under circumstances that tend to be less uncertain and fragile than is the case for the utilization of noncosmopolitan knowledge.

By the same token, novel knowledge that is highly dependent for its implementation on the control of multiple conditions of action (relational skills, expensive infrastructures) will hardly benefit from knowledge policies designed to encourage its relocation. The transmission costs are high and the investments in infrastructural improvements are significant, as is the time required to generate returns. In economic terms, such knowledge extends primarily to the production of nonstandardized and nonroutinized goods and delivery of services. The conditions of action in this case are characterized by greater uncertainty and fragility. The conscious efforts required to manage and achieve successful coordination of actions under conditions of pervasive uncertainty are, of course, considerable.

Which countries are likely to agree to international regulative political measures and sign agreements that impose rules and regulation on the use of new scientific knowledge and technical devices? Such a question is most difficult to answer, and the only evidence available that might be helpful in arriving at estimates is the experience with international environmental treaties.

The experience so far demonstrates clearly that nation-states take rather different postures when it comes to international environmental legislation. Some countries have embraced international environmental legislation, such as the Montreal Protocol on CFC emissions, or proposals that originated with the United Nations Conference on Environment and Development in Rio de Janeiro in 1992. Other countries have rejected such agreements. The most prominent example is the rejection by U.S. President George W. Bush of the Kyoto Protocol. The U.S. Administration declared in March 2001 that it would not submit the Kyoto Protocol to the U.S. Senate for ratification. The president, as a spokesman quoted him, did not support the Kyoto treaty because it was not in the United States' best economic interest. The U.S. government would devise different strategies to deal with climate change.[17] In general, the willingness of nations to agree to international environmental treaties reflects "widely different internal state policies towards the environment and in the priority given to enforcement of environmental legislation" (Roberts, 1996: 38).

Notes

1. Despite the rapid diffusion across the world of certain kinds of modern technologies and certain forms of knowledge, as well as the presence of major corporations in many countries, we are still far removed from an even distribution in the production of major

knowledge-intensive goods and services. "The core technology- and knowledge-intensive outputs of the world economy continue to be produced in relatively few places on the globe" (Storper, 1966: 262). For the critics of the politics of globalization this is, of course, among the best evidence for the asymmetry of the globalizing process, which "aims to extend to the whole of the world, but without reciprocity, one way (which is to say in association with isolationism and particularism), the model most favorable to the dominant" (Bourdieu, 2001: 4).

2. There is a growing literature on the interrelations between globalization and regulation, especially in the field of business affairs (e.g., Piccotio and Mayne, 1999; Drahos and Braithwaite, 2000; Newell, 2001). Although transnational (reactive) regulatory activities in the field of agricultural biotechnology are already extensive but diverse and they are beginning to be studied (Newell, 2003), it is too early to expect the same reflexive attentiveness to the question of knowledge politics and globalization.

3. "Pregnancy created using infertile woman's egg nucleus," *New York Times,* October 14, 2003; and "Ban on scientists trying to create three-parent baby," *Independent,* October 14, 2003.

4. A "phenotypic" view of globalization, which privileges matter over information, might see the "achievement" of global cultural processes as an outcome of the application of biological knowledge.

5. The universalistic (global) aspirations of the political movements of socialism and liberalism during much of the past century, and their affinity to the rationalization or modernization process, have their functional equivalent in the universalistic ambitions of such social movements as environmentalism and feminism. Environmentalism, for example, is global in at least two senses: (1) It stresses global impacts, interdependencies, and amelioration; and (2) it emphasizes global social, economic, and political action (Frank, Hironaka, Meyer, Schofer, and Tuma, 1999; Frank, Hironaka, and Schofer, 2000; Buttel, 2000b).

6. Pierre Bourdieu (2001: 3), for example, observed in one of his last publications that the term globalization "(and the model it expresses) embodies the most accomplished form of *the imperialism of the universal,* which consists, for a society, of universalizing its own characteristics by tacitly establishing them in a universal model."

7. Whether economic globalization, or the nature of the relations of humans to their environment, is the greater source of instability is a contentious matter. Dunn (1993: 255) advances a clear vision in this regard when he observes, "There is ... good reason to believe that, within the national economies of the world as these now exist and are likely to develop in the near future, even the bemusing challenges of international economic operation are a less drastic and alarming source of instability than the interaction between human beings and the natural habitat within which they live out their lives."

8. Hall (1999) counters the apparent force of the economic globalization thesis by asserting that it is premature to speak of the demise of the nation-state in the face of contemporary economic developments. The strong globalization theory oversimplifies the intricate, reciprocal relations between globalizing dynamics and the nation-state. Zysman (1996: 180) observes that in recent decades "national developments have driven the changes in the global economy," for example, as the result of the entrance of Asia's developing economies and of Japan into the world market. Zysman adds that the national institutional foundations of several market systems have not disappeared, nor has the importance of differentially shaped national economic and political developments.

9. The sovereignty of even small nations in the areas of education, citizenship, migration, and immigration policies continues to be relatively strong (Koopmans and Statham, 1999).

10. Horkheimer and Adorno ([1944] 1972: 121), for example, describe developments toward greater social homogeneity as a "circle of manipulation and retroactive need in which the unity of the system grows ever stronger."

11. Compare, for example, the following observations about the weakening relationship between state authority, the legal system, and modern technology: "The legal system as the foundation and stabilizing force of state authority will lose in importance to the extent to which modern information and communication technologies displace traditional means of administrative authority in the form of dossiers" (Wolf, 1988: 170; also Friedman, 1996).

12. The claim that knowledge can be forgotten, or that it remains dormant, only to be rediscovered at a later time, is by no means an unusual observation; but this fact apparently needs to be rediscovered periodically (cf. Sorokin, 1958; Gouldner, 1980; Douglas, 1995). See also Karl Mannheim's conviction that "nothing of value in the history of the human spirit is lost forever" (Mannheim, [1922–24] 1982).

13. Mayer-Schönberger and Brodnig (2001), who examine the impact of the "information revolution" on power structures in international relations, suggest that the "denationalization" of information infrastructures has prompted significant shifts in information access and, in its wake, changes in the structure of international relations.

14. *Contingent knowledge,* that is, knowledge that is highly specific to a particular domain (Fleck, 1997: 390–394) might be a competing term for local cognitive representations—but then all knowledge is in some sense contingent.

15. Banri Asanuma (1989: 210), in an investigation of manufacturer-supplier relationships in Japanese industry, designates relation-specific skills as the skills that are required to respond effectively to the needs of the core firm: "Formation of this skill requires that learning through repeated interactions with a particular core firm be added to the basic technological capability which the supplier has accumulated."

16. Patel and Pavitt (1991: 18) put the matter of the national concentration of the location of the production sites of high technology firms in their study as follows: "Certain key features related to major innovations may help explain the advantages of geographical concentration: the primacy of multidisciplinary and tacit knowledge inputs and the commercial uncertainties surrounding outputs. Physical proximity facilitates the integration of multidisciplinary knowledge that is tacit and therefore 'person-embodied' rather than 'information-embodied.' It also facilitates the rapid decision-making needed to cope with uncertainty."

17. The new U.S. climate policy strategies were announced in February 2002. The climate policy calls for a gradual and modest approach to global warming that banks on incentives and new technological developments leading to a decades-long decline in emissions ("U.S. planning gradual curb on emissions, taking years," *New York Times,* February 6, 2002). Noteworthy is the fact that the new policy relies on voluntary efforts to slow, but not halt, the growth in emissions of greenhouse gases. Progress is to be measured by tracking the growth of emissions relative to the growth of the economy.

Outlook

> Our ability to effectively control and implement existential conditions is, despite the immense capacity to change them, limited, and even more restricted is the possibility to derive a state of happiness from such transformations.
>
> *Friedrich H. Tenbruck,* Zur Kritik der Planenden Vernunft

The massive changes and additions to human capacities to act within just a century may well be represented by two "bookmarks": By 1945 humans had produced the capacity to destroy life on earth on a grand scale, while by 2045 or earlier it might be possible to create life on a grand as well as a minute scale (see Baldi, 2001: 163). Thus it seems that the speed with which new capacities to act are generated forces us to alter our conceptions of who we are and, even more consequentially, may in fact change who we are. The promises and anxieties raised by these prospects are the motor of knowledge politics in modern societies. The boundaries of what was once clearly beyond the control of all of us are rapidly shifting.

The political landscape is changing as a result of new scientific discoveries and new technological innovations. The *kind* of regulative knowledge politics now in demand is new. Present mechanisms and institutions are unprepared to cope. But governments will be forced to face up to new problems and novel standards; they will have to develop new rules, and they will be judged as to whether they are successful in meeting new goals. The nation-state will continue to be of consequence, but less so as an autonomous corporate actor that shapes knowledge politics. The knowledge politics of the nation-state will frequently have to or (in the case of deliberate policy transfers) desire to enact policies supporting wider global institutions, international treaties, and social movements. However—and this can already be detected—the tempo with which solutions to new problems are found will be far outdistanced by the accumulation of new political challenges.

With the advent and the advance of knowledge politics upwards on the political ladder of importance, one can expect that the general lack of attention the scientific community has paid to what is done with their discoveries in society will also change. The scientific detachment and autonomy which began as a useful barrier against threats to the unencumbered, single-minded pursuit of knowledge will increasingly be seen as an isolating boundary, and will be challenged by the consequences of knowledge politics for scientific work. The atomic bomb, of course, shattered the isolation of science first. But the new capacities of knowledge, their apprehended impact on the individual and society, and the enlargement of what is possible will be equally powerful forces that should transform the relations between science and society and the social engagement of scientists. Current public debates already demonstrate that in increasing numbers, scientists are leaving their laboratories and studies in order to take part in political debates about the future of science and the social consequences of scientific developments.

As I have emphasized, efforts to regulate knowledge are not entirely novel, but a strong case can be made that we are about to reach a new stage in the next few decades in efforts by various corporate actors to police new knowledge. Past legal and regulatory practices will probably prove to be of limited value as guides and precedents for future practices. For example, the regulatory system adopted to assess and deal with the risks associated with chemicals developed over the last fifty years in many countries, representing a form of knowledge politics, will be insufficient, even useless, when it comes to dealing with genetically modified plants. The standardized tests available for chemicals do not exist for microorganisms (Krimsky, 1995). The disputes, debates, and dilemmas over what discourse (for example, political, normative, military, or economic) should be decisive in decisions that draft and enact knowledge policies is bound to escalate.

The limits to our capacities to act rapidly expand. As far as is possible to see, this enlargement of knowledge does not imply an elimination of the limits of the power of knowledge. The realization of knowledge still occurs in and requires control over relevant conditions of action in specific social contexts. The limits of the power of knowledge may be shifting, but various constraints, including novel limits, remain in place. It is impossible to say how much and in what ways the world will be transformed by our expanding knowledge. Perhaps nothing will be left unchanged.

What is less uncertain is that *expectations* that the world will change dramatically, as a consequence of our enlarged knowledge and therefore enhanced human capabilities, are growing at a rapid pace. Expectations that the world will witness a spectacular knowledge-based transformation are on the rise, even though most individuals' distance from the knowledge base is increasing, and their understanding of it shrinking, with similar speed.

Efforts to slow the production of knowledge, to police knowledge, and to defend society against some of the anticipated, yet uncertain, effects of the utilization of recent gains in knowledge have ultimately done little, at least in the long term, to seriously limit its application in one way or the other. But this will not keep various societal agents from trying. There are no universally accepted moral codes that could mediate differences or transcend conflicts between the various interests that believe it is necessary to act, or to bridge the gap between understanding the need to act and the capacity to put such understanding into practice. Nor is there a central societal vantage point, an objective perspective, or even a globally accepted construct that could somehow overcome such tensions. We live in essentially fragile societies. Despite the growing realization that insecurity and contingency are constitutive of modern societies, large social institutions—for example politics—still present themselves to the public as corporate actors capable of managing societal risks and dangers. Not infrequently, however, disappointed expectations are the outcome of promises that are difficult to live up to. Even science is rarely capable of producing solutions to societal problems; instead science too generates uncertainty and risks.

One of the most immediate controversial questions that awaits regulation and resolution, as the result of evolving knowledge about susceptibility to certain health risks associated with specific genes, is the question of how insurance companies (and other organizations and institutions), in particular health insurance companies, will use such information.

Private health insurance companies in Germany have announced that they plan to continue using established procedures when it comes to calculating the risks individual applicants represent (*Frankfurter Allgemeine Zeitung,* July 21, 2000, p. 17; also Murray, 2000: 242–245; Task Force on Genetic Information and Health Insurance, 1993). That is, full disclosure of all relevant information by the applicant is required, though the applicant is under no obligation to disclose information she or he does not happen to have.[1] A genome analysis will not, the insurers indicate, become a prerequisite for issuing a policy. However, individuals who happen to have such information—for example, as the result of taking part in a research study—are expected to divulge the genetic information.

But how is one to ensure that insurance companies limit their usage of such information voluntarily? What exactly is genetic information? How broad or narrow can or should one define genetic information? And how does one treat the interaction between genetic and nongenetic "causes"? How does one attribute responsibility? Can an insurer acquire genetic information indirectly, for example, on the basis of a family history? Are special legal norms required? What constitutes (public and/or private) genetic discrimination?

Genetic tests are bound to become more common, more accessible, and less and less expensive. In its wake, the rifts that the availability of genetic information is bound to create are not limited to the relations between insurance companies and their customers. Policing knowledge looks like an uphill quest, work that Sisyphus might recognize, and constantly enhanced knowledge produces more and more Sisyphean labor.

Given the openness of human conduct and what anchors such action, many would argue, as I do, that the policing and restriction of the use of new knowledge is inherently difficult, and that meaningful and effective decision-making should be at the point of the fabrication of knowledge, and not at the point of its application. However, resistance to limits on the production of knowledge and the persuasiveness of arguments for the preservation of open possibilities for individuals and collectivities alike will, for the time being, perhaps be even greater (at least from the scientific community) than will be political maneuvers to restrict the application of new knowledge. As Ernest Gellner (1964: 115) reminds us, openness and liberty are essential if new knowledge is to be brought into being.[2] The social utilization of new technical artifacts and new knowledge, in contrast, does not require liberty and freedom, as we know. Yet the privileged status of theory rests on its distinction from action. As the two merge in new forms of knowledge, the foundation of their separation becomes questionable (see Jonas, [1976] 1979: 38). In any event, the extent to which future societies will be confronted with immense conflicts and difficulties in the field of knowledge politics is almost self-evident.

Unintended, unplanned, but still consequential barriers to the formulation and implementation of knowledge politics may have their origin in societal transformations that are difficult, if not impossible, to anticipate and to direct. How future policymaking in the field of knowledge politics will evolve and be implemented can only be discovered from observing the future practice of knowledge and its results. Since increasing knowledge is the source of economic growth and societal change, any massive intervention in and restriction of the application of novel capacities to act represents an incursion into the biography of individuals, not to mention the course of economic development of a society and its wealth.

It will be very difficult to develop, implement, and somehow firmly embed a broad-minded, progressive perspective in the field of knowledge politics—a perspective that will continue to guarantee the freedom and autonomy of research, that will help prevent abuses of novel scientific knowledge, that will respect the right of the individual to social justice and privacy, that will not suppress conflicts, and that will allow for a democratically organized regulation of knowledge gains. With these essential insecurities we have to live; we are aware that we have to live with a rather restrained degree of trust and without a lot of confidence in more secure prospects in the future (Luhmann, [1991] 1993: 143; Bauman, 2001).

The currently constant and controversial public debates about the consequences of new scientific knowledge and technical artifacts, and calls for their regulation and administration, are expanding the public sphere in modern societies. The organization of the public sphere is changing, and participatory demands and contributions to the regulation of knowledge are bound to become more routine. More generally, we will see significant transformations of the political culture and the realignment of the major institutions of modern society as the result of the emergence of knowledge politics as new field of political activity. Whether a new "social contract for science" (see Ravetz, 1990: 284–300) is possible or desirable, the future will have to decide.

Notes

1. The "private" dilemmas for individuals who have genetic information are equally difficult. "The scientific advances [in genetics] have created debates about public policy on genetic discrimination. But the private effects on family dynamics are just as complex, as patient and health professionals adjust to thinking about family not just as flesh and blood,

but flesh and blood and genes" ("Boom in gene testing raises questions about sharing results," *New York Times,* July 21, 2000).

2. For a counterexample, compare Loren Graham's review of Richard Louries' book *Sakharov–A Biography,* "'Saharov': From the H-Bomb to Human Rights," *New York Times,* April 7, 2002.

Bibliography

Under each author's name the most recent works are listed first. In the case of translations and revised or later editions, the original date of publication is also shown, within square brackets.

Adorno, Theodore W. ([1966] 1984), *Negative Dialektik: Jargon der Eigentlichkeit. Gesammelte Schriften,* Band 6, Frankfurt am Main: Suhrkamp.

Albrecht, Johan, and Niko Gobbin (2001), "Schumpeter and the rise of modern environmentalism," *http://papers.ssrn.com/paper.taf?abstract_id=275871*

Albrow, Martin (1990), "Introduction," in Martin Albrow and Elisabeth King, eds., *Globalization, Knowledge and Society.* London: Sage, pp. 3–13.

Aldhous, Peter (2003), "Time to choose. In some countries, transgenic plants are already a part of mainstream farming. Will the rest of the world soon follow suit?" *Nature* 425: 655.

Allee, Verna (1997), *The Knowledge Evolution: Expanding Organizational Intelligence.* Boston: Butterworth-Heinemann.

Altieri, Miguel A. (2001), "Genetically engineered crops: Separating the myths from the reality," *Bulletin of Science, Technology and Society* 21: 130–146.

American Association for the Advancement of Science (2003), *Regulating human cloning.* Washington, D.C.: AAAS (*www.aaas.org/spp/cstc/issues/cloningreport.pdf*)

Amidon, Debra M. (1997), *Innovation Strategies for the Knowledge Economy.* Boston: Butterworth-Heinemann.

Andrews, Richard N.L. (1999), *Managing the Environment, Managing Ourselves: A History of American Environmental Policy.* New Haven, CT: Yale University Press.

Antonelli, Christiano (1999), "The evolution of the industrial organisation of the production of knowledge," *Cambridge Journal of Political Economics* 23: 243–260.

Apel, Karl-Otto (2000), "First things first: Der Begriff primordialer Mit-Verantwortung. Zur Begründung einer planetaren Makroethik," in Matthias Kettner, ed., *Angewandte Ethik als Politikum.* Frankfurt am Main: Suhrkamp, pp. 21–50.

Appadurai, Arjun (1996), *Modernity at Large.* Cultural Dimensions of Globalization. Minneapolis: University of Minnesota Press.

Appleyard, Bryan (1998), *Brave New Worlds: Staying Human in the Genetic Future.* New York: Viking.

Arntzen, Charles J., Andy Coghlan, Brian Johnson, Jim Peacock, and Michael Rodemeyer (2003), "GM crops: Science, politics and communication," *Nature Review Genetics* 4: 839–843.

Aron, Raymond ([1966] 1968), *The Industrial Society: Three Essays on Ideology and Development.* New York: Praeger.

Aron, Raymond ([1962] 1967), *Eighteen Lectures on Industrial Society.* London: Weidenfeld and Nicolson.

Arrow, Kenneth (1962a), "Economic welfare and the allocation of resources of invention," in Richard R. Nelson, ed., *The Rate and Direction of Inventive Activity: Economic and Social Factors.* A Report of the National Bureau of Economic Research. Princeton, NJ: Princeton University Press, pp. 609–625.

Arrow, Kenneth (1962b), "The economic implications of learning by doing," *Review of Economic Studies* 29: 155–173.

Arundel, Anthony (2000), "Measuring the use and planned use of biotechnologies by firms." Paper presented at the Research Workshop, "The Economic and Social Dynamics of Biotechnology," Ottawa, February 24–25.

Asanuma, Banri (1989), "Manufacturer-supplier relationships in Japan and the concept of relation-specific skills," *Journal of the Japanese and International Economies* 3: 1–30.

Ashford, Tony (1996), "Regulating agricultural biotechnology: Reflexive 'modernisation' and the European Union," *Policy and Politics* 24: 125–135.

Asimov, Isaac (1983), "Popularizing science," *Nature* 306 (November 10): 119.

Attewell, Paul (1992), "Technology diffusion and organizational learning: The case of business computing," *Organization Science* 3: 1–19.

Attewell, Paul (1987), "Big brother and the sweatshop: Computer surveillance in the automated office," *Sociological Theory* 5: 97–99.

Baldi, Pierre (2001), *The Shattered Self: The End of Natural Evolution.* Cambridge, MA: MIT Press.

Barber, Bernard (1952), *Science and the Social Order.* New York: Free Press.

Barnes, Barry (1999), "Biotechnology as expertise," in Patrick O'Mahony, ed., *Nature, Risks and Responsibility: Discourses on Biotechnology.* New York: Routledge, pp. 52–66.

Bateson, Gregory (1972), *Steps to an Ecology of Mind.* New York: Ballantine.

Baudrillard, Jean ([1970] 2001), "Consumer society," in *Selected Writings.* Edited and introduced by Mark Poster. 2nd ed. Stanford, CA: Stanford University Press, pp. 32–59.

Bauman, Zygmunt (2001), "The great war on recognition," *Theory, Culture and Society* 18: 137–150.

Bauman, Zygmunt (1998), *Work, Consumerism and the New Poor.* Buckingham: Open University Press.

Bechmann, Gotthard, and Nico Stehr (2002), "The legacy of Niklas Luhmann," *Society* 39: 67–75.

Bechmann, Gotthard, and Nico Stehr (2000), "Risikokommunikation und die Risiken der Kommunikation wissenschaftlichen Wissens—zum gesellschaftlichen Umgang mit Nichtwissen," *Gaia* 9: 113–201.

Becker, Gary S. (1983), "A theory of competition among pressure groups for political influence," *Quarterly Journal of Economics* 98: 371–400.

Bell, Daniel (1990), "Resolving the contradictions of modernity and modernism," *Society* 27: 43–50.

Bell, Daniel (1979), "The social framework of the information society," in Michael L. Dertouzos and Joel Moses, eds., *The Computer Age: A Twenty-Year View,* Cambridge, MA: MIT Press, pp. 163–211.

Bell, Daniel (1973), *The Coming of Post-Industrial Society: A Venture in Social Forecasting.* New York: Basic Books.

Bell, Daniel (1968), "The measurement of knowledge and technology," in Eleanor B. Sheldon and Wilbert E. Moore, eds., *Indicators of Social Change: Concepts and Measurements.* Hartford, CT: Russell Sage Foundation, pp. 145–246.

Bell, Daniel (1964), "The post-industrial society," in Eli Ginzberg, ed., *Technology and Social Change,* New York: Columbia University Press, pp. 44–59.

Bell, Daniel (1960), *The End of Ideology.* Glencoe, IL: Free Press.

Benatar, Solomon R. (1997), "Just healthcare beyond individualism: Challenges for North American bioethics," *Cambridge Quarterly of Healthcare Ethics* 6: 397–415.

Benhabib, Seyla (1999), "Citizens, residents, and aliens in a changing world: Political membership in the global era," *Social Research* 66: 709–744.

Beniger, James R. (1986), *The Control Revolution: Technological and Economic Origins of the Information Society.* Cambridge, MA: Harvard University Press.

Berkowitz, M. (1970), *The Conversion of Military Oriented Research and Development to Civilian Uses.* New York: Praeger.

Berlin, Isaiah ([1998] 2002), "My intellectual path," in *The Power of Ideas.* Edited by Henry Hardy. Princeton, NJ: Princeton University Press, pp. 1–23.

Berman, Jerry, and Paul Bruening (2001), "Is privacy still possible in the twenty-first century?" *Social Research* 68: 306–317.

Bernal, John D. (1939), *The Social Functions of Science.* London: George Routledge and Sons.

Berrill, Kenneth, ed. (1964), *Economic Development with Special Reference to East Asia.* New York: St. Martins Press.

Bhalla, Ajit S., and A.G. Fluitman (1985), "Science and technology indicators and socioeconomic development," *World Development* 13: 177–190.

Bimber, Bruce (1996), *The Politics of Expertise in Congress: The Rise and Fall of the Office of Technology Assessment.* Albany, NY: State University of New York Press.

Bishop, Jerry E., and Michael Waldholz (1990), *Genome.* New York: Simon and Schuster.

Blackler, Frank (1995),"Knowledge, knowledge work and organizations: An overview and interpretation," *Organization Studies* 16: 1021–1046.

Blumenberg, Hans ([1973] 1983), *The Legitimacy of the Modern Age.* Cambridge, MA: MIT Press.

Bodewitz, Henk J.H.W., Henk Buurma, and Gerard H. de Vries (1987), "Regulatory science and the social management of trust in medicine," in Wiebe E. Bijker, Thomas P. Hughes, and Trevor Pinch, eds., *The Social Construction of Technological Systems: New Directions in the Sociology and History of Technology,* Cambridge, MA: MIT Press, pp. 243–259.

Böhme, Gernot (1992), *Coping with Science.* Boulder, CO: Westview Press.

Böhme, Gernot (1981), "Wissenschaftliches und lebensweltliches Wissen am Beispiel der Verwissenschaftlichung der Geburtshilfe," in Nico Stehr and Volker Meja, eds., *Wissenssoziologie.* Opladen: Westdeutscher Verlag, pp. 445–463.

Bolz, Norbert (1989), *Auszug aus der entzauberten Welt: Philosophischer Extremismus zwischen den Weltkriegen.* Munich: Fink.

Borgmann, Albert (1999), *Holding on to Reality: The Nature of Information at the Turn of the Millennium.* Chicago: University of Chicago Press.

Bourdieu, Pierre (2001), "Uniting to better dominate," *Items* (Social Science Research Council) 2: 1–6.

Bourdieu, Pierre ([1979] 1984), *Distinction: A Social Critique of the Judgment of Taste.* London: Routledge and Kegan Paul.

Bowker, Geoffrey (1994), "Information mythology," in Lisa Bud-Frierman, ed., *Information Acumen: The Understanding and Use of Knowledge in Modern Business.* London: Routledge, pp. 231–247.

Bowles, Mark D. (2000), "Liquefying information: Controlling the flood in the cold war," in Miriam R. Levin, ed., *Cultures of Control.* Amsterdam: Harwood, pp. 225–246.

Brave, Ralph (2001), "Governing the genome," *Nation,* December 10, 2001.

Brill, Winston J. (1986), "The impact of biotechnology and the future of agriculture," in Kevin B. Byrne, ed., *Responsible Science: The Impact of Technology on Society.* San Francisco: Harper and Row.

Brimblecombe, Peter (1987), *The Big Smoke: A History of Air Pollution in London since Medieval Times.* London: Methuen.

Brooks, Harvey (1984), "The resolution of technically intensive public policy disputes," *Science, Technology, and Human Values* 9: 39–50.

Brooks, Harvey (1965), "Scientific concepts and cultural change," *Daedalus* 94: 66–83.

Brooks, Harvey (1964), "The scientific advisor," in Robert Gilpin and Christopher Wright, eds., *Scientists and National PolicyMaking.* New York: Columbia University Press.

Brooks, Harvey, and Raymond Bowers (1970), "The assessment of technology," *Scientific American* 222: 13–20.

Brown, John S., and Paul Duguid (2000), *The Social Life of Information.* Cambridge, MA: Harvard Business School Press.

Bruce-Briggs, Barry (1979), *The New Class?* New Brunswick, NJ: Transaction Books.

Brüggemann, Anne, and Helmut Jungermann (1998), "The whole and the parts of genetic engineering: The importance of structuring the assessment of opinions about biotechnology with respect to specificity," in Papers FS II 98–111, Forschungsschwerpunkt Technik, Arbeit und Umwelt, Wissenschaftszentrum. Berlin, Germany, pp. 23–38.

Bruner, Jerome (1990), *Acts of Meaning.* Cambridge, MA: Harvard University Press.

Buchmann, Marlis (1995), "The impact of resistance to biotechnology in Switzerland: A sociological view of the recent referendum," in Martin Bauer, ed., *Resistance to New Technology: Nuclear Power, Information Technology, Biotechnology.* Cambridge: Cambridge University Press, pp. 207–224.

Buchner, Bradley J. (1988), "Social control and the diffusion of modern telecommunications technologies: A cross-national study," *American Sociological Review* 53: 446–453.

Bud, Robert (1991), "Biotechnology in the twentieth century," *Social Studies of Science* 21: 415–457.

Burke, John G. (1972), "Bursting boilers and the federal power," in Melvin Kranzberg and W Davenport, eds., *Technology and Culture.* New York: New American Library, pp. 93–118.

Burke, Peter (2000), *A Social History of Knowledge: From Gutenberg to Diderot.* Oxford: Polity Press.

Burton-Jones, Alan (1999), *Knowledge Capitalism: Business, Work, and Learning in the New Economy.* Oxford: Oxford University Press.

Bush, Vannevar (1945), "As we may think," *Atlantic Monthly* 176 (July): 101–108.

Buttel, Fred (2000a), "The recombinant BGH controversy in the United States: Toward a new consumption politics of food?" *Agriculture and Human Values* 17: 5–20.

Buttel, Frederick H. (2000b), "World society, the nation-state and environmental protection: Comment on Frank, Hronaka, and Schafer," *American Sociological Review* 65: 117–121.

Buttel, Fred (1999), "Agricultural biotechnology: Its recent evolution and implications for agrofood political economy." *Sociological Research Online,* www.socresonline.org.uk/ -socresonline/-1995/1/buttel.html

Buttel, Fred (1989), "How epoch-making are high technologies? The case of biotechnology," *Sociological Forum* 4: 247–261.

Cable, Vincent (1995), "The diminished nation-state: A study in the loss of economic power," *Daedalus* 124: 23–53.

Callahan, Daniel (2003), *What Price for Better Health: The Hazard of the Research Imperative.* Berkeley: University of California Press.

Callahan, Daniel (1999), "The social sciences and the task of bioethics," *Daedalus* 128: 275–294.

Callon, Michel (1999), "Actor network theory—the market test," in John Law and John Hassard, eds., *Actor Network Theory and After.* Oxford: Blackwell, pp. 181–195.

Callon, Michel (1994), "Is science a public good?" *Science, Technology, and Human Values* 19: 395–424.

Callon, Michel (1992), "The dynamics of techno-economic networks," in Rod Coombs, Paolo Saviotti, and Vivien Walsh, eds., *Technological Change and Company Strategies,* London: Academic Press, pp. 132–161.

Cambrosio, Alberto, and Camille Limoges (1991), "Controversies as governing processes in technology assessment," *Technology Analysis and Strategic Management* 3: 377–396.

Cambrosio, Alberto, and Peter Keating (1988), "'Going monoclonal': Art, science, and magic in the day-to-day use of hybridoma technology," *Social Problems* 35: 244–260.

Campbell, John L., and Leon N. Lindberg (1991), "The evolution of governance regimes," in John L. Campbell, J. Rogers Hollingsworth, and Leon N. Lindberg, eds., *Governance of the American Economy.* Cambridge: Cambridge University Press, pp. 319–366.

Caplan, Arthur L. (1978), *The Sociobiology Debate: Readings on the Ethical and Scientific Issues concerning Sociobiology.* New York: Harper and Row.

Carey, William D. (1985), "Force, foresight and science," *Society* 22: 507.

Carley, Kathleen (1986), "Knowledge acquisition as a social phenomenon," *Instructional Science* 14: 381–438.

Carroll, James D. (1971), "Participatory technology: Citizen participation in the public development, use, and regulation of technology is examined," *Science* 171: 647–653.

Cash, David W. (2001), "'In order to aid in diffusing useful and practical information': Agricultural extension and boundary organizations," *Science, Technology and Human Values* 26:431–453.

Casper, Barry M. (1979), "Value conflicts in restricting scientific inquiry," in Keith M Wulff, ed., *Regulation of Scientific Inquiry: Societal Concerns with Research.* Boulder, CO: Westview Press, pp. 15–20.

Casper, Barry M. (1977), "Laser enrichment: A new path to proliferation?" *Bulletin of Atomic Scientists* 33: 28–41.

Castells, Manuel (1996), *The Information Age: Economy, Society and Culture.* Volume 1: The Rise of the Network Society. Oxford: Blackwell.

Castells, Manuel (1989), *The Informational City: Information Technology, Economic Restructuring, and the Urban-Regional Process.* Oxford: Basil Blackwell.

Cerny, Philip G. (1999), "Reconstructing the political in a globalising world: States, institutions, actors and governance," in Frans Buelens, ed., *Globalisation and the Nation-State.* Cheltenham: Edward Elgar, pp. 89–137.

Cerny, Philip G. (1991), "The limits of deregulation: Transnational interpenetration and policy change," *European Journal of Political Research* 19: 173: 196.

Chargaff, Erwin (1976), "[Letter] On the dangers of genetic meddling," *Science* 192: 938–940.

Chargaff, Erwin (1975), "Profitable wonders: A few thoughts on nucleid acid research," *The Sciences* 17: 21–26.

Chubin, Daryl, and Sol Restivo (1983), "The 'mooting' of science studies: Research programmes and science policy," in Karin Knorr-Cetina and Michael Mulkay, eds., *Science Observed.* London: Sage, pp. 53–83.

Cohen, Wesley M., Richard P. Nelson, and John P. Walsh (2000), "Protecting their intellectual assets: Appropriability conditions and why U.S. manufacturing firms patent (or not)." Working Paper 7552. Cambridge, MA: National Bureau of Economic Research.

Collingridge, David, and Colin Reeve (1986), *Science Speaks to Power: The Role of Experts in Policymaking.* London: Frances Pinter.

Collins, Harry M. (1993), "The structures of knowledge," *Social Research* 60: 95–116.

Collins, Harry M. (1987), "Certainty and the public understanding of science: Science on TV," *Social Studies of Science* 17: 689–713.

Conrad, Peter (1999), "A mirage of genes," *Sociology of Health and Illness* 21: 228–241.

Conrad, Peter (1997), "Public eye and private genes: Historical frames, news constructions, and social problems," *Social Problems* 44: 139–154.

Cooper, Fredrick (2001), "What is the concept of globalization good for? An African historian's perspective," *African Affairs* 100: 189–213.

Cowan, Robin, Paul A. David, and Dominique Forey (1999), "The explicit economics of knowledge certification and tacitness," paper prepared for the third TIPIK workshop, Strasbourg, France, April.

Cowan, Ruth Schwartz (1993), "Aspects of the history of prenatal diagnosis," *Fetal Diagnosis and Therapy* 8 (supplement 1): 10–17.

Crombie, Alistair C. (1961), *Augustine to Galileo.* Cambridge, MA: Harvard University Press.

Crook, Stephen (2000), "Science, technology and the relevance of sociology," in John Eldridge, John MacInnes, Sue Scott, Chris Warhurst, and Anne Witz, eds., *For Sociology: Legacies and Prospects.* Durham, UK: Sociologypress, pp. 160–173.

Crouch, Colin, and Wolfgang Streeck, eds. (1997), *Political Economy of Modern Capitalism. Mapping Convergence and Diversity.* London: Sage.

Crow, Michael (2001), Harnessing science to benefit society," *Chronicle of Higher Education,* March 9.

Crozier, Michael ([1963] 1964), *The Bureaucratic Phenomenon.* Chicago: University of Chicago Press.

Daele, Wolfgang van den (1996), "Objektives Wissen als politische Ressource: Experten und Gegenexperten im Diskurs," in Wolfgang van den Daele and Friedhelm Neidhardt, eds., *Kommunikation und Entscheidung.* Berlin: Sigma, pp. 297–326.

Daele, Wolfgang van den (1992), "Concepts of nature in modern societies and nature as a theme in sociology," in Meinolf Dierkes and Bernd Biervert, eds., *European Social Science in Transition: Assessment and Outlook.* Frankfurt am Main: Campus, pp. 526–560.

Daele, Wolfgang van den, Wolfgang Krohn, and Peter Weingart, eds. (1979), *Geplante Forschung: Vergleichende Studien über den Einfluß politischer Programme auf die Wissenschaftsentwicklung.* Frankfurt am Main: Suhrkamp.

Dahl, Edgar, Klaus-Dieter Hensch, Manfred Beutel, and Burkhard Brosig (2003), "Preconception sex selection for nonmedical reasons: A representative survey from the UK," *Human Reproduction* 18: 2238–2239.

Dam, K.W. (1994), "The economic underpinnings of patent law," *Journal of Legal Studies* 23: 247–271.

Daniels, Norman, Bruce P. Kennedy, and Ichiro Kawachi (1999), "Why justice is good for our health: The social determinants of health inequalities," *Daedalus* 128: 215–251.

Dasgupta, Partha S., and Paul A. David (1994), "Toward a new economics of science," *Research Policy* 23: 487–521.

Dasgupta, Partha S., and Paul A. David (1986), "Information disclosure and the economics of science and technology," in George F. Feiwel, ed., *Arrow and the Ascent of Modern Economic Theory*. London: Macmillan, pp. 519–542.

Davenport, Thomas H., David W. DeLong, and Michael C. Beers (1998), "Successful knowledge management projects," *Sloan Management Review* 39: 43–57.

David, Paul A. (2000), "The digital technology boomerang: New intellectual property rights threaten global 'open science,'" *World Bank Conference Volume* (forthcoming).

Davis, Joel (1991), *Mapping the Code*. New York: Wiley.

DeBresson, Christian, and F. Amesse (1991), "Networks of innovators: A review and introduction to the issue," *Research Policy* 20: 363–379.

Dei, George J. Sefa, Budd L. Hall, and Dorothy Goldin Rosenberg, eds., (2000), *Indigenous Knowledges in Global Contexts: Multiple Readings of Our World*. Toronto, ON: University of Toronto Press.

Dempsey, Gillian (1999), "Revisiting intellectual property policy: Information economics for the information age," *Prometheus* 17: 33–40.

Derber, Charles (1982), "Toward a new theory of professionals as workers: Advanced capitalism and postindustrial labour," in Charles Derber, ed., *Professionals as Workers: Mental Labour in Advanced Capitalism*. Boston: Hall, pp. 193–208.

de Soto, Hernando (2000), *The Mystery of Capital: Why Capitalism Triumphs in the West and Fails Everywhere Else*. New York: Basic Books.

Dewey, John ([1927] 1954), *The Public and Its Problems*. Athens: Ohio University Press.

Dierkes, Meinolf, ed., (2001), *Handbook of Organizational Learning and Knowledge*. New York: Oxford University Press.

Dijick, José van (1998), *Imagenation: Popular Images of Genetics*. New York: New York University Press.

Dosi, Giovanni (1996), "The contribution of economic theory to the understanding of a knowledge-based economy," in Organisation for Economic CoOperation and Development (1996b), *Employment and Growth in the Knowledge-Based Economy,* Paris: OECD, pp. 81–92.

Dosi, Giovanni, Keith Pavitt and Luc Soete (1990), *The Economics of Technical Change and International Trade*. New York: New York University Press.

Douglas, Mary (1995), "Forgotten knowledge," in Marilyn Strathern, ed., *Shifting Contexts: Transformations in Anthropological Knowledge*. London: Routledge, pp. 13–29.

Douglas, Mary, and Baron Isherwood (1979), *The World of Goods*. New York: Basic Books.

Drahos, Peter, and John Braithwaite (2002), *Information Feudalism: Who Owns the Knowledge Economy?* London: Earthscan.

Drahos, Peter, and John Braithwaite (2001), "The globalization of regulation," *The Journal of Political Philosophy* 9:103–128.

Drahos, Peter, and John Braithwaite (2000), *Global Business Regulation*. Cambridge: Cambridge University Press.

Dror, Yehezkel (1968), *Public Policymaking Reexamined.* Scranton, PA: Chandler.

Drucker, Peter F. (1993), *Post-Capitalist Society,* New York: HarperBusiness.

Drucker, Peter F. (1969), *The Age of Discontinuity: Guidelines to our Changing Society,* New York: Harper and Row.

Dunkmann, Karl (1929), *Angewandte Soziologie: Probleme und Aufgaben.* Berlin: Verlag von Reimar Hobbing.

Dunn, John (1993), "Political science, political theory and policymaking in an interdependent world," *Government and Opposition* 28: 242–260.

Durant, John R., Anders Hansen, and Martin Bauer (1996), "Public understanding of the new genetics," in Theresa Marteau and Martin Richards, eds., *The Troubled Helix: Social and Psychological Implications of the New Genetics.* Cambridge: Cambridge University Press, pp. 235–248.

Durant, John R., Geoffrey A. Evans, and Geoffrey P. Thomas (1992), "Public understanding of science in Britain: The role of medicine in the popular representation of science," *Public Understanding of Science* 1: 161–182.

Durant, John R., Geoffrey A. Evans, and Geoffrey P. Thomas (1989), "The public understanding of science," *Nature* 340: 11–14.

Duster, Troy (1990), *Backdoor to Eugenics.* New York: Routledge.

Dutton, Diana B. (1988), *Worse than the Disease: Pitfalls of Medical Progress.* Cambridge: Cambridge University Press.

Dworkin, Roger B. (1996), *Limits: The Role of Law in Bioethical Decision Making.* Bloomington: Indiana University Press.

Eagleton, Terry (2003), *After Theory.* London: Allen Lane.

Easterbrook, Frank H. (1982), "Insider trading, secret agents, evidentiary privileges, and the production of information," *Supreme Court Review* 11: 309–365.

Ellis, Richard J., and Fred Thompson (1997), "Seeing green: Cultural biases and environmental preferences," in Richard J. Ellis and Michael Thompson, eds., *Culture Matters: Essays in Honor of Aaron Wildavsky.* Boulder, CO: Westview Press, pp. 169–188.

Elsom, Derek (1995), "Atmospheric pollution trends in the United Kingdom," in Julian Simon, ed., *The State of Humanity.* Oxford: Blackwell, pp. 476–490.

Epstein, Stephan R. (1998), "Craft guilds, apprenticeship, and technological change in preindustrial Europe," *Journal of Economic History* 58: 684–713.

Epstein, Steven (1996), *Impure Science: AIDS, Activism, and the Politics of Knowledge.* Berkeley: University of California Press.

Epstein, Steven (1991), "Democratic science? AIDS activism and the contested construction of knowledge," *Socialist Review* 91: 35–64.

Ettore, Elizabeth (1999), "Experts as 'storytellers' in reproductive genetics: Exploring key issues," *Sociology of Health and Illness* 21: 539–559.

Eulau, Heinz (1973), "Social revolution and the consultative commonwealth," *American Political Science Review* 67: 169–191.

Faulkner, Wendy (1994), "Conceptualizing knowledge used in innovation: A second look at the science-technology distinction and industrial innovation." *Science, Technology and Human Values* 19: 425–458.

Faulkner, Wendy, Jacqueline Senker, and Lea Velho (1995), *Knowledge Frontiers: Industrial Innovation and Public Sector Research in Biotechnology, Engineering Ceramics, and Parallel Computing.* Oxford: Oxford University Press.

Featherstone, Mike (1991), *Consumer Culture and Postmodernism.* London: Sage.

Feenberg, Andrew (1995), *Alternative Modernity: The Technical Turn in Philosophy and Social Theory.* Berkeley: University of California Press.

Feyerabend, Paul (1980), *Erkenntnis für freie Menschen,* rev. ed. Frankfurt am Main: Suhrkamp.

Feyerabend, Paul (1978), *Science in a Free Society.* London: Verso.

Fiorino, Daniel J. (1990), "Citizen participation and environmental risk: A survey of institutional mechanisms," *Science, Technology and Human Values* 15: 226–243.

Fleck, James (1997), "Contingent knowledge and technology development," *Technology Analysis and Strategic Management* 9: 383–397.

Fleising, Usher ([1991] 1999), "Public perceptions of biotechnology," in Vivian Moses and Ronald E. Cape, eds., *Biotechnology: The Science and the Business,* 2nd ed. Edited by Derek G. Springham. Amsterdam: Harwood, pp. 89–103.

Forest, Chris E., Peter H. Stone, Andrei P. Sokolov, Myles R. Allen, and Mort D. Webster (2002), "Quantifying uncertainties in climate system properties with the use of recent climate observations," *Science* 295: 113–117.

Forey, Dominique (2001), "Continuities and ruptures in knowledge management practices," in John de la Mothe and Dominique Foray, eds., *Knowledge Management in the Innovation Process.* Boston: Kluwer, pp. 43–52.

Foucault, Michel ([1978] 2000), "Governmentality," in *Power. The Essential Works of Foucault, 1954–1984.* Volume 3. New York: The New Press, pp. 201–222.

Foucault, Michel (1977), "Prison talk: An interview," *Radical Philosophy* 16: 10–15.

Frank, David John (1997), "Science, nature, and the globalization of the environment, 1870–1990," *Social Forces* 76: 409–437.

Frank, David John, Ann Hironaka, and Evan Schofer (2000), "The nation-state and the natural environment over the twentieth century," *American Sociological Review* 65: 96–116.

Frank, David John, Ann Hironaka, John W. Meyer, Evan Schofer, and Nancy Brandon Tuma (1999), "The rationalization and organization of nature in world culture," in John Boli and George M. Thomas, eds., *Constructing World Culture: International Non-Governmental Organizations since 1875.* Stanford, CA: Stanford University Press, pp. 81–99.

Freeman, Chris (1991), "Networks of innovators: A synthesis of research issues," *Research Policy* 20: 499–514.

Freidson, Eliot (1994), *Professionalism Reborn: Theory, Prophecy and Policy.* Chicago: University of Chicago Press.

Freidson, Eliot (1983), "The theory of the professions: State of the art," in Robert Dingwall and Philip Lewis, eds., *The Sociology of the Professions: Doctors, Lawyers and Others.* London: Macmillan, pp. 19–37.

Frenkel, Stephen J., Marek Korcynski, Karen A. Shire, and May Tam (1999), *On the Front Line: Organization of Work in the Information Economy.* Ithaca, NY: Cornell University Press.

Friedman, Jonathan (1996), "The implosion of modernity," in Michael J. Shapiro and Hayward R. Alker, eds., *Challenging Boundaries: Global Flows, Territorial Identities.* Minneapolis: University of Minnesota Press, pp. 247–256.

Friedman, Jonathan (1995), "Global system, globalization and the parameters of modernity," in Mike Featherstone, Scott Lash, and Ronald Robertson, eds., *Global Modernities.* London: Sage, pp. 69–90.

Friedman, Jonathan, ed., (1994), *Consumption and Identity.* London: Harwood.

Fukuyama, Francis (2002), *Our Postmodern Future: Consequences of the Biotechnology Revolution.* New York: Farrar Straus and Giroux.

Fukuyama, Francis (1992), *The End of History and the Last Man.* New York: Free Press.

Fukuyama, Francis, and Caroline S. Wagner (2000), *Information and Biological Revolutions: Global Governance Challenges—Summary of a Study Group.* Santa Monica, CA: Rand.

Fuller, Steve (2001), *Knowledge Management Foundations.* London: Butterworth-Heinemann.

Fuller, Steve (2000a), *The Governance of Science: Ideology and the Future of the Open Society.* Buckingham: Open University Press.

Fuller, Steve (2000b), "The coming biological challenge to social theory and practice," in John Eldridge, John MacInnes, Sue Scott, Chris Warhurst, and Anne Witz, eds., *For Sociology: Legacies and Prospects.* Durham, UK: Sociologypress, pp. 174–190.

Fuller, Steve (1993), *Philosophy, Rhetoric, and the End of Knowledge: The Coming of Science and Technology Studies.* Madison, WI: University of Wisconsin Press.

Fuller, Steve (1988), *Social Epistemology.* Bloomington, IN: Indiana University Press.

Funtowicz, Silvio O., and Jerome R. Ravetz (1990), *Uncertainty and Quality in Science Policy.* Dordrecht: Kluwer.

Gaisford, James D., Jill E. Hobbs, William A. Kerr, Nicholas Perdikis, and Marni D. Plunkett (2001), *The Economics of Biotechnology.* Cheltenham: Elgar.

Galbraith, John K. ([1967] 1971), *The New Industrial State.* Boston: Houghton Mifflin.

Galbraith, John K.(1983), *The Anatomy of Power.* Boston: Houghton Mifflin.

Gamble, Andrew, and Gavon Kelly (1996), "The new politics of ownership," *New Left Review* 220: 62–97.

Garfinkel, Simson, and Deborah Russel (2001), *Database Nation: The Death of Privacy in the Twenty-First Century.* Cambridge, MA: O'Reilly.

Gath, M., and Alvensleben, R. V. (1997), "The potential effects of labeling GM foods on consumer decisions." Preliminary Report. Institute for Agricultural Economics. Universität Kiel.

Gehlen, Arnold (1949), *Sozialpsychologische Probleme der industriellen Gesellschaft.* Tübingen: J.C.B. Mohr (Paul Siebeck).

Gellner, Ernest (1964), *Thought and Change.* London: Weidenfeld and Nicolson.

Geroski, Paul (1994), *Market Structure, Corporate Performance and Innovative Activity.* New York: Oxford University Press.

Gibbons, Michael, Camille Limoges, Helga Nowotny, Simon Schwartzman, Peter Scott, and Martin Trow (1994), *The New Production of Knowledge: The Dynamics of Science and Research in Contemporary Societies.* London: Sage.

Giddens, Anthony (1984), *The Constitution of Society: Outline of the Theory of Structuration.* Cambridge: Polity Press.

Giddens, Anthony (1981), *A Contemporary Critique of Historical Materialism. Vol. 1: Power, Property and the State.* London: Macmillan.

Gilbert, Nigel G., and Michael Mulkay (1984), *Opening Pandora's Box.* Cambridge: Cambridge University Press.

Ginsberg, Theo (1986), "Wissen ohne Gewissen ist Macht ohne Verantwortung. Gedanken zum technischen Fortschrift," in Otto Neumaier, ed., *Wissen und Gewissen: Arbeiten zur Verantwortungsproblematik.* Vienna: VWGÖ, pp. 125–141.

Glass, Bently (1971), "Science: Endless horizons or golden age?" *Science* 171 (January 8): 23–29.

Gofton, Les, and Erica Haimes (1999), "Necessary evils? Opening up in sociology and biotechnology," *Sociological Research Online* http: //www.socresonline.org.uk/-socresonline/-1995/1/gofton.html

Goodell, Rae S. (1979), "Public involvement in the DNA controversy: The case of Cambridge, Massachusetts," *Science, Technology, and Human Values* No. 27: 36–43.

Goslin, David A. (1985), "Decision-making and the social fabric," *Society* 22: 7–11.

Gottweis, Herbert (1995), *Governing Molecules: The Discursive Politics of Genetic Engineering in Europe and the United States.* Cambridge: MIT Press.

Gould, Steven J. (1977), *Ontegeny and Phylogeny.* Cambridge, MA: Harvard University Press.

Gouldner, Alvin W. (1980), "Is amnesia in sociology discontinuous, and the problem of permeable boundaries in culture." Paper presented at an international conference on "The Political Realization of Social Science Knowledge," Institute for Advanced Studies, Vienna, June 18–20, 1980.

Gouldner, Alvin W. (1979), *The Future of Intellectuals and the Rise of the New Class.* New York: Continuum.

Gouldner, Alvin W. (1976), *The Dialectic of Ideology and Technology: The Origins, Grammar and Future of Ideology.* New York: Seabury Press.

Graham, Loren R. (1978), "Concerns about science and attempts to regulate inquiry," *Daedalus* 107: 1–22.

Green, Harold P. ([1978] 1979), "The recombinant DNA controversy: A model of public influence," in Keith M. Wulff, ed., *Regulation of Scientific Inquiry: Societal Concerns with Research.* Boulder, CO: Westview Press, S. 115–122.

Green, Harold P. ([1977] 1979), "The boundaries of scientific freedom," in Keith M. Wulff, ed., *Regulation of Scientific Inquiry: Societal Concerns with Research.* Boulder, CO: Westview Press, pp. 139–143.

Green, Harold P. (1976), "Law and genetic control: Public-policy questions," in Marc Lappé and Robert S. Morrison, eds., *Ethical and Scientific Issues posed by Human Uses of Molecular Genetics.* Annuals of the New Academy of Sciences. Volume 265. New York: New York Academy of Sciences.

Grundahl, Johs (1995), "The Danish consensus conference model," in Simon Joss and John Durant, eds., *Public Participation in Science: The Role of Consensus Conferences in Europe.* London: Science Museum, pp. 31–40.

Grundmann, Reiner, and Nico Stehr (2001), "Why is Werner Sombart not part of the core of classical sociology?" *Journal of Classical Sociology* 1: 257–287.

Grundmann, Reiner, and Nico Stehr (2002), "Die Entzauberung der Wissenschaft: Wissenschaft als Lieferant politischer Probleme und systematischer Unsicherheiten," Manuscript.

Grundmann, Reiner, and Nico Stehr (2000), "Social science and the absence of nature," *Social Science Information* 39: 155–179.

Guerlain, Pierre (1997), "The ironies and dilemmas of America's cultural dominance: A transcultural approach," *American Studies International* 35: 30–51.

Guston, David H. (2001), "Boundary organizations in environmental policy and science: An introduction," *Science, Technology, and Human Values* 26: 399–408.

Guston, David H. (2000), *Between Politics and Science: Assuring the Integrity and Productivity of Research.* Cambridge: Cambridge University Press.

Guston, David H. (1999), "Stabilizing the boundary between U.S. politics and science: The role of the Office of Technology Transfer as a boundary organization," *Social Studies of Science* 29: 87–112.

Habermas, Jürgen (2001), *Die Zukunft der menschlichen Natur: Auf dem Weg zu einer liberalen Eugenik?* Frankfurt am Main: Suhrkamp.

Habermas, Jürgen ([1998] 2001), "An argument against human cloning: Three replies," in *The Postnational Constellation: Political Essays.* Oxford: Polity Press.

Habermas, Jürgen (1987), *Die neue Unübersichtlichkeit.* Frankfurt am Main: Suhrkamp.

Habermas, Jürgen (1981), *Theorie des kommunikativen Handelns.* 2 Volumes. Frankfurt am Main: Suhrkamp.

Habermas, Jürgen ([1965] 1971), "Knowledge and human interest: A general perspective," in *Knowledge and Human Interest.* Boston: Beacon, pp. 301–317.

Habermas, Jürgen ([1969] 1970), "Technology and science as 'ideology,'" in *Toward a Rational Society: Student Protest, Science, and Politics.* Boston: Beacon Press.

Habermas, Jürgen (1964), "Dogmatismus, Vernunft und Entscheidung—Zur Theorie und Praxis in der wissenschaftlichen Zivilisation," pp. 231–257 in *Theorie und Praxis.* Neuwied: Luchterhand.

Hacking, Ian (1990), *The Taming of Chance.* Cambridge: Cambridge University Press.

Haeckel, Ernst ([1899] 1902), *The Riddle of the Universe.* New York: Harper.

Haeckel, Ernst (1878), *Freie Wissenschaft und freie Lehre: Eine Entgegnung auf Rudolf Virchow's Münchener Rede über "Die Freiheit der Wissenschaft im modernen Staat."* Stuttgart: E. Schweizerische Verlagbuchhandlung (E. Koch).

Hall, John A. (1999), "Globalization and nationalism," *Thesis Eleven,* No. 63: 63–79.

Hamstra, A (1995), "The role of public instruments of constructive technology assessment," in Simon Joss and John Durant, eds., *Public Participation in Science: The Role of Consensus Conferences in Europe.* London: Dillon.

Harding, Sandra (1991), *Whose Science? Whose Knowledge? Thinking from Women's Lives.* Ithaca, NY: Cornell University Press.

Hayek, Friedrich A. ([1945] 1948), "The use of knowledge in society," in *Individualism and Economic Order.* Chicago: University of Chicago Press, pp. 77–91.

Held, David (1995), *Democracy and the Global Order: From the Modern State to Cosmopolitan Government.* Stanford, CA: Stanford University Press.

Hennen, Leonhard (1995), "Discourses on technology—public debates on technology," in René van Schomberg, ed., *Contested Technology.* Tilburg: International Centre for Human and Public Affairs.

Hill, Christopher T. (1997), "The congressional Office of Technology Assessment: A retrospective and prospects for the post-OTA world," *Technological Forecasting and Social Change* 54: 191–198.

Hindmarsh, Richard, Geoffrey Lawrence, and Janet Norton (1998), "Bio-utopia: The way forward," in Richard Hindmarsh, Geoffrey Lawrence, and Janet Norton, eds., *Altered Genes. Reconstructing Nature: The Debate.* London: Allen and Unwin, pp. 3–23.

Hippel, Eric von (1994), "'Sticky information' and the locus of problem solving: Implications for innovation," *Management Science* 40: 429–439.

Hippel, Eric von (1991), "The impact of 'sticky information' on innovation and problem-solving." Sloan School of Management, MIT, Working Papers BPS 33147 (revised).

Hirschman, Albert O. (1994), "Social conflicts as pillars of democratic market society," *Political Theory* 22: 203–218.

Hirschman, Albert O. (1977), *The Passions and the Interests.* Princeton, NJ: Princeton University Press.

Hirschman, Albert O. (1970), *Exit, Voice and Loyalty.* Cambridge, MA: Harvard University Press.

Hirshleifer, Jack (1971), "The private and social value of information and the reward to inventive activity," *American Economic Review* 61: 561–574.

Hirst, Paul, and Grahame Thompson (1997), "Globalization in question: International economic relations and forms of public governance," in J. Rogers Hollingsworth and Robert Boyer, eds., *Contemporary Capitalism: The Embeddedness of Institutions.* Cambridge: Cambridge University Press, S. 337–360.

Hirst, Paul, and Grahame Thompson (1996), *Globalisation in Question*. Cambridge: Polity Press.

Hirst, Paul, and Grahame Thompson (1992), "The problem of 'globalization': International economic relations, national economic management and the formation of trading blocs," *Economy and Society* 21: 357–396.

Hollingsworth, J. Rogers, and Robert Boyer (1997), "Coordination of economic actors and social systems of production," in J. Rogers Hollingsworth and Robert Boyer, eds., *Contemporary Capitalism: The Embeddedness of Institutions*. Cambridge: Cambridge University Press, pp. 1–47.

Hollingsworth, Rogers, and Leon Lindberg (1985), "The governance of the American economy: The role of markets, clans, hierarchies, and associative behavior," in Wolfgang Streeck and Philippe C. Schmitter, eds., *Private Interest Government: Beyond Market and State*. London: Sage, pp. 221–254.

Holt, Robert T. (1977), "Technology assessment and technology inducement mechanism," *American Journal of Political Science* 21: 283–301.

Holton, Gerald (1992), "How to think about the 'anti-science' phenomenon," *Public Understanding of Science* 1: 103–128.

Holton, Gerald (1986), "The Advancement of science and its burdens," *Daedalus* 115: 77–104.

Horgan, John (1996), *The End of Science: Facing the Limits of Knowledge in the Twilight of the Scientific Age*. New York: Addison Wesley.

Horkheimer, Max ([1932] 1972), "Notes on science and the crisis," in *Critical Theory: Selected Essays*. New York: Continuum.

Horkheimer, Max, and Theodor W. Adorno ([1947] 1972), *Dialectic of Enlightenment*. New York: Herder and Herder.

Horowitz, Irving L. (1985), "Elite roles and democratic sentiments," *Society* 22: 16–19.

House, Tamzy J., et al. (1996), "Weather as a force multiplier: Owning the weather in 2025," US Air Force Research Paper. http://www.au.af.mil/au/2025/

Howe, Henry, and John Lyne (1992), "Gene talk in sociobiology," *Social Epistemology* 6: 109–163.

Indyk, Debbie, and David A. Rier (1993), "Grassroots AIDS knowledge: Implications for the boundaries of science and collective action," *Knowledge* 15: 197–212.

Inglehart, Ronald (1995), "Changing values, economic development and political change," *International Social Science Journal* 145: 379–403.

Inglehart, Ronald, and Wayne E. Baker (2000), "Modernization, cultural change and the persistence of cultural values," *American Sociological Review* 65:19–51.

Inkeles, Alex (1998), *One World Emerging? Convergence and Divergence in Industrial Societies*. Boulder, CO: Westview Press.

Irwin, Alan, and Brian Wynne (1996) "Conclusions," in Alan Irwin and Brian Wynne, eds., *Misunderstanding Science? The Public Reconstruction of Science and Technology*. Cambridge: Cambridge University Press, pp. 213–221.

James, William F. (1890), *The Principles of Psychology*. Volume 1. New York: Dover Publications.

Jasanoff, Sheila (1996), *Science at the Bar: Law, Science and Technology in America*. Cambridge, MA: Harvard University Press.

Jasanoff, Sheila (1995), "Product, process, or program: Three cultures and the regulation of biotechnology," in Martin Bauer, ed., *Resistance to new Technology: Nuclear Power, Information Technology, Biotechnology*. Cambridge: Cambridge University Press, pp. 311–334.

Jasanoff, Sheila (1990), *The Fifth Branch: Science Advisors as Policymakers*. Cambridge, MA: Harvard University Press.

Jasanoff, Sheila (1986), *Risk Management and Political Culture*. New York: Russell Sage Foundation.

Jessop, Bob (1990), "Regulation theories in retrospect and prospect," *Economy and Society* 19: 153–216.

Joerges, Bernward ([1979] 1996), "Die Macht der Sachen über uns," in *Technik Körper der Gesellschaft*. Frankfurt am Main: Suhrkamp, pp. 15–32.

Jonas, Hans (1982), *The Phenomenon of Life: Toward a Philosophical Biology*. Chicago: University of Chicago Press.

Jonas, Hans ([1976] 1979), "Freedom of scientific inquiry and the public interest," in Keith M. Wulff, ed., *Regulation of Scientific Inquiry: Societal Concerns with Research*. Boulder, CO: Westview Press, pp. 33–39.

Jonas, Hans (1974), *Philosophical Essays: From Ancient Creed to Technological Man*. Englewood Cliffs, NJ: Prentice Hall.

Jørgensen, Torben (1995), "Consensus conference in the health care sector," in Simon Joss and John Durant, eds., *Public Participation in Science: The Role of Consensus Conferences in Europe*. London: Science Museum, pp. 17–29.

Joss, Simon, and John Durant (1995), "The UK national conference on plant biotechnology," *Public Understanding of Science* 4: 195–204.

Joy, Bill (2000), "Why the future doesn't need us," *Wired* 8.04 (April).

Kahn, Herman, and B. Bruce-Briggs (1972), *Things to Come: Thinking about the Seventies and Eighties*. New York: Macmillan.

Kay, John (1999), "Money from knowledge," *Science and Public Affairs* (April): 12–13.

Kay, Lily E. (2000). *Who Wrote the Book of Life? A History of the Genetic Code*. Stanford, CA: Stanford University Press.

Keller, Evelyn Fox (2000), *The Century of the Gene*. Cambridge, MA: Harvard University Press.

Keller, Evelyn Fox (1992), "Nature, nurture, and the human genome project," in Daniel J. Kevles and Leroy Hood, eds., *The Code of Codes: Scientific and Social Issues in the Human Genome Project*. Cambridge, MA: Harvard University Press, pp. 281–299.

Kemeny, John G. (1980), "Beyond technocracy: The lessons of Three Mile Island," *Technology Review* 82: 65–75.

Keynes, John Maynard (1936), *The General Theory of Employment, Interest and Money*. London: Macmillan.

Keynes, John M. ([1930] 1984 "Economic possibilities for our grandchildren," in *Collected Writings. Volume IX: Essays in Persuasion*. Cambridge: Cambridge University Press, pp. 321–334.

Kilminster, Richard (1997), "Globalization as an emergent concept," in Alan Scott, ed., *The Limits of Globalization: Cases and Arguments*. London: Routledge, pp. 257–283.

King, Lauriston R., and Philip H. Melanson (1972), "Knowledge and politics: Some experiences from the 1960s," *Public Policy* 20: 83–101.

Kitch, Edmund W. (1980), "The law and the economics of rights in valuable information," *Journal of Legal Studies* 9: 683–723.

Kleinman, Arthur (1999), "Moral experience and ethical reflection: Can ethnography reconcile them? A quandary for 'the new bioethics,'" *Daedalus* 128: 69–97.

Kleinman, Daniel L. (1998), "Beyond the science wars: Contemplating the democratization of science," *Politics and the Life Sciences* 16: 133–145.

Klitgaard, Robert (1997), "Applying cultural theories to practical problems," in Richard J.

Ellis and Michael Thompson, eds., *Culture Matters: Essays in Honor of Aaron Wildavsky.* Boulder, CO: Westview Press, pp. 191–202.

Kloppenburg, Jack Jr., and Beth Burrows (2001), "Biotechnology to the rescue? Ten reasons why biotechnology is incompatible with sustainable agriculture," in Brian Tokar, ed., *Redesigning Life? The Worldwide Challenge to Genetic Engineering.* Montreal: McGill–Queen's University Press, pp. 103–110.

Klüver, Lars (1995), "Consensus conferences at the Danish Board of Technology," in Simon Joss and John Durant, eds., *Public Participation in Science: The Role of Consensus Conferences in Europe.* London: Science Museum, pp. 41–49.

Konrád, György, and Ivan Szelényi (1979), *The Intellectuals on the Road to Class Power: A Sociological Study of the Role of the Intelligentsia in Socialism.* Brighton, Sussex: Harvester Press.

Koopmans, Ruud, and Paul Statham (1999), "Challenging the liberal nation-state? Postnationalism, multiculturalism, and the collective claims-making of migrants and ethnic minorities in Britain and Germany," *American Journal of Sociology* 105: 652–696.

Kornhauser, William (1959), *The Politics of Mass Society.* Glencoe, IL: Free Press.

Krimsky, Sheldon (1995). "Letter: biotechnology regulation," *Science* 267: 945.

Krimsky, Sheldon (1982), *Genetic Alchemy: The Social History of the Recombinant DNA Controversy.* Cambridge, MA: MIT Press.

Krohn, Wolfgang, and Günter Küppers (1989), *Die Selbstorganisation der Wissenschaft.* Frankfurt am Main: Suhrkamp.

Krohn, Wolfgang, and Johannes Weyer (1989), "Gesellschaft als Labor: Die Erzeugung sozialer Risiken durch experimentelle Forschung," *Soziale Welt* 40: 349–373.

Krugman, Paul (1994), *The Age of Diminished Expectations: U.S. Economic Policy in the 1990s,* rev. ed. Cambridge, MA: MIT Press.

Kuisel, Richard (1993), *Seducing the French: The Dilemma of Americanization.* Berkeley: University of California Press.

Kyrtsis, Alexandros-Andreas, Vasilios Koulaidis, and Gerassimos Kouzelis (1998), "The cultural background of quantitative research on public understanding of science and technology," in Papers FS II 98–111, Forschungsschwerpunkt Technik, Arbeit und Umwelt, Wissenschaftszentrum Berlin, Germany, pp. 3–21.

LaFleur, William (1992), *Liquid Life: Abortion and Buddhism in Japan.* Princeton, NJ: Princeton University Press.

Laird, Frank N. (1993), "Participatory analysis, democracy, and technological decision making," *Science, Technology, and Human Values* 18: 341–361.

Lammers, Cornelius J. (1974), "Mono- and poly-paradigmatic developments in natural and social sciences," in Richard Whitley, ed., *Social Processes of Scientific Development.* London: Routledge and Kegan Paul, pp. 123–147.

Landes, David (2000), "Culture makes almost all the difference," in Lawrence E. Harrison and Samuel P. Huntington, eds., *Culture Matters: How Values Shape Human Progress.* New York: Basic Books, pp. 2–13.

Landry, Réjean, and Nabil Amara (2001), "Creativity, innovation and business practices in the matter of knowledge management," in John de la Mothe and Dominique Foray, eds., *Knowledge Management in the Innovation Process.* Boston: Kluwer, pp. 55–79.

Lane, H. Clifford, and Anthony S. Fauci (2001), "Bioterrorism on the home front: A new challenge for American medicine," *Journal of the American Medical Association* 286: 2595–2597.

Lane, Robert E. (1966), "The decline of politics and ideology in a knowledgeable society," *American Sociological Review* 31: 649–662.

Lanza, Robert P., Arthur L. Caplan, Lee M. Silver, Jose B. Cibelli, Michael D. West, and Ronald M. Green (2000), "The ethical validity of using nuclear transfer in human transplantation," *Journal of the American Medical Association* 284: 3175–3179.

Larsen, Otto N., Jr. (1985), "Social science of the closet," *Society* 22: 16–19.

Lash, Scott (1996), "Introduction to the ethics and difference debate," *Theory, Culture and Society* 13: 75–78.

Lash, Scott, and John Urry (1994), *Economies of Signs and Spaces,* London: Sage.

Latour, Bruno (1998), "From the world of science to the world of research?" *Science* 280: 208–209.

Latour, Bruno ([1991] 1993), *We Have Never Been Modern.* Cambridge, MA: Harvard University Press.

Lave, Jean (1993), "The practice of learning," in Seth Chaiklin and Jean Lave, eds., *Understanding Practice: Perspectives on Activity and Context.* Cambridge: Cambridge University Press. pp. 3–32.

Lederer, Emil (1992), *Grundzüge der ökonomischen Theorie: Eine Einführung.* Tübingen: J.C. B. Mohr (Paul Siebeck).

Leibniz, Georg Wilhelm (1951), *Selections.* New York: Scribner.

Lenger, Friedrich (1996), "Werner Sombart als Propagandist eines deutschen Krieges," in Wolfgang J. Mommsen, ed., *Kultur und Krieg: Die Rolle der Intellektuellen, Kuenstler und Schriftsteller im Ersten Weltkrieg.* Munich: Oldenbourg, pp. 65–76.

Lessig, Lawrence (2001), *The Future of Ideas: The Fate of the Commons in a Connected World.* New York: Random House.

Levin, Miriam R. (2000), "Contexts of control," in Miriam R. Levin, ed., *Cultures of Control.* Amsterdam: Harwood, pp. 13–39.

Levitt, Norman, and Paul Gross (1994), "The perils of democratizing science," *Chronicle of Higher Education* (October 5): B1–B2.

Lewontin, Richard (2001), "Genes in the food," *New York Review of Books* 48 (June 21): 81–84.

Limoges, Camille (1993), "Expert knowledge and decision-making in controversy contexts," *Public Understanding of Science* 2: 417–426.

Lipset, Seymour M. ([1979] 1985), "Predicting the future: The limits of social science," in *Consensus and Conflict: Essays in Political Sociology.* New Brunswick, NJ: Transaction Books, pp. 329–360.

Lopata, Helen Z. (1976), "Expertization of everyone and the revolt of the client," *Sociological Quarterly* 17: 435–447.

Lowe, Adolph (1971), "Is present-day higher learning 'relevant'?" *Social Research* 38: 563–580.

Lowenthal, David (1990), "Awareness of human impacts: Changing attitudes and emphases," in Billie L. Turner, et. al., eds., *The Earth as Transformed by Human Action: Global and Regional Changes in the Biosphere over the Past 300 Years.* Cambridge: Cambridge University Press, pp. 121–135.

Lübbe, Hermann (1977), *Wissenschaftspolitik.* Planung-Politik- Relevanz. Zurich: Interfrom.

Luhmann, Niklas (1997a), "Grenzwerte der ökologischen Politik," in Petra Hiller, Petra and Georg Krücken, eds., *Risiko und Regulierung: Soziologische Beiträge zur Technikkontrolle und präventiver Umweltpolitik.* Frankfurt am Main: Suhrkamp, pp. 195–221.

Luhmann, Niklas (1997b), "Globalization or world society: How to conceive of modern society?" *International Review of Sociology* 7: 67–79.

Luhmann, Niklas ([1991] 1993), *Risk: A Sociological Theory.* New York: de Gruyter.

Luhmann, Niklas (1988), *Die Wirtschaft der Gesellschaft.* Frankfurt am Main: Suhrkamp.

Luhmann, Niklas ([1981] 1987), "Gesellschaftsstrukturelle Bedingungen und Folgeprobleme des naturwissenschaftlich-technischen Fortschritts," in *Soziologische Aufklärung 4.* Opladen: Westdeutscher Verlag, pp. 47–63.

Luhmann, Niklas (1979), "Erleben und Handeln," in Hans Lenk, ed., *Handlungstheorien interdisziplinär.* Volume 2. Munich: Fink, pp. 235–253.

Lynd, Robert S. (1939), *Knowledge for What?* Princeton, NJ: Princeton University Press.

Lyotard, Jean-François (1989), "Defining the postmodern," in Lisa Appignanesi, ed., *Postmodernism.* London: Free Association Books, pp. 7–10.

Macer, Darryl R. J. (1992), "Public acceptance of human gene therapy and perceptions of human genetic manipulation," *Human Gene Therapy* 3: 511–518.

Machlup, Fritz (1983), "Semantic quirks in studies of information," in Fritz Machlup and Una Mansfield, eds., *The Study of Information.* New York: Wiley.

Machlup, Fritz (1980), *Knowledge: Its Creation, Distribution, and Economic Significance. Volume 1: Knowledge and Knowledge Production.* Princeton, NJ: Princeton University Press.

Machlup, Fritz (1979), "Use, value, and benefits of knowledge," *Knowledge* 1: 62–81.

Machlup, Fritz (1968), "Patents," *International Encyclopedia of the Social Sciences.* Volume 11: 461–472.

Mannheim, Karl ([1928] 1993), "The problem of generations," in Kurt H. Wolff, ed., *From Karl Mannheim.* 2nd ed. New Brunswick, NJ: Transaction Books, pp. 351–395.

Mannheim, Karl ([1922–24] 1982), *Structures of Thinking.* Edited by David Kettler, Volker Meja, and Nico Stehr. London: Routledge and Kegan Paul.

Mannheim, Karl ([1929] 1936), *Ideology and Utopia.* London: Routledge.

Marcuse, Herbert (1964), *One-Dimensional Man: Studies in the Ideology of Advanced Industrial Society.* Boston: Beacon Press.

Marcuse, Herbert (1941), "Some social implications of modern technology," *Studies in Philosophy and Social Science* 9: 414–439.

Margalit, Avishai (2001), "Privacy in a decent society," *Social Research* 68: 255–268.

Marquard, Odo (1986), *Apologie des Zufälligen.* Stuttgart: Reclam.

Marshall, Alfred (1920), *Principles of Economics.* 8th ed. London: Macmillan.

Martin, Ben L. (1973), "Experts in policy processes: A contemporary perspective," *Polity* 6: 149–173.

Martin, Brian, and Eveleen Richards (1995), "Scientific knowledge, controversy, and public decision-making," in Sheila Jasanoff, Gerald E. Markle, James C. Petersen, and Trevor Pinch, eds., *Handbook of Science and Technology Studies.* London: Sage, pp. 506–526.

Martin, John Levi (1999), "The myth of the consumption-oriented economy and the rise of the desiring subject," *Theory and Society* 28: 425–453.

Mayer-Schönberger, Victor, and Gernot Brodnig (2001), "Information power: International affairs in the cyber age," John F. Kennedy School of Government, Harvard University, Faculty Research Working Paper Series, RWP01–044.

Mazur, Allan ([1989] 1999), "Connections: Biomedical sciences in supermarket tabloids," *Knowledge, Technology, and Policy* 12: 19–26.

Mazur, Allan (1973), "Disputes between experts," *Minerva* 11: 243–262.

Mendelsohn, Everett (1978), "'Frankenstein at Harvard': The public politics of recombinant DNA research," in Everett Mendelsohn, Dorothy Nelkin, and Peter Weingart, eds., *The Social Assessment of Science.* Science Studies Report 13. Bielefeld: Forschungsschwerpunkt Wissenschaftsforschung, pp. 57–78.

Mendelsohn, Everett, and Peter Weingart (1978), "The social assessment of science: Issues and perspectives," in Everett Mendelsohn, Dorothy Nelkin, and Peter Weingart, eds., *The Social Assessment of Science*. Science Studies Report 13. Bielefeld: Forschungsschwerpunkt Wissenschaftsforschung, pp. 3–21.

Mendelsohn, Everett, Dorothy Nelkin, and Peter Weingart (1978), "Foreword," in *The Social Assessment of Science*. Science Studies Report 13. Bielefeld: Forschungsschwerpunkt Wissenschaftsforschung, pp. 1–2.

Merton, Robert K. (1973), *The Sociology of Science: Theoretical and Empirical Investigations*. Chicago: University of Chicago Press.

Merton, Robert K. (1957), *Social Theory and Social Structure*. Glencoe, IL: Free Press.

Meyer, John, John Boli, George M. Thomas, and Francisco O. Ramirez (1997), "World society and the nation-state," *American Journal of Sociology* 103: 144–181.

Miles, Ian, Birgitte Andersen, Mark Boden, and Jeremy Howells (2000), "Service processes and property," *International Journal of Technology Management* 20: 95–115

Miller, Clark (2001), "Hybrid management: boundary organizations, science policy, and environmental governance in the climate regime," *Science, Technology, and Human Values* 26: 478–500.

Miller, Jon D. (1983), *The American People and Science Policy*. New York: Pergamon.

Miller, Jon D., R. Pardo and F. Niwa (1997), *Public Perceptions of Science and Technology: A Comparative Study of the European Union, the United States, Japan, and Canada*. Chicago: Chicago Academy of Sciences.

Miller, Peter, and Nikolas Rose (1997), "Mobilizing the consumer: Assembling the subject of consumption," *Theory, Culture and Society* 14: 1–36.

Mills, C. Wright (1956), *The Power Elite*. New York: Oxford University Press.

Milward, Alan S. (1992), *The European Rescue of the Nation-State*. Berkeley: University of California Press.

Mitnick, Barry M. (1980), *The Political Economy of Regulation: Creating, Designing, and Removing Regulatory Forms*. New York: Columbia University Press.

Moffat, Anne Simon (1993), "New meetings tackle knowledge conundrum," *Science* 259: 1253–1255.

Moore, Wilbert E., and Melvin M. Tumin (1949), "Some social functions of ignorance," *American Sociological Review* 14: 787–795.

Moravec, Hans (1999), *Robot: Mere Machine to Transcendent Mind*. New York: Oxford University Press.

Morgenthau, Hans J. (1972), *Science: Servant or Master?* New York: New American Library.

Morrison, Robert S. (1978), "Introduction," *Daedalus* 107: vii–xvi.

Mukerji, Chandra (1989), *A Fragile Power: Scientists and the State*. Princeton, NJ: Princeton University Press.

Mulkay, Michael (1997), *The Embryo Research Debate: Science and the Politics of Reproduction*. Cambridge: Cambridge University Press.

Mulkay, Michael (1993), "Rhetorics of hope and fear in the great embryo debate," *Social Studies of Science* 23: 721–742.

Mulkay, Michael (1972), *The Social Process of Innovation*. Basingstoke: Macmillan.

Münch, Richard (1992), "The dynamics of societal communication," in Paul Colomy, ed., *The Dynamics of Social Systems*. London: Sage, pp. 56–71.

Münch, Richard (1991), *Die Dialektik der Kommunikationsgesellschaft*. Frankfurt am Main: Suhrkamp.

Münch, Richard (1990), "Differentiation, rationalization, interpenetration: The emergence of modern society," in Jeffrey C. Alexander and Paul Colomy, eds., *Differentiation Theory and Social Change*. New York: Columbia University Press, pp. 441–464.

Murray, Thomas H. (2000), "Das Humangenomprojekt, das ELSI-Programm und die Demokratie," in Matthias Kettner, ed., *Angewandte Ethik als Politikum.* Frankfurt am Main: Suhrkamp, pp. 229–252.

Narr, Wolf-Dieter ([1979] 1985), "Toward a society of conditioned reflexes," in Jürgen Habermas, ed., *Observations on "The Spiritual Situation of the Age."* Cambridge, MA: MIT Press. pp. 31–66.

National Bioethics Advisory Commission (1999), *Ethical Issues in Human Stem Cell Research.* Washington, DC: National Bioethics Advisory Commission.National Science Board (2000), *Science & Engineering Indicators—2000.* Arlington, VA: National Science Foundation.

Nederveen Pieterse, Jan (2001), "Hybridity, so what? The anti-hybridity backlash and the riddles of recognition," *Theory, Culture and Society* 18: 219–245.

Neidhardt, Friedhelm (1993), "The public as a communication system," *Public Understanding of Science* 2: 339–350.

Nelkin, Dorothy (2001a), "Beyond risk: Reporting about genetics in the post-Asilomar press," *Perspectives in Biology and Medicine* 44: 199–207.

Nelkin, Dorothy (2001b), "Molecular metaphors: The gene in popular discourse," *Nature Cell Biology* 2: 555–559.

Nelkin, Dorothy (1995), "Science controversies: The dynamics of public disputes in the United States," in Sheila Jasanoff, Gerald E. Markle, James C. Petersen, and Trevor Pinch, eds., *Handbook of Science and Technology Studies.* Thousand Oaks, CA: Sage, pp. 444–456.

Nelkin, Dorothy (1992), *Controversy.* London: Sage.

Nelkin, Dorothy (1978a), "Value conflict and modes of intervention in biomedical research," in Everett Mendelsohn, Dorothy Nelkin, and Peter Weingart, eds., *The Social Assessment of Science.* Science Studies Report 13. Bielefeld: Forschungsschwerpunkt Wissenschaftsforschung, pp. 22–35.

Nelkin, Dorothy (1978b), "Threats and promises: Negotiating the control of research," *Daedalus* 107: 191–209.

Nelkin, Dorothy (1977), "Technology and public policy," in Ina Spiegel-Rösing and Derek de Solla Price, eds., *Science, Technology and Society: A Cross-Disciplinary Perspective.* London: Sage, pp. 393–441.

Nelkin, Dorothy (1975), "The political impact of technical expertise," *Social Studies of Science* 5: 35–54.

Nelkin, Dorothy, and Laurence Tancredi (1989), *Dangerous Diagnostics: The Social Power of Biological Information.* New York: Basic Books.

Nelkin, Dorothy, and Michael Pollak (1981), *The Atom Besieged: Extraparliamentary Dissent in France and Germany.* Cambridge, MA: MIT Press.

Nelkin, Dorothy, and Michael Pollak (1975), "Public participation in technological decisions: Reality or grand illusion," *Technology Review* (August/September): 55–64.

Nelson, Richard R., and Gavin Wright (1992), "The rise and fall of American technological leadership: The postwar era in historical perspective," *Journal of Economic Literature* 30: 1931–1964.

Nemetz, Peter N., William T. Stanbury, and Fred Thompson (1986), "Social regulation in Canada: An overview and comparison with the American model," *Policy Studies Journal* 14: 580–603.

Newell, Peter (2003), "Globalization and the governance of biotechnology," *Global Environmental Politics* 3: 56–71.

Newell, Peter (2001), "Managing multinationals: The governance of investment for the environment," *Journal of International Development* 13: 907–919.

Nivola, Pietro S. (1997), *Comparative Disadvantages? Social Regulations and the Global Economy.* Washington, DC: Brookings Institution.

Novas, Carlos, and Nikolas Rose (2001), "Genetic risk and the birth of the somatic individual," *Economy and Society* 29: 485–513.

Nowotny, Helga, Peter Scott, and Michael Gibbons (2001), *Re-thinking Science: Knowledge and the Public in an Age of Uncertainty.* Cambridge: Polity Press.

Nye, Joseph S., and William A. Owens (1996), "America's information edge," *Foreign Affairs* 75: 20–34.

Ogburn, William F. [1922] 1950), *Social Change: With Respect to Culture and Original Nature.* New York: Viking Press.

Ogburn, William F., and Meyer F. Nimkoff (1947), *A Handbook of Sociology.* London: Kegan Paul, Trench, Trubner and Co.

Olson, Mancur (1990), "Is Britain the wave of the future? How ideas affect societies," in Michael Mann, ed., *The Rise and Decline of the Nation State.* Oxford: Blackwell, pp. 91–113.

Olson, Mancur (1982), *The Rise and Decline of Nations.* New Haven, CT: Yale University Press.

O'Mahony, Patrick, ed., (1999), *Nature, Risk and Responsibility: Discourses of Biotechnology.* New York: Routledge.

Organisation for Economic Co-Operation and Development (2000), *Knowledge Management in the Learning Society.* Paris: OECD.

Organisation for Economic Co-Operation and Development (1999), *Science, Technology and Industry Scoreboard 1999: Benchmarking Knowledge-Based Economies.* Paris: OECD.

Organisation for Economic Cooperation and Development (1988), *Biotechnology and the Changing Role of Government.* Paris: OECD.

Ostrum, Vincent, and Elinor Ostrum (1977), "Public goods and public choices," in Emanuel S. Savas, ed., *Alternatives for Delivering Services: Toward Improved Performance.* Boulder, CO: Westview Press.

Packard, Vance ([1957] 1960), *The Hidden Persuaders.* Harmondsworth: Penguin.

Park, Robert E. (1940), "News as a form of knowledge: A chapter in the sociology of knowledge," *American Journal of Sociology* 45: 669–686.

Parsons, Talcott (1970), "The impact of technology on culture and emerging new modes of behavior," *International Social Science Journal* 22: 607–627.

Patel, Pari, and Keith Pavitt (1991), "Large firms in the production of the world's technology: An important case of 'non-globalisation,'" *Journal of International Business Studies* 22: 1–21.

Paul, Diane B. (1992), "Eugenic anxieties, social realities, and political choices," *Social Research* 59: 663–683.

Pavitt, Keith (1987), "The objectives of technology policy," *Science and Public Policy* 14: 182–188.

Perrow, Charles (1986),"Lernen wir etwas aus den jüngsten Katastrophen?" *Soziale Welt* 37: 390–401.

Petermann, Thomas (1999), "Technikfolgen-Abschätzung—Konstituierung und Ausdifferenzierung eines Leitbilds," in Stephan Bröchler, Georg Simonis, and Karsten Sundermann, eds., *Handbuch der Technikfolgenabschätzung.* Volume 1. Berlin: edition sigma, pp. 17–49.

Petit, Pascal, and Luc Soete (1999), "Globalization in search of a future," *International Social Science Journal* 51: 165–181.

Phelps, Bob (1998), "Genetic engineering: The campaign frontier," in Richard Hindmarsh, Geoffrey Lawrence, and Janet Norton, eds., *Altered Genes, Reconstructing Nature: The Debate*. London: Allen and Unwin, pp. 186–198.

Piccottio, Sol, and Ruth Mayne (1999), *Regulating International Business: Beyond Liberalisation*. Basingstoke: MacMillan.

Pinch, Trevor, and Wiebe Bijker (1984), "The social construction of facts and artifacts: Or how the sociology of science and the sociology of technology might benefit each other," *Social Studies of Science* 14: 399–441.

Plein, L. Christopher (1991), "Popularizing biotechnology: The influence of issue definition," *Science, Technology and Human Values* 16: 474–490.

Polanyi, Michael (1967), *The Tacit Dimension*. New York: Doubleday.

Polanyi, Michael (1958), *Personal Knowledge: Towards a Post-Critical Philosophy*. London: Routledge and Kegan Paul.

Polanyi, Michael ([1946] 1973), *Science, Faith and Society: Fifth Impression*. Chicago: University of Chicago Press.

Pollock, Friedrich (1935), "Review: Werner Sombart, *Deutscher Sozialismus*," *Zeitschrift für Sozialforschung* 4: 105–108.

Popitz, Heinrich (1968), *Über die Präventivwirking des Nichtwissens*. Tübingen: J.C.B. Mohr (Paul Siebeck).

Porter, Michael E. (2000), "Attitudes, values, beliefs, and the microeconomics of prosperity," in Lawrence E. Harrison and Samuel P. Huntington, eds., *Culture Matters: How Values Shape Human Progress*. New York: Basic Books, pp. 14–28.

Porter, Michael E. (1990), *The Competitive Advantage of Nations*. London: Macmillan.

Porter, Theodore (1965), *Trust in Numbers: The Pursuit of Objectivity in Science and Public Life*. Princeton, NJ: Princeton University Press.

Posner, Richard (1974), "Theories of economic regulation," *Bell Journal of Economics* 5:335–358.

President's Council on Bioethics (2003), *Beyond Theraphy: Biotechnology and the Pursuity of Happiness. http://bioethics.gov/reports/beyondtherapy/beyond_therapy.pdf*

Price, Don K. (1978), "Endless frontier or bureaucratic morass," *Daedalus* 107: 75–92.

Rabe, Barry G., and William R. Lowry (1999), "Comparative analyses of Canadian and American environmental policy," *Policy Studies Journal* 27: 263–266.

Rabinow, Paul (1999), *French DNA: Trouble in Purgatory*. Chicago: University of Chicago Press.

Radnitzky, Gerard (1986), "Responsibility in science and in the decisions about the use or non-use of technologies," in Otto Neumaier, ed., *Wissen und Gewissen: Arbeiten zur Verantwortungsproblematik*. Vienna: VWGÖ, pp. 99–124.

Rapoport, Anatole (1988), "Risiko und Sicherheit," *Leviathan* 16: 123–136.

Rauch, Jonathan (2003), "Will Frankenfood save the planet?" *Atlantic* (October 2003).

Ravetz, Jerome R. (1990), *The Merger of Knowledge with Power*. London: Mansell.

Ravetz, Jerome (1977), "Criticisms of science," in Ina Spiegel-Rösing and Derek de Solla Price, eds., *Science, Technology and Society: A Cross-Disciplinary Perspective*. London: Sage, pp. 71–89.

Ravetz, Jerome (1971), *Scientific Knowledge and its Social Problems*. New York: Oxford University Press.

Rees, Martin (2003), *Our Final Hour. A Scientist's Warning: How Terror, Error, and Environmental Disaster Threaten Humankind's Future in this Century—on Earth and Beyond*. New York: Basic Books.

Reiss, Albert J. Jr. (1979), "Conditions and consequences of consent in human subject

Knowledge Politics

research," in Keith M. Wulff, ed., *Regulation of Scientific Inquiry: Societal Concerns with Research.* Boulder, CO: Westview Press, pp. 161–184.

Rescher, Nicholas (1987), *Forbidden Knowledge and other Essays on the Philosophy of Science.* Dordrecht: Reidel.

Rescher, Nicholas (1984), *The Limits of Science.* Berkeley: University of California Press.

Rescher, Nicholas (1978), *Scientific Progress.* Oxford: Blackwell.

Richter, Emanuel (1992), *Der Zerfall der Welteinheit: Vernunft und Globalisierung in der Moderne.* Frankfurt am Main: Campus.

Ridley, Matt (2003), *Nature via Nurture: Genes, Experience and What Makes us Human.* London; Fourth Estate.

Riesman, David ([1950] 1961), *The Lonely Crowd: A Study of the Changing American Character.* New Haven, CT: Yale University Press.

Rissler, Jane, and Margaret Mellon (2000), *The Ecological Risks of Engineered Crops.* Cambridge, MA: MIT Press.

Robert, J. S., and F. Baylis (2003), "Crossing species boundaries," *American Journal of Bioethics* 3: 1–13.

Roberts, J. Timmons (1996), "Predicting participation in environmental treaties: A world-system analysis," *Sociological Inquiry* 66: 38–57.

Robertson, Roland (1992), *Globalization: Social Theory and Global Culture.* London: Sage.

Robertson, Roland (1990), "Mapping the global condition: Globalization as the central concept," in Mike Featherstone, ed., *Global Culture: Nationalism, Globalization and Modernity.* A Theory, Culture and Society Special Issue. London: Sage, pp. 15–30.

Robinson, John, and Jon Tinker (1997), "Reconciling ecological, economic and social imperatives: Towards an analytical framework," in Ted Schrecker, ed., *Surviving Globalism: Social and Environmental Dimensions.* New York: St. Martin's Press, pp. 71–94.

Robinson, William I. (1996), "Globalisation: Nine theses on our epoch," *Race and Class* 38: 13–31.

Roco, Mihail C., and William Sims Bainbridge (2002), *Converging Technologies for Improving Human Performance: Nanotechnology, Biotechnology, Information Technology and Cognitive Science.* Washington, DC: National Science Foundation and U.S. Department of Commerce (Prepublication on-line version, June).

Rose, Hilary (1995), "Social criticism and the Human Genome Project programme: Some reflections on the limits of a limited social science," *Genetic Engineer and Biotechnologist* 15: 169–179.

Rose, Nikolas (1999), *Powers of Freedom: Reframing Political Thought.* Cambridge: Cambridge University Press.

Rose, Steven, and Lisa Appignanesi, eds., (1986), *Science and Beyond.* Oxford: Blackwell.

Rosen, Jeffrey (2001), "Out of context: The purposes of privacy," *Social Research* 68: 209–220.

Rosen, Jeffrey (2000), *The Unwanted Gaze: The Destruction of Privacy in America.* New York: Random House.

Rosenberg, Charles E. (1999), "Meanings, policies, and medicine: On the bioethical enterprise and history," *Daedalus* 128: 27–46.

Rosenberg, Nathan (1969), "The direction of technological change: Inducement mechanisms and focusing devices," *Economic Development and Cultural Change* 18: 1–24.

Rossini, Frederick A., and Alan L. Porter (1984), "Public participation and professionalism in impact assessment," in James C. Petersen, ed., *Citizen Participation in Science Policy.* Amherst: University of Massachusetts Press.

Rouse, Joseph (1991), "Policing knowledge: Disembodied policy for embodied knowledge," *Inquiry* 34: 353–364.

Rovere, Richard H. ([1958] 1963), "The invasion of privacy: Technology and the claims to community," in Hendrik M. Ruitenbeek, ed., *The Dilemma of Organizational Society.* New York: E.P. Dutton.

Rueschemeyer, Dietrich (1986), *Power and the Division of Labor.* Stanford, CA: Stanford University Press.

Rueschemeyer, Dietrich, and Theda Skocpol, eds., (1995), *States, Social Knowledge, and the Origins of Modern Social Policies.* Princeton, NJ: Princeton University Press.

Rüstow, Alexander (1951), "Kritik des technischen Fortschritts," *Ordo* 4:373–407.

Russell, Bertrand (1924), *Marriage and Morals.* London: Allen and Unwin.

Ryan, Michael P. (1998), *Knowledge Diplomacy: Global Competition and the Politics of Intellectual Property.* Washington, DC: Brookings Institution Press.

Samuelson, Paul (1954), "The pure theory of public expenditures," *Review of Economics and Statistics* 94: 1002–1037.

Scarf, Maggie (2001), "Secrets for sale," *Social Research* 68: 333–338.

Schauer, Frederick (2001), "The legal construction of privacy," *Social Research* 68: 51–54.

Schelsky, Helmut (1961), *Der Mensch in der wissenschaftlichen Zivilisation.* Cologne/ Opladen: Westdeutscher Verlag.

Schelsky, Helmut (1954) "Zukunftsaspekte der industriellen Gesellschaft," *Merkur* 8: 13–28.

Schiller, Dan (1997), "The information commodity: A preliminary view," in Jim Davis, Thomas A. Hirschl, and Michael Stack, eds., *Cutting Edge: Technology, Information Capitalism and Social Revolution.* London: Verso, pp. 103–120.

Schmidt, Vivien A. (1995), "The new world order, incorporated: The rise of business and the decline of the nation-state," *Daedalus* 124: 75–106.

Schmitter, Philippe C. (1997), "The merging Europolity and its impact upon national systems of production," in J. Rogers Hollingsworth and Robert Boyer, eds., *Contemporary Capitalism: The Embeddedness of Institutions.* Cambridge: Cambridge University Press, pp. 395–430.

Schofer, Evan (1999), "Science associations in the international sphere, 1875–1990: the rationalization of science and the scientization of society," in John Boli and George M. Thomas, eds., *Constructing World Culture: International Non-Governmental Organizations since 1875.* Stanford, CA: Stanford University Press, pp. 249–268.

Schofer, Evan, Francisco O. Ramirez, and John W. Meyer (2000), "The effects of science on national economic development, 1970 to 1990," *American Sociological Review* 65: 866–887.

Schon, Donald A. (1967), *Technology and Social Change: The Impact of Invention and Innovation on American Social and Economic Development.* New York: Dell.

Schot, Johan W., and Arie Rip (1997), "The past and future of constructive technology assessment," *Technology Forecasting and Social Change* 54: 251–268.

Schott, Thomas (1993), "World science: Globalization of institutions and participation," *Science, Technology, and Human Values* 18: 196–208.

Schott, Thomas (1988), "International influence in science: Beyond center and periphery," *Social Science Research* 17: 219–238.

Schumpeter, Joseph A. ([1942] 1962), *Capitalism, Socialism and Democracy.* New York: Harper.

Schwartz, Barry (1999), "Capitalism, the market, the 'underclass,' and the future," *Society* 37: 33–42.

Sclove, Richard (1996), "Town meetings on technology," *Technology Review* (July): 25–31.

Sen, Amartya (1981), "Ingredients of famine analysis: Availability and entitlements," *Quarterly Journal of Economics* 96: 433–464.

Serwer, Daniel P. (1978), "Radiation protection standards: Scientific and public roles," in Everett Mendelsohn, Dorothy Nelkin, and Peter Weingart, eds., *The Social Assessment of Science*. Science Studies Report 13. Bielefeld: Forschungsschwerpunkt Wissenschaftsforschung, pp.136–155.

Shakespeare, Tom (1999), "'Losing the plot'? Medical and activist discourses of contemporary genetics and disability," *Sociology of Health and Illness* 21: 669–688.

Shapin, Steven (2001), "Proverbial economies: How an understanding of some linguistic and social features of common sense can throw light on more prestigious bodies of knowledge, science for example," *Social Studies of Science* 31: 731–769.

Shapin, Steven (1992), "Why the public ought to understand science-in-the-making," *Public Understanding of Science* 1: 27–30.

Shattuck, Roger (1996), *Forbidden Knowledge: From Prometheus to Pornography*. San Diego, CA: Harcourt Brace & Company.

Shea, Christopher (2000), "Don't talk to humans. The crackdown on social science research," *Lingua Franca* 10.

Shields Rob (1992), *Lifestyle Shopping: The Subject of Consumption*. New York: Routledge.

Shiva, Vandana (2001), "Biopiracy: The theft of knowledge and resources," in Brian Tokar, ed., *Redesigning Life: The Worldwide Challenge to Genetic Engineering*. Montreal: McGill–Queen's University Press, pp. 283–289.

Shiva, Vandana (2000), *Stolen Harvest: The Hijacking of the Global Food Supply*. London: Zed Books.

Shiva, Vandana (1998), *Biopiracy: The Plunder of Nature and Knowledge*. London: Zed Books.

Simerly, Calvin, et al. (2003), "Molecular correlates of primate nuclear transfer failure," *Science* 300: 297.

Simmel, Georg ([1911/12] 1968), "On the concept and tragedy of culture," in *The Conflict in Modern Culture and other Essays*. New York: Teachers College Press, pp. 27–46.

Simmel, Georg ([1907] 1978), *The Philosophy of Money*. London: Routledge and Kegan Paul.

Simmel, Georg ([1900] 1907), *Philosophie des Geldes*. 2ⁿᵈ ed. Leipzig: Dunker and Humblot.

Simmel, Georg ([1907] 1989), *Philosophie des Geldes*. Volume 6 of the Collected Works. Frankfurt am Main: Suhrkamp.

Simonis, Georg (1999), "Vorwort," in Stephan Bröchler, Georg Simonis, and Karsten Sundermann, eds., *Handbuch der Technikfolgenabschätzung*. Volume 1. Berlin: edition sigma, pp. 13–16.

Sinsheimer, Robert L. (1978), "The presumptions of science," *Daedalus* 107: 23–35.

Sinsheimer, Robert L. (1976a), "Comment," *Hastings Center Report* (August): 18.

Sinsheimer, Robert L. (1976b), "Recombinant DNA—On our own," *BioScience* 26: 599.

Smith, H. Jeff (1994), *Managing Privacy: Information Technology and Corporate America*. Chapel Hill: University of North Carolina Press.

Smithson, Michael (1985), "Toward a social theory of ignorance," *Journal for the Theory of Social Behavior* 15: 151–172.

Smits, Ruud, Jos Leyten, and Pim den Hertog (1995), "Technology assessment and technology policy in Europe: New concepts, new goals, new infrastructures," *Policy Sciences* 28: 271–299.

Snow, David A., and Richard Machalek (1982), "On the presumed fragility of unconventional beliefs," *Journal for the Scientific Study of Religion* 21: 15–26.

Sombart, Werner (1934), *Deutscher Sozialismus*. Berlin: Buchholz and Weisswange.

Sombart, Werner ([1916] 1921), *Der moderne Kapitalismus: Historisch-systematische Darstellung des gesamten Wirtschaftslebens von seinen Anfaengen bis zur Gegenwart*. Erster Band: Einleitung—Die vorkapitalistische Wirtschaft—Die historischen Grundlagen des modernen Kapitalismus. Erster Halbband. Munich and Leipzig: Duncker and Humblot.

Sombart, Werner (1911), "Technik und Kultur," *Verhandlungen des ersten Deutschen Soziologentages in Frankfurt am Main*, 19–22. Oktober 1910. Tübingen: J.C. B. Mohr (Paul Siebeck).

Sorokin, Pitirim A. (1958), *Fad and Foibles in Modern Sociology and Related Sciences*. London: Mayflower Publishing and Vision Press.

Spallone, Pat, Tom Wilkie, Elizabeth Ettore, Erica Haimes, Tom Shakespeare, and Meg Stacey (2000), "Putting sociology on the bioethics map," in John Eldridge, John MacInnes, Sue Scott, Chris Warhurst, and Anne Witz, eds., *For Sociology: Legacies and Prospects*. Durham, U.K: Sociologypress, pp. 191–206.

Spengler, Oswald (1938), "Zur Weltgeschichte des zweiten vorchristlichen Jahrtausends," in Hildegrad Kornhardt, ed., *Reden und Äufsätze*. 2nd ed. Munich: C.H. Beck.

Starbuck, William H. (1992). "Learning by knowledge-intensive firms." *Journal of Management Studies* 29: 713–740.

Steevens, Valerie (2000), "Privacy, property and policy: Hidden implications for the information highway," in John de la Mothe and Gilles Paquet, eds., *Information, Innovation and Impacts*. Norwell, MA: Kluwer, pp. 221–237.

Stehr, Nico (2002a), *Knowledge and Economic Conduct: The Social Foundations of the Modern Economy*. Toronto, ON: University of Toronto Press.

Stehr, Nico (2002b), "The social role of knowledge," in Nikolai Genov, ed., *Advances in Sociological Knowledge*. Paris: International Social Science Council, 2002, pp. 84–113.

Stehr, Nico (2001a), *The Fragility of Modern Societies: Knowledge and Risk in the Information Age*. London: Sage.

Stehr, Nico (2001b), "The grammar of productive knowledge," in John de la Mothe and Dominique Foray, eds., *Knowledge Management in the Innovation Process*. Boston: Kluwer, pp. 193–204.

Stehr, Nico (2000b), "Knowledge, markets and biotechnology," in John de la Mothe and Jorge Niosi, eds., Boston: Kluwer Academic Publishers, pp. 205–214.

Stehr, Nico (1999), "The future of inequality," *Society* 36: 54–59.

Stehr, Nico (1992a), *Practical Knowledge*. London: Sage.

Stehr, Nico (1992b), "Experts, counsellors and advisors," in Nico Stehr and Richard V. Ericson, eds., *The Culture and Power of Knowledge*. New York: de Gruyter, pp. 107–155.

Stehr, Nico (1978), "The norms of science revisited: Social and cognitive norms," *Sociological Inquiry* 48: 172–196.

Stehr, Nico, and Reiner Grundmann (2001), *Werner Sombart: Economic Life in the Modern Age*. New Brunswick: Transaction.

Steinberg, D. L. (1997), *Bodies in Glass: Genetics, Eugenics, Embryos, Ethics*. Manchester: Manchester University Press.

Steinmetz, George, ed. (1999), *State/Culture: State-Formation after the Cultural Turn*. Ithaca, NY: Cornell University Press.

Steinmetz, George (1993), *Regulating the Social: The Welfare State and Local Politics in Imperial Germany*. Princeton, NJ: Princeton University Press.

Stent, Gunther S. (1969), *The Coming of the Golden Age: A View of the End of Progress.* Garden City, NY: Natural History Press.

Stewart, Thomas A. (1997), *Intellectual Capital: The New Wealth of Organizations.* New York: Doubleday.

Stich, Stephen P. (1982), "Genetic engineering: How should science be controlled," in Tom Regan and Donald VandeVeer, eds., *And Justice for All: New Introductory Essays in Ethics and Public Policy.* Totowa, NJ: Rowman and Littlefield.

Stigler, George J. (1980), "An introduction to privacy in economics and politics," *Journal of Legal Studies* 9: 623–644.

Stigler, George J. (1971), "The theory of economic regulation," *Bell Journal of Economics* 2: 3–21.

Stiglitz, Joseph E. (1999), "On liberty, the right to know, and public discourse: The role of transparency in public life," Oxford Amnesty Lecture, Oxford, UK, January 27, 1999.

Stiglitz, Joseph E. (1987), "Learning to learn, localized learning and technological progress," in Partha S. Dasgupta and Paul Stoneman, eds., *Economic Policy and Technological Performance.* Cambridge: Cambridge University Press, pp. 125–153.

Storper, Michael (1996), "Institutions of the knowledge-based economy," in Organisation for Economic Cooperation and Development, *Employment and Growth in the Knowledge-Based Economy,* Paris: OECD, pp. 255–283.

Strange, Susan (1997), "The future of global capitalism; or, will divergence persist forever?" in Colin Crouch and Wolfgang Streeck, eds., *Political Economy of Modern Capitalism: Mapping Convergence and Diversity.* London: Sage, pp. 182–191.

Swazey, Judith P. (1978), "Protecting the 'animal of necessity': Limits to inquiry in clinical investigations," *Daedalus* 107: 129–145.

Swazey, Judith P., and Renee C. Fox (1970), "The clinical moratorium: A case study of mitral valve surgery," in Paul Freund, ed., *Experimentation with Human Subjects.* New York: Braziller, pp. 315–357.

Swedberg, Richard (1994), "Markets as social structures," in Neil J. Smerlser and Richard Swedberg, eds., *The Handbook of Economic Sociology.* Princeton, NJ: Princeton University Press, pp. 255–282.

Task Force on Genetic Information and Insurance (1993), *Genetic Information and Health Insurance.* Bethesda, MD: National Institutes of Health, National Center for Genome Research.

Teece, David J. (1977), "Technology transfer by multinational firms: The resource cost of transferring technological know-how," *Economic Journal* 87: 242–261.

Tenbruck, Friedrich H. (1972), *Zur Kritik der planenden Vernunft.* Freiburg im Breisgau: Alber.

Tenbruck, Friedrich H. (1969), "Regulative Funktionen der Wissenschaft in der pluralistischen Gesellschaft," in Herbert Scholz, ed., *Die Rolle der Wissenschaft in der modernen Gesellschaft.* Berlin: Duncker & Humblot, pp. 61–85.

Theocharis, T., and M. Psimopoulos (1987), "Where science has gone wrong," *Nature* 329: 595–598.

Tiger, Lionel (2002), "Biology as precedent," *Social Science Information* 41:25–34.

Tokar, Brian, ed., (2001), *Redesigning Life: The Worldwide Challenge to Genetic Engineering.* Montreal: McGill–Queen's University Press.

Tomlinson, John (1999), *Globalization and Culture.* Chicago: University of Chicago Press.

Touraine, Alain ([1995] 1997), "The crisis of 'Progress,'" in Martin Bauer, ed., *Resistance to New Technology: Nuclear Power, Information Technology and Biotechnology.* Cambridge: Cambridge University Press.

Touraine, Alain ([1992] 1995), *Critique of Modernity*. Oxford: Blackwell.

Touraine, Alain ([1984] 1988), *Return of the Actor: Social Theory in Postindustrial Society*. Minneapolis: University of Minnesota Press.

Tribe, Laurence (1972), "Policy science: analysis or ideology," *Philosophy and Public Affairs* 2: 66–110.

Turner, R. Steven (2001), "On telling regulatory tales: rBST comes to Canada," *Social Studies of Science* 31: 475–506.

Turner, Stephen (2001), "What is the problem with experts?" *Social Studies of Science* 31: 123–149.

Turney, Jon (1998), *Frankenstein's Footsteps: Science, Genetics and Popular Culture*. New Haven, CT: Yale University Press.

Vaitsos, Constantine V. (1989), "Radical technological changes and the new 'order' in the world-economy," *Review* 12: 157–189.

Valladão, Alfredo G. A. (1996), *The Twenty-First Century Will Be American*. London: Verso.

Vanderburg, William H. (2000), *The Labyrinth of Technology*. Toronto, ON: University of Toronto Press.

Virchow, Rudolf ([1885] 1922), "Über Akklimatisation," in Karl Sudhoff, *Rudolf Virchow und die Deutschen Naturforscherversammlungen*. Leipzig: Akademische Verlagsgesellschaft, pp. 214–240.

Virchow, Rudolf (1877), *Die Freiheit der Wissenschaft im modernen Staat: Rede gehalten in der dritten allgemeinen Sitzung der fünfzigsten Versammlung deutscher Naturforscher und Aerzte zu München am 22. September 1877*. Berlin: von Wiegand, Hempel and Perry.

Vogel, David (2003), "The hare and the tortoise revisited: The new politics of consumer and environmental regulation in Europe," *British Journal of Political Science* 33:557–580.

Vogel, David (1986), *National Styles of Regulation: Environmental Policy in Great Britain and the United States*. Ithaca, NY: Cornell University Press.

Wambugu, Florence (1999), "Why Africa needs agricultural biotech," *Nature* 400: 15–16.

Watson, James D. (1990), "The human genome project: Past, present, future," *Science* 248: 44–48.

Weber, Max ([1922] 1978), *Economy and Society*. Two volumes. Edited by Guenther Roth and Claus Wittich. Berkeley, CA: University of California Press.

Weber, Max ([1921] 1980), *Gesammelte politische Schriften*. Tübingen: J.C.B. Mohr (Paul Siebeck).

Weber, Max ([1919] 1992), "Wissenschaft als Beruf," in *Gesammelte Aufsätze zur Wissenschaftslehre*. Tübingen: J.C.B. Mohr (Paul Siebeck), pp. 524–579.

Weber, Max (1922), *Gesammelte Aufsätze zur Wissenschaftslehre*. Tübingen: J.C.B. Mohr (Paul Siebeck).

Webster, Frank, and Kevin Robins (1993), "I'll be watching you: Comment on Sewell and Wilkinson," *Sociology* 27: 243–252.

Webster, Frank, and Kevin Robins (1989), "Plan and control: Towards a cultural history of the information society," *Theory and Society* 18: 323–351.

Webster, Frank, and Kevin Robins (1986), *Information Technology: A Luddite Analysis*. Norwood, NJ: Ablex.

Whitaker, Reg (1999), *The End of Privacy: How Total Surveillance Is Becoming a Reality*. New York: New Press.

Wikström, Solveig, and Richard Normann (1994), *Knowledge and Value: A New Perspective on Corporate Transformation*. London: Routledge.

Wilson, Edward O. (1975), *Sociobiology: The New Synthesis.* Cambridge, MA: Harvard University Press.

Wingerson, Lois (1990), *Mapping Our Genes.* New York: Dutton.

Winner, Langdon (1992), "Citizen virtues in a technological order," *Inquiry* 35: 341–361.

Winner, Langdon (1977), *Autonomous Technology: Technics out of Control, a Theme in Political Thought.* Cambridge, MA: MIT Press.

Wolf, Rainer (1988), "'Herrschaft kraft Wissen' in der Risikogesellschaft," *Soziale Welt* 39: 164–187.

World Bank (1999), *World Development Report: Knowledge for Development.* New York: Oxford University Press.

Wright, Robert (1990), "Achilles' helix," *New Republic* 202: 21–31.

Wright, Susan (1993), "The social warp of science: Writing the history of genetic engineering policy," *Science, Technology, and Human Values* 18: 79–101.

Wright, Susan (1986a), "Recombinant DNA technology and its social transformation," *Osiris* 2: 303–360.

Wright, Susan (1986b), "Molecular biology or molecular politics? The production of scientific consensus on the hazards of recombinant DNA technology," *Social Studies of Science* 16: 593–620.

Wright, Susan (1978), "Molecular politics in Great Britain and the United States: The development of policy for recombinant DNA technology," *South California Law Review* 51: 1383–1434.

Wulff, Keith M. (1979), *Regulation of Scientific Inquiry: Societal Concerns with Research.* Boulder, CO: Westview Press.

Wynne, Brian (1992), "Misunderstood misunderstanding: Social identities and public uptake of science," *Public Understanding of Science* 1: 281–304.

Wynne, Brian (1991), "Knowledges in context," *Science, Technology, and Human Values* 16: 111–121.

Wynne, Brian (1975), "The rhetoric of consensus politics: A critical review of technology assessment," *Research Policy* 4: 108–158.

Zuckerman, Harriet (1986), "Uses and control of knowledge: Implications for the fabric of society," in James F. Short Jr., ed., *The Social Fabric: Dimensions and Issues.* Beverly Hills, CA: Sage, pp. 334–348.

Zysman, John (1996), "The myth of a 'global' economy: Enduring national foundations and emerging regional realities," *New Political Economy* 1: 157–184.

Zysman, John (1994), *How Institutions Create Historically-Rooted Trajectories of Growth.* Oxford: Oxford University Press.

Indexes

Name Index

Subject Index